CANADIAN SOCIAL POLICY

AN INTRODUCTION

Fourth Edition

JOHN R. GRAHAM
University of Calgary

KAREN J. SWIFT
York University

ROGER DELANEY
Lakehead University

Toronto

Vice-President, Editorial Director: Gary Bennett
Editor-in-Chief: Michelle Sartor
Editor, Humanities and Social Sciences: Joel Gladstone
Marketing Manager: Lisa Gillis
Supervising Developmental Editor: Madhu Ranadive
Project Manager: Richard di Santo
Manufacturing Coordinator: Susan Johnson
Production Editor: Purnima Narayanan, MPS Limited, a Macmillan Company
Copy Editor: Deborah Cooper-Bullock
Proofreader: Tara Tovell
Compositor: MPS Limited, a Macmillan Company
Art Director: Julia Hall
Cover Designer: Julia Hall
Cover Image: Getty Images

Credits and acknowledgments borrowed from other sources and reproduced, with permission, in this textbook appear on the appropriate page within the text.

10 9 8 7 6 5 4 3 2 1   RRD-H

Library and Archives Canada Cataloguing in Publication

Graham, John R. (John Russell), 1964–
Canadian social policy : an introduction / John R. Graham, Karen J. Swift, Roger Delaney. — 4th ed.

Includes index.
ISBN 978-0-13-231061-1

1. Canada—Social policy—Textbooks. I. Swift, Karen II. Delaney, Roger III. Title.

HV108.G735 2012   361.6'10971   C2011-902727-5

ISBN 978-0-13-231061-1

For Peter and for Marie and Austin

This edition is also dedicated to the memory of Brian Wharf for his invaluable contributions to our understanding of Canadian social policy.

Brief Contents

Contents

Preface

There are numerous books on social policy in the United Kingdom and the United States. *Canadian Social Policy: An Introduction* is a response to the need for a Canadian perspective. It is a single-volume introduction to a highly diversified field, one that provides a framework for analyzing social policies. The book stresses concepts and policies as parallel and equal means to a framework. Our thinking owes much to recent forces in social policy practice and scholarship, particularly as they relate to feminist, postmodern, and social diversity writings, widely construed, and to the concerns of social justice raised by this scholarship.

Social policy is a fundamental component of social work practice and should never be seen as an ethereal or aloof add-on to the curriculum. It is important in other ways, perhaps more so than at any other time either in our country's history or in the history of the social work profession. The now prolonged assault on universal programs, the evermore limited scope of policies, the ascendancy of neo-conservative ideology, the growth of globalization, the imperative of diversity—these issues, among other phenomena, will greatly influence social work practice and social policy analysis in future years. It is essential, therefore, that students introduced to Canadian social policy understand these dynamics and have at their disposal an analytical frame of reference that will make them sensitive to the nuances of policy work and to the diverse needs of society's most marginalized people.

Canadian Social Policy: An Introduction examines major social policy considerations in Canada. It is intended for an audience of graduate, senior undergraduate, and senior community college students in social work, and for professionals who want to update their knowledge of current policy contexts. It is also intended to offer insights to students and practitioners of other disciplines, such as anthropology, business administration, Canadian studies, clinical psychology, development studies, divinity, economics, education, geography, history, nursing, occupational therapy, political science, public administration, rehabilitation studies, and sociology.

This textbook has been a number of years in the making. It started out as a proposal submitted by Roger Delaney. Once a publishing contract was received and the work begun, Roger invited John Graham and Karen Swift to be co-authors. The textbook's initial focus then expanded to place greater emphasis on the historical origins of Canadian social policies and on the impact of social diversity on all aspects of policy formation and analysis. The writing process has been truly collaborative, with each author contributing to the others' sentences, paragraphs, references, and ideas, and acting as a sounding board for all matters related to authorship. Roger took the lead in Chapters 1, 8, and 9; John in Chapters 2, 3, 4, and the first part of Chapter 5; and Karen in the latter part of Chapter 5 and in Chapters 6 and 7; but the entire final product has each scholar's imprint.

The authors have been fortunate for so many things, including the kind encouragement of readers and our press. We greatly appreciate the supportive and useful advice from reviewers and from readers. The second edition, released in 2003, expanded beyond the first edition to include greater discussion of Canada's welfare-state institutions, social welfare theory, socio-economic class, social policy practice, globalization, the physical ecology, and social movements. The third edition considerably updated the analysis and provided further analysis of social policy practice and social policy development in a market-state era of less government and ascendant liberal capitalist ideology.

In the fourth edition, Chapter 1 outlines some conceptual ideas that form a foundation for social policy analysis and application. Chapter 2 considers historic influences on Canadian social policies; Chapter 3, some of the country's major social welfare programs; and Chapter 4, significant policy-related ideological, social, and economic facets. Chapter 5 covers globalization, the environment, social inclusion, and social movements. Chapter 6 introduces the key notion of diversity to social policy formation; and Chapter 7 presents how social policies are applied to social work practice and to social service delivery in general. The final two chapters examine the policy-making process in Canada, from stages and structures through to analysis, implementation, and assessment.

This fourth edition expands the scope of analysis used in the third edition in several respects. The entire book has been updated with new secondary literature on Canadian social policy and social policy writ large (written for Canadian and non-Canadian audiences). It has likewise been updated with new social policy theories that emphasize the increasing importance of globalization, the escalation of income inequality, neo-liberalism, and the changing patterns of international relations as emerging economic powers in the developing world grow in power and influence. The book cites policies, programs, and statistics on social policy usage, as well as demographic changes, and all such references have been updated. Chapter 4 has been rewritten to emphasize the significance of economic inequality in Canada and internationally (within and between countries), and Chapters 2 and 5 have been changed considerably to draw attention to social policy as of the great recession of 2008 and in light of changing international and domestic political–economic arrangements in which emerging countries, such as Brazil, China, India, and Indonesia, are holding greater sway and importance while the influences of traditionally powerful countries are declining proportionately. Chapter 5 also discusses some new ideas about civil society and the increasing use of the Internet to fuel social movements and shape public opinion. A case study has been incorporated into Chapter 8. As in previous editions, we pay particular attention to writing clear and precise prose and to trying to present social policy as the relevant, important thing that it is.

SUPPLEMENTS

CourseSmart for Instructors (ISBN 978-0-13-231081-9)

CourseSmart goes beyond traditional expectations—providing instant, online access to the textbooks and course materials you need at a lower cost for students. And even as students save money, you can save time and hassle with a digital eTextbook that allows you to search for the most relevant content at the very moment you need it. Whether it's evaluating textbooks or creating lecture notes to help students with difficult concepts, CourseSmart can make life a little easier. See how when you visit **www.coursesmart.com/instructors**.

CourseSmart for Students (ISBN 978-0-13-231081-9)

CourseSmart goes beyond traditional expectations—providing instant, online access to the textbooks and course materials you need at an average savings of 60 percent. With instant access from any computer and the ability to search your text, you'll find the content you need quickly, no matter where you are. And with online tools such as highlighting and note-taking, you can save time and study efficiently. See all the benefits at **www.coursesmart.com/students**.

Technology Specialists

Pearson's Technology Specialists work with faculty and campus course designers to ensure that Pearson technology products, assessment tools, and online course materials are tailored to meet your specific needs.

This highly qualified team is dedicated to helping schools to take full advantage of a wide range of educational resources, by assisting in the integration of a variety of instructional materials and media formats. Your local Pearson Education sales representative can provide you with more details on this service program.

MySearchLab

MySearchLab offers extensive help to students with their writing and research project and provides round-the-clock access to credible and reliable source material.

Research

Content on MySearchLab includes immediate access to thousands of full-text articles from leading Canadian and international academic journals, and daily news feeds from The Associated Press. Articles contain the full downloadable text—including abstract and citation information—and can be cut, pasted, emailed, or saved for later use.

Writing

MySearchLab also includes a step-by-step tutorial on writing a research paper. Included are sections on planning a research assignment, finding a topic, creating effective notes, and finding source material. Our exclusive online handbook provides grammar and usage support. Pearson SourceCheck™ offers an easy way to detect accidental plagiarism issues, and our exclusive tutorials teach how to avoid them in the future. And MySearchLab also contains AutoCite, which helps to correctly cite sources by using MLA, APA, CMS, and CBE documentation styles for both endnotes and bibliographies. To order this book with MySearchLab access at no extra charge, use ISBN 978-0-13-282387-6.

Take a tour at **www.mysearchlab.com**.

Pearson Custom Library

For enrollments of at least 25 students, you can create your own textbook by choosing the chapters that best suit your own course needs. *To begin building your custom text, visit www.pearsoncustomlibrary.com.* You may also work with a dedicated Pearson Custom editor to create your ideal text—publishing your own original content or mixing and matching Pearson content. Contact your local Pearson Representative to get started.

Acknowledgments

Many people, too numerous to mention, were extremely influential in the completion of this text. Special thanks are extended to Tanjeem Azad, Helen Boukos, Andreas Breuer, Cathryn Bradshaw, Xiaobei Chen, Stefanie Kaiser, Patricia Bianchini, Susan Graham, Sarah Meagher, Nikoo Najand, Louise Querido, and Micheal Shier in particular, for extremely helpful and timely research assistanceship. The fourth edition relied heavily on Andrea Newberry, David Sandoz, Josée Couture, Heath McLeod, and Elena Esina, to whom we extend sincere thanks. Likewise, thank you to Leslie Stirritt for his contribution to the HST case study. John Graham's father, Russell Graham, read the entire first-edition manuscript and provided, as always, exceptionally valuable editorial advice. Staff at Pearson Education Canada remain unendingly cooperative and encouraging.

In the early 1970s, the late Albert Rose of the Faculty of Social Work, University of Toronto, conceived a social policy chart for teaching purposes. In light of substantial policy changes since then, part of the conceptualization in Chapter 3 is loosely based on Dr. Rose's original chart and is dedicated to his memory. A major contributor to the development of Figures 4.2 and 8.2 is Raika Abdulahad, a Ph.D. student at the University of Calgary. Keith Brownlee, Issam Dawood, Paul DeBakker, M.D., Gayle Gilchrist-James, Jacqueline Ismael, Margaret McKee, and Bob Luker were among colleagues who provided much-appreciated support and advice. Funding from the University of Calgary Starter Grant for newly recruited faculty provided money for research assistanceship for the first edition; particular thanks are extended to the University of Calgary and the Alberta government for this critical support. Grateful acknowledgment is extended for grant support from SSHRC to the Caring Labour Network and the project on "Risk and risk assessment in child welfare." A Senate Research Grant from Lakehead University was likewise instrumental in moving the manuscript toward completion. Finally, thanks are extended to the Caledon Institute of Social Policy, the Canadian Council on Social Development, Human Resources and Skills Development Canada, the National Council of Welfare, Statistics Canada, and those publishing companies that allowed us to cite various research.

The editors and authors would like to thank the following reviewers for their helpful commentary on previous editions: Robert Marino of King's College, University of Western Ontario; Francis Turner of Wilfrid Laurier University; Brian Wharf of the University of Victoria; Sheila Neysmith of the University of Toronto; Douglas Durst of the University of Regina; Michael J. Holosko of the University of Windsor; Lynda E. Turner of Kwantlen University College; Thérèse Jennissen of Carleton University; Horatio Sam-Aggrey of Carleton University; Bruce Northey of the College of New Caledonia; Mojgan Rahbari of the University of Ontario Institute of Technology; and Kimberley Wilson of the University of Guelph.

Chapter (1)

Introduction to Canadian Social Policy

Social policy is premised in the past, implemented in the present, and directed toward the future. It is profoundly influenced by societal values and ideologies, by domestic and international factors, and it should be sensitive to the diversities that constitute Canadian society. A thorough understanding of social policy is essential to effective social work practice. This text, therefore, presents Canadian social policy from a framework that takes into account the imperatives of history, diversity, and relevance to direct practice in Canada. Likewise, the book consciously affirms the empowerment of all Canadians—particularly those who have historically been marginal within local, regional, national, and international power structures.

For a beginning student, one of the most immediate means of understanding social policy is through terminology. This chapter, therefore, introduces several key concepts and concludes with a look at the relationship of policy to direct practice, a theme that is elaborated in Chapter 7. The student is also encouraged to refer to the glossary at the end of the book, which contains core definitions used in the present chapter and throughout the text.

Human beings believe in a wide range of religions and philosophies, organize around a wide range of political and social principles, and value different human attributes and characteristics. However, there is a common attribute—the fact that each of us is a human being. Moreover, these world views and physical and human attributes *describe* human beings but do not *define* human beings. In other words, gender, religion, skin colour, physical attributes, social norms, ideologies, intelligence, physical fitness, gender preference, age, and other physical and mental attributes describe what is different about people, but not who we are as human beings.

These differences represent our world views. World views are constructed from values drawn from religious, political, social, and physical information about humans and the societies they create. Once accepted by a group of people, these world views become *agreement realities* (Babbie, 1986). Agreement realities become the *truth* for all those with a similar world view, and this truth is passed down from generation to generation.

1

If you were born and raised only in Canada after 1970, then the many elements that currently make up Canadian society probably make sense to you. If you live in an organized community (such as a city or town) that elects officials (such as mayors, reeves, and councillors) to govern the community, this process of governance seems normal to you. Other things that would be normal to you would include electing provincial and federal members to provincial, territorial, and federal parliaments to represent you (representative democracy); having your basic health-care costs paid for by government (medicare); having free public education to Grade 12; being free to travel throughout Canada without a passport; working for a salary or profits in a competitive marketplace; and having police forces that are accountable to elected officials.

You would also be acquainted with the rules that govern people's conduct in Canada, such as criminal laws that make such activities as murder, theft, kidnapping, and physical and sexual assault illegal. You would be aware of rules that govern conduct in the workplace, such as those dealing with harassment, exploitation, and injury. You would be aware that there are rules that also protect the vulnerable, such as children and the elderly, from being exploited or injured. Finally, you would also have discovered a number of rules that govern our activities, such as traffic laws, snowmobile and boating laws, and hunting and fishing laws.

You would also be aware that Canada is made up of many different people who speak different languages, believe in different religions, live different lifestyles, and value different things, all of which are protected from discrimination by Canada's Charter of Rights and Freedoms.

More importantly, in addition to these shared world views, how you experience all of the above elements of Canadian society is influenced by such factors as whether you are rich or poor; white or a person of colour; male or female; heterosexual or gay or lesbian; married or single; renting or owning; working, unemployed, or retired; young or old; citizen or immigrant; professional or minimum-wage worker; full-time employed or part-time employed; or healthy, injured, or ill. Most of us will experience life in Canada from perspectives shaped by many combinations of the above attributes over the course of our lives.

Because people experience Canada differently, they can also differ about what they believe is in Canada's best interest. If people are rich, powerful, and respected, they may very well want Canada to remain as it is or to change only in ways that benefit them. Philosopher Karl Mannheim (1936) calls this *ideological thinking*. On the other hand, if people are poor, unemployed, and living in slum conditions, they may very well want Canada to change drastically and in ways that benefit them. Mannheim (1936) called this *utopian thinking*.

The study of social policy helps us to understand how world views influence the way in which members of social arrangements (i.e., societies, communities, families, or clubs) feel about such things as

➤ social power, including personal powers and freedoms;

➤ social justice, including social equality, social status, roles, and prerogatives;

> ➤ human, civil, and social rights;
> ➤ human and social diversity;
> ➤ the nature of society;
> ➤ the relationship between people and society; and
> ➤ the nature of human relationships.

These are all very big issues; because they are so big, social policies can affect human beings in every aspect of their lives. Social workers and other human service professionals support the notion that society is about people and that, when properly resourced physically, emotionally, and spiritually, human beings will strive to become more fully human, whether that be by achieving higher order needs (see Chapter 4) or by fulfilling a human ontological vocation (Freire, 1994) to become more fully human. This view is not shared by some people in our industrialized societies, who offer a view of society governed by economic or human attribute supremacy. For example, Payne (1998) argues that social work failed when the profession accepted the position that environment (unemployment/underemployment, racism, ageism, ghettos, poverty) significantly affects human behaviour because social work then created a society of expectant giving with no personal responsibility. In his view, the Charity Organization Society had it right: poverty and social alienation are a result of personal failure and inadequate character. Should this view become the social policy basis for societal public policies on welfare, then the poor would be blamed as the cause of their own poverty. Simply put, if you cause your own problems, why should society be responsible for you? When society refuses to take responsibility, the poor are made black against the night; they simply disappear from public consciousness. The views expressed by Payne have been embraced by the political right, who hold increasingly greater power in Canada and other industrialized countries (including Great Britain and France).

Social policy is about making decisions that are—in the perception of those making them—in the best interests of Canada and Canadians. Because these perceptions are very subjective, it is essential to ask certain questions in order to understand what impact social policies will have on society. Specifically, who has the power to make social policy decisions? Whose views of life in Canada are driving the policy-making process? Who is benefiting from these policies? Who is not benefiting from these policies? How consistent are these policies with societal norms?

One of the most important aspects of social policy for beginning students is the multitude of approaches available to study it. Among the many approaches that will be explored throughout the book are the contrasting perceptions of social policy as comprehensive versus incremental, global versus local, and value-driven versus scientifically derived. These variations in approach reflect the social work profession's and society's confusion about just what social policy is.

What Are Social Policies?

The late British scholar Richard Titmuss (1974) examined social policy by first exploring the meaning of the terms *social* and *policy*. To him, *social* referred to all of the non-economic factors that affect people in society and relate to people as social beings. *Policy*, Titmuss insisted, is about enduring the dilemmas of choice created when one objective must be selected over others.

Exploring various definitions and perceptions about social policy can be a frustrating journey into subtle abstract differences or esoteric debates. Moreover, many social workers and human service workers often confuse just what social policy is. For example, it is not uncommon to hear social workers talk about their agency's *social policy* rather than the correct term, *agency policy* or *public policy*.

The following social policy definition is intended to provide you with a framework to ground your study of social policy. Throughout the book, you will be able to use this definition to analyze social policy debates.

Social policy describes societal visions—that is, values and beliefs that people hold about what a society should look like, based on a notion about human beings, the nature of society, and the way society and humans interact. For example, different political parties talk about programs and policies that they believe will benefit society. Different interest and advocacy groups also have visions about what a society should look like. These visions make it possible to identify social policy positions related to different competing groups in a society. We can also assume that groups of like-minded people will support a common vision and will disagree with the different visions of other groups. If all people agreed on one societal vision, then society would have only one social policy position.

Those elected to form a government are in a unique position. They can translate their social policy vision into law, thus creating new public policies that reflect their vision, revising existing public policies and repealing others. Public policies guide public programs and laws and are binding to all citizens. Therefore, if you gain power, you can implement your social policies and require all citizens to live under the societal vision reflected in your social policies. People who disagree with the new laws are left with limited options, such as supporting a party with an opposing policy vision to help it win the next election, using social and/or economic power to prevent or discourage an elected government from implementing policies, or revolting against the existing government and taking power through force.

Public policies inform social programs and define both the nature of the programs and the citizens whom the programs serve. Agencies, government departments, and ministries (the formal social organizations) are empowered and financed to provide these social programs within the framework provided by the enabling act and subsequent regulations. In turn, agencies and government services have organizational cultures that influence how services are delivered even within their guiding legislation.

In summary, social policy positions influence legislation, which in turn influences programs, which in turn influence services. Whoever has the power to implement his or her social policy position or to prevent others from implementing their positions determines the quality, range, and availability of social programs.

Definitions of Social Policy

Richard Titmuss—Models of Social Policy

Richard Titmuss (1974) argued that social policy is basically about "choices between conflicting political objectives and goals and how they are formulated" (49). These choices are influenced by views of what constitutes a good society, based on that which "culturally distinguishes between the needs and aspirations of social man [sic] in contradiction to the needs and aspirations of economic man [sic]" (49). Titmuss argues that social policy can best be understood in terms of the following three models or functions:

1. *The Residual Welfare Model of Social Policy:* This model argues that the private market and the family are responsible for meeting an individual's needs. Only when these options break down should social welfare institutions intervene. As discussed in Chapter 3, proponents of neo-conservative and liberal ideologies favour this model.

2. *The Industrial Achievement-Performance Model of Social Policy:* This model argues that social needs should be met on the basis of merit, work perform-ance, and productivity. Known as the *Handmaiden Model*, it is favoured by positivists (Federico, 1983) and other economic and psychological theorists who advocate incentives, effort, and reward.

3. *The Institutional Redistributive Model of Social Policy:* This model argues that social welfare should be a major integrated institution in society, provid-ing universal services outside the market, based on the principle of need.

Policy can emerge from these approaches only in areas of life where choices exist. Without choices, there is no policy; rather, there is a law, either natural or legislated. For example, since people cannot control the weather, societies have no policies concerning weather control. However, should science ever learn how to control weather, then societies would have to make choices about how to control the weather. Tension might arise between people who want warm sunshine and farmers who want rain (*preferential choices*). Further, controlling the weather might cause well-known ecological effects, such as sterilizing some insects or wildlife (*anticipated consequences*). Finally, controlling the weather might have detrimental effects that are not even known (*unanticipated consequences*). In this example, the choice to control weather would result in an anticipated consequence for insects and wildlife, some potential unanticipated consequences, and a decision about whether the farmer gets rain or the public gets sunshine.

Martin Rein—Value-Driven Policy

The weather example shows that values and beliefs are important to decisions in social policy. The American scholar Martin Rein (1974) suggested that "social policy is, above all, concerned with choice among competing values" (298). From Rein's perspective, society consists of people holding diverse values (world views), and these people compete with one another and one another's values in an effort to achieve maximum power. So ingrained are values in every aspect of social, economic, and public policies that many social policy theorists—such as Rein (1983), Gil (1998), and Wharf and McKenzie (2010)—warn that a major role of policy-makers is to learn how to control their own values and prejudices. This warning is further discussed in Chapter 8.

Rein suggests that values influence social policy in five major ways:

1. Values influence the definition of the purpose of the policy, especially policies dealing with "moral" decisions. An example would be a policy addressing abortion.

2. Values influence priorities by assigning greater "value" to some courses of action than to others. An economic example would be the decision to reduce the rate of inflation by increasing interest rates. This decision assigns higher value to the protection of business interests and lower value to the mainte-nance of employment levels.

3. Values demand change when they are formally and legally articulated. Once a position is articulated and the means to bring it about are put in place, people will assign it importance (which is value-derived) simply because it exists (has form). As a result, society may have to change in order to allow that form to exist. For example, the North American Free Trade Agreement has caused significant changes to the Canadian economy, leading to the closure of some industries, the increase in some markets, the decrease in others, and so on.

4. Values focus on usefulness and feasibility. Policy-makers can become preoc-cupied with usefulness and political feasibility rather than societal need. An example is the federal government's Axworthy social policy reform document of 1994, which many people think has done little to change social policies, since few of the proposals were ever implemented.

5. Values influence the interpretation and evaluation of outcomes. One example is the claim that certain poverty lines do not really describe poverty. As dis-cussed in Chapter 3, Canada has many different poverty lines, each with its own threshold below which a person's annual income is declared "in pov-erty"; ultimately, the threshold level is determined by some value of what is seen to be fair (adapted from Rein, 1974, 298).

Since social policy is often articulated as public policy, public policy documents reflect values that gain dominance. Public policies are legislated acts, regulations, and bylaws (including all associated policies in the ministerial, agency, and public arenas) at the federal, provincial, and municipal levels of gov-ernment (Doern & Aucoin, 1971). As such, public policies are *social statements* reflecting the values and ideology of the political party or parties sponsoring them. Because public policies are encased in law, they have three distinct attributes:

1. Public policies are *legitimate*. Although an issue may be heavily debated—gun control, for example—once a policy is legislated, it is the law and is right or legitimate. Those who opposed the issue must now accept it as law, even if they are working to change it.

2. Public policies are *universal*—that is, they apply to everyone.

3. Because government *controls* (much, but not all) *coercion* in society, public policies can be enforced. Governments control enforcement agencies, such as the police, government investigators (e.g., income tax and welfare fraud investigators), and, in the case of the federal government, the army. These enforcement agencies ensure that the government can enforce the law.

Public policies provide boundaries and controls to regulate citizen behaviour, either directly (e.g., game and fishing policy, housing policy, taxation policy) or indirectly (e.g., foreign policy). As such, public policies play an instrumental part in all aspects of societal life.

David Gil—Social Justice

David Gil (1970), who, along with Rein, and Wharf and McKenzie, is discussed in greater length in Chapter 8, suggested that social policies are concerned not only with the life-sustaining activities that ensure minimum basic needs, but also with those that stimulate our human potential. But the range of possibilities for these activities is as great as the range of world views that influence them. From a *polycentric perspective*, variation in views allows a more complete world view to emerge. A polycentric perspective, first articulated by McPherson and Rabb (1994), argues that

radically different world views not only reveal something about culture and language, but about reality itself and the ways different people have come to know it. Therefore, each world view reveals something about the total picture, which can never be fully known. An accurate picture of reality is only possible by attempting to accommodate and reconcile as many world views as possible. (Delaney, 1995, 13)

Moreover, Gil (1998) saw a need for social transformation. Systemic inequalities based on world views supporting "inequality, individualism, selfishness, domination, competition, and disregard for community (from local to global)" (35) need to be replaced by world views "affirming equality, individuality, liberty, cooperation, community and global solidarity" (35). Fundamental to this perspective is the view that human beings have physical, emotional, and spiritual dimensions and that human social functioning is impeded without the resources that meet these physical, emotional, and spiritual dimensions. The result would be humans whose potential is limited or constrained. Should one group of people attempt to ensure that their physical, emotional, and spiritual dimensions are satisfied at the expense of another group, then this action would be one of oppression.

Other approaches to social policy tend to reflect the comprehensive–incremental continuum.

Braybrooke and Lindblom—Incrementalism

Braybrooke and Lindblom (1963) identified *incrementalism* as a key feature of social policy. They suggested that the world is just too complex and organic to allow for comprehensive policy and planning. For one thing, comprehensive policy-makers themselves have to fill in variables about society and people about which they do not have valid and reliable information, thus allowing their own values to influence the design of social policies. Instead, these authors suggested that throughout history, people have simply corrected problems as they arose, and, over time, made substantive changes.

This incrementalist approach to social policy analysis is limited to considerations of alternative policies that are only incrementally different from the status quo. Because incrementalist theory has no major framework, the overall policy approach tends to be disjointed. Because different people are preparing policies for different problems independently, the term *disjointed incrementalism* is often applied to examples of this approach, which displays the following characteristics:

1. Analysis is limited to a few familiar alternatives.
2. Analysis of policy goals is intertwined with empirical aspects of the problem.
3. Analysis is concerned with remedying ills rather than with seeking positive goals.
4. Policies undergo a sequence of trials, errors, and revised trials.
5. Analysis of only some of the important consequences of those alternatives is considered.
6. Analytical work is fragmented among many partisan participants in policy-making (Hogwood & Gunn, 1984).

Some observers argue that incrementalism closely approximates *functionalism*. Functionalism suggests that every social system must meet four functional prerequisites in order to persist. These four prerequisites apply to all social systems:

1. *Adaptation:* The policy is adapted to the external environment;
2. *Goal attainment:* The policy co-ordinates collective activities to reach certain goals;
3. *Integration:* The policy integrates members of society to maintain solidarity and harmony; and
4. *Pattern maintenance (or latency):* The policy ensures that the activities required by members are performed with optimum compliance.

Functionalists view social welfare activities as a means of helping to create harmony among social institutions and individuals and hence maintain communal solidarity. The essential framework of functionalism is to value stability and continuity above social change. In other words, society as it currently exists is considered to be good; therefore, only when something goes wrong should it be changed.

Critics of functionalism, such as Mishra (1981), suggest that the increase in poverty, privilege, and exploitation in the United States and the universal problems of racism and sexism have served to undermine the validity of the functionalist model. Mishra and other scholars argue that the dominant metaphor for social organization is conflict between groups in society, rather than social stability, as functionalist theory implies.

But more important than incrementalist and functionalist approaches is the question of who determines the priorities, the structure, and the method of implementation of social welfare programs.

Turner and Yelaja—Group Goals and Objectives

Canadian scholar Francis Turner views social policy as statements of the social goals and objectives to which various groups—professional, governmental, or private—are committed. "They are the mission statements of various groups, and . . . vary widely in a country such as ours. . . . [A]s responsible citizens in a democratic country, we have a responsibility to understand this important component of our lives. This responsibility exists whether our goal is to become a social worker, a member of other related professions, a better-informed recipient of services, an advocate for social change, or a fully participating member of society" (1995, 10).

While reflecting the competition among values held by various groups for domination, Turner's view also states that social policy is culturally relevant—that is, Canadian social policies are not the same as those of other countries.

Another rather comprehensive definition of social policy comes from Canadian scholars Shankar Yelaja (1987), Ann Westhues (2003), and Rosalie Chappell (2006), whose definitions of social welfare reflect a social administration approach. For Yelaja, social policy is concerned with

the public administration of welfare services, that is, the formulation, development and management of specific services of government at all levels, such as health, education, income maintenance, and welfare services. Social policy is formulated not only by government, but also by institutions such as voluntary organizations, business, labour, industry, professional groups, public interest groups, and churches. Furthermore, social policy is to be understood within the framework of societal ends and means, which are interdependent. (1987, 2)

Westhues (2003) furthers Yelaja's position by viewing social policies as courses of "action or inaction chosen by public authorities to address a given problem or interrelated set of problems" (8). Public authorities include decision-makers in government, social service organizations, and collective agreements. Moreover, Westhues (2006) cautions that not only can the social policy process be very slow and resource (time, energy, and financial) intensive, but also its outcomes may not be congruent with social justice principles, let alone gain political approval. Chappell (2006) views social policies as sets of guidelines that provide structure and direction to Canada's social welfare programs. According to this perspective, social policy reflects social reality within a cultural context.

Gilbert and Specht; Marshall, Rice, and Prince; Mishra, Finkel, and Lightman—Social Action

American scholars Gilbert and Specht (1974) tried to teach social workers how policies affect the populations they work with. They define the institution of social welfare as "that patterning of relationships which develops in society to carry out mutual support functions" (5). A British social policy theorist with a similar social administration orientation is T.H. Marshall (1965), who notes that *social policy* is not a technical term with an exact meaning; instead, it refers to

the policy of governments with regard to action having a direct impact on the welfare of the citizens by providing them with service or income. The central core consists, therefore, of social insurance, public (or national) assistance, the health and welfare services, [and] housing policy. (7)

Marshall argues that the best way to ensure the welfare of citizens is to cultivate a sense of the right (or entitlement) to the following three things:

1. civil rights, which guarantee individual liberty and equality before the law;
2. political rights, which ensure the right to vote and seek political office; and
3. social rights, which ensure equal access and opportunities to all social institutions.

To ensure these rights, social policy advocates rely on the legal system to monitor and correct any abuses of these rights. However, Drover (2000) warns that globalization requires a redefinition of Marshall's notion of social citizenship, because nations now have restricted ability to respond to the rights of their citizens.

Rice and Prince (2000) envision a cooperative union between the forces driving economic policies and social policies, where social policy is treated as a partner of economic policy rather than as a drain of national and international economies.

Mishra (1981) defines social policy as referring "to the aims and objectives of social action concerning needs as well as to the structural patterns or arrangements through which needs are met" (x). For Mishra, social policy is concerned with deliberately and rationally matching ends and means through social institutions designed for that purpose.

Finkel (2006) views social policy as "the set of non-market decisions, public or private, that determine the distribution of wealth to individuals and families and the degree of availability of human services to all members of society" (3). Clearly, Finkel's view calls for an analysis of those who hold power and how their decisions influence those without power.

Lightman (2003) views Canadian social policy as a spectrum. At one end is a set of values, programs, and practices designed to (theoretically) bring Canadians together as a community by relating to shared experiences and mutual interdependence. At the other end of the spectrum, social policies are sets of programs designed for Canada's poor and vulnerable populations. Lightman views social policies as the choices made with respect to a group, community, or collective, and these choices have real consequences and costs for people and society.

In a similar argument, Lafitte (1962) claimed that social policy is "an attempt to steer the life of society along lines it would not follow if left to itself" (9).

Freeman and Sherwood (1970) view social policy as consisting of "conclusions reached by persons concerned with the betterment of community conditions and social life, and with the amelioration of deviance and social disorganization" (13).

Quality-of-Life Approach

Another perspective that allows comparisons of the impact of social policies is the *quality-of-life approach*. This approach is used by the United Nations, which makes statements about the social health of nations on the basis of data collected on quality-of-life indicators. Quality-of-life indicators include the following:

> ➢ physical and mental health;
> ➢ education and occupational achievements;
> ➢ development in the arts and science;
> ➢ production and consumption;
> ➢ wealth and income (including child poverty);
> ➢ conditions of the natural environment;
> ➢ patterns of recreation;
> ➢ patterns of social participation;
> ➢ patterns of social morality; and
> ➢ social deviance and alienation.

Quality-of-life indicators allow social workers to compare their country's social welfare programs internationally. In recent years, the amount of money Canada spends on social programs has slipped considerably and the number of poor children and families has increased.

The social policy theories described above all seek to explore the following questions: Is society organized around the needs of human beings? Are human beings organized around the needs of society? Are the needs of human beings and the needs of society interdependent? While these questions may sound rather simplistic, their resolution is not simplistic: ideologies and world views seek to make certain questions central to all social policy statements. For example, the current dominant social policy approach in Canada is based on the economic model of people, which advocates that human beings be organized around the economic needs of society. To challenge this view is also to challenge the power establishment, not just in Canada but internationally. As globalization creates more treaties among nations, giving substantial power to economic interests, national governments have less say in the quality-of-life and social program issues that affect their people.

Social Policy in a Time of Mistrust and Cynicism

One of the unfortunate consequences of the replacement of the Canada Assistance Plan (CAP) with the Canada Health and Social Transfer (CHST) in the 1990s was that it unleashed the *ideology of mistrust*. The CAP, which was hailed by many countries as positive and progressive social welfare legislation, provided a standard of social assistance across Canada for people in need or likely to be in need. Originally designed to share welfare costs with the provinces on a fifty–fifty basis, the CAP had slowly begun to decrease cost-sharing with the provinces during the late 1980s and early 1990s. With the passing of the CHST, responsibility for the funding of social services devolved from the federal government to the provinces and even to local communities in some of these provinces. Moreover, the removal of the CAP increased the privatization of social services across Canada. This issue will be discussed further in Chapter 3.

The ideology of mistrust suggests that poor people are "guided by an 'acquisitive instinct,' that is, they are out to get all they can by any means" (Macarov, 1995b, 147). Mistrust has existed for centuries. The Law of Less Eligibility (also referred to as *wage stop*) is one example. Passed in 1834, this law required all people receiving charity to be given less money or goods than the lowest paid worker in the parish. This law was designed to starve those who were "lazy" or "immoral" back to work. The nineteenth-century English workhouses, which encouraged brutal and cruel treatment of unemployed workers, are another example of social policy being driven by the ideology of mistrust. Similarly, the "ideology of the elite" argues that while most people are deserving and trustworthy, people receiving charity or social assistance are not trustworthy or deserving because they lack moral character and cannot plan and think for themselves. This view also supports "the politics of conduct," which argues that a person's conduct should determine both the quality and quantity of services provided.

The resulting mistrust of poor people can lead to public announcements that welfare cheats are being hunted down and will be punished. Certainly, the news media are more attracted to welfare cheaters being caught than to the many stories of those who are trying to both subsist and exist as people on social assistance. Consider how often you have heard people who are not poor speak knowingly about youth who are abusing Employment Insurance, women who are having babies in order to live off the public purse, immigrants who are sending their welfare money to support terrorists, youth who are committing horrible crimes and getting away with it, homeless people who are all mentally ill or lazy, unions who are trying to destroy business, gays who want extra rights, or children of the poor who are "just no good" like their parents.

As the ideology of mistrust becomes more pervasive in Canadian society, that society becomes more cynical. It quickly becomes evident that people who are rich demand and have opportunities that those who are not rich do not have. For example, while medicare attends to the health needs of the general population, those with sufficient money can go to the United States and receive medical attention and procedures more quickly.

Political and Social Consequences

Lerner (1997) believes that the current ethos of cynicism and selfishness has led to an economy-first attitude. People feel more and more insecure if they are not among those who are "winning" in today's economic marketplace. Lerner envisions an alliance of the shrinking middle class with the poor to work on combating the selfishness, materialism, and corporatism (Saul, 1995) espoused by the rich and by multinational conglomerates. For Lerner, the *politics of meaning* is a political process aimed at achieving the following five goals:

1. to create a society that "encourages and supports love and intimacy, friendship and community, ethnic sensitivity, and spiritual awareness" (55);
2. to redefine production and profit in terms of practices that foster spiritual harmony, loving relationships, mutual recognition, and work that promotes the common good;
3. to construct social conditions that promote the material, emotional, and spiritual uniqueness, sanctity, and infinite preciousness of every human being;
4. to design a society that recognizes the need and provides for the opportunity to develop our inner lives; and
5. to create a society that instills awe and joy in how we relate to the world and one another.

For social workers whose value and ethical base is grounded in principles of social justice, social equality, and respect for the inner being of all humans, these goals, while seemingly idealistic, speak to the very heart of their profession. Many other twentieth-century writers, such as Fromm (1955, 1967), Teilhard de Chardin (1955), Freire (1968, 1985, 1994), Frankl (1969), Gil (1970, 1992, 1998), and Titmuss (1970) have all supported aspects of Lerner's five goals.

Titmuss studied the effects of encouraging altruism (1970) and noted that the donation of blood in such countries as Britain and Canada is done voluntarily and without financial payment, while in other countries, such as the United States, donors are paid for their blood. Titmuss examined whether the altruistic act of donating blood created different results from the market mechanism of purchasing blood. Titmuss concludes that the selling of blood

represses . . . altruism, erodes the sense of community, lowers scientific standards, sanctions . . . the profits in hospitals and clinical laboratories, legalizes hostility between doctor and patient, subjects . . . medicine to the laws of the marketplace, places immense social costs on those least able to bear them . . . [and] increases the danger of unethical behaviour. (245–246)

In effect, blood systems that purchase blood may create a situation in which blood and blood products are transferred from the poor to the rich. Moreover, where blood is given voluntarily, supplies and the quality of these supplies of blood are expected to be superior to those within systems where blood is purchased.

As elaborated in Chapters 5 and 9, there are profound implications to the current ethos of cynicism, as it relates to the environmental movement, global economic and political structures, and the decrease of social service programs.

Social Policy and Social Welfare Policy

Many beginning students of social policy are confused about the terms *social policy* and *social welfare policy*. What is apparent from the various approaches to social policy that we have discussed is the lack of consensus about how *social policy* ought to be defined. The generally prevailing view of social policy is that it is concerned with the "big picture" of society and with the big issues in society, such as social justice, social equality, human rights and freedoms, empowerment and human authenticity, progressive distribution of wealth, full employment, medicare, criminal justice, and mutual aid (Mullaly, 1993).

Because social policy deals with major social issues, it is concerned with the espoused visions and social remedies articulated by such groups as political communities, business communities, professional communities, labour communities, multicultural communities, interest groups, and special-needs communities representing people who are poor, physically challenged, and homeless.

Issues of social power and social control are also important concerns for social policy. In a very real way, social workers who work in the area of social policy become monitors of social conditions and public policies. In this capacity, they play an important role in educating the social work profession and society-at-large regarding anticipated or unanticipated consequences of new or revised public policies or of changes in government and business practices in Canada.

Social policy is also concerned with "politics," trade agreements, environmental issues, hiring practices, taxation, racism, gender and sexual preference discrimination, economics, and other related subjects. Advocates for social justice often use the social policy forum to promote political solutions for social problems (Gil, 1998; Carniol, 1995; Mullaly, 1993); they view the role of the social worker as one of promoting social justice and social equality not only in the service community, but also in the population-at-large. Social change based on humanistic values drives this agenda for change and promotes a collaborative partnership in Canadian policy-making.

Social welfare policy, on the other hand, is concerned with welfare programs and the relationship between public and business policies and welfare programs. As such, it is less abstract and global than social policy and deals with very concrete issues, such as the quality and effectiveness of social service programs, citizen participation in policy and service issues, the role of community, and the actual impact of public policies on people. By studying social welfare policy, social workers directly observe the impact of public policies on the lives of people. As a result, social welfare policy advocates deconstruct the social myths that drive current social programs and encourage people to be directly involved with finding solutions to their life problems.

Social welfare policy advocates are very concerned with the role of the community in the lives of its members (Delaney, Brownlee, & Sellick, 1999; Wharf & McKenzie, 1998; Cassidy, 1991). Wharf and McKenzie (2004) describe community governance by using the metaphor of a three-rung ladder. The first rung represents community programs essentially under community control, such as water and sewage, garbage, parking, and recreation programs. The second rung represents programs mandated by provincial, territorial, or federal government levels but operated by the community. This level includes such programs as child welfare and health services. The third rung is concerned with principles of equity and requires a collaborative partnership between government and the community. Included on this rung are such programs as Social Assistance and Employment Insurance. Wharf and McKenzie (2010) conclude that community governance models provide "more space for more people to participate, to develop a constituency for the human services, and to increase the sense of the participants' self-worth" (142). Moreover, community governance can provide a forum where people who are significantly affected by these outcomes get the opportunity to reform the policy process and policy outcomes.

It is in the area of citizen participation that social welfare policy excels. While social policy tends to deal comprehensively in the political and societal arenas, social welfare policy lends itself to involving people in policy development and renewal. On the one hand, the issues that social welfare policy addresses are issues that people know about and that affect everyday living. People can more readily see the cause–effect relationship between how programs operate and how these programs affect them. It is much easier to involve people in actions that are clear, local, and achievable. On the other hand, advocacy in social policy tends to be national, provincial, or territorial; it also tends to be ideological, value-based, and complex. This makes it much harder to involve people. For example, in a university or college setting, it is always much easier to get students to participate in a march against rising tuition fees than it is to get students to join a political party to influence its educational policies in favour of lowering tuition fees.

A final consideration is the distinction between policy-making and policy advocacy. Jansson (1990) suggests that policy advocates must have analytical skills (for policy evaluation and development), political skills (for development and implementation of political strategies), interactional skills (for development of collaborative partnerships), and values-clarification or ethical-reasoning skills. Both policy advocates and policy-makers must be able to perform six policy tasks: setting agendas, analyzing problems, making proposals, enacting policy, implementing policy, and assessing policy. As Jansson notes,

When presenting problems to agency, community, and legislative decision makers, the [policy practitioners and policy advocates] engage in agenda-setting tasks. When they use social science research . . . practitioners use problem-analyzing tasks. They also analyze social problems, such as homelessness, in classifying homeless persons, gauging the problem's prevalence in various communities, and seeking its causes. (13)

Social Work and Social Policy

All schools of social work have at least one course that deals with social policy. One reason for this is that social policy and social welfare policy govern the environment in which most social workers work. Another reason is that the quality of services available and the attitudes of those who rely on these services for their well-being depend on social policy. As the following section discusses, there are still other reasons why social policy is important to social work.

As subsequent chapters will explain, every social work intervention—be it with an individual, a family, a group, an organization, or a community—is somehow referenced to a social policy. Assisting a family to seek adequate housing invariably relates to social housing policies; assisting an individual to re-enter the community after a prolonged period of incarceration may relate to vocational policies. These considerations therefore influence the nature of Canadian social work education.

From a curriculum perspective, the Educational Policy Statements of *The Manual of Standards and Procedures for the Accreditation of Canadian Programs of Social Work Education* (1996), approved by the Canadian Association of Schools of Social Work (CASSW), state that the social work curriculum at the first university level (HBSW) shall ensure that social work students learn "critical analysis of social work and social welfare history, and social policy as socially constructed institutions and their implications for social work practice" (CASSW, 1996, 3). Accreditation Standard Article 5.8 (d) states that social work students in the first university level shall have "transferable analysis of the multiple and inter-secting bases of oppression and related practice skills" (CASSW, 1996, 6).

Although this explains why schools of social work teach social policy, it does not explain why you should study social policy. Perhaps the following narrative will help.

While driving home from work one day in 1979, I heard on the radio that the city was going to increase swimming pool rates from 10 cents per child to 25 cents per child. I thought to myself that inflation is striking everywhere and, while annoyed, gave this no further thought. After all, a 15-cent raise is not the end of the world.

Three days later, I was listening to the same station's call-in show, and I heard a mother relate the following. She was a single mother with five children, living on social assistance. Each summer, she saved money to allow her children to go swimming three times a week at a cost of $1.50. However, with the new rates, this would now cost her $1.25 per day or $3.75 for the three days. She could not afford this and would have to cut back the time her children could go swimming.

She was greatly distressed, as swimming was one of the few activities to which she could afford to send her children. Now her children would become even more isolated from other children, and she was helpless to do anything about it. When asked why she could not just save more money, the mother replied that she was giving up meals for herself in order for the children to go swimming under the old rates.

I was embarrassed as I listened to this mother and angry that she even had to tell such a story. As a social worker, I should have been more sensitive to the price hike. Worse, since I could afford to pay the extra 15 cents, I did not even consider that there were those who could not. This is one policy I vowed to fight and one new awareness that allows me to assess policies better. I just hope I did learn.

The study of social policy can increase our sensitivity to the people we serve. Because we know the circumstances under which many of our clients live, we can become proponents for policies that will enhance their well-being and advocates against policies that negatively impact them.

The study of social policy also allows you to learn how social inequalities, disempowerment, marginalization, and oppression can seep into political agendas and affect those least able to fight against them. Bishop (1994) sees these elements as part of a "power-over" agenda. A power-over agenda seeks to create a world of systems designed to keep people unequal. It uses four types of power over people. The first type, *political power*, concentrates power in the hands of fewer and fewer people because those making decisions build up the power of their own group. The second type, *economic power*, occurs when one group has access to more economic resources than others. The third type, *physical force*, uses the army and the police to back up economic and political power. The fourth type, *ideological power*, allows one group to influence thought and shape popular ideas of what is possible, desirable, and valuable (36–37).

Understanding how groups gain social, economic, and political power through social policy is important for social workers. Wharf (1990) suggests that social work insufficiently oriented to social change fails in four ways. First, it makes the assumption that once a problem is identified, change will occur and the problem will be solved. This situation is rarely the case in real practice. Second, it ignores power and its distribution in Canada. Third, because society does not assign social workers responsibility for bringing about change, some agencies may become the problem and not the solution. Fourth, the issue of auspices is not addressed: because social workers are employed in agencies that receive their mandates from those holding political power, each agency's political and social agendas limit the social workers' efforts to change the system (Wharf, 1990, 23–25).

By understanding the policy-making process, social workers can learn to advocate for social changes that benefit those in society least able to fend for themselves. Many current beliefs about leadership, privilege, hierarchy, power, and wealth have developed over long periods of history and have created patterned inequalities of status and rights (Gil, 1970, 1992). By exposing these historical inequalities and confronting the metaphors that support social inequality, social workers can participate in the policy debate. In fact, both the American and Canadian Social Work Codes of Ethics make the study of social justice a practice requirement.

It is important for social workers to understand and be sensitive to the different life experiences of Canadians. Moreover, understanding social policies' impact on issues of human diversity is critical for social workers who live in a pluralist society. Social workers are asked to play a variety of practice roles—teacher, enabler, facilitator, mediator, organizer, advocate, case manager, and administrator, among others. Social policy gives an added contextual dimension to these roles because it places the client situation within the social arena—an arena that too often has little or no regard for the client or the client's situation.

The following story outlines one of the authors' experiences with social policy and its direct impact on people.

One day, I reported to my deputy minister, who informed me that a prominent author was coming to the province to assist us with reforms to our institutions for children. A major presentation involving the premier, several provincial and federal ministers, and the prominent author was being planned, and I was asked to be the spokesperson for the province. Flattered but anxious, I read every article and book written by this prominent author until I had prepared a speech that I believed would reflect both the province's and the author's position on reform.

On the day of the presentation, which was being held in the province's largest children's institution, I arrived in a very nervous state. As I walked down the rather dingy corridor leading to the elevator, I could not help but notice the children wandering in the corridor. As I looked at each child, I told myself that I was giving this speech for this child. I kept repeating this thought child by child, and I began to feel energized and confident. After all, I had a cause.

Just as I approached the elevator, I saw a young girl stretched out in a wheelchair. The child had no recognizable face. Her skin was pale and wrinkled, and her nose was two holes on her face. Mucus was running from her nose into a gaping mouth.

As I was giving my speech, I noticed the smiles from the officials on the stage, including the author. I was pleased. After the speeches were finished, the moderator asked whether there were any questions. Among the several hundred people in the audience was a woman who, after a few polite and complimentary questions had been asked by others, said, "This is all well and good, but these children need someone to love them, to hold them, to comfort them. How are your changes going to achieve this if you don't give us more staff?" Politely brushed off, she repeated the same question in many ways until those sitting near her began to physically indicate by their body positions that they were not with her.

I was really angry with this woman because I sensed she had taken the edge off the presentations and, after all, I had been one of the presenters. However, the deputy minister came over to me, shook my hand, congratulated me on an excellent speech, and invited me to join the dignitaries for lunch. Flattered, I said I would be along shortly but I wanted to help package our equipment first. Actually, I just needed to work off energy.

Eventually I went into the elevator and upon leaving had this overwhelming urge to turn around. When I did, I saw the woman who had irritated me holding the little girl who had been in the wheelchair in her arms while she was feeding her. I saw the love on this woman's face as she gazed into the girl's eyes and I sensed the love this little girl returned. I stood transfixed, totally shattered, shamed, and humbled.

This is one of those events in my life that was a gift, albeit a very painful one. Before my eyes was a reminder to me that I chose to be a social worker and I had unconsciously drifted from my own values and belief in human beings. I told myself over and over that social and public policies are about people, and policy and people cannot be compartmentalized. As a policy analyst, I use this moment to understand the human face in policy and the beauty that this rugged woman taught me. I wish every policy analyst and social planner had a moment like mine when the intellect is awakened to human potential and the power of love.

I did not go to lunch. I did not give another speech for five years. But I did learn a beautiful but painful lesson about the human spirit and about the purpose of social policy.

This story is a reminder that policy is about people, not just facts, statistics, laws, rules, manuals, power, and politics. Social workers whose values put people first and promote the human imperative to become more fully human (Freire, 1968) are positioned to play a vital role in the development of Canada's social policy and social welfare policy.

Finally, social policy provides a wealth of information on such issues as how our current social structures came to be; who is benefiting from these structures; who has the real power to make social changes; what the most effective approaches to citizen participation are; who is being oppressed, isolated, or ignored in society; and what array of ideological powers exist to maintain the current social agenda regarding the distribution of wealth, powers, and privilege.

Conclusion

Social policy helps social workers to better understand people. It does this by describing both the social context in which people live and the forces that created this context. It allows us to appreciate that the world in which we live did not just happen. Rather, it was created on the basis of decisions people made about what this society would look like and what values and beliefs would drive the development of this society. The inequalities that exist in Canada are not accidental. Moreover, as this chapter points out, there are different ways of conceptualizing social policy and differences between social policies and social welfare policies, and there is considerable interface between all levels and fields of social work practice and social policies, and such social values as cynicism and ideology have a profound effect on how social policies are created and carried out. The next chapter discusses how understanding the historic origins of social policies means appreciating how social policies evolved, what the major factors in this evolution were, and what might be a reasonable basis for thinking about their present and future development.

Discussion

To help you explore the issue of equality and its importance to social policy, the following exercise is intended to provide a source of discussion.

Are You a Number One?

Issues of equality are of enormous concern to advocates of progressive social welfare in Canada. However, for beginning (and sometimes advanced) students of social policy, this concept can be deceptive, simply because a "living" society is enormously difficult to understand.

Equality does not view human beings as "the same," which is what the political right attempts to say. In fact, it is just the opposite. Equality recognizes that every human being is unique and capable of human development. In essence, equality promotes the notion that every person is entitled to the same chance to develop and evolve her or his human potential.

This exercise uses the number 1.0 to illustrate just how complex this concept of inequality is. Assume that a society assigns every human being in that society the value of 1.0. In a democracy, every eligible citizen has one vote and therefore a 1.0 value. But the term *eligible citizen* suggests that there must be people who are not eligible to vote and who politically are assigned a value of less than 1.0, or in this case, 0. At the turn of the twentieth century, Canada did not allow people who were mentally ill, criminals, women, children, immigrants, refugees, Aboriginals, and others the right to vote. Advocacy groups fought to gain the value of 1.0 for some of these people but not for all. At the turn of the twenty-first century, some of those listed here are still assigned the value of 0 (e.g., immigrants and people who are mentally ill). In other words, they have no voice in the Canadian political election system.

You can apply the number 1.0 to assess how any situation values participants, including individual value, social value, organizational value, and human value at political, civil, and social levels of societal interactions. Obviously, this type of analysis can become very complex very quickly. Experiment by using the number 1.0 to analyze family situations, relationships, social groups, and others. You may wish to read Gil (1998), Saul (1995), Swift (1995), and/or Bishop (1994) for more information on equality.

Chapter 2

Historical Influences

Social policies are in a constant state of change, but their roots may be traced back to the earliest stages of human evolution. Familiarity with history therefore provides you with tools for thinking about how social policies could be constructed for today and tomorrow. Rather than being constrained by the present-day circumstances of time or place, your imagination can be free to consider possibilities. You can readily challenge prevailing assumptions, rather than benignly accepting them. You can also use creative approaches, rather than overlooking them or assuming that they are untenable.

This chapter examines several areas of English Canadian social welfare history; further elaboration of the experiences of Aboriginal peoples and of French-speaking Canada appears in Chapter 6. Although this chapter also presents data in chronological order, the following 12 themes are evident throughout:

1. Policies are in a constant state of evolution—they have taken on different forms during different periods of history.

2. Social policies are "cultural constructs"—they are profoundly influenced by myriad cultures, values, and ideologies in a society.

3. Social policies sometimes represent the highest aspects of being human. At their very best, they reflect a basic concern for other people, a recognition of our interdependence, and an impulse to act upon this recognition.

4. Social policies have a contradictory nature. Among recipients, some aspects have been beneficial, while others, as will be seen, have not. Motivations among proponents of social policies, whether conscious or not, have been just as variable. As a result, social policies may reflect motivations and/or have consequences that are troubling: the drive to contain social unrest, to maintain social control, or to reproduce social inequalities with respect to gender, ethnicity, race, range of mental or physical ability, or other areas of diversity.

5. Social policies have different impacts on different groups in society. Recipients of a particular policy, for instance, may have an experience disparate from that of the person who is paid to carry out the policy.

6. Various concepts in the history of policy development remain with us to the present day, such as the distinction between deserving and undeserving poor, or the local responsibility for social welfare.

7. In contemporary times, social policies have mirrored the growing social and economic complexity of modern life: the increasing mobility of people, the spread of urbanization, the deep impact of industrial capitalist development, and the gradual appreciation of human diversity. Corresponding also with industrial capitalist development has been the increasingly atomized, stratified nature of society, and the rise of bureaucratic structures, of which social work has been an important part.

8. The arrangements of capitalism during the past several decades have eroded the range of social policies and their comprehensiveness. Across the globe, more flexible forms of capital accumulation, labour market organization, and consumption patterns have prevailed. These, in turn, are seen by many observers to have compromised the range of social policy choices available to political leaders. International industrial capitalism and its multinational corporations have been increasingly freed from earlier notions of national responsibility. Environmental policy, workplace conditions, job security, wages, and social policies may well be determined less by national policy and more by the market-driven, lowest-bidder ethos of an increasingly international and competitive industrializing world.

9. The state has increasingly relinquished social service delivery to the private realm, a process often called the *privatization of social services*. This development reflects current national and international trends that emphasize the private marketplace over the direct role of government.

10. More and more, the economy requires a flexible workforce made up of part-time jobs, underemployment, and limited employment in the form of contract jobs of short duration. Social workers, like their clients, will be expected to respond to this new workplace environment, where, among other things, lifelong learning and vocational flexibility prevail.

11. Reflecting the inherently political nature of social policies, the Constitution of Canada is significant in determining which level of government has a particular administrative or financing authority. At the beginning of the twentieth century, local or municipal governments funded and administered most social services. But over the course of the century social welfare responsibilities gradually emerged among provincial and, in particular, federal jurisdictions.

12. The conceptualization of social welfare has transformed from a "residual" to an "institutional" perspective (Wilensky & Lebeaux, 1958) and then finally to a "market-state" perspective (Bobbitt, 2002).

It is this final theme that provides a framework for exploring the preceding ones, as these terms—*residual, institutional,* and *market state*—describe approaches that represent the three major periods in which Canadian social welfare history occurred from European contact to the present time.

The Residual Approach

In Canada, the residual concept of social welfare predominated until the twentieth century. During times of sickness, unemployment, or interrupted or insufficient income, the family and the economic marketplace were considered the "normal" channels of help. For example, if sickness made it impossible for a family member to go to work, alternative sources of income—credit, a loan, or a different family member taking on additional employment—were sought. Alternatively, the family could turn to relatives for temporary assistance. Only after these sources were exhausted would other parties intervene, including members of the immediate community, religious institutions, or, later, charities (Emery & Emery, 1999). This residual model of social welfare contrasts with the institutional approach. The institutional model emphasizes the role of government in responding to social needs, and is elaborated later in this chapter.

Classical Civilizations

The impulse to come to another's assistance is a fundamental part of what it is to be human. Indeed, anthropologists have observed that sharing is an essential characteristic of some of the earliest forms of human organization (Berman, 2000). Among early hunting–gathering societies, when food became scarce and hunger acute, generosity and sharing prevailed over hoarding. This tendency was more than a simple matter of etiquette, because the maintenance of social bonds was essential to determining a group's fertility and rate of survival (Dolgoff & Feldstein, 1984, 16, 26). Given the threat of raids from other tribes or species, and the hazards of eking out an existence amid a harsh physical climate, an individual could not survive without belonging to the collective. In the real life and death context, people were aware of the symbiotic benefits of doing good unto their neighbours.

The present discussion of hunting–gathering societies indicates how the responses we make to those in our identified group differ from those we make to people who are considered outsiders. Traditional societies often differentiate their treatment of members inside their own group from those outside it. In the same manner, contemporary social policies provide benefits for members of Canadian society, yet not to members of other societies. Social welfare assistance is an example of a program that applies only to Canadians living in Canada. Canadian social policies have other subtle ways of distinguishing between insiders and outsiders. As will be seen, particularly in Chapter 6, various areas of diversity—such as race, ethnicity, gender, range of ability, sexual orientation, and others—influence social policies.

Many ancient cultures throughout the world expressed social responsibilities in religious terms. As early as 2000 BC, Sumerian society placed a divine value on the protection of widows, orphans, and the poor. In fourth-century-BC China, Confucian ideals of humane and righteous leadership compelled rulers to target public funds toward the care of the aged, the poor, orphans, or those affected by natural disasters, as well as toward the creation of public lands for the gathering of wood and herbs (Dolgoff & Feldstein, 1984, 28–30). Aboriginal societies in present-day North America continue to use such symbols as the medicine wheel to express the sacred bond between humanity and the physical and spiritual planes of existence (Bopp, Bopp, Brown, & Lane, 1985; Feehan & Hannis, 1993). In the Judeo-Christian tradition, several Old Testament injunctions compel part of an annual harvest to be donated to the poor (Leviticus 19:9–10) and to the widowed and strangers (Deuteronomy 24:19–22). The New Testament instructs Christians to care for the disadvantaged (Matthew 25:31–46) and to forsake the love of material possessions (Luke 6:20–38). Muslims also have a strong tradition of concern for the poor. In fact, one of the Five Pillars of Islam, alms-giving, is described not as a tax or a charity, but as a religious duty (Sura 9:60).

Such widespread religious ideals were manifest in tangible forms. Ancient Grecian temples served as medical centres and care stations for the poor. In Roman society, a system of public charity was so advanced that, during the second century AD, as much as half of Rome's population relied on some form of public assistance. In the Byzantine East, a complex system of maternity hospitals, medical facilities, and food rationing was provided from the revenues of the Orthodox Christian patriarchs (Dolgoff & Feldstein, 1984, 31–40). In our own time, social legislation has been the bedrock of the welfare state and is far from a historical aberration or a peculiarity of our own time. Indeed, one of the earliest explicit social policies, the 1349 Statute of Labourers, occurred in medieval England. In the aftermath of the Black Plague, this statute froze workers' wages to their pre-plague levels and limited the mobility of labour outside of one's home parish (de Schweinitz, 1943, 1–2).

The Medieval and Elizabethan European Heritage

Many of the direct roots of Canadian social policy are derived from a European heritage. Three non-governmental forms of European institutionalized charity gradually developed and were particularly significant. The first of these were the medieval guilds, representing various merchant classes and artisans. Acting as mutual aid societies and charitable organizations for their members, the guilds built and maintained hospitals, distributed food to the needy, provided lodgings for the travelling poor, and gave other forms of incidental help. The second form of charity, the private foundations, were established by affluent benefactors and devoted to the construction and maintenance of hospitals, almshouses, and other such institutions. By the early sixteenth century, there were 460 such foundations in England alone. The third source of charity was the Church, providing assistance through various monastic orders among the thousands of local parishes across the continent. In Western Europe, among other parts of Christendom, tithing to the Church was compulsory, and one-third of all collections went to the poor (Dolgoff & Feldstein, 1984, 39–44). The tithe may be seen as an early precursor to the contemporary income tax system, which helps to finance the modern welfare state.

This elaborate system of medieval charity was turned upside down by the sixteenth-century Protestant Reformation. In England, as in other parts of Europe, Protestant sects emerged, and Roman Catholic monasteries were dissolved. A new system of English social welfare was established and enshrined in the Elizabethan Poor Laws of 1601. Earlier voluntary modes of charity now fell to the local (Parish) governments on a national scale, with accompanying punishments for non-compliance. Each parish was required to appoint an overseer of the poor, who, in consultation with church wardens, dispensed relief to the poor. The significance to the present day is twofold. First, the overseer was an obvious precursor to the modern-day social worker. The role of overseer also had an obvious social control function. Indeed, the fact of Elizabethan overseers provides an excellent reminder that not all of social work's roots have been altruistic. Secondly, these changes meant that for the first time in history, social welfare responsibility became, in practice and in legislation, a formalized, local arrangement. Voluntary forms of charity, including orphanages, hospitals, and almshouses for the old, remained alongside other local arrangements (Leiby, 1978, 38–41). The establishment of a comprehensive state role, a concept that emerged in its complete form in the twentieth century, saw its beginnings, therefore, in the sixteenth century. Up to the present time, this strong presence of local jurisdictions in social service delivery has persisted.

Other aspects of the Elizabethan Poor Laws remain with us today. The principle of local residency was legislated, requiring that an individual receiving alms (or, in contemporary usage, welfare) within a particular parish had to be a resident of that parish. In our own time, local governments as well as provinces have legislated that recipients must live within a particular province or municipality for a certain length of time before being entitled to receive social assistance (Stedman Jones, 2004).

A final feature of Elizabethan welfare was the differentiation made between deserving and undeserving poor, an aspect that had been part of previous forms of charity but which was now outlined in legislation. While present-day terminology and practices may be different, this compulsion to distinguish between those who are worthy and those who are not has endured. In Elizabethan times, the classification was threefold: the impotent poor—that is, those who could not work (pregnant women, extremely sick men or women, those over the age of 60)—were allowed to live in what became known as poorhouses; any able-bodied people who could not seek employment or were temporarily unemployed were consigned to workhouses; and "unregenerate idlers" were placed in houses of correction (Bruce, 1961, 26; Dolgoff & Feldstein, 1984, 46). Today, income security programs differentiate among classes of eligibility. Able-bodied individuals who temporarily cannot work because of work-related illness or injury may apply for Workers' Compensation. Able-bodied individuals who are capable of working but are between jobs may be eligible to receive Employment Insurance (EI), or if EI entitlements run out, provincially/locally administered social assistance programs under various names, including Ontario Works, may be granted. Those who cannot work because of physical or psychiatric incapacity may receive Workers' Compensation long-term disability, Canada Pension Plan long-term disability, or provincially administered income security programs. Those who cannot work because of the responsibilities of single parenthood may receive benefits from provincially administered income security programs (Graham, 2008).

The Elizabethan Poor Laws also distinguished between men and women. For example, women were classed in the impotent poor category. In our own time, as will be seen, social policies have continued to be constructed differentially for men and women.

In the 1600s, as in previous centuries, the plight of the poor was deplorable. Hospitals, poorhouses, workhouses, and other such institutions were invariably overcrowded, lacked public health standards familiar to the contemporary reader, and were the loci of such deadly diseases as cholera, tuberculosis, and typhoid (Desert, 1976; Gonthier, 1978). Marginalized members of society—vagrants and those who were sick or disabled, among others—were forced into poorhouses that were as wretched as—and were sometimes one and the same as—local jails. Levels of alms were deliberately minimal. To seek assistance beyond the residual bounds of one's immediate family or the economic marketplace could be the source of frequent and intense public derision. Idle men refusing work were whipped, sent to prison, or both. Others were permanently maimed in an effort to rid them of their idleness. For these and other reasons, people were known to turn to prostitution, theft, or other crimes to avoid the disgrace and hardships of receiving alms (de Schweinitz, 1943, 20–22; Dolgoff & Feldstein, 1984, 49).

Before leaving the Elizabethan period in England, one final point should be emphasized: the Reformation Protestant theology of Calvin, Luther, and other thinkers influenced virtually all aspects of society, social welfare included. This thinking, moreover, continues to resonate in those twenty-first-century countries, such as Canada, where the historical influence of a Protestant theology remains strong. In Calvinist terms, work was a divine vocation and therefore a religious activity; idleness and worldly temptations interfered with the glory of God. Personal responsibility, discipline, and intense individualism were all revered (Weber, 1930/1958). As for social welfare, a legacy of punitive and repressive approaches found new rationalization. In this Protestant world view, pauperism was thought to result from the character defects of an individual or the flaws of a family. For moral and religious reasons, indiscriminate alms-giving was condemned, and the poor were visited by Poor Law overseers or by other community representatives, such as clergy, to root out the drunk, the idle, and other undesirables (Dolgoff & Feldstein, 1984, 46–47).

The Nineteenth-Century European Heritage

For several centuries, the principles established during the Elizabethan era predominated, but in the early nineteenth century, changes came about because of two issues of public concern: the rising costs of British poor relief and the rising numbers of relief recipients. A three-year royal commission was struck, resulting in the Poor Law Reforms of 1834. These reforms established several new principles. The first was the "less eligibility" principle, which stated that the basic provisions one received while on relief were to be *less* than the lowest-paying available job. The rationale was to dissuade people from receiving relief and to encourage self-reliance via the economic marketplace. This "less eligibility" principle continues to dominate social welfare thinking in our own time. Throughout the 1990s, economists and other analysts referred to and supported the development of policies to encourage swift return to work rather than reliance on income security programs (Burns, Batavia, & DeJong, 1994; Lewin & Hasenfeld, 1995; Schansberg, 1996; Shah & Smith, 1995; Smith, 1993). Beginning in the mid-1990s, social assistance programs in Canada, as in the United States, increasingly tied benefit entitlement to job skill development, job search, and, in some jurisdictions, welfare for work. In the provinces of Alberta and Ontario, for example, social assistance programs have been renamed to "Alberta Works" and "Ontario Works," respectively, to reflect this greater emphasis on job retention. Furthermore, over the last decade, some politicians and policy analysts have called for further reductions in social welfare entitlements, described in the next chapter.

The second 1834 principle was delineation between outdoor and indoor relief, the forerunner of the current Canadian system of provincially/municipally administered social assistance. Outdoor relief provided material assistance to a select category of recipients who were allowed to live at home: the sick, the aged, the orphaned, or the widowed. Indoor relief, in contrast, was limited to able-bodied men who were deemed employable. Indoor relief could not be received at home. Recipients were obliged to live in workhouses and to undertake hard, manual labour—for example, breaking piles of large stones—in compensation for work. The intention was to punish and to limit the appeal of relief so as to encourage the able-bodied to fend for themselves.

This distinction in legislation between outdoor and indoor relief spelled out different categories of the poor and was reminiscent of comparable Elizabethan notions. Also present were various assumptions anchored to the Protestant Reformation: that those poor who had been responsible for their own poverty were morally at fault, but, at the same time, were capable of "uplift"—to use a term from the Victorian era—through discipline, thrift, hard work, and righteous living.

Three prominent thinkers of the nineteenth century also reinforced Poor Law thinking. The first was the Reverend Thomas Malthus, who in the late eighteenth century wrote that the human population was increasing at a greater rate than such means of subsistence as the food supply. This idea, to many, was a clarion call to limit the appeal of relief: if the dependent classes were "coddled," or so the thinking went, they would multiply too quickly and start to exert undue pressure on society's limited material wealth. The second individual was the economist Adam Smith, who saw a natural harmony between the self-seeking of an individual and the well-being of society. His view was typical of the strongly individualist outlook of the eighteenth and nineteenth centuries, which encouraged minimal standards of relief. The third thinker was philosopher Jeremy Bentham, who introduced the utilitarian notion that society should promote the greatest possible good for the greatest possible numbers (Bruce, 1961, 46–47, 78): a form of collectivism, but one that tended to promote the views of the majority and to minimize the benefits for those who were poor or in other ways disempowered.

A final historical experience bears emphasis. The Speenhamland experiment of 1795 was a remarkable example of a social policy that challenged prevailing assumptions. Because of a short harvest and a severe winter, local justices of the peace of the Speenhamland area of England decided to pay subsidies to low-income employed individuals who had families to support—setting a minimum based on the price of bread and scaled according to family size. The Speenhamland experiment, as it later became known, spread to other parts of England. Following its implementation, familiar criticisms led to its abolition. Some argued that individual initiative would cease, the numbers of dependent people would grow, productivity would drop, and costs of relief would rise inordinately. Others argued, in hindsight, that its major problems were the maintenance of artificially low market wages, and the creation of artificial barriers to labour mobility (Bruce, 1961, 41, 76–77; de Schweinitz, 1943, 72–73; Dolgoff & Feldstein, 1984, 55). While historically brief, the Speenhamland experiment highlights the issue of wage supplementation for low-income citizens, which contemporary governments continue to debate. Some Canadian provinces have provisions in their welfare programs to defray additional expenses that recipients face when they start working, such as daycare, transportation, work clothing, and tools. Others have considered programs that ease the transition from welfare to work via a "top-up" income supplementation program during the initial re-entry into the workforce (National Council of Welfare, 2006b). The Speenhamland experiment demonstrates that wage supplementation has historical roots.

Canada Up to 1945

The European heritage blended with a North American context to create a distinctly Canadian approach to social welfare. One of the most significant and tragic aspects of North American history is the colonization of Aboriginal peoples. Sporadic attempts by the Vikings to live along the northeast coast in the tenth century were followed by the permanent settlement of French habitants in the sixteenth century. The habitants lived largely along the St. Lawrence River, in a land they named Nouvelle France. The French—and, after the 1759 conquest of Nouvelle France, the British—forever changed North America. The continent's Aboriginal peoples, decimated by disease and war, were forced onto reserves of land in the late nineteenth and early twentieth centuries, where they were further marginalized—economically, politically, and socially. As elaborated in Chapter 6, the resolutely Eurocentric orientation of Canadian social policies contributed much to the tragedy of the colonization of Aboriginal peoples.

Nouvelle France and, later, British North America possessed an isolating geography, tormenting physical elements, and numerous forms of social misfortune: poverty, vagrancy, alcoholism, illegitimate births, and debtor classes, among others. Long-standing models of European social organization, however, could be adapted only haphazardly to the patterns of sparse inhabitation of frontier settlement. In Nova Scotia and New Brunswick, locally financed overseers of the poor administered Poor Laws. Present-day Quebec, like Newfoundland, relied on the Roman Catholic Church to administer and dispense a complex system of social welfare, in addition to public education and health services. In Ontario, the absence of either Poor Law legislation or a strong Roman Catholic influence meant that spontaneous forms of community concern had to prevail (Boychuk, 1998; Graham, 1995; Splane, 1965).

These machineries of social welfare carried on into the seventeenth, eighteenth, and early nineteenth centuries. But they were later transformed, mirroring the ferment of economic, social, and political changes of the day. Throughout this period, a series of primary economic staples dominated the economy. The cod fisheries of present-day Newfoundland became important in the sixteenth century, and they were supplemented in the sixteenth to the nineteenth centuries by the fur trade, corresponding with the slow but persistent westward pattern of human settlement. The latter gave way to a timber trade in the nineteenth century, and then to a wheat staple, first in present-day Central Canada, and then, after the 1880s, in Western Canada. Over the last quarter of the nineteenth century and into the twentieth, Canada experienced an industrial revolution, making Montreal and Toronto the leading urban centres of a growing network of national cities (Easterbrook & Aitken, 1956).

During this time, there were several waves of immigration, highlighted by Loyalist settlement from south of the border after the American Revolution, significant British immigration during the middle of the nineteenth century, followed by a more diverse European settlement, much of it westward bound, during and after the 1880s (Lower, 1958, 187). From a scattered population of 70 000 in 1759, there appeared significant demographic growth. In 1851, present-day Ontario, Quebec, and the Maritime provinces had a combined population of 2.5 million people. In 1901, Canada's population had risen to 5.37 million, and in 1921, to 9 million (Easterbrook & Aitken, 1956, 395, 400; Prentice et al., 1988, 108). Meanwhile, the percentage of Canadians living in urban centres steadily climbed from 13 percent in 1851, to 35 percent in 1901, to 47 percent in 1921, and to 52.5 percent by 1931 (Artibese & Stelter, 1985, 1887).

In 1867, the former colonies of British North America united to form Canada. Equally significant, the effects of industrialization, urbanization, and demographic growth transformed Canada from a small, resource-based mercantilist economy into an industrializing nation. As society became increasingly complex, social welfare had to adapt accordingly. Houses of Industry—in effect, workhouses for the poor—emerged in Canada in the 1830s, through the influence of the British Poor Law Reforms of that decade. These institutions tended to be administered on a local basis and alongside local and provincial hospitals, with the latter signalling governments' growing responsibility for social welfare. The voluntary sector at the same time remained vital, and a profusion of publicly and privately founded specialized charities were established over the next 80 years, among them: Houses of Providence, Boys' and Girls' Homes, city missions, Protestant and Roman Catholic orphanages, Jewish philanthropic organizations, hospitals for the sick, and refuges for the old. A distinct form of charity also came into being in the late nineteenth century—the settlement house, wherein the well-to-do, often university students, lived among and sought to help a city's poor. These settlement houses were often significant loci of community social change (Desroches, 2009; Irving, Parsons, & Bellamy, 1995). The voluntary sector and the government had a close relationship; neither worked in isolation, nor did the government ever replace the voluntary sector, despite the former's growing involvement in social welfare over the early nineteenth century through to the late twentieth century. As one sociologist points out, "At least since the 1830s, governments [in English-speaking Canada] have been in the business of regulating and funding charities. And the expansion of the voluntary sector historically, as in the contemporary context, has always hinged on substantial government involvement" (Maurutto, 2009, 159).

Likewise, nineteenth-century social welfare institutions and social movements were inextricably linked. For example, religious organizations provided tangible services and a moral rationale for expanded activities, and proved to be a political force compelling greater state intervention into the country's social milieu. The Social Gospel Movement, a loose coalition of Protestant denominations influenced by British and American counterparts, emerged in Canada in the 1890s, applying Christian principles to prevailing social and economic issues. Similar forces were evident in twentieth-century Quebec, where, through the *Semaines sociales*, Roman Catholic clergy and laity discussed social issues. The Social Service Council of Canada, so named in 1913, was a public education and advocacy organization; originally created in 1907, it included representatives from the Anglican, Methodist, Presbyterian, and Baptist churches, as well as the Trades and Labour Congress of Canada (Guest, 1997, 34). Protestant clergymen had been particularly important in the creation, leadership, and perpetuation of the Co-operative Commonwealth Federation (renamed the New Democratic Party in 1961), a social democratic political party elected to national and provincial legislatures and advocating a more comprehensive welfare state (Allen, 1971).

In the late 1880s, what has become known as an *urban reform movement* emerged—a loose coalition of journalists, clergy, charity workers, government officials, and other interested parties. It pursued a broad array of public causes: public control of utilities, including public transit; better public health provisions, including the expansion of public health nursing services, improved sanitation, improved housing standards, and improved standards of meat processing and water quality; the establishment of more green spaces (parks and playgrounds) in urban areas; and improved standards of relief, child welfare, and other social programs (Stelter & Artibese, 1977). A leading proponent was Toronto *Globe* journalist J.J. Kelso, founder of the Toronto Humane Society in 1887, later renamed the Children's Aid Society (Fingard, 1989, 171; Jones & Rutman, 1981). Another was Herbert B. Ames, a well-to-do Montreal manufacturer who published an 1897 study titled *City on the Hill*, documenting the deplorable living conditions endured by Montreal's working class (Copp, 1974).

The working class itself did much to assist the working poor; nineteenth-century workers organized fraternal societies, with each member contributing a small regular amount to a fund from which they could draw if sickness or an accident interfered with work. Canadian trade unions helped to raise standards of living, protect workers' wages, and improve workplace conditions (Kealey, 1980;

Palmer, 1979). Women were responsible for fundraising and service provision within many local charities. By the end of the nineteenth century, these women's activities had expanded to include a number of reform organizations, many now national in scope. The National Council of Women (established in 1893), the Woman's Christian Temperance Union (1874), and the Young Women's Christian Association (established nationally in 1895), to name three, sought numerous social improvements, including women's right to vote (obtained federally in 1918 and provincially shortly before and afterwards), and social policies that would assist women and children (Kealey, 1979; Strong-Boag, 1976).

One of the most important social effects of industrialization was the segregation of people according to gender. In earlier economies, a family's income would often focus on agricultural production and take place at home, relying on the work of men, women, and children within families. But in an industrial economy, a family's livelihood depended more and more on men's employment outside the home; some literature refers to this as the phenomenon of the *breadwinner male*. Increasingly, women in the industrial economy remained at home and focused their attention increasingly on such domestic work as raising children, cooking, laundering, and sewing, and less on producing goods for trade or barter; certain literature refers to this phenomenon as *women's domesticity*, or *the domestication of women*. In an industrial society, there emerged a gendered split between the public realm outside the home, dominated by men, and the domestic realm of women and children. However, women's social advocacy and charitable activities, it should be stressed, did take women outside the home. And they were important precedents to the growing presence of women employed outside the home during the post-1960s period.

Patriarchy was and still is a major theme of social welfare history. The political franchise had been extended in the nineteenth century to include men who did not hold property. But only in the post–World War I period did women achieve the right to vote in federal elections—a right that was established in the West during the war and that spread to other provinces until 1940, when Quebec women got the right to vote. Another landmark was the 1929 Famous Five court challenge, in which five Canadian women successfully sought legal recognition as persons under the British North America Act.

The Industrial Revolution of the nineteenth century ushered in massive disparities in health and standards of living between those who worked in factories and those of greater means. It also created large concentrations of urban poverty (Ball & Gready, 2006). Unions were at the fore of the charge to change these inequalities, always against concerted opposition. After much effort, a nine-hour day was successfully obtained in 1872, and the Canadian Labour Union was created but then abolished that same decade. The Royal Commission on the Relations of Labour and Capital (1887) ultimately recognized the social value of unions. By the 1890s, there were 240 unions nationwide, and with a growing urban reform and women's movement, positive change was occurring. By 1894, labour had become so respectable that the first Monday in September became a national holiday (now known as *Labour Day*). In 1900, the federal government established the Department of Labour to mediate disputes between workers and owners.

The nineteenth and twentieth centuries also covered the tragic story of oppression of Aboriginal peoples—first by the experience of European contact, disease, and economic exploitation; and then, during the development of Nouvelle France, British North America, and Canada, by the taking over of an entire continent by colonizers. A series of land treaties were negotiated between successive colonizing governments, and the 1876 Indian Act enshrined this colonial orientation—defining what was meant by *Indian*, extending power to the Canadian government to regulate Aboriginal peoples, providing federal government guardianship over Aboriginal lands, and restricting the political franchise to those who assimilated. An infrastructure of assimilation emerged during the post-Confederation period, during which some Christian churches and government officials collaborated to provide residential schooling for Aboriginal children. The legacy of residential schooling has traumatized generations of Aboriginal peoples and continues to have massive negative repercussions to this day. Also during the post-Confederation period, Aboriginal peoples were relegated to reserves of land, many of which remain chronically underserviced for basic urban infrastructures and became places of high unemployment and high despair. Chapter 6 elaborates.

Chapter 6 also discusses the impact of racism on Canadian society—a major theme in the history of Canadian social policy, as in Canadian history in general. Prior to the early 1960s, Canadian immigration policy was overtly racist, stating preferences for immigration to certain preferred ethnic and racial backgrounds. The state promoted racist policies. It interned Ukrainian Canadians during World War I and Japanese Canadians during World War II; in 1885, it imposed a head tax on people of Chinese background to reduce immigration, and in 1923, it excluded Chinese immigration entirely (rescinded in 1947).

The Canadian social work profession in its early years therefore was largely white. It also had strong roots in national organizations that represented women, churches, and trade unions, as discussed above. It was likewise influenced by the Charity Organization movement, which was preceded by American and British counterparts and which sought to rationalize charity, to make it more efficient, more humane, and more proficient in its techniques. The world's oldest schools of social work opened in Great Britain in 1890 and the United States in 1903, and Canada's first school appeared soon afterwards, at the University of Toronto in 1914. It was followed by similar schools at McGill University (1918), the University of British Columbia (1928), the Université de Montréal (1939), and at an independent institution that ultimately became affiliated with Dalhousie University (1941) in Halifax, Nova Scotia. The Canadian Council on Child Welfare was founded in 1920 (renamed the Canadian Welfare Council in 1935 and the Canadian Council on Social Development in 1969). The Canadian Association of Social Workers was founded in 1926, and two years later, the First International Conference of Social Work was convened, spawning the International Association of Schools of Social Work. These were among the myriad organizations that sought more comprehensive social policies at the provincial, national, and international levels (Graham, 1996b).

Social Policies

Among the most significant pieces of social policy legislation before World War II was the Workmen's Compensation Act of 1914, first established in Ontario but soon imitated by other provinces. It provided injured workers with regular cash income as a right, rather than as something that followed often lengthy litigation against an employer. As early as 1919, the federal government was pledging to create national systems of health insurance and unemployment insurance (UI, now named Employment Insurance or EI). But a national system of health insurance did not come into being until 1966. UI finally came into force in 1940, several decades after the establishment of comparable programs in Britain and other advanced industrialized nations. Its introduction had been delayed for decades because of the federal government's reluctance to amend the Canadian Constitution to allow the federal government jurisdiction in this area. Meanwhile, in 1916, Manitoba became the first province to introduce Mother's Pensions, a selective program providing a small, means-tested income to widows and divorced or deserted wives and their children (Guest, 1997). The next major piece of legislation—also selective—was the 1927 Old Age Pensions Act, the cost of which was shared on a fifty–fifty basis by the federal and provincial governments.

Under Section 92 of the Canadian Constitution (the British North America Act, 1867, renamed in 1982 as the Constitution Act, 1867), the areas of education, health, and welfare were (and remain to this day) provincial prerogatives. But by strength of precedent, local governments continued to take on funding and administrative responsibilities for many social programs. As creatures of the provinces with no constitutionally prescribed autonomy of their own, municipalities could be created and disbanded by provincial writ and tended to have a limited tax base. But because of the unprecedented extent and duration of unemployment during the 1930s, local governments could not withstand the financial and administrative commitments of unemployment relief, among other social programs for which they had always been held responsible. Over the course of that decade, higher levels of government consequently took on greater financial responsibility (Graham, 1995). In the process, social welfare was massively transformed.

The Institutional Approach

Canada, 1945–1973

Canada changed dramatically after World War II. Immigration levels increased significantly. New immigration selection practices came into effect in 1962, intending to introduce principles that were universal and non-discriminatory; in 1967, further selection practice changes led to the introduction of what was intended to be a more objective points system. This is not to suggest, however, that Canadian immigration practices became entirely objective. Indeed, as several scholars point out, there remain discriminatory standards, sometimes less obvious and sometimes different from earlier practices. Excellent current examples relate to the rules and procedures that categorize immigrants in three main groups (family class, economic class, and refugee class), that set the number of individuals to admit in each of these categories, and that emphasize integration into Canadian society in relation to societal barriers for immigrants in each of these categories (Beach, Green, & Reitz, 2004).

The country's growing racial and ethnic diversity, discussed in Chapter 6, was further reinforced by the federal government's introduction of an official policy of multiculturalism in 1971, the Charter of Rights and Freedoms in 1982, and the Canadian Multiculturalism Act in 1987. In addition to being significantly more diverse, the country's population was also more numerous. In 1971, Canada consisted of 21.6 million people, nearly a twofold increase from 1941. In the same year, 1971, the percentage of Canadians living in urban centres had increased to 76.1 percent.

Social work grew proportionately. In 1941, the census reported 1767 social workers in Canada. By 1981, there were more than 27 590 (Drover, 1988, 2034). An earlier reliance on a two-year, post-BA diploma (and before this a one-year, post-BA certificate) gave way, in the post-war era, to the dominance of the Bachelor of Social Work/Master of Social Work sequence.

The country's first Doctor of Social Work program was inaugurated at the University of Toronto in 1952. Moreover, by 1949, there were eight Canadian social work schools—nearly a threefold increase over a ten-year period—and by 1970, there were twelve (Graham, 1996a, 129). Numerous social workers forever changed the face of Canadian society. Harry Cassidy (1900–1951), an economist at the University of Toronto School of Social Work, wrote numerous studies on Canadian social security programs. Charlotte Whitton (1896–1975), director and driving force behind the Canadian Welfare Council (later named the Canadian Council on Social Development), was responsible for several aspects of the profession's history. Yet although she crusaded for improved standards of child welfare and for changes in social policies, she also advocated harsh welfare assistance eligibility requirements for single mothers, among other practices that might be considered less than progressive by today's standards (Rooke & Schnell, 1987). Bessie Touzel (1904–1997) was trained in the 1920s at the University of Toronto and held a succession of appointments of increasing responsibility, such as chief of the Ottawa Public Welfare Department, executive secretary of the Toronto Welfare Council, and executive director of the Ontario Welfare Council. A staunch advocate of improved casework practices, she wrote numerous policy studies, was an adviser to the Marsh Commission (see below), and served with the United Nations in Tanzania (Obituaries, *The Globe and Mail*, April 26, 1997).

Social Policies

Everything changed after the 1943 *Report on Social Security for Canada* (the Marsh Report), written by economist Leonard Marsh, who taught social work at McGill University. The Marsh Report echoed the famous 1942 Beveridge Report in Great Britain. Both were blueprints for a comprehensive and largely universal welfare state in their respective countries, and both provided a rationale for what scholars describe as an institutional model of social policy. In contrast to the residual approach, the institutional approach saw the welfare services as normal, "first line" functions of modern industrial society, a proper, legitimate function of modern industrial society in helping individuals to achieve self-fulfillment (Wilensky & Lebeaux, 1958, 138). The tendency to construct stigmatizing programs was much reduced, and means testing, under a universal program, was no longer the primary requirement for eligibility. Under universal programs, a sense of entitlement, or right of citizenship, prevailed (Graham, 2008).

As noted in Figure 2.1, spending for social programs increased markedly over the following several decades. Following the introduction of UI, the next major Marsh Report proposal, a universal Family Allowances (FA) program, came into being in 1944: regardless of family income, *all* Canadian mothers of children under the age of 16 would receive a monthly allowance (Blake, 2009). The next major development after that was the 1951 conversion of the Old Age Security (OAS) program from a selective to a universal program. As of that year, all seniors over the age of 70 would receive a pension, regardless of their level of income.

A universal system of health insurance first appeared in Saskatchewan, under the political leadership of the first social democratic government elected in North America: the Co-operative Commonwealth Federation. In 1945, Premier Tommy Douglas set up a social assistance medical care plan covering old age pensioners, recipients of mothers' allowances, blind pensioners, and wards of the state. This selective program was supplemented in 1947 by the introduction of universal, state-administered hospital insurance, and in 1959, by universal, province-wide medical insurance. Meanwhile, in 1956, the federal government initiated the Hospital Insurance and Diagnostic Services Act, a negotiated cost-sharing

FIGURE 2.1   Total Social Spending in Canada, 1945–46 to 1992–93

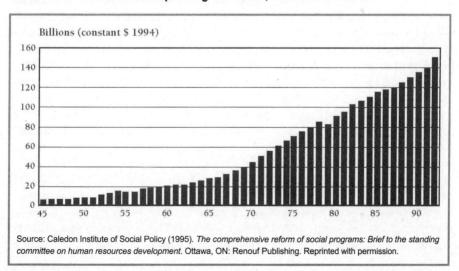

Source: Caledon Institute of Social Policy (1995). *The comprehensive reform of social programs: Brief to the standing committee on human resources development.* Ottawa, ON: Renouf Publishing. Reprinted with permission.

agreement between Ottawa and the provinces, covering a basic range of in-patient hospital services. Again, following the lead of Saskatchewan, the federal government installed a universal health-care system in 1966; and by 1972, every province and territory was administering its own health services. The story of social policy has been one of intense competition between groups in society, and health care was no exception. Companies that had provided private health insurance resisted what some perceived to be the intrusion of the state. So, too, did many physicians acting individually and through professional associations, claiming that physicians' autonomy would be compromised, and that access to comprehensive health-care services would be reduced (Naylor, 1986).

As the legislation described it, "programs for the provision of assistance and welfare services to and in respect of persons in need" were cost-shared equally, on a fifty–fifty basis, by the federal government and each province under the Canada Assistance Plan (CAP). The Medical Care Act (1966) was another cost-sharing plan. Under the CAP, provinces also set up and administered such social services as child welfare protection, rehabilitation, home support for the elderly and people who were disabled, employment programs, child care, and social assistance. The federal government, with massive revenue sources from the income tax system, corporate taxes, and tariffs, was expected to provide otherwise vulnerable programs with a solid basis of funding.

As early as 1966, the federal government had introduced the Canada Pension Plan (CPP), providing social insurance protection for retirement and disability, as well as survivors' benefits. A national program (with the exception of Quebec, which legislated the equivalent in the Quebec Pension Plan), the CPP was a compulsory plan tied to workplace earnings and was portable if the individual moved or took on a different job within Canada. The CPP and OAS were supplemented in 1966 by an income-tested pension plan for low-income earners, the Guaranteed Income Supplement.

But as Andrew Jackson and Matthew Sanger (2003) point out, "from the 1950s through to the mid-1970s, even as state provision of direct care expanded, the voluntary social services sector" increased in like proportion (30). In Canada, voluntary sectors were not ipso facto replaced by an increasingly robust government responsibility for social well-being: "It is wrong to see a process of one-dimensional evolution from voluntaristic charity provision" of the residual era to the formal, state structures of institutionalism. "As the welfare state grew, so did the non-profit sector" (2003, 30).

On the international scene, the seeds of an emerging globalization of the market-state era had already been sown. Post–World War II economic arrangements were concluded by the Bretton Woods Agreements (1944), which culminated in the development of the International Monetary Fund (IMF), the International Bank for Reconstruction and Development (later renamed the World Bank, or WB), and a proposal for an international trading organization (developed in 1947 as the General Agreement on Tariffs and Trade—GATT—later, in 1994, developing into the World Trade Organization, or WTO). These new international economic institutions were driven by American economic and foreign policy

(Hobsbawm, 1995) and coincided with the emergence of more powerful transnational corporations (Ellwood, 2006). Europe in the post–World War II period experienced the Marshall Plan (1947), in which billions of dollars of aid and technical assistance poured into those European countries that had joined the Organisation for Economic Co-operation and Development (OECD, established 1948). In the 1960s, a comparable Marshall Plan was proposed for an emerging, post-colonial Africa but was rejected by Global North policy elites—a move that development economist Jeffrey Sachs has labelled racist.

Several important international institutions had emerged after World War I, including the precursor to the United Nations: the League of Nations (1919); its member agency, the International Labour Organization (1919), which intended to promote the rights of labour worldwide; and the International Council on Social Welfare (1928). In the aftermath of World War II, the United Nations was established in 1945, and with it came the emergence of a battery of social welfare institutions at the international level, including the World Health Organization (1948), the United Nations Children's Fund (UNICEF) (1946), and the United Nations Development Programme (1965). The 1948 Universal Declaration of Human Rights is an exemplary international covenant adopted by the United Nations, and a succession of other policies followed: the International Covenant on Economic, Social, and Cultural Rights (1966); the International Covenant on Civil and Political Rights (1966); and the Convention on the Rights of the Child (1984), among others (Ball & Gready, 2006).

The Market-State Approach

By the late 1960s and early 1970s, it seemed as though many of the basic programs had been established, and continued policy initiatives would simply fill in the gaps that had been overlooked or had developed. The UI program was considerably expanded in 1971 by increasing benefit rates, widening the program's compulsory coverage to include nearly all employees and easing qualifying conditions. During the same decade, the CPP benefit rates were also elevated, and OAS benefits were extended to recipients' widows (Guest, 1997, 173, 188). A growing awareness of female poverty led to the 1975 introduction of the Spouse's Allowance, a means-tested supplement paid to old age pensioners' spouses. Several studies in the late 1960s and 1970s, including a Senate Committee report, *Poverty in Canada* (1971), revealed as many as one in five Canadians living in poverty (Guest, 1997, 156). The report called for a Guaranteed Annual Income (GAI), which would have provided, had it been adopted, a minimum threshold of income below which no individual would fall. There also emerged a gradual recognition of poverty and inequality as a reflection of such social diversities as gender, ethnicity, race, Aboriginal status, range of ability, and geography. These, given their critical significance, are examined in greater depth in Chapter 6.

Historian Philip Bobbitt considers the rise of the twentieth-century welfare-state period in a broad historical context, from the mid-fifteenth-century emergence of the European princely state (which was founded when people rallied around a prince for mutual protection) through to the late nineteenth-century nation-state, when the twentieth-century welfare state began to unfold (Bobbitt, 2002). The post-welfare-state period of the mid-1970s to the present is manifestly different, a cataclysmic shift from the nation-state structure to a market-state structure (Bobbitt, 2002).

Just as many countries of the previous period, Canada included, could be described as nation-states, so too are many countries in addition to Canada now market states. The market state is characterized by a number of factors, including computer technology and communication on a global scale, the decentralization of governments, the reduced scope and sanction of government, the increased significance of liberal ideology (as elaborated in the next chapter), and the increasing importance of the private sector. The "market" has become a defining metaphor, the benchmark by which government and non-government sectors operate. In a market state, the growing authority of the private and voluntary sectors has replaced the old era of governments funding and delivering a welfare state. The state's primary purpose, although limited in scope, is to support private-sector goals and the economic growth and accumulation that represent them. As Bobbitt (2002) points out, governments within the market state are no longer mandated to provide for the welfare of the nation. The extent of the social welfare responsibilities of government are entirely reduced from that which Marsh and Beveridge envisioned in the mid-1940s. In the institutional period, Canadians were citizens; in the market-state era, Canadians are consumers. As Chapter 1 describes, this period can be aptly viewed as an age of cynicism.

Social Policies

As the market state emerged in the mid-1970s, several factors conspired to gradually erode Canadian social policies, and this erosion marks the underlying difference between the institutional and market-state models of social policy. Seven aspects relating to the market-state period are of particular significance. The first is that government funding for social programs, when adjusted for inflation, has remained largely the same since the mid-1970s (see Figures 2.2 to 2.7). But, overall, the amount of social spending compared with the percentage of Gross Domestic Product (GDP, the value of goods and services produced in the economy based on earnings inside the country) has dropped several points since the early 1990s, essentially demonstrating the reduced spending in this budgetary sector. The turning point in the history of social spending in Canada occurred in the early 1990s. These figures show income security expenditures and demonstrate increases into the early 1990s for all levels of government and for per capita spending, followed by a decade-long period of marginal decreases in spending relative to total GDP, total spending, and total social spending. The latter category of comparison is significant because it signifies the changing trajectory of social policy and program financing. For example, social spending has remained relatively consistent, but the proportion that funds income security programs has diminished. Greater analysis is needed to determine precisely what is considered social policy amid the decreases in traditional programs developed during the welfare-state period.

FIGURE 2.2   Total Social Spending in Canada, 1978 to 2007

Note: All data was converted to constant 2007 dollars, as calculated by the Bank of Canada Inflation Calculator at www.bankofcanada.ca/en/rates/inflation_calc.html.

Sources: Human Resources and Social Development Canada (2005). *Social security statistics Canada and provinces 1978–79 to 2002–03*. Ottawa: Author. www.hrsdc.gc.ca/encs/sp/sdc/socpol/tables/page2/shtml. Reproduced with the permission of Her Majesty the Queen in Right of Canada 2010.

Statistics Canada CANSIM database. http://estat.statcan.gc.ca/cgi-win/cnsmcgi.exe?Lang=E&EST-Fi=EStat/English/CII_1-eng.htm. Table no. 385-0001. Reproduced with permission from Statistics Canada, 2010.

FIGURE 2.3   Total Social Spending in Canada Per Capita, 1978–79 to 2002–06

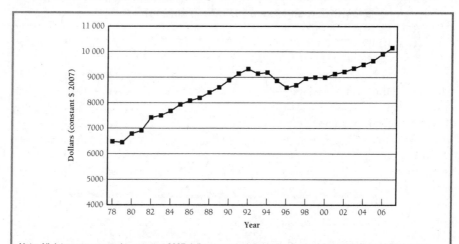

Note: All data was converted to constant 2007 dollars, as calculated by the Bank of Canada Inflation Calculator at www.bankofcanada.ca/en/rates/inflation_calc.html.

Sources: Human Resources and Social Development Canada. (2005). *Social security statistics Canada and provinces 1978–79 to 2002–03*. Ottawa: Author. www.hrsdc.gc.ca/encs/sp/sdc/socpol/tables/page2/shtml. Reproduced with the permission of Her Majesty the Queen in Right of Canada 2010.

Statistics Canada CANSIM database. http://estat.statcan.gc.ca/cgi-win/cnsmcgi.exe?Lang=E&EST-Fi=EStat/English/CII_1-eng.htm. Table nos. 385-0001; 051-0001. Reproduced with permission from Statistics Canada, 2010.

FIGURE 2.4   Total Social Spending in Canada as Percentage of GDP, 1978–79 to 2002–06

Note: All data was converted to constant 2007 dollars, as calculated by the Bank of Canada Inflation Calculator at www.bankofcanada.ca/en/rates/inflation_calc.html.

Sources: Human Resources and Social Development Canada (2005). *Social security statistics Canada and provinces 1978–79 to 2002–03*. Ottawa: Author. www.hrsdc.gc.ca/encs/sp/sdc/socpol/tables/page2/shtml. Reproduced with the permission of Her Majesty the Queen in Right of Canada 2010.

Statistics Canada CANSIM database. http://estat.statcan.gc.ca/cgi-win/cnsmcgi.exe?Lang=E&EST-Fi=EStat/English/CII_1-eng.htm. Table nos. 385-0001; 380-0002. Reproduced with permission from Statistics Canada, 2010.

FIGURE 2.5   Total Government (Federal, Provincial, and Municipal) Income Security Expenditures, 1978–79 to 2002–07

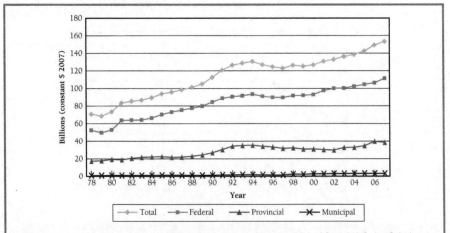

Note: All data was converted to constant 2007 dollars, as calculated by the Bank of Canada Inflation Calculator at www.bankofcanada.ca/en/rates/inflation_calc.html.

Sources: Human Resources and Social Development Canada (2005). *Social security statistics Canada and provinces 1978–79 to 2002–03*. Ottawa: Author. Retrieved May 15, 2007, from www.hrsdc.gc.ca/en/cs/sp/sdc/socpol/tables/page02.shtml. Reproduced with the permission of Her Majesty the Queen in Right of Canada 2010.

Statistics Canada (2009). *Government transfer payments to persons*. Retrieved July 27, 2010, from http://www40.statcan.gc.ca/l01/cst01/govt05a-eng.htm. Reproduced with permission from Statistics Canada, 2010.

FIGURE 2.6   Total Government (Federal, Provincial, and Municipal) Income Security Expenditures Per Capita, 1978–79 to 2002–06

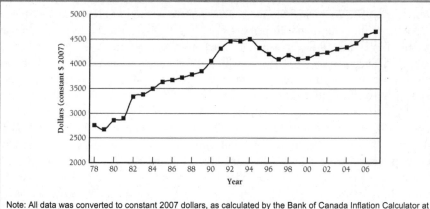

Note: All data was converted to constant 2007 dollars, as calculated by the Bank of Canada Inflation Calculator at www.bankofcanada.ca/en/rates/inflation_calc.html.

Sources: Human Resources and Social Development Canada (2005). *Social security statistics Canada and provinces 1978–79 to 2002–03*. Ottawa: Author. Retrieved May 15, 2007, from www.hrsdc.gc.ca/en/cs/sp/sdc/socpol/tables/page02.shtml. Reproduced with the permission of Her Majesty the Queen in Right of Canada 2010.

Statistics Canada CANSIM database at http://estat.statcan.gc.ca/cgi-win/cnsmcgi.exe?Lang=E&EST-Fi=EStat/English/CII_1-eng.htm. Table no. 051-0001. Reproduced with permission from Statistics Canada, 2010.

Statistics Canada (2009). *Government transfer payments to persons*. Retrieved July 27, 2010, from http://www40.statcan.gc.ca/l01/cst01/govt05a-eng.htm. Reproduced with permission from Statistics Canada, 2010.

FIGURE 2.7   Total Government (Federal, Provincial, and Municipal) Income Security Expenditures as Percentage of GDP, Total Social Security Spending, and Total Spending, 1978–79 to 2002–07

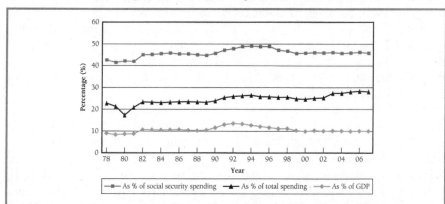

Sources: Human Resources and Social Development Canada (2005). *Social security statistics Canada and provinces 1978–79 to 2002–03*. Ottawa: Author. Retrieved from www.hrsdc.gc.ca/en/cs/sp/sdc/socpol/tables/page02.shtml. Reproduced with the permission of Her Majesty the Queen in Right of Canada 2010.

Statistics Canada CANSIM database. http://estat.statcan.gc.ca/cgi-win/cnsmcgi.exe?Lang=E&EST-Fi=EStat/English/CII_1-eng.htm. Table nos. 380-0002; 385-0001; 384-0009. Reproduced with permission from Statistics Canada, 2010.

Several factors have influenced the erosion of these traditional social policies. A primary factor is the decline of federal government transfer payments to provinces, which began under the CAP in the 1970s and accelerated up to 1992–93, when the federal share of CAP transfers to the country's three wealthiest provinces was down to 28 percent in Ontario and 36 percent in British Columbia and Alberta (National Council of Welfare, 1995, 7). The CAP itself was replaced in 1996 by the Canada Health and Social Transfer (CHST), which reduced federal government contributions to education, health care, and social welfare by another 15 percent during the first two years of its implementation (Graham, 2008). The CHST also reduced the federal government's ability to enforce standards as to how the money would be spent and to which of the three major block areas money would be allocated (National Council of Welfare, 1995). Following the CHST, in 2004, two separate transfer programs were created: the Canada Health Transfer and the Canada Social Transfer. Changes in the 2007–08 Federal Budget sought to improve the transparency of how transfer money is spent. Provincial governments, meanwhile, have tended to reduce transfers to local governments for the delivery of programs administered and partially financed by municipalities. These programs vary from province to province but, depending on the province, may include child welfare, general welfare assistance, homemaking, rehabilitation services, and other forms.

At the same time, the contributions of individuals and their employers to various programs such as UI/EI (see below) and CPP have increased steadily. Funding reductions of the CAP and of social programs not associated with the CAP (e.g., UI, FA, CPP, OAS) have helped to create a second feature of the market-state era: the persistent and definite shrinkage in the comprehensiveness and extent of social programs. For example, after 50 years of funding the UI program, the federal government removed its financial support in 1990, making the program fully funded by employer and worker contributions. In the same year, more restrictive eligibility criteria were introduced, alongside shortened benefit periods, higher premiums, and more severe penalties to claimants quitting their jobs without "just cause" (Human Resources and Social Development Canada, 2007; Chappell, 2006, 49). In 1996, UI was changed to Employment Insurance (EI), and various reforms, intended to produce further savings of $1.9 billion, sought to reduce the maximum stay on insurance, penalize repeat users, and take back a proportion of payments from wealthier recipients (Battle, 2001).

While health care has undergone significant erosion in its funding base, the federal government released an important 1984 policy document, the Canada Health Act (CHA), which was widely viewed as an instrument to maintain federal standards. The document reaffirms five principles of our universal health-care system: its universality, comprehensiveness, accessibility (minimal barriers to services), portability (transferability of services from province to province), and public administration. In the 2007–08 Federal Budget, the government reaffirmed its commitment to these principles; but its ability to enforce these standards may be impaired. Enduring tensions throughout the last decade can be illustrated by the struggle over funding experienced in Alberta. Its government released *A Framework for Reform: Report of the Premier's Advisory Council on Health* in 2002 to lead policy decisions "on what health services are publicly insured in addition to those required under the Canada Health Act" (Government of Alberta, 2002). Many questioned the intention of the report, warning that the onus of increasing the quality of services by way of sustainability and competition would point the province in the direction of privatization (Makarenko, 2007). Opponents argued that diversifying revenue streams through the introduction of user fees and extra-billing contrary to the CHA would jeopardize the very nature of the health system and erode the principle of fair and equitable access.

Fears seem to have been put to rest since the 2008 inception of Alberta Health Services, a publicly funded province-wide authority that co-ordinates the delivery of all health services. More recently, the province's vision was reconfirmed in *Becoming the Best: Alberta's 5-Year Health Action Plan 2010–2015*, a document published in November 2010 that assures the government's five-year commitment to Alberta Health Services of almost $50 billion (Alberta Health Services, 2010). Following the creation of a new Alberta Health Act, the plan established a series of initiatives that correspond with the pioneering funding policy. Despite these developments, criticism persists regarding the Alberta government's aggressive tactics of debt elimination and its resultant $17 billion Sustainability Fund, which is meant to protect the very institutions whose funding was cut (Statistics Canada, 2010b). Suspicions of policy shifts toward privatization of health care, delisting of services, and the permissibility of flexible legislation continue to make headlines in the province (Kleiss, 2010).

A third and related aspect of welfare-state retrenchment is the replacement of universal programs with selective programs. An excellent example is the 1992 replacement of the universal Family Allowances (FA) with the Child Tax Benefit, which combines the former FA and child tax credits into one refundable, income-tested child tax credit. In addition, the 1989 introduction of a claw back on OAS payments to upper-income Canadians essentially abolished the universal basis of this program. As one policy document observes, the de-indexing against inflation of the threshold beyond which the OAS is taxed back means that an increasing number of Canadians will receive partial or no benefits (Battle & Torjman, 1993, 4). These are but two examples of the trend to move away from universal programs.

A fourth aspect underlying many of the above changes is the growth of government debt. The debt is a cumulative, multiyear calculation based on the total amount of money that the government owes. It is different from a deficit, which is a yearly calculation of annual operating costs where spending exceeds revenue. While all levels of government experience debts and deficits, the present analysis, for sake of illustration, considers only the federal scene. In 2007, the federal government's total debt was $588 billion, or $17 939 for every Canadian. This amount is a considerable increase from 1965, when the deficit was $17 billion, or roughly $860 per person. Between 1965 and 1975, the federal government deficits were still below 2 percent of GDP, and the debt was a low 18 percent. A combination of circumstances—a recession, accelerated borrowing, and an inability to match revenues with expenses—increased the debt to 48 percent of GDP by 1982, and by 1994 it was 71 percent ("Fair Taxes", 1995). During the following decade, reduced interest rates on the debt and drastic trimming of program expenditures helped to spur an economic climate of recovery in the country. In 2001, the debt ratio fell to 53 percent (Little, 2001), and by 2006 it decreased to 35 percent (Department of Finance Canada, 2006). Despite lengthy and costly military involvement in Afghanistan and a recent recession, the current debt-to-GDP ratio is estimated at 35.4 percent (Stittle, March 4, 2010). The Canadian government aspires to reduce it to 31.9 percent by 2014–15. Yet, extensive cost-saving strategies, including capping investments to International Assistance, thinning the annual increase in military spending, and other policy directives, will only slow down the growth of the national debt. Its $566.7 billion price tag will continue to escalate and is expected to reach $622.1 billion by 2014–15. It is not debt in itself that matters, however, but rather how policy analysts, politicians, and others interpret the causes and significance of debt. When social programs are considered the cause of debt, then these programs get cut.

A fifth theme is the gradual recognition—through federal and provincial human rights legislation, the 1982 Charter of Rights and Freedoms, and other policy initiatives—of the rights of historically disempowered peoples, such as Aboriginal peoples, members of ethnoracial and religious minority communities, women, gays and lesbians, and people with disabilities, among others. Yet some of the institutions that had sought these rights in the past are disappearing. In 2009, 29.9 percent of Canadian workers belonged to a union, prolonging a steady downward trend from 38 percent in 1981 (Human Resources and Skills Development Canada, January 15, 2010). Younger workers, particularly those under age 35, experienced more pronounced declines in union membership than older workers (Morissette, Schellenberg, & Johnson, 2005). In addition, as Chapter 5 points out, new conceptions of community and individual rights are developing. This development is a sea change in social policy: moving from an institutional era of justice as distribution and redistribution, to a market era of justice as the politics of recognition and individual rights (Bakan, 1997; Fraser, 1995).

Likewise, a sixth theme, as elaborated in Chapter 4, is the rise of a neo-liberal ideology. This includes the primacy of financial markets, where even public pension funds, traditional instruments of the institutional state era, are now heavily invested in financial markets (Blackburn, 2002). For example, since 1999, state investors have increasingly been moving the CPP from the relatively safe purview of bonds to funds in far more volatile financial markets (Cooke, 2003).

A seventh and final theme, also elaborated in Chapter 5, is the impact of globalization on social policy and of new relationships between civil society and the state (Rice & Prince, 2000). The "third sector," or "civil society," is becoming increasingly important. On December 17, 2010, Statistics Canada released a report that stated that the GDP of the non-profit sector rested at $35.4 billion for 2008, accounting for 2.4 percent of Canada's total GDP and 7.1 percent (a figure representing $106.4 billion) of all national economic activity in that year (Statistics Canada, 2010d). It is estimated that there are more than 160 000 charities and non-profit organizations in Canada (Canadian Association of Gift Planners, 2010), which, in 2003, boasted 139 million memberships (Hall et al., 2004).

The non-profit sector depends on receiving income from a variety of sources. Of a total amounting to $80 billion in 2008, "sales of goods and services accounted for 45% of total income . . . government transfers were also significant at 21%" and "membership fees [accounted for] (17.1%) and donations from households [accounted for] (11.2%)" (Statistics Canada, 2010d). Interestingly, a study conducted in 2006 pointed out that businesses ranked at the bottom of those who give money to non-profit organizations (Waldi, 2006), a finding since corroborated by official data. Statistics Canada reported that businesses contributed a mere 2.1 percent of the total income received by the non-profit sector in 2008 and that investment income comprised only 3.6 percent (Statistics Canada, 2010d).

Although arduous economic times have befallen Canadians in the past couple of years, and charity tax fraud has been of considerable concern (The Canadian Press, 2010), government records indicate that 5.6 million tax-filers donated $7.75 billion to charity in 2009 (Statistics Canada, 2010a). Statistics Canada also shows that the GDP of the non-profit sector is still growing at a faster rate than average compared with the rest of Canada's industries (Statistics Canada, 2010d). At the same time, as elaborated in Chapter 6, human rights take on growing importance.

Conclusion

As this chapter demonstrates, the historical experience is profoundly important in shaping the current nature of social policies. To best understand the present, social work students need to learn about the past and to have some commensurate appreciation of the future prospects of social policies. The next chapter, which emphasizes ideological, political, social, and economic aspects of Canadian social policies, will help you to better appreciate the contexts in which social policies are conceived, carried out, and changed.

Chapter ③

Contemporary Social Policy Structures

This chapter examines some major social policy structures in Canada. As discussed in Chapter 2, between the mid-1940s and the mid-1970s, Canada could have been considered a welfare state. But up to and after the early 1990s, so much retrenchment has occurred that few would describe Canada today as a welfare state. The welfare state refers to those governments that commit themselves to the development of social policies for the collective well-being of all. This commitment occurs via social policy structures, and the following pages outline several ways in which these commitments can take. Despite the welfare state's decline, governments remain important to the funding and delivery of social policies. But not all social policies are available through government auspices. Armitage (2003) outlines seven types of programs and services; some are offered through government structures and others by non-government structures:

1. cash programs, such as Old Age Security, Canada Child Tax Benefit, Canada Pension Plan, and postsecondary student loans;
2. fiscal measures, including tuition-fee deductions, child-care expense deductions, and RRSP exemptions;
3. goods and services measures, such as hospital insurance, legal aid, and education;
4. measures related to employment, including minimum-wage legislation and employment equity programs;
5. occupational welfare measures, such as pension and insurance plans, and sports and recreational facilities;
6. family care and dependency programs, such as home-care provisions; and
7. voluntary/charitable programs, such as shelters, soup kitchens, and food banks.

This chapter and the next touch on many of these largely governmental components, particularly income security. The chapter first introduces the political and fiscal arrangements in Canada that make contemporary welfare-state institutions possible. It then focuses on income security programs and concludes by discussing several related emerging social policy issues in Canada.

But we need to stress, too, the enduring importance of what is called the "third sector," or "civil society": those voluntary civic and social organizations and institutions that fall between the private sector of companies and the public sector. There are also non-governmental organizations (sometimes called *NGOs*) that have a diverse array of similar designations, such as advocacy groups and networks, interest associations, local organizations, membership organizations, non-profit or not-for-profit organizations, people's organizations, quasi–non-governmental organizations, self-help organizations, and volunteer organizations (Lewis & Kanji, 2009, 9). Civil society can include things that occur both seemingly without traditional institutional structures and through the social media via Twitter, Facebook, blogs, and the Internet (Shirky, 2008). In all instances, civil society is responsible for a vast array of social change. In its electronic format, it can be responsible for many significant social movements, including, for example, the 2010 election in Calgary of Canada's first Muslim mayor.

Also noteworthy is the rise of social entrepreneurship: a response to a social problem by using the principles of entrepreneurship to organize, fund, and administer an institution, which can be either for-profit or not-for-profit (Bornstein & Davis, 2010). Its advocates can be extraordinarily confident of its impacts and derisive of what might be deemed "traditional," including governmental, means of responding to social need. "For social entrepreneurs, the bottom line is to maximize some form of social impact, usually by addressing an urgent need that is being mishandled, overlooked, or ignored by other institutions. . . . Unlike governmental efforts, it flows from the bottom up" (Bornstein & Davis, 2010, 30). Social entrepreneurs "can recruit talented executives more easily than government . . . because nobody has to worry about being attacked in the press for joining a citizen organization. (Many executives cringe at the thought of putting themselves forward for high-level governmental posts.)" (Bornstein & Davis, 2010, 34, 36). Such things as charter schools, microfinance, and independent living centres can be attributed to the efforts of social entrepreneurs. Over the past several decades, a further development has been consolidated, that of "corporate social responsibility," wherein the private sector sponsors activities in the social services through either cash donations or employee volunteerism, and often with the explicit understanding that the corporation will be widely acknowledged as a sponsor (thus deriving recognition for its work).

Fiscal and Political Arrangements in the Canadian State

The Context

Most of the world's countries are unitary; that is, political power is centralized in one central or national level of government. Canada is among the world's approximately 20 countries that are federal states; political power in Canada is divided between a central or national level of government and several provincial levels of government. Canada has 10 provinces, as well as three territories: the Northwest Territories, Yukon Territory, and Nunavut. The provinces have clearly defined jurisdiction areas and tend to have large governments. The territories do not have the constitutionally prescribed autonomy that provinces have; each is governed by the federal government and by territorial governments that have been delegated authority. Since the 1970s, the federal government, through the minister of Indian and Northern Affairs Canada, has increasingly devolved responsibilities to territorial legislatures. Similarly, Aboriginal peoples have assumed either delegated or inherent powers to raise revenues and deliver services to people living on reserves, as elaborated in Chapter 6.

The Canadian Constitution defines the framework for working out social policy within the federal political system by giving both the national and the provincial governments sovereign yet interdependent jurisdictions. As a pre-welfare-state document, the Constitution (known as the British North America Act in 1867) was not entirely clear whether the federal or provincial governments were responsible for social welfare. Sections 91 through 95 of the Constitution outline the main division of powers and responsibilities; powers not expressly given to the provinces were to remain the domain of the federal government (Irving, 1987). Only a few social issues are mentioned at all. Under Section 91, the federal government has jurisdiction over quarantine and marine hospitals, penitentiaries, and Aboriginal peoples; Section 92 makes provincial governments responsible for building and maintaining hospitals, asylums, charities, and public or reformatory prisons (Chappell, 1997, 80).

Over several decades, major legal decisions tended to place social welfare under provincial rather than federal jurisdiction (Irving, 1987; Thomlison & Bradshaw, 1999). Irving (1987) suggests two reasons for these decisions. First, the Great Depression highlighted the imbalance between community-based social welfare initiatives and the ability of local communities to pay for these; for this reason, responsibility for social welfare moved to the provinces. Second, the courts began to interpret the provinces' property and civil rights responsibilities as a mandate to deal with social problems; and the federal government, in contrast, was mandated responsibility for those issues not directly associated with social problems, namely "peace, order, and good government." Thus, responsibility for social welfare, health care, and employment services became principally under provincial control.

Many social policies, such as Unemployment Relief in the 1930s, were historically delivered at the municipal or local level of government. In some regions, local governments continue to be responsible or co-responsible for the funding and delivery of social assistance, supported housing, home care, daycare, and other services. Types of Canadian local governments include cities, towns, villages, and municipalities (which range from rural municipalities to regional and metropolitan governments that serve major urban areas). Under the Constitution, local governments are creations of the provinces; provincial governments can create or disband them, as recent amalgamations of such major urban centres as Toronto, Ottawa, and Montreal illustrate. Municipal powers are set out by provincial legislation often known as the Municipal Act, the Local Government Act, the Cities and

Towns Act, or a similar name. Local governments, like their provincial and federal counterparts, are democratically accountable; legislation determines cycles of municipal elections of mayors, councillors, or their equivalents. Local councils make and carry out policies and receive revenue, principally through municipal taxes on real property and grants from provincial governments.

In addition to receiving transfers from provincial governments, local governments also receive specific-purpose transfers from the federal government, usually for infrastructure and transportation services. In both cases, the higher level of government tends simply to impose specific rates and amounts, rather than negotiating, in the way that federal and provincial governments negotiate federal–provincial transfers. Just as the federal government has been criticized for off-loading responsibilities for funding major social programs to provincial governments, provincial and federal governments—particularly provincial governments—have been criticized for off-loading to local governments, without commensurate increases in cash transfers (Graham, 1995). Municipal budgets for social services have become constrained.

In 1988, transfers from federal, provincial, and territorial governments accounted for 23 percent of the total revenue collected by municipal governments (Statistics Canada, 2006a). Much of the 1990s was punctuated by drastic transfer cuts, as the federal, provincial, and territorial governments strove to eliminate their deficits. By 2001, higher levels of government were contributing 16 percent of municipalities' income, a figure that has not significantly improved since (Statistics Canada, 2006a). Making do with much less revenue and being saddled with the responsibility of an increasing number of services, municipalities were forced to slash their own expenditures and endure larger deficits. In 1988, the total municipal deficit was $800 million; by 2005, this figure had grown to $2.2 billion (Statistics Canada, 2006a). By increasing fees and taxes and benefiting from greater generosity in terms of transfers, local governments ran a deficit of $1.1 billion for the 2008 fiscal year (Statistics Canada, 2010b). Downloading from higher to lower levels of government is occurring in many advanced industrial countries, not just Canada, and the commensurate impacts are affecting the social and economic well-being of communities worldwide (Kahn & Kamerman, 1998).

Higher levels of government became involved more extensively in the Canadian welfare state over the course of the early twentieth century, with accelerated presence in the aftermath of the Great Depression of the 1930s. As the need for health and welfare services increased across Canada during that calamitous decade, the financial burden became too heavy for the provinces and their municipal counterparts to carry (Graham, 1995). Most taxation powers resided with the federal government. A constitutional dilemma ensued: how to develop strategies for securing federal monies without violating the provincial jurisdictions of social welfare delivery. After World War II, in particular, with the rise of a more comprehensive welfare state, the federal government developed cost-sharing programs as a means of providing financial assistance for the delivery of social programs by the provinces and the territories. These arrangements facilitated the development of our current social policies. Federal powers, such as the responsibility for public debt and property and the ability to raise monies by taxation, were important for supporting social policies. Through the spending power of the federal parliament, social welfare transfer monies became available to the provinces and the territories without changing much of the original constitutional jurisdiction.

Note that not all social programs are cost-shared and provincially delivered, as the following pages will show. Several, such as Employment Insurance, are federally administered and employer–employee funded.

The Fiscal Context

Intergovernmental finance refers to the web of financial flows that link governments in a federal system. Since the federal government has especially comprehensive tax-raising capacities, a considerable portion of intergovernmental finance involves federal-to-provincial transfers; provincial-to-municipal transfers and federal-to-municipal transfers also occur.

The literature often refers to seven types of transfers (also noted in the glossary at the end of this book). Some intergovernmental grants are *block grants* (or general-purpose grants), while others are *specific-purpose grants*. A block grant is a cash transfer provided by one level of government to another, the amount of the transfer being fixed independently of the purpose to which the funds are put. Its opposite is a specific-purpose grant, the amount of which is tied to its intended purpose. An example would be a matched or shared-cost program.

Thirdly, there are unconditional grants, or *equalization payments*, which require no particular commitment by the recipient government to tie the grant to an expected type of expenditure. Equalization payments are intended to address two types of imbalances. The first is a *horizontal imbalance* between provinces—differences in fiscal capacity between "richer" and "poorer" provinces. The second is a *vertical imbalance*—differences in fiscal capacity between the federal government and a particular province. *Fiscal capacity* refers to a particular level of government's ability to change the total or composition of its revenues (e.g., taxes) or expenditures (e.g., social programs). The final type of transfer is a *conditional grant*, which is tied directly to an expected type of service delivery. An example of a conditional grant is the Canada Assistance Plan (1966–1996), which provided federal transfers to provincial governments to cover the provincial delivery of health, education, and social services.

Horizontal imbalances between provinces can be addressed in two ways. First, the federal government can take over a particular responsibility. For example, Unemployment Insurance was inaugurated in 1941 as a federal, rather than a provincial, social program. A second way of addressing a horizontal imbalance is the direct transfer of federal monies to a province, via either an unconditional grant (equalization payment) or a conditional grant. Vertical imbalances are usually addressed through equalization payments from the federal government to "poorer" provinces.

As indicated in Figure 3.1, in the 2009–10 fiscal year, the federal government transferred roughly $63.8 billion to provincial and territorial governments, which included $24 billion for the Canada Health Transfer (CHT), $10.9 billion for the Canada Social Transfer (CST), $14.2 billion for equalization payments, and a further $12.2 billion for the funding of various other programs (Department of

FIGURE 3.1 Total Federal Transfers, 2009–10 $63.8 Billion to Provinces and Territories

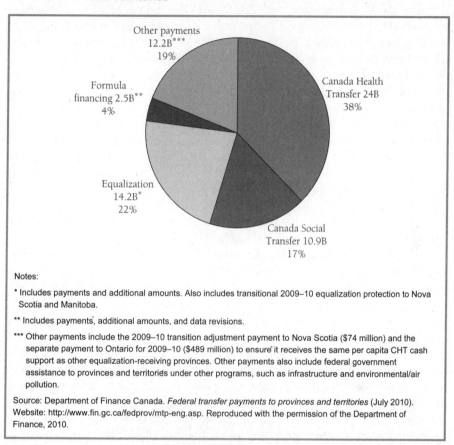

Other payments
12.2B***
19%

Formula
financing 2.5B**
4%

Canada Health
Transfer 24B
38%

Equalization
14.2B*
22%

Canada Social
Transfer 10.9B
17%

Notes:

* Includes payments and additional amounts. Also includes transitional 2009–10 equalization protection to Nova Scotia and Manitoba.

** Includes payments, additional amounts, and data revisions.

*** Other payments include the 2009–10 transition adjustment payment to Nova Scotia ($74 million) and the separate payment to Ontario for 2009–10 ($489 million) to ensure it receives the same per capita CHT cash support as other equalization-receiving provinces. Other payments also include federal government assistance to provinces and territories under other programs, such as infrastructure and environmental/air pollution.

Source: Department of Finance Canada. *Federal transfer payments to provinces and territories* (July 2010). Website: http://www.fin.gc.ca/fedprov/mtp-eng.asp. Reproduced with the permission of the Department of Finance, 2010.

Finance Canada, 2010). According to estimates, next year these transfers will total more than $64 billion, accounting for about 19 percent of aggregate provincial and territorial estimated revenues. Precise values vary by province and are more significant for less financially wealthy provinces than more prosperous provinces. For example, according to the 2010–11 provincial budgetary estimates, federal payments will represent 32 percent of revenue in Nova Scotia, compared to just 9 percent in Alberta (Department of Finance Canada, 2010).

Equalization Payments

Initial arrangements for Canada's system of intergovernmental finance were set out in the Canadian Constitution and have been revised periodically as federal–provincial relations and governmental services have become more complex.

The first formal equalization program was introduced in 1957 as a cost-shared program, in order to ensure that per capita revenues of all provinces—personal income taxes, corporate taxes, and succession duties—matched those of the country's wealthiest provinces, which were British Columbia and Ontario at the time. In the first of the required five-year revisions to these arrangements, the level to which these transfers were equalized became the all-province average, rather than the wealthiest two provinces. Also in this first revision, recipient provinces were guaranteed revenues equal to 50 percent of the all-province per-capita resource revenues. The system evolved during the 1960s until the present time, with changes to actuarial formulas for determining how to measure a fair transfer of revenue. Such changes were generally determined via conferences of federal and provincial first ministers. The last five-year arrangement was introduced in 2004 but was scrapped in 2007 for a formula that attempts to be more responsive to several concerns regarding the inequality within the entire system of equalization. But a 2005 critique describes it as a program with "reasonable origins" that has become "a self-propelling monster based on obscure calculations" and that discriminates against certain provinces (Naylor & Martin, 2005).

One of the more recent contentious equalization issues, one of the more contentious equalization issues is a perceived disincentive for equalization-receiving provinces to develop revenue capacities. For example, the federal government would "claw back" in equalization payments the amount that a province such as Newfoundland or Nova Scotia collected in offshore oil or onshore mineral production projects. In fact, the two provinces have entered into agreements with the federal government to protect their industries and economies from consequent reductions (Government of Canada, 2008), a move that has foreshadowed upcoming changes to the equalization program. In response to this criticism, adjustments were made to the equalization payment formula subsequent to reforms introduced in the Conservatives' 2007–08 Federal Budget (Makarenko, 2008). Today, a national standard is calculated by using the fiscal capacity of all 10 provinces, and those provinces that fall below the average are entitled to payments. In terms of protecting provinces against the loss of equalization dollars, the new formula includes only 50 percent of revenue collected from non-renewable resources. This change also alleviates a degree of inflation for which the previous benchmark did not account by reducing the effect of extreme figures, such as revenues generated by oil in Alberta. Arguments continue to linger regarding the constitutionality of such policies, the dependence they create, the burden they encumber on rich provinces, and the unfair advantages that materialize from their allowance (Harischandra & Palacios, 2007). Yet the Constitution is clear that the federal government is responsible for ensuring delivery of reasonably comparable levels of public services at reasonably comparable levels of taxation to all Canadians, regardless of where they live. Depending mostly on population and natural resources, the capacity of generating revenue is vastly disparate across the country (Makarenko, 2008). This reason, to many, is the rationale for continuing equalization, in the face of calls for its modification.

The Canada Health Transfer (CHT) and the Canada Social Transfer (CST), 2004

Perhaps the apex of the creation of a universal welfare state in Canada occurred after the 1966 introduction of the Canada Assistance Plan (CAP, 1966–1996). The CAP was a funding agreement that enabled the federal government to cost-share with the provinces for the delivery of education, health, and social service commitments. The CAP was a landmark social policy, allowing the federal government to ensure minimum standards of service delivery and relatively equal standards of services across the provinces.

The CAP started to unravel in the mid-1970s, as reductions in cost-sharing arrangements eroded the amount of money transferred to provinces. By 1992–93, the federal share of CAP transfers to the country's three wealthiest provinces was down to 28 percent in Ontario and 36 percent in British Columbia and Alberta (National Council of Welfare, 1995, 7). The CAP had ceased to be a fifty–fifty cost-shared relationship. Many provinces, in turn, downloaded significant financial responsibility to local governments, such as social assistance, supported housing, home care, daycare, and other services.

The Canada Health and Social Transfer (CHST) replaced the CAP in 1996 and resulted in a 15 percent decrease in federal transfers intended for health, postsecondary education, and social services over the following two years (Scott, 1998, xv). In response, provinces reduced benefit rates for social assistance and other programs. The CHST therefore eroded enforceable federal government standards, leaving provinces free to allocate the funds however they wished—even if this meant substantial reductions in program entitlements and restrictions on eligibility and access. One of the country's foremost social policy think tanks, the Caledon Institute of Social Policy (CISP), contended that this change in enforceability "constitute[d] one of the worst mistakes in the history of our social security system." In fact, the CISP continues, it turns back "the social policy clock" to a period of minimal standards and far greater risks for society's most vulnerable (Torjman & Battle, 1995a, 5). A second CISP document warns, "There will be no guarantee of a safety net in the country" (Torjman & Battle, 1995b, 2).

This one piece of legislation—passed in the federal House of Commons in 1995—highlighted the extent to which social policy directs social work practice and affects the lives of many social work clients. For example, the federal government's CHST cutbacks to provincial governments for the cost-shared funding of health services, social services, and education had an impact on provincial government delivery of services, as well as on the relative role of each level of government (federal, provincial, and municipal) in social policy. One observer insists that the "relative power of the provinces over social policy" increased as a result of these cutbacks, as well as the devolution of labour market social programs, such as employment training, to the provinces (Battle, 2001, 16). Yet the federal government "dominates income security policy" and the provinces deliver "most welfare, social service, and health care" policies, depending on cost-sharing arrangements with the federal government (16). As a result of new imbalances, federal–provincial fiscal and administrative relations are in "full evolutionary flight" (16). Another expert continues, "There is no status quo" (Courchene, 1996, as cited in Inwood, 2000, 128); in effect, the federal government had erased the norms of the previous system. But the funding of health and social programs continued to evolve. In 2004, the CHST was divided into two separate block transfer programs: the Canada Health Transfer (CHT, 2004) and the Canada Social Transfer (CST, 2004).

The CHT governs the main transfer of federal money to the provinces in support of health care, and the CST governs the funding arrangements in support of education, social services and social assistance, and child development programs. One goal of these two transfer programs is to provide greater spending accountability. First, the creation of two separate block transfer programs clarifies how much federal transfer money was spent specifically on each program area. Second, and of greater significance, the block transfer nature of these grants makes clear what proportions of the transfers are to be spent on each program area. While the new funding arrangements do not replace the restrictions and levels of accountability on provincial spending and program delivery that were present during the time of the CAP, they provide a greater check on government spending and program funding than was present during the period of the CHST.

In 2011–12, provinces and territories will receive $57.6 billion through major transfers. These consist of the CHT and the CST, already discussed, and a system of "equalization," which is intended to even out fiscal disparities between richer and poorer provinces/territories in Canada (Department of Finance, 2011). The relative balance of participation of the provincial and federal governments, and the dynamics that create these ever-shifting arrangements, are examined in greater detail in the next section.

Federal–Provincial Relations

Canadian federalism has never been static. With the increased scope of the post–World War II Canadian welfare state, and with federal and provincial responsibilities for social welfare becoming more complex, federal–provincial relationships have become increasingly important to government and to the country's policy-making processes. Indeed, most of the important areas of contemporary social policy cut across loosely defined boundaries of federal and provincial jurisdiction. National policies can often be carried out only with some degree of provincial cooperation; and most provincial responsibilities rely on some degree of federal cooperation—in social policy, this "cooperation" often means the transfer of federal monies to provinces.

The Political Context

Federal–provincial relations take place in many arenas. They range from informal, sometimes daily, contact between federal and provincial civil servants, to formal contact that includes large-scale conferences of provincial and federal first ministers (i.e., the prime minister and provincial premiers). Contact itself covers the widest gamut of jurisdictions—from international trade to fiscal arrangements to economic development. Each year, formal contacts usually number in the hundreds, while less formal contacts are far more numerous. Joint federal–provincial agreements are essential to many types of social policies, particularly in relation to joint funding arrangements.

The tone and nature of federal–provincial relations have changed significantly through history. Some scholars argue that the end of World War II until the early 1960s was an era of "cooperative federalism," in which federal–provincial relations were relatively cordial. During the late 1960s and 1970s, an era of "executive federalism"—as one scholar describes it—emerged: federal–provincial relations became more acrimonious (Smiley, 1976, 54). Several factors may have precipitated this changing dynamic. Provincial responsibilities had grown in scope and magnitude since the cooperative federalism era. In addition, during the 1960s, a Quiet Revolution was occurring in Quebec: a renewed sense of nationality was propelling the Quebec government to assert its right to withdraw from certain federal social welfare programs, such as the CPP (and to create its Quebec counterpart, the QPP), and its right to modernize Quebec social and political affairs (Trofimenkoff, 1983). During the 1970s and afterward, Western provinces were likewise increasingly asserting their rights (Inwood, 2000, 129). Moreover, federal–provincial constitutional struggles became increasingly visible, with more elaborate and formal federal–provincial "diplomacy": institutionalized first ministers' conferences and the creation of entire specialist bureaucracies to support these exchanges (Inwood, 2000, 129).

Several major attempts at re-establishing a Canadian constitutional framework over the past 30 years have had a significant, incremental impact on federal–provincial relations. In 1976, the Parti Québécois was elected in Quebec; and in 1980, it held a provincial referendum on sovereignty association with Canada. Sovereignty association referred to the political sovereignty of Quebec, with economic and other types of ties with Canada, including a common currency, a free-trade zone, a common tariff, and a court of justice composed of equal numbers of Canadians and Québécois to oversee this associative arrangement. The referendum was defeated by a 60 percent No to 40 percent Yes return. During that referendum, during which Prime Minister Pierre Trudeau campaigned for the No side, Trudeau promised to repatriate Canada's Constitution—then called the British North America Act, which was still held in London, England. In 1982, the federal government repatriated the Canadian Constitution and added to it the Charter of Rights and Freedoms. However, the government of Quebec had never agreed to the repatriation process and refused to sign the new constitution; and Quebec's premier, René Lévesque (whose government had lost the 1980 referendum), publicly expressed a feeling of betrayal of Quebec by the other premiers and Prime Minister Trudeau.

In 1987, a new federal government under Brian Mulroney sought to induce the government of Quebec to officially accept repatriation of the Constitution through the Meech Lake Accord, a set of new constitutional reforms. The Accord's five basic points, proposed by Quebec Premier Robert Bourassa, included a guarantee of Quebec's special status as a "distinct society" and a commitment to Canada's linguistic duality; increased provincial powers over immigration; provincial input

in appointing Supreme Court judges; restricted federal spending power; and resto-
ration of the provincial right to constitutional veto. Prime Minister Mulroney and
all the provincial premiers agreed to the Accord on April 30, 1987, although the
premiers of Ontario and Manitoba, several women's groups, and Native groups
expressed strong objections. The Accord died on June 22, 1990, when the legislatures of Newfoundland and Manitoba failed to approve it before the deadline. This
led to a national referendum in 1992 over a proposed constitutional renewal (the
Charlottetown Accord), which contained several provisions, including Quebec's
special status within the Canadian federation. The Charlottetown national referendum of 1992 was defeated nationally by 54 percent of votes cast. It did, however,
receive approval in New Brunswick, Newfoundland, Prince Edward Island, the
Northwest Territories, and, by the narrowest of margins, Ontario. Three years
later, in 1995, the sovereigntist government in Quebec held a referendum on
whether or not Quebec should become sovereign, after having made a formal offer
to Canada for a new economic and political partnership. This referendum narrowly
lost by a vote of 50.6 percent against and 49.4 percent for.

Since then, federal–provincial relations have been relatively cordial, but Quebec
has remained on the periphery of some federal–provincial agreements. One example is the 1999 social union agreement struck between the federal government and
all provinces except Quebec. Its goal was to improve transparency, accountability,
and mutual collaboration in social policy, and it remains an important benchmark
for current federal–provincial relations in this area (Inwood, 2000, 128; Federal/
Provincial/Territorial Ministerial Council on Social Policy Renewal, 2003).

An excellent example of the spirit of intergovernmental cooperation is the
Canada Child Tax Benefit (CCTB) program. The CCTB consists of the Canada
Child Tax Benefit, which provides federal income support to all low- and middle-
income families with children; the Child Disability Benefit, a benefit provided to
families caring for a child with a mental and/or physical disability; and the National
Child Benefit (NCB) supplement for low-income families (National Council of
Welfare, 2001, 43). The CCTB is the culmination of a much-simplified federal
approach to child poverty, blending several older programs (Family Allowances,
children's tax exemption, and the refundable child tax credit) into one federal benefit. Moreover, it introduced new provincial income-tested child benefits to be
administered on behalf of the provinces by the federal government through the
income tax system (Battle, 2001, 40). Because of the joint nature of the CCTB,
federal and provincial governments shared administrative data in these areas.

Some analysts assert that at the best of times, Canada's federal system creates
a form of "institutional fragmentation" that limits the state's capacity to create
social policies (Banting, 1985, 49). This drawback is precisely what the CCTB
attempted to overcome. But there is a long historical legacy of fragmentation, as
the following section on income security illustrates. The federal government is
responsible for such programs as Employment Insurance, Old Age Security, and
the Canada Pension Plan. Provinces have jurisdiction over social assistance and
Workers' Compensation. These different federal and provincial roles, as pointed
out in Chapter 2, evolved for historically specific reasons.

Income Security Programs

Canadian social policies cover a wide range of health, education, and income security measures. The present chapter, for purposes of brevity, concentrates on income security programs—that is, those social programs that provide cash payments to recipients. As Chapter 2 emphasizes, prior to the development of a comprehensive welfare state in the 1940s and 1950s, Canadians living in poverty had few avenues of assistance. They were expected to be self-reliant. If, however, they had no options but to seek help from others, they would ordinarily go first to family, then to friends, and then to such community sources as a church or a charity (Graham, 1992; Splane, 1965). When these were exhausted, "unemployment relief"—the precursor to contemporary social assistance—was accessed (Graham, 1996c; Struthers, 1983).

In today's world, a far more elaborate system of income security exists, encompassing all three levels of government (and hence different offices with which a social worker might be in contact) and falling under a wide spectrum of categories. Different income security programs have been designed for the following, among other categories:

> lone-parent families (income support programs—the exact name varies by province);

> families with children (Canada Child Tax Benefit; Universal Child Care Benefit);

> individuals experiencing lengthy periods of unemployment (income support programs—the exact name varies by province);

> individuals experiencing a short period of unemployment (Employment Insurance);

> youth without guardian support (income support programs—the exact name varies by province);

> individuals who are injured at work (Workers' Compensation);

> people with a disability (income and health benefits programs, the exact name varies by province; or Canada Pension Plan; or Workers' Compensation);

> the elderly (Canada Pension Plan, International Benefits, and Old Age Security—which includes the Guaranteed Income Supplement and Spousal Allowance programs; some provinces have top-up programs for the elderly poor);

> refugees new to Canada receiving Government of Canada assistance (Resettlement Assistance Program); and

> veterans of wars (War Veterans' Allowance).

Social workers need to be fully familiar with this system in order to help clients to identify the programs for which they are eligible and to ensure prompt and full access to these programs. The social worker's success may be of crucial significance to the client. It may make the difference, for example, between a client's going hungry or having food, being homeless or being able to secure accommodations, being in despair or feeling hopeful, being trapped in poverty or having the means to better their standard of living.

Some Key Terms and Concepts

There are two major forms of income security programs in Canada: selective and universal. Each has its own assumptions. We will discuss additional income security program terms at the end of this section, which includes comments about demogrants, social assistance, and social insurance.

Selective Programs

Selective programs have a long history, extending to Elizabethan poor relief in England, and were brought to Canada with European colonization. Unemployment Relief was a selective program, as is its contemporary successor, general welfare assistance, also called *social assistance*, *social allowance*, or, more recently, *income support* or *social benefit*. The usual form of a selective payment involves a transfer of money from a level of government to an individual. Eligibility for selective programs is based on a means test. Means tests are carried out to evaluate, first, a person's financial resources—such as income, assets, debts, and other obligations—and second, other criteria, such as number of dependants or health status of the applicant.

Selective programs are subject to several criticisms. One criticism is that they personalize problems of poverty, rather than focusing attention on broader societal structures that create the conditions for poverty. The economy is one example of a societal structure. Say, for instance, that a weak economy leads to the closure of a pulp and paper mill in a one-industry town. This external condition would cause job losses, leading individuals to apply for assistance.

Moreover, selective programs, critics contend, may stigmatize people who, through factors outside their immediate control, experience temporary or permanent loss of income. Selective programs devote considerable administrative resources to monitoring the lives of individual clients, rather than focusing on broader community and societal changes that might improve the opportunities of a client. Proponents, on the other hand, believe that selective programs are the most efficient means of targeting money to those in need. As well, some believe means tests may motivate recipients to return to the workforce.

Universal Programs

Universal programs provide cash benefits to *all* individuals in a society who fall into a certain category. They differ from selective programs in that eligibility is a right of citizenship, rather than an entitlement that has to be proven through a means test. The implications are several-fold. A recipient's level of specific needs, or economic status, is not taken into account when determining eligibility. Where selective programs focus attention on an individual claimant's worthiness to receive benefits, universal programs operate under manifestly different assumptions. The state expresses responsibility to provide income security for all citizens, and society implicitly recognizes the presence of conditions beyond an individual's control that may impede economic well-being. Stigma has little place in a universal program, since all people, regardless of level of need, may have access to benefits as long as they fulfill eligibility conditions (such as age for Old Age Security or children under the age of 6 in the case of the Universal Child Care Benefit).

While universal programs may target money to a greater number of people, including the well-to-do, many argue that the income tax system can be used to counterbalance payments to the rich—and not the social program itself. In a progressive income tax system, the proportion of taxes paid increases with earnings; those with a greater ability to pay end up paying more taxes. In contrast, in a regressive tax system, taxes are not collected on an ability-to-pay basis. The most extreme instance of a regressive tax—such as a sales tax—is one that is levied equally. How so? Whether a person paying a sales tax is below the poverty line or the president of a major bank, the sales tax charged remains the same, even though the poor person has much less ability to pay this tax. Canada's tax system is somewhat—although far from completely—progressive. Thus, higher income earners pay a greater proportion of their money on income tax than do those in lower income categories. Governments try to offset the regressive nature of sales taxes through refund cheques to people who qualify. Some people might argue that universal programs do *not* wrongfully direct money to the better off, given the existence (or potential existence) of a progressive income tax system and refund programs (Muszynski, 1987). But some argue that with everyone receiving benefits from a universal program, the middle and upper classes are politically co-opted into supporting the program. This means that benefits are less likely to be reduced in scope or eligibility than in a selective program that is geared toward only the less politically powerful poor (Titmuss, 1958, 1987).

Universal programs came to the fore during the World War II period. But they have eroded over the past 25 years, as selective programs have found new favour. The reasons for these changes were elaborated in Chapter 2.

Demogrants, Social Assistance, and Social Insurance

Several other terms are used to describe income security programs. Familiarity with them is essential to social work practice. A *demogrant* is a cash payment to an individual or family based on a demographic characteristic (usually age), as opposed to need; an example is Old Age Security. *Social assistance* refers to selective income security programs that use a means or needs test to determine eligibility; these are often administered at the provincial or local governmental level, depending on the province. *Social insurance* refers to income security programs in which eligibility for benefits is determined by a previous record of contribution and on the occurrence of a particular contingency, such as unemployment, retirement, injury, or widowhood; examples include the Canada Pension Plan and Employment Insurance (Armitage, 1996, 190–195).

Major Income Security Programs in Canada

Several levels of government deliver income security programs. These programs constitute part of, but not the entirety of, transfers to persons and transfers to governments. The following programmatic descriptions are deliberately succinct and simplified, covering major aspects of eligibility and benefits but omitting minor details that are too numerous to discuss. Many programs are not discussed because of the need for brevity. Greater elaboration is found in Graham (2008), Guest (1997), and McGilly (1998).

Federal Government Programs

Employment Insurance (EI, 1996–) Employment Insurance was previously known as Unemployment Insurance (1940–1996). There are three ways to obtain EI: loss of job because of termination, temporary disruption of work because of illness, and application for maternity/parental benefits. EI is based on hours worked, rather than weeks worked—which is a fairer practice for part-time and multiple-job-holding workers. The entrance requirements have become more stringent over the past 15 years but continue to vary depending on job type and rate of unemployment in the region where the claimant lives. For example, in areas with high unemployment (above 13 percent), a minimum of 420 hours is needed, whereas in places of low unemployment (below 6 percent), 700 hours are needed (Human Resources and Social Development Canada, 2007). Furthermore, if a worker happened to be unemployed for a period greater than two years or was entering the labour market for the first time, they would have to prove 910 worked hours prior to qualifying for Employment Insurance benefits (Service Canada, 2007). These restrictions have resulted in a large percentage of jobless people not qualifying for benefits. In 2004, 42 percent of jobless individuals in Canada did not qualify for Employment Insurance benefits (Human Resources and Skills Development Canada, 2004). Most recipients receive up to 55 percent of their average weekly insured earnings (up to a particular ceiling); however, during the 1970s, entitlement was as high as 64 percent of working wages (Battle, 2002). As of July 19, 2010, the maximum benefits payment is $457 per week. The program used to be funded by the federal government and employer–employee contributions but is now funded only by employer–employee contributions. Furthermore, the length of time an individual can receive Employment Insurance benefits is restricted, based on where an individual resides. The maximum time ranges between 36 and 45 weeks (Human Resources and Social Development Canada, 2007).

Canada Pension Plan/Quebec Pension Plan (CPP/QPP, 1966–) Canada and Quebec Pension Plans are insurance plans to which people must contribute during their working years. Both were created the same year and are similar in design; the QPP is administered by the Quebec provincial government and is solely for people working in that province; the CPP is administered by the federal government and is for those in all provinces and territories other than Quebec. CPP and QPP also comprise survivor's pensions for the spouses of deceased pensioners, disability pensions, children's benefits, and death benefits. Eligibility is based on past contributions to the plan. In instances of retirement (as distinct from disability or spousal death), it is paid to contributing claimants over the age of 60 and is intended to replace about 25 percent of the income the claimant was earning while paying into the plan. As of July 19, 2010, the maximum benefits are $934.17 per month for retirement payments, $1126.76 for disability payments, $560.50 for spousal survivors' payments (age 65 or over), and $214.85 for children's survivor payments. The program is funded by employer and employee contributions. The program is considered social insurance.

Old Age Security (OAS, 1952–) The Old Age Security pension is a monthly benefit for people 65 years of age or over. It originated in 1927 as a selective, means-tested program but was transformed into a universal program in 1951. Because it is a universal program, employment history does not play a part in eligibility, and a claimant need not be retired. Those on an OAS pension pay both federal and provincial income tax on the money they receive. Those with higher incomes repay part or all of their benefit through the tax system. As such, some argue that OAS ceases to be a universal program, because of this claw back of benefits from higher-income-earning Canadians. As a result, it excludes many people from full entitlement and a substantial number from ever receiving any compensation. Moreover, claw-back amounts have systematically increased since the late 1980s. As of July 19, 2010, the maximum benefits were $518.51 per month. The program is financed from federal government general tax revenues and is considered a demogrant.

Guaranteed Income Supplement (GIS, 1966–) The Guaranteed Income Supplement was established to supplement the earnings of low-income OAS recipients and is administered under the OAS program. Eligibility is determined by need and may increase or decrease according to a claimant's overall yearly income. As of July 19, 2010, the maximum benefits are $654.47 per month for a single applicant and $432.19 for individual applicants who are married. The program is funded through federal government general tax revenues and is considered social insurance.

Spouse's Allowance (SPA, 1976–) The Spouse's Allowance was established to provide income to the spouse of an OAS pensioner or to a widow or widower. Like the GIS, eligibility is based on need, and the SPA is provided only to those within certain income limits. The SPA stops when the recipient turns 65 and becomes eligible for the OAS, or if the recipient leaves the country or dies. As of July 19, 2010, the maximum benefits were $950.70 per month for a beneficiary married to an OAS pensioner, and $1,053.83 for a widow or widower of a former OAS pensioner. The program is funded from federal government general tax revenues and is considered social insurance.

Veterans' Pensions (VP, 1919–) Those members of the armed forces who incur a disability during wartime (Active Force), peacetime (Special Duty Area), or other military service are eligible for the Veterans' Pension. The amount of pension is determined by degree of disability and varies accordingly; maximum rates for

2011 are $2,478.08 for the pensioner and $619.52 for spousal recipients (Veterans Affairs Canada, 2009). The program is funded from federal government general tax revenues and is considered a demogrant.

War Veterans Allowances (WVA, 1930–) This income-related program ensures a minimum annual income for wartime/peacetime service veterans who served in World Wars I or II or the Korean War. Eligibility is based on need and a minimum qualifying age of 60 for a man and 55 for a woman. Survivors' allowances are also available. As of March 31, 2010, the maximum benefits were $1,273.88 per month for single claimants and $1,937.69 for those living with a spouse and/or a child (The Royal Canadian Legion-Ontario Provincial Command, 2009). This program is funded from federal government general tax revenues and is considered a form of social assistance.

Resettlement Assistance Program (RAP, 1998–) Administered by Citizenship and Immigration Canada (CIC), the Resettlement Assistance Program provides financial assistance for up to one year after arrival to government-assisted refugees arriving to Canada. In many instances, funding may also be provided via cost-sharing sponsorship agreements between CIC and sponsorship agreement holders at the local, regional, and national levels.

Almost all newcomers to Canada are independent-class immigrants or are sponsored by others, such as Canadian family members. A small proportion of immigrants are refugees, defined as having "a well-founded fear of persecution in his or her country of origin because of race, religion, nationality, membership in a social group, or political opinion" (Government of Canada, 2007). RAP is only for refugee-class immigrants. Benefit levels are consistent with provincial social assistance programs and are intended to provide the necessary financial resources for food, shelter, and clothing. The program also seeks to provide opportunities for new Canadians to enrol in English or French language classes and to develop the means to secure employment. RAP is parallel to the Immigrant Loans Program, which is also intended to assist the resettlement process. Local, regional, and national immigration-service organizations provide hands-on transition assistance to help a refugee to secure housing, education, employment, and other services, and RAP is delivered in collaboration with these organizations. The program is funded through federal government general tax revenues and is considered a form of social assistance.

Canada Child Tax Benefit (CCTB, 1998–) The Canada Child Tax Benefit (formerly the Child Tax Benefit, 1993–1998) replaced the following three benefits: the Family Allowance (1944–1992) and refundable and non-refundable tax credits. Under the CCTB, the federal government provides payments to parents or guardians on behalf of children under the age of 18. Payments are usually made to the mother of the child if the child lives with her. The amount differs according to the family income, the number of children, and the children's ages. This program also coincides with comparable programs at the provincial and territorial levels; eligibility for those programs is determined by information provided for the CCTB application. The three main components of the CCTB are the base benefit, the

National Child Benefit (NCB) supplement, and the Child Disability Benefit. The CCTB is tax free; and as of July 20, 2010, in all provinces except Alberta, the benefits can be as much as $3,436.00 per child per year. The NCB supplement, an important component of the system, is a federal, provincial, and territorial initiative designed to tackle child poverty and is available to low-income families. In July 2010, the supplement provides $174.00 per month for the first child and $154.00 for the second child in families with an annual income of less than $23,855 (Canada Revenue Agency, 2010). The CCTB is an example of a formerly universal program (the Family Allowance) that has been replaced by a selective/income-tested program (the CCTB). Some commentators criticize the program for providing inadequate benefits in light of pervasive child poverty (Freiler & Cerny, 1998; National Council of Welfare, 2001).

Provincial Programs

Workers' Compensation (WC, 1914–) Workers' Compensation is designed to make payments to and cover rehabilitation and medical costs for workers who have been injured on the job. In the case of workplace death, it also provides payments to an employee's survivors. It was first introduced in Ontario and subsequently spread to other provinces. Assistance levels vary from province to province. Eligibility criteria are stricter now than in the past, and benefits have been reduced in scope. In Alberta, for example, benefits as of 2011 are 90 percent of net income up to $82,800.00 (The Workers' Compensation Board-Alberta, 2010). In Ontario, 85 percent of net income is covered up to $79,600.00 (Workplace Safety and Insurance Board of Ontario, 2010). The program is funded by worker and employer contributions and is considered a form of social insurance.

Social Assistance (SA, various years) Social assistance, often called welfare or public assistance, helps people in need who are not eligible for other benefits and is one of the most important income security programs with which a social worker should be familiar. It is typically delivered to three broad categories of people: families with dependent children in need (often this is long-term need), individuals with disabilities (often this is long-term need), and individuals or families in short-term need. These three categories may have different names and may be administered out of different offices. The last category—short-term assistance—is seen as an income program of last resort. Benefit payments help to pay for food, shelter, fuel, clothing, prescription drugs, and other health services.

Eligibility rules and amounts of payment differ from province to province and from municipality to municipality in provinces where municipalities administer and/or partially fund programs. Especially for short-term need assistance, means tests are common. Applicants must be of a certain age, usually between 18 and 65, but some provinces have provisions for minors under the age of 18 not living with a legal parent or guardian. Under certain circumstances, full-time students in post-secondary education may be eligible for assistance in some provinces but not in others. Single parents seeking assistance must have already tried to secure court-ordered maintenance and child support from the other spouse if they were entitled to it. Workers on strike are usually not eligible for assistance, nor are sponsored refugees or sponsored family-class immigrants during their period of sponsorship. In general, social assistance is granted if a household's net assets are less than the cost of regularly recurring basic needs for food, shelter, and other necessities.

Fixed and liquid assets are usually assessed in the application process. Most provinces exempt the value of a car, a principal residence, furniture, clothing, Retirement Savings Plans that are locked in, and Registered Education Savings Plans. Other allowable assets—cash, bonds, securities that are readily convertible to cash, the value of life insurance—are limited by household size and employability. Applicants are usually required to convert non-exempt fixed assets into liquid assets and deplete those assets before qualifying for welfare (National Council of Welfare, 2006b).

Benefit rates fall well below low-income cut-off (LICO) poverty lines, as indicated in Table 3.1. (The calculation of poverty lines is elaborated in Chapter 4.) Benefit rates and definitions of eligibility have also tightened in recent years. For example, in 1995, during its first term in administration, the Ontario Conservative government slashed social assistance by a remarkable 21 percent. Because of

TABLE 3.1   Social Assistance Nationwide, 2008

	Total Income	Poverty Line*	Poverty Gap	Total Welfare Income as Percentage of Poverty Line
Newfoundland and Labrador				
Single, employable	$ 9 448	$15 538	−$ 6 090	61%
Person with disability	$10 977	$15 344	−$ 4 367	71%
Lone parent, one child	$19 015	$18 911	$ 104	101%
Couple, two children	$21 968	$29 378	−$ 7 410	75%
Prince Edward Island				
Single, employable	$ 6 672	$15 344	−$ 8 672	43%
Person with disability	$ 8 765	$15 344	−$ 6 579	57%
Lone parent, one child	$16 033	$18 676	−$ 2 643	86%
Couple, two children	$23 267	$29 013	−$ 5 746	80%
Nova Scotia				
Single, employable	$ 6 300	$15 538	−$ 9 238	41%
Person with disability	$ 9 140	$15 538	−$ 6 398	59%
Lone parent, one child	$14 851	$18 911	−$ 4 060	79%
Couple, two children	$20 703	$29 378	−$ 8 675	70%
New Brunswick				
Single, employable	$ 3 687	$15 538	−$11 851	24%
Person with disability	$ 8 496	$15 538	−$ 7 042	55%
Lone parent, one child	$15 868	$18 911	−$ 3 043	84%
Couple, two children	$19 376	$29 378	−$10 002	66%

TABLE 3.1   Social Assistance Nationwide, 2008 (continued)

	Total Income	Poverty Line*	Poverty Gap	Total Welfare Income as Percentage of Poverty Line
Quebec				
Single, employable	$ 7 143	$18 373	−$11 230	39%
Person with disability	$10 630	$18 373	−$ 7 743	58%
Lone parent, one child	$17 231	$22 361	−$ 5 130	77%
Couple, two children	$22 134	$34 738	−$12 604	64%
Ontario				
Single, employable	$ 7 352	$18 373	−$11 021	40%
Person with disability	$12 647	$18 373	−$ 5 726	69%
Lone parent, one child	$16 683	$22 361	−$ 5 678	75%
Couple, two children	$21 215	$34 738	−$13 523	61%
Manitoba				
Single, employable	$ 6 426	$18 373	−$11 947	35%
Person with disability	$ 9 332	$18 373	−$ 9 041	51%
Lone parent, one child	$14 742	$22 361	−$ 7 619	66%
Couple, two children	$21 319	$34 738	−$13 419	61%
Saskatchewan				
Single, employable	$ 8 120	$15 538	−$ 7 418	52%
Person with disability	$10 477	$15 538	−$ 5 061	67%
Lone parent, one child	$16 413	$18 911	−$ 2 498	87%
Couple, two children	$22 626	$29 378	−$ 6 752	77%
Alberta				
Single, employable	$ 5 426	$18 373	−$12 947	30%
Person with disability	$ 8 773 (AB-IS)		−$ 9 600	48% (AB-IS)
	$13 377 (AB-AISH)	$18 373	−$ 4 996	73% (AB-AISH)
Lone parent, one child	$14 094	$22 361	−$ 8 267	63%
Couple, two children	$20 710	$34 738	−$14 028	60%
British Columbia				
Single, employable	$ 7 770	$18 373	−$10 603	42%
Person with disability	$11 382	$18 373	−$ 6 991	62%
Lone parent, one child	$16 808	$22 361	−$ 5 553	75%
Couple, two children	$21 016	$34 738	−$13 722	60%

* The poverty line used in the table comes from Canada's after-tax low-income cut-off, as reported in the National Council of Welfare's *Welfare Incomes 2008*.

Sources: Adapted from National Council of Welfare (2010). *Welfare incomes 2008*. Bulletins 1–4. Website: http://ncw.gc.ca/l.3bd.2t.1ils@-eng.jsp?lid=91. Reproduced with the permission of the Minister of Public Works and Government Services Canada, 2010.

tightened eligibility requirements nationwide, one million Canadians who would have qualified for benefits in 1994 no longer qualified in 2004 (Greenaway, 2004). One major cause of this shrinkage in numbers is the relative prosperity in the 2000s in Canada; another is the new restrictions placed on those qualifying to receive benefits. Some provinces have also introduced workfare. Workfare requires recipients to undergo training programs and/or other forms of work-related activities in return for benefits. The program is funded by federal and provincial monies under the CST and, in some instances, partially by municipal governments.

The CISP points out that it may be wiser to approach social assistance as a human resource strategy issue rather than as workfare (Torjman, 1996a). On the one hand, workfare implies compulsory labour and mandatory participation in designated activities. A human resource strategy, on the other hand, is voluntary. Both, ideally, are collaborative with numerous stakeholders—industries, educators, social welfare, and justice. Both are also supposed to provide a range of opportunities, including job search, academic upgrading and skills training, and employment creation; but some argue that workfare emphasizes these less. A human resource strategy also ensures "that appropriate supports are in place—notably, high-quality, affordable childcare and transportation subsidies—so that recipients can move off welfare" (Torjman, 1996a, 1). Finally, and perhaps most important, a human resource strategy promotes, rather than destroys, human dignity and well-being.

Some provincial governments have sought to revise their social assistance programs previously targeted for children and families to align these with the federal CCTB. British Columbia was the first to consider a federal–provincial integrated child benefits system payable to low-income families with children (Battle & Mendelson, 1997, 2). Other provinces have followed suit. Earnings supplement programs for working-poor families are also available in several provinces.

Provincial Top-Ups for the Elderly (various years) The combined OAS and GIS supplements are low enough to qualify most elderly couples in most provinces for social assistance. To avoid having the elderly as SA recipients, some provinces have introduced seniors' income supplemental programs. Benefit rates vary from province to province and are intended to raise incomes of recipients to roughly the income levels of public assistance recipients. Not all provinces have these particular benefits programs. An example of a provincial top-up for the elderly is the Seniors Income Plan, which, as of July 19, 2010, provided a maximum of $190 per month to single claimants and $155 each to married claimants (Government of Saskatchewan, 2010). Another program, the Ontario Guaranteed Annual Income System (GAINS), provides a maximum of $83 per month for a single claimant, an amount that has remained unchanged since before May 1, 2007 (Government of Ontario, 2010). Provincial top-ups for the elderly are selective social assistance programs, funded jointly by federal and provincial monies under the CST.

Conclusion

Income security policies work best when they are integrated with other social and economic policies and when they successfully address categories of people who are most in need. The disgraceful incidences of poverty among Aboriginal peoples, children, people with disabilities, and women, among other social groups, ought to compel more comprehensive and successful policy responses. Disability pensions within the CPP, for example, have been criticized for not allowing beneficiaries who can work irregularly or part-time to do so—unless they are willing to forfeit all benefits (Torjman, 1997). Some likewise argue that social assistance programs should be designed to provide income top-ups to low-income labourers and that social programs should provide special transportation, childcare, and other supports necessary to full and vital functioning in and beyond the workplace (Torjman, 1996a, 1996b, 1997, 1998a, 1998b, 1999).

So, too, might policies be delivered in ways that more sensitively appreciate how age, ethnicity, gender, geography, race, religion, and range of ability, among other parameters, affect need. In 2002, new Canadians during their first year in Canada were 3.5 times more likely to be in a low-income category than Canadian-born citizens, which fell only slightly to 3.2 times greater in 2004 (Picot, Hou, & Coulombe, 2007). Other research also suggests that immigrants who have been in Canada for 10 years are at risk of being in, or falling into, poverty (in Picot, Hou, & Coulombe, 2007). The implications are considerable. People new to Canada may have little appreciation of or experience with a welfare state and may require especially skilful and competent social work assistance to gain access to income security programs. Further research is needed to address the often profound and troubling questions regarding immigrant access to labour markets (Galabuzi, 2006).

These issues of diversity are examined in further detail in Chapter 6. But before discussing them, the following two chapters examine some social, economic, and political consequences of social welfare (Chapter 4), as well as some broader contextual issues, such as globalization, social movements, social inclusion, and social welfare retrenchment (Chapter 5).

Chapter 4

Ideological, Social, and Economic Influences

Chapter 1 points out that the various definitions of social policy influence how policies are conceived and carried out. Chapter 2 shows that history is important in determining how policies developed into their current state (Chapter 3) and in determining their future prospects. This chapter builds further on the preceding three chapters. It considers the ideological, social, and economic factors that influence social policy development. After reading the chapter, you will have a better understanding of how such dynamics influence social policies—and hence how they affect the lives of social work clients. In addition, this chapter will help you to appreciate why social workers who are genuinely concerned about the people they work with are interested in such forces; and why, as a result, social workers and their professional associations ought to be continuously engaged in social advocacy leading toward social change.

Ideology and the Political Spectrum

Ideology refers to a shared way of thinking based on a set of ideas that reflect the values, beliefs, attitudes, and experience of a particular person or group. Ideological beliefs focus on the nature of the ideal political system, the ideal economic order, and the ideal social goals. Political ideology places a special emphasis on the role government should play in economic and social matters.

Ideology provides a way of interpreting problems and designing appropriate solutions. Ideological considerations are not the only factors that influence political decisions about social policy and social problems; but political parties attempt to shape social policy decisions from their ideological base. Individuals such as social workers also embrace particular ideologies because all social policy decisions influence the work social workers perform. Social policy decisions affect the funding and delivery of social services, as well as who will receive what services.

FIGURE 4.1   Major Political Ideologies: The Political Spectrum

This section very briefly explores different ideological approaches to social policy and then relates these approaches to the way the major Canadian political parties think about social policy. But before beginning either, we will cover a few core definitions for terms that are key to ideology: *communism, socialism, liberalism, Toryism, neo-conservatism,* and *fascism* (see Figure 4.1). Note that there is tremendous diversity of views within each term; as a result, consider the following to be a short and necessarily non-comprehensive paraphrase of major attributes within each.

The six political ideologies presented in Figure 4.1 are ordered along a continuum from communism on the extreme political left to fascism on the extreme political right. It is important to remember, as you read about these political ideologies, that they do not necessarily represent the Canadian political parties that may bear the same name. The Liberal Party of Canada, as an example, has some aspects that are liberal in ideology and others that are not. Though political parties may have their foundations in certain ideological positions, each party has been uniquely shaped by historical, economic, and social forces as much as by ideological values and beliefs. Those to the left of the spectrum have tended to emphasize an institutional perspective to social welfare, as discussed in Chapter 2. The neo-conservative ideology on the right end of the spectrum tends to emphasize the market state. Tory and liberal ideologies have emphasized both institutional and market-state perspectives, depending on the moment in history.

Because most political ideologies have something to say about the social unit of attention—the collective (society) or the individual—the following concepts, individualism and collectivism, and egalitarianism and elitism, are often used in ideological descriptions:

> *Individualism* emphasizes the individual's freedom, worth, and self-determination in the political, social, and economic spheres.

> *Collectivism*, by way of contrast, places the rights and welfare of the group or society above those of any and all individuals.

> *Egalitarianism* is the belief that all people should have equal political, social, and economic rights.

> *Elitism* is the organization of society around interrelated but unequal functional groups, usually with those in the political or economic leadership group

referred to as the *elite*. Elitism is a hierarchical rather than an egalitarian organizational view.

The central organizing principles of each political ideology will be discussed according to its stance on such dimensions as liberty or regulation, equality or hierarchical organization, and individualism or collectivism.

Communism

Distinguishing between Marxist, radical, and communist perspectives is important; since each of these ideologies is based on particular assumptions, they should not be used interchangeably. As one author points out, "Whereas Marxist social work is certainly radical, the reverse is not necessarily true" (Webb, 1981, 145). As elaborated in Chapter 7, *radical social work* emerged from a variety of theoretical traditions that included labelling theory and new criminology (Webb, 1981, 145). Marxism, for the purposes of this chapter, represents a variety of approaches based on the writings of Karl Marx; as such, Marxism is one part of the broader rubric of communist political ideology.

Although the term *communism* has roots extending back centuries, as a contemporary ideology, it owes much to the contributions of such nineteenth- and early-twentieth-century thinkers as Karl Marx, Vladimir Ilyich Lenin, and Friedrich Engels. Communism often brings to mind the twentieth-century communist regimes of the Soviet Union, China, and Cuba (Krieger, 1993) and is a distinct version of socialism. Communism has become associated with a political movement directed by the working class to establish an alternative to capitalist societies and also with a societal ideal of egalitarianism.

The focus of communism is collectivism—that is, social ownership and control of lands as well as the *means of production* (the land, labour, and capital used by a society to produce material goods). State ownership and production is directed toward meeting human need rather than for profit, as in a capitalist state. Communism assumes that citizens will regard themselves as co-owners of the means of production, acknowledge their true needs and the needs of fellow citizens, and work diligently to produce what is necessary to accomplish these ends (Krieger, 1993; Marchak, 1988). According to some communists, these goals have to be organized under a dictatorship of the proletariat; for example, during the Russian Revolution, the Communist Party assumed political control in Russia without democratic elections and created a classless, communist society. In summary, the core ideological principles of communism are a highly communal and egalitarian social and economic order (Chappell, 2006).

The Communist Party of Canada was founded in 1921, preceded by various activities within trade unions, collectives, and former political organizations, such as the Socialist Party of Canada (British Columbia, founded 1904). Until 1937, the Communist Party was illegal under the Canadian Criminal Code, and its members were persecuted. Party members took leadership positions in some trade unions and were elected to the federal legislature (Fred Rose, 1943) and provincial legislature (W.A. Kardash, Manitoba, 1941; A.A. MacLeod and J.B. Salsberg, Ontario, 1943), as well as to many municipal councils. One of the party's founders,

Jacob Penner, served on Winnipeg City Council between 1931 and 1960; his son Roland became the province's Attorney General in 1981. The Communist Party (Marxist-Leninist), founded in 1970, espouses similar ideology to the Communist Party of Canada (Penner, 1992).

Social Democracy

Contemporary social democracy finds its roots in nineteenth-century Europe, which was strongly associated with labour activism and criticism of both capitalism and an unbridled free-market economy (Krieger, 1993). Social democrats believe that free-market economies cannot ensure the efficient and effective allocation of economic resources to meet the needs of all citizens. Most support the market economy model, but with some important state interventions; the degree of support for either may vary from one social democrat to the next. Social democrats often focus on economic issues, such as the ownership and regulation of basic or key economic resources. From this perspective, the state is responsible for planning, directing, and regulating economic sectors as well as providing social welfare services for those in need. In the Western world, socialism has most often become associated with social democrats as opposed to communists. Social democrats advocate free elections and democracy.

Unlike communism, in which a dictatorship of the proletariat without recourse to democratic elections may exist, social democrats limit the extent of state control to that determined by a democratic election process, and temper capitalism with egalitarianism through government legislation and regulation (Chappell, 2006; Krieger, 1993). Texts often cite Sweden and other Scandinavian countries as quintessential examples of social democracy (although there have been shifts to the political right in these countries); to some extent, the province of Quebec retains some social democratic traditions more obviously than other parts of Canada. In summary, social democracy seeks collective and egalitarian means to moderate the effects of capitalist, free-market economic forces.

It is important to reiterate that these definitions are "ideal types": conceptually precise terms that have divergent applications in real life. While the New Democratic Party (NDP) in Canada is seen as a major locus of our country's social democratic ideas, there are many social democrats who disagree with the NDP's approach to current social, political, and economic issues, perceiving them to be too right-wing. These same criticisms may be applied to social democratic parties in other industrialized countries, such as France, Germany, and Great Britain.

Toryism

In the eighteenth century, conservatism was a movement to counter the liberalization of traditional ideals and the advent of egalitarian ideologies that threatened the status quo (Hoover, 1992). A "Tory" conservative ideology contrasts with American brands of "liberal conservatism" because it retains its British roots (Horowitz, 1970; Mishra, 1995). The traditional Canadian attitude of deference to authority is seen as an expression of Tory elitism (Horowitz, 1970). Toryism also sees itself as collectivist in an organic sense of society, because the ideal of social and economic hierarchies contributes to economic security and social stability (Mishra, 1995). Toryism's social "law and order" orientation contrasts with liberalism's individual liberty and freedom perspective. Marchak (1988) places Toryism as slightly right of centre on the egalitarian–elitist and the individualist–collectivist spectrum, but left of the neo-conservative position on these dimensions. Historically, the term Tory has been used to describe members of the former Progressive Conservative Party of Canada. But, as we shall see, political parties change. Although some Conservatives are still Tory, many Conservatives these days are in fact liberal or neo-conservative in ideology. Some conservative thinkers in social work, on the other hand, have a great deal in common with their Tory predecessors (Thyer, 2010).

Liberalism

The ideology of liberalism evolved in the eighteenth and nineteenth centuries as a change-oriented perspective that emphasized individual development in a social, political, and economic order unencumbered by government restraints (Krieger, 1993). Modern liberal doctrine for many liberals acknowledges the constraints of capitalism and the free-market economy in the unequal distribution of wealth and its attendant status and power (Chappell, 1997). This realization has led to a tempered liberal outlook with stronger humanistic values becoming more prominent. The liberal ideology is strongly individualistic, though its proponents claim it staves off the extremes of the left and the right by developing policies that reduce economic and social inequalities (see Krieger, 1993, for a more extensive historical review). Nineteenth-century liberalism in economic matters was often referred to as *laissez-faire*, which called for no government interference in the marketplace. But liberalism has since moved from a belief that individual differences accounted for economic and social inequalities to a recognition that some government intervention is needed to facilitate equality of opportunity (Marchak, 1988). The extent of this intervention would be less, as a rule, than what a social democrat might advocate. The Liberal Party of Canada should not be confused with the ideology of liberalism described here. The terms *Liberal*, with a capital letter and describing the Canadian political party, and *liberal*, with a lower-case letter and describing the ideology, are not the same. Only *some* Liberals are liberal in ideology; others have social democratic leanings, and others are neo-conservative.

Neo-Conservatism

Conservatism recognizes the inequalities among people but sees differences as more important than similarities (Hoover, 1992). Neo-conservatism refers to the "new right"—the rejection of collectivist values and the return to laissez-faire economics, which advocates less government and a more minimalist position toward social and economic affairs. Hoover (1992) identifies neo-conservatives as "individualist conservatives," sharing much in common with liberals. More traditional Tories and "red Tory" conservatives accept inequality less willingly, whereas neo-conservatives more strongly revere freedom and personal initiative. Many policy scholars use the terms *neo-liberal* and *neo-conservative* interchangeably in the popular media. One can consider the two terms as synonymous.

Fascism

Fascism refers to a government or political philosophy that is typically totalitarian, extreme right-wing, and nationalist. Twentieth-century fascist political parties rose to power between the two world wars in Mussolini's Italy and Hitler's Germany. Payne (1992) describes fascism as an ideology opposed to almost all other political ideologies of the time—communism, socialism, and liberalism. The strong, radical, nationalist stance of fascism arose out of several forces, among them an intense fear of communist and socialist ideology, and a racist assertion of nationality. Fascism gave rise to a one-party authoritarian state that maintained an active control of the economy, but without socialist ownership of the means of production. Like communism, fascism is inherently undemocratic. Once a fascist government comes to power, it tends to ban open elections. In addition, fascists embrace a radical collectivist stance (i.e., a particular form of nationalism, often racially and/or ethnically based). They place the interest of the nation or groups within a nation ahead of any particular class or individual. They also reject the egalitarian perspective of communism and socialism and maintain an elitist or class structure in society, *but* with the belief that the class structure should be subordinate to the social cohesion of the nation.

Mainstream Canadian Political Parties

There are numerous political parties in Canada, and many that do not have representatives in federal or provincial legislatures represent theoretical concerns of interest. But for purposes of brevity, this section examines four divergent political ideologies as represented in mainstream Canadian political parties: neo-conservatism, Toryism, liberalism, and social democracy. Common to all the major political parties of Canada are some basic values, such as the inherent right of citizens to self-determination, a belief in democracy, and a commitment to varyingly regulated forms of industrial capitalism—depending on the political ideology. But among our major political parties, and indeed within society, principles of egalitarianism appear to be weakening, as liberal tenets of individualism gain greater currency.

It is best, though, to appreciate the complex, sometimes contradictory and divergent ideological base within the same party. Holding each party together and determining its social policy stance is a complex set of interactions among ideological, historical, economic, political, and social forces. For example, some scholars have characterized the Liberal and former Progressive Conservative parties as governing by "brokerage" politics since the 1960s: this means that their respective ideological tenets hold only a marginal place in decision-making processes and outcomes (Carty, Cross, & Young, 2000; Turner, 1995). It is important, too, to appreciate that the parliamentary and economic (political, civil society, business, media, and others) mechanisms often cause non-incremental change to party policies, some of which are unpredictable and some of which vary from issue to issue (Gormley, 2007). Further details of these mechanisms are noted in Chapter 9.

Liberal Party of Canada

The Liberals, or "Grits," were part of Canada's political structure at its founding in 1867. Christian and Campbell (1990) characterize the Liberals as comprising two ideological factions: business liberalism and welfare liberalism. These party factions are held together by the common traditional liberal values of liberty and individualism. Welfare liberalism, on the one hand, places human rights above the economic rights of individuals. This type of liberalism expresses itself in the policies that impose taxation and other forms of economic regulation, as well as those that facilitate the development of social welfare programs. Business liberalism, on the other hand, interprets taxes and regulation as economic restraints to individual freedom. The business faction of the Liberal Party prefers minimizing government law-making and regulation, especially in economic matters.

Any interpretation of Liberal social policy must begin by assessing which side of the business–welfare liberalism tension is in the ascendancy position within the party. When business liberalism dominates, social policy focuses on costs and thus limits access to and reduces emphasis on universal programs. In contrast, when welfare liberals speak for the party, they emphasize universal access and standards in social policies. At these times, emphasis on the costs of *not* providing these services overrides concerns about the financial costs of providing them.

Conservative Party of Canada

The country's conservative tradition originated with the original Conservative Party (1867–1942) and the Progressive Conservative Party (1942–2003). The Progressive Conservative Party always had a wide spectrum of proponents. Those in the "Tory" tradition of eighteenth- and nineteenth-century England were conscious of the interdependence of socio-economic classes and were more open to government involvement in the economy and society than many liberals. This group was once so powerful in the party that the Progressive Conservatives were known as *the Tories*. Others in this party were stauncher advocates of the free market and individualism. In 1987, the Reform Party of Canada arose in Western Canada as a populist right-wing protest party, rejecting the "Toryism" of the Progressive Conservatives. Its presence split the right-wing vote, assuring a succession of Liberal Party governments in the late 1980s and 1990s. The Reform Party (renamed the Alliance Party in 2000) amalgamated with the federal Progressive Conservative Party in 2003, creating a new Conservative Party that came to federal power in 2005. At the provincial level, Progressive Conservative Parties remain in most Canadian provinces. The new Conservative Party of Canada, like its provincial counterparts, has strong ideological anchors in neo-liberalism/neo-conservatism. As a result, social policy proposed by the Conservative Party of Canada tends to promote reduced government involvement in social policy and increased reliance on self, families, and the economic marketplace. This approach has a lot in common with the market-state stage of social policy discussed in Chapter 2. A final point bears emphasis. Keep in mind that this entire definition emphasizes general principles only. For example, while it is true, on balance, that the Conservative

Party of Canada prefers selective programs, some Conservative policies retain certain universal programs, as occurred with the creation of the Universal Child Care Benefit (2006).

New Democratic Party

The New Democratic Party is a social-democratic–oriented party that originated as the Co-operative Commonwealth Federation (CCF) party, established during the Great Depression of the 1930s, among trade unions and farmer cooperatives. It was renamed the New Democratic Party (NDP) in 1961. The NDP has ideological roots in welfare liberalism and is a reaction to the Tory hierarchical view of society. A collectivist but egalitarian stance characterizes the Canadian socialism portrayed by the NDP. Legal equality and equality of opportunity are major features of its view of Canadian social democracy. NDP social policy tends to support universal programming, with broad access and a uniformity of distribution across Canada. To many party faithful, the costs of sustaining these social programs should be borne more prominently by corporate Canada.

Bloc Québécois Party

The Bloc Québécois, a federal political party that elected its first leader in 1991, has had as its principal mandate the promotion of Quebec sovereignty. In 1993, the Bloc gained the second largest number of seats in the general election and therefore became the official opposition (McMenemy, 1995). Although the Bloc has a very clear and precise political agenda, it has had support from diverse parts of Quebec society. For example, it is currently centrist but has also had trade union support and other social democratic influences. The Bloc, whose political fortunes declined in 2011, is also closely associated with the Parti Québécois, a provincial political party founded in 1968 and also devoted to the sovereignty of Quebec.

A final point on these four political parties bears emphasis. Political parties are elected at the provincial and federal levels to govern for a maximum of five years. Governments can be elected with a majority of seats (half the seats plus one) or a minority of seats (less than half of the seats but with more seats than any other party). When acting as a majority, a governing party can pass legislation regardless of opposition if all members of that party vote. For minority governing parties, any legislation can be defeated if all members of the opposition vote against it. Thus, minority governments often need to negotiate with the other parties.

Theories of Social Welfare/The Welfare State

Ideology is the foundation of social welfare theory and the extent of programs and services delivered through the welfare state. Figure 4.2 illustrates the interconnection of ideology and the welfare state by demonstrating, in general terms, the relationship between ideology and social responsibility. For example, at the left end of the political spectrum, there is strong emphasis on societal responsibility, which

FIGURE 4.2   Model of Social Responsibility and Social Capital

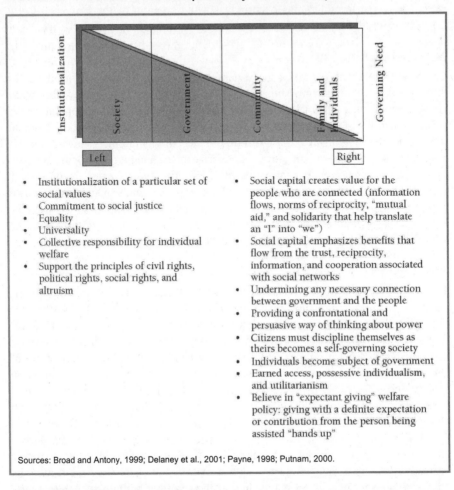

- Institutionalization of a particular set of social values
- Commitment to social justice
- Equality
- Universality
- Collective responsibility for individual welfare
- Support the principles of civil rights, political rights, social rights, and altruism

- Social capital creates value for the people who are connected (information flows, norms of reciprocity, "mutual aid," and solidarity that help translate an "I" into "we")
- Social capital emphasizes benefits that flow from the trust, reciprocity, information, and cooperation associated with social networks
- Undermining any necessary connection between government and the people
- Providing a confrontational and persuasive way of thinking about power
- Citizens must discipline themselves as theirs becomes a self-governing society
- Individuals become subject of government
- Earned access, possessive individualism, and utilitarianism
- Believe in "expectant giving" welfare policy: giving with a definite expectation or contribution from the person being assisted "hands up"

Sources: Broad and Antony, 1999; Delaney et al., 2001; Payne, 1998; Putnam, 2000.

results in an institutionalized approach to social welfare. Alternatively, at the other end of the spectrum, individuals are challenged to meet their own basic needs, with emphasis placed on the development of social or human capital. A current example is the use of welfare-to-work programs: these programs emphasize the development of individual skills to create greater social capital. *Social capital* is defined as the attitude, spirit, and willingness of people to engage in collective civic activities or networks of relationships with people in their community and family.

As with any continuum, the political spectrum contains a wide range of ideological beliefs, each with a distinct interpretation of social responsibility. This discussion is based on Mulvale's outline of theoretical approaches to social welfare (2001, 15–29)—practice frameworks used within the social work profession. Adapting Mulvale, we have eight perspectives.

The first, a social democratic perspective, assumes that the welfare state emerged out of democratic political pressures, be it via trade unions, political parties, or other social institutions. Often these pressures come from the left end of the political spectrum (Struthers, 1994).

The second perspective, premised on Marxist thought, deems the welfare state an instrument of social control; for instance, it forestalls class insurrection. The welfare state serves the needs of capital accumulation—ensuring, for example, economic growth and relative peace with labour. It also serves the needs of the state: post–World War II economic growth financed a burgeoning welfare state, which in turn kept unemployment relatively low; political parties were elected in part on their ability to help to facilitate these outcomes (Offe, 1984). Many Marxists believe social welfare has contradictory purposes in meeting the needs of the state and of capital. Some, in fact, accept right-wing arguments that some welfare programs create disincentives for work and diminish profit margins (Offe, 1984). Most see the post–World War II universal welfare state as decidedly a thing of the past. As elaborated in Chapter 2, economic growth in the 1970s faltered and governments abandoned the principles of intervening in the economy. Consequently, "two legs (high levels of employment and consumer demand, both premised on strong economic growth)" of the welfare state became wobbly; the third, the government's commitment to social welfare programs, was weakened as a result (Mulvale, 2001, 19).

A third perspective, based on feminist thought, sees the welfare state as having profoundly reinforced dependency of women and children on the breadwinner male. Women are fundamental actors in social welfare: as the clients, reformers, and state employees of the welfare state (Ursel, 1992). Yet the welfare state has been modest at best in meeting women's needs, and oppressive at worst in reproducing gender inequalities that arise within patriarchal structures. Income security programs, for instance, have been bifurcated into insurance-based entitlements for men and needs-tested, stigmatizing programs for women. Feminist theorists call for greater support for women in the workplace, the expansion of affordable daycare, and the transformation of income security programs to reflect women's needs, among many other measures. These concerns are elaborated in Chapter 6.

A fourth perspective is an anti-racist critique of the welfare state. One writer describes the double process of disadvantage experienced by members of ethnoracial communities. Their less-advantaged positions on economic and social grounds make them more reliant on the welfare state. Yet the welfare state treats them "on systematically less favourable terms than members of the majority community" (Pierson, 1991, as cited in Mulvale, 2001, 23). This perspective is also discussed in Chapter 6.

Fifth, a green critique sees the welfare state as "embedded in an industrial order"—meaning an economy based on growth that is no longer sustainable (Pierson, 1991, as cited in Mulvale, 2001, 23). Green critics assert that the welfare state is premised on an expanded economy that overproduces, depletes resources, and creates pollution (Payne, 2010). These concerns are elaborated in Chapter 5.

A sixth perspective calls for a shift in social welfare from compensation to empowerment. Rather than emphasizing individual deficits and providing an agreed-upon community standard, such as a poverty line, empowerment social welfare assumes that all people require help in order to develop (Drover & Kerans, 1993, as cited in Mulvale, 2001, 26–27). Central to this view is a critique of the way needs are interpreted and claims are made.

The market state, discussed in Chapter 2, challenges several of these perspectives—particularly the social democratic perspective and any others that do not adhere to individualist or liberal assumptions. The market state represents a seventh and important perspective unto itself. While many social workers do not adhere to it, some may; and many governments, particularly those of the right, do.

The final perspective was honed in the late 1990s and the first decade of the twenty-first century by British prime minister Tony Blair. It emphasizes what sociologist Anthony Giddens (1998) coined a "Third Way" in that it attempts to combine market-state principles with social democratic principles. Giddens and a colleague at the London School of Economics, Julian Le Grand, advised Blair extensively, and Le Grand writes that the best solution for social services is to offer choice to users and encourage competition among providers (Le Grand, 2007). Others see choice as a Trojan Horse that could eventually lead to the privatization of social, health, and educational services by "piecemealing it and starving it of funds" (Sadava, 2010, 29).

Social Welfare as a Response to Need

Social welfare programs may be categorized as functioning in one of the following three ways (Macarov, 1995a):

1. Intervention is made before a problem arises. This function of social welfare is perhaps the least addressed, given that scarce resources are most often used to address existing cases of economic hardship.
2. Maintenance is provided for at-risk individuals or groups, such as families with children, who receive various tax credits in the hope that they will not slip into the poverty ranks.
3. Social policy is directed at the amelioration of existing problems through such programs as social assistance. This category is the most commonly used. Governments and social agencies strive to develop clear indicators for identifying when personal economic troubles should fall within the realm of a social economic problem.

There is a great deal of debate about how to define the need worthy of social intervention, as well as how to respond to identified need. It is important to remember that there is a direct relationship between how a social problem is defined and its perceived solution. In this section, we will consider how poverty is defined and the solutions that these definitions imply. To do this, we will distinguish needs from wants, categorize types of economic need, and examine how benchmarks for measuring economic need that societal intervention will address are created.

Need versus Want

A four-part typology helps social workers to determine the exact nature of a particular human need. The types include felt needs, expressed needs, normative needs, and comparative needs (Chappell, 2006):

> *Felt needs* are defined on a personal or subjective level.

> *Expressed needs* are felt needs that are communicated to others.

> *Normative needs* are determined by someone other than the individual by applying a benchmark or standard to the individual case.

> *Comparative needs* are determined by comparing one individual or group to another.

Establishing the benchmarks for normative needs and the boundaries of specific social groups, such as those living in poverty, is of major concern for the creators and administrators of social policy.

Theoretical and/or ideological perspectives influence how social policy planners determine the nature of a human need. Psychologist Abraham Maslow's *hierarchy of needs* theory (see Figure 4.3) is an excellent means of considering these distinctions (Maslow, 1954; Macarov, 1995b). Maslow's theory categorizes needs according to a hierarchy ranging from *having* (physiological needs) to *loving* (social needs) and finally to *being* (self-actualizing needs) (Macarov, 1995b). Maslow defined the basic physiological needs (i.e., food, shelter, and clothing) as essential survival needs. Social policy is most often directed at this "having" aspect of need. Maslow's theory is based on the principle of deficiency needs; that is, if a particular need is not being sufficiently met, then the person or group will seek to make up for this deficiency. This theory highlights a motivational element in meeting common human needs (adapted from Chappell, 2006).

Differential Human Needs

While Maslow's hierarchy distinguishes types of common needs, it does not address special conditions that create these specific needs. Macarov (1995b) identified five categories of people with special needs:

1. the *incapable*, such as children;
2. the *unprepared*, such as recent immigrants to a new country and those who cannot read;
3. *disaster victims*, such as victims of war or environmental situations;
4. the *unconforming*, or those who do not abide by societal norms; and
5. the *unmotivated*, or people who lack the motivation to meet their own needs.

All five categories are essential to social policies.

Besides common human needs and special needs, some needs are created by society (Macarov, 1995b). Institutionalized discrimination—along lines of race, gender, culture, or other areas of social diversity—may create obstacles to developing

FIGURE 4.3   Maslow's Hierarchy of Needs

- **Self-Actualization**
  * Realizing one's own potential
  * Self-development activities
  * Behaving creatively
  * Problem-centred orientation to life
  * Identifying the problems of humanity
  * Acceptance of self and others

- **Self-Esteem**
  * Self-confidence * Independence * Achievement
  * Competence * Knowledge * Status
  * Personal recognition * Respect

- **Social**
  * Love and affection * Friendships * Association with others * Affiliation

- **Safety**
  * Shelter * Protection from immediate or future danger to physical well-being
  * Protection from immediate future threat to psychological economic well-being

- **Physiological**
  * Hunger * Thirst * Sex * Sleep * Rest * Exercise * Elimination * Pain avoidance * Oxygen consumption

Source: Haber, A., & Runyon R. (1986). *Fundamentals of psychology* (4th ed.). New York: McGraw-Hill Company. Reprinted with permission from publisher, 2010.

and implementing social policy. These include, but are not restricted to, lack of access to services, inadequate funding and representation in community-based programs, and ethnocentric values and practices in existing services and programs policy (Galabuzi, 2006). Discriminatory policies are examined in greater depth in Chapter 6.

Denying the impact of institutionalized discrimination affects the definition of the problems and, therefore, the anticipated solutions. This denial may lead to an interpretation of needs based on membership in the unconforming and/or the unmotivated categories mentioned earlier. As a result, social needs—for housing, income security, or other things—may be restricted or even denied to a particular person or group, because they are evaluated as deserving or undeserving.

As society changes, the social attention to needs may also change. Policy-makers decide how and when societal resources are directed at certain needs and when social norms dictate that social institutions other than social welfare (e.g., the individual, family, or informal social networks) should be directed at finding a solution.

Measurements of Well-Being

There are several ways to measure well-being. Measuring the strength of a country's economy by means of the Gross Domestic Product (GDP) and Gross National Product (GNP) is one. GDP is "a measure of the total flow of goods and services produced by the economy over a specified time period" (Bannock, Baxter, & Davis, 1998a). GNP is a more comprehensive measure, which includes "gross domestic product plus the income accruing to domestic residents arising from investment abroad less income earned in the domestic market accruing to foreigners abroad" (Bannock, Baxter, & Davis, 1998b). Unemployment levels are another measure; a full employment economy means that unemployment levels are 3 percent or less: anyone wanting a job could have one (albeit not necessarily a well-paying job). According to Vosko (2006), *precarious employment* refers to

Forms of work involving limited social benefits and statutory entitlements, job insecurity, low wages, and high risks to health. It is shaped by employment status (i.e., self-employment or wage work), form of employment (i.e., temporary or permanent, part-time or full-time), and dimensions of labour market insecurity as well as social context (such as occupation, industry, and geography) and social location (the interaction between social relations, such as gender and race, and political and economic conditions. (3–4)

New immigrants and racialized groups are overrepresented among Canada's precariously employed (Galabuzi, 2006).

Several conditions related to precarious employment—such as job insecurity, excessive work hours, work–life conflict, effort–reward imbalance, and job strain—are also work-related determinants of health (Raphael, 2004, 97). The social determinants of health determine the conditions of a person's life. Table 4.1 lists other social determinants of health (Raphael, 2004, 13).

TABLE 4.1   Social Determinants of Improved Health

1. Don't be poor. If you can, stop. If you can't, try not to be poor for long.
2. Don't have poor parents.
3. Own a car.
4. Don't work in a stressful, low-paid, manual job.
5. Don't live in damp, low-quality housing.
6. Be able to afford to go on a foreign holiday and sunbathe.
7. Practise not losing your job, and don't become unemployed.
8. Take up all benefits you are entitled to, if you are unemployed, retired, sick, or disabled.
9. Don't live next to a busy major road or near a polluting factory.
10. Learn how to fill in the complex housing benefit/asylum application forms before you become homeless and destitute.

Source: Dennis Raphael (Ed.). (2004). *Social determinants of health: Canadian perspectives.* Toronto: Canadian Scholars' Press. Reprinted with permission from Canadian Scholars' Press Inc., 2010.

In 1990, the United Nations created a popular measure of human well-being called the Human Development Index (HDI). HDI is based on three indicators: longevity, education, and standard of living. These constructs are measured by analyzing the rates of life expectancy, adult literacy, enrolment in education facilities, purchasing power parity, and income. Canada often scores high; in 1992 and 1994 through to 2000, it had the world's highest HDI. In 2010, Canada ranked eighth out of 169 countries—following Norway, Australia, New Zealand, the United States, Ireland, Liechtenstein, and the Netherlands (United Nations Development Programme, 2010).

Another recent measure of well-being results from people evaluating the well-being within their own lives: subjective well-being (SWB). SWB is measured by personal perceptions of life satisfaction as they relate to, for example, one's moods and emotions and one's living and work situations (Graham, Trew, Schmidt, & Kline, 2007). Understanding well-being in this manner is largely individualistic, but it provides a picture of a wide range of conditions that influence a person's happiness. According to SWB, happiness is more than simply monetary gains—in contrast to the corporate message promulgated through the popular media (Graham, 2008). SWB has been used as an official indicator of well-being in such countries as France, and much empirical research is used via World Values Surveys to determine SWB levels within and between countries (Kingdon & Knight, 2007).

Conceptualizing and Defining Poverty

Perhaps the most important concept of well-being in social policy is the notion of poverty. The concept of poverty dates back to ancient times. *Poverty* is a state of deficiency in money or the means of subsistence. Welfare-state governments want to know how many citizens live in a state of poverty, and these governments are not content to rely on subjective assessment. To this end, governments and organizations set *poverty lines* that measure the necessary amount of money for living at a determined *standard of living*. A standard of living refers to the "necessities, luxuries, and comforts" needed to sustain oneself or one's family at a determined level (Barker, 1991).

Defining poverty with a poverty line means measuring the difference between *what is* and *what should be*. As indicators of an income level below which living would be seriously difficult, poverty lines may be set at absolute or relative levels. Absolute and relative definitions of poverty are based on destitution and disparity models, respectively. *Absolute need* definitions of poverty answer the question "What is the bare minimum (destitution) level in order for an individual or family to survive?" Writing for the Canadian Council on Social Development, policy analysts Ross, Scott, and Smith (2000) set an absolute poverty line at about $2000 per person per annum in Canada (6). Adjusting this figure for inflation, in 2010 the absolute poverty line would be approximately $2440 per person per annum. This amount is a mere survival rate that includes using all local resources such as basic provincial health care, community shelters, food banks, and thrift shop clothing. In contrast, *relative need* definitions are based on social values, rather than absolute needs, and start with a prevailing standard of living and then deduce the level below this standard that is intolerable to society. Relative poverty lines are concerned with what *should* be; they establish the norm against which an individual or family can be compared.

Normative Basis of the Poverty Line

How do Canadians define poverty? Table 4.2 summarizes major indexes for defining Canadian poverty lines, and shows that Canadians cannot agree on a definition of poverty. Statistics Canada's low-income cut-off (LICO) definition is the best known of these indicators. The LICO has been a standard since 1959 and is based on a 1959 survey of family spending patterns conducted by Statistics Canada. The survey showed that the average Canadian family spent 50 percent of its gross income on essentials: food, shelter, and clothing. It was estimated that any family spending more than 50 percent on these essentials was living in constrained circumstances, and any family spending more than 70 percent on essentials was designated as *low-income*. In essence, these definitions created a poverty line. In subsequent years, the poverty cut-off has been adjusted by using the same formula (i.e., spending on essentials for the average Canadian family, plus 20 percent). For example, in the *2008 Survey of Household Spending*, one-fifth of Canadian households with the lowest incomes spent almost 52 percent of their gross family spending budget on essential expenditures. Since 1973, Statistics Canada has also

TABLE 4.2   Measuring Poverty

Poverty Lines in 2007/2008	Cut-Off Income for Household of Four[*]
Sarlo Basic Needs[**] (Canada)	$23 355
Montreal Diet Dispensary (minimum adequate standard)[***]	$30 306
Market-Based Measure[****]	Toronto: $31 729 Quebec community with population between 30 000–99 999: $24 283
After-Tax Low-Income Measure (Canada)[*****]	$32 050
After-Tax Low-Income Cut-Off (community of 500 000+)[*****]	$33 946
Before Tax Low-Income Measure (Canada)[*****]	$36 456
Before Tax Low-Income Cut-Off (community of 500 000+)[*****]	$40 259

Notes:

[*] A *household of four* refers to households with two adults and two children, or one adult and three children.

[**] Sarlo Basic Needs updated to 2007 by the National Council of Welfare by using the Consumer Price Index.

[***] Source: National Council of Welfare (2009). *Poverty profile 2007.* Retrieved July 21, 2010, from http://www.ncwcnbes.net/en/research/poverty-pauvrete.html. Reproduced with permission from publisher, 2010.

[****] Source: Human Resources and Skills Development Canada (2009). *Low income in Canada: 2000–2007 using the market basket measure.* Catalogue No. HS28-49/2009E. Ottawa: Author. Reproduced with permission from publisher, 2010.

[*****] Source: Income Statistics Division, Statistics Canada (2007). *Low-income cutoffs for 2008 and low income measures for 2007.* Income Research Paper Series, Catalogue No. 75F00002M. Ottawa: Minister of Industry. Reproduced with permission from Statistics Canada, 2010.

distinguished among five different sizes of urban and rural communities—the larger the community, the higher the LICO for any family (Statistics Canada, Income Statistics Division, 2010).

In 1991, Statistics Canada calculated a second poverty line, based on median after-tax incomes rather than the average gross income. This measurement became known as the *low income measure* (LIM). The LIM is based not on the proportion of income spent on food, clothing, and shelter, but rather on income itself. It is calculated on the basis of one-half of median net (i.e., after-tax) income, where median income is first adjusted for family size. Be careful not to confuse *median* with *average*: the median income represents the income that half of all income earners earn more than and half earn less than, while an average income represents the sum of all incomes divided by the number of income earners (Statistics Canada, Income Statistics Division, 2010). An after-tax index may be a truer standard than the commonly used gross or before-tax measures. Statistics Canada nonetheless continues to use its LICO measurement as the standard for assessing poverty. As Table 4.2 makes clear, the LIM approach and the LICO provide different measurements. The LIM tends to reduce the number of people in poverty by two or three percentage points.

Another measure of poverty is the market basket measure (MBM). The MBM is distinct from the other two measures discussed here because it creates a measure of poverty that is based on the actual calculated market costs of shelter, food, clothing and footwear, transportation, and other goods and services—such as hygiene products and furniture (Human Resources and Social Development Canada, 2006). The MBM includes a greater spectrum of necessary goods and services for living a decent life, and is also calculated to a specific community, rather than being calculated as an average applicable to all Canadians.

Defining the Problem, Defining the Solution In 1984, the Canadian Council on Social Development (CCSD) outlined the following four rationales for establishing poverty lines, all of which are still relevant today:

1. Poverty lines are needed to determine the number of people living in poverty. In Canada, the Statistics Canada LICO measurement is most frequently used to determine this figure.

2. Poverty indicators are used to inform and perhaps motivate those receiving and administering social service programs. This rationale explains why social assistance payments are set at a minimal level: to motivate people to view this financial program as temporary.

3. Poverty lines help to set the parameters of an accepted "market basket" (the amount of goods and services consumed by a family or individual over the course of a typical month). This market basket approach contributes to the development of only a few of the major poverty indicators, such as Social Planning Toronto's budget guides and the Montreal Diet Dispensary's budget guidelines of basic needs.

4. Poverty indexes inform future social policy planners, especially with respect to setting income security levels.

The various poverty lines described above can be pegged across the political spectrum. The conservative "right" of the political spectrum is represented by the Fraser Institute (also referred to as the *Sarlo measure*, named after Dr. Christopher Sarlo of the Fraser Institute) and Montreal Diet Dispensary definitions of poverty. This position asserts that poverty levels using other standards are grossly exaggerated. The Social Planning Toronto figures represent the "left" or social democratic end of the political spectrum, or a more social-justice or equality focus. Statistics Canada maintains poverty measures that are closer to the political centre.

It should be stressed that the agreed-upon definition of poverty is the one that Canadian society accepts. In the face of rising numbers of persons living in poverty, society ultimately has three options, none of which are mutually exclusive. Society can:

1. decide to leave more and more people behind;
2. find ways to distribute wealth more efficiently and equitably; or
3. hope to find ways for people to receive more income from their own efforts and work.

Economic inequality is a growing problem worldwide. A shocking 1 percent of the world's population holds 40 percent of its entire wealth, and 10 percent hold 85 percent of its wealth. At the other end of the continuum, 1 percent of the world's wealth is shared by 50 percent of its population—3 billion people (Davies, Sandstrom, Shorrocks, & Wolff, 2009). According to a study published in *Perspectives on Labour and Income*, the top 20 percent of families in Canada held 75 percent of total household wealth in 2005, compared to 73 percent in 1999 and 69 percent in 1984. The study was based on the results of the 1984 Assets and Debts Survey and the Surveys of Financial Security conducted in 1999 and 2005 (Statistics Canada, 2010c). The share of all income going to the richest 1 percent almost doubled between 1982 and 2007, rising from 7.9 percent to 13.8 percent (Yalnizyan, 2010). In addition, economic inequality, measured by income or consumption, seems to be worsening in Canada and throughout much of the westernized world (Heisz, 2007). A recent Statistics Canada study revealed that inequality in after-tax family income increased between 1976 and 2004, driven by widening differences in family market income (the sum of earnings from employment and net self-employment income, investment income, and private retirement income, for all family members). Indeed, the report concludes that "This increase occurred at the same time as a reduction in the generosity of several income transfer programs, including the Employment Insurance and Social Assistance Programs (in some provinces), and decreases in income tax rates. This potentially reflects a weakening of the redistributive role of the Canadian state" (Heisz, 2007, 5). As discussed later in this chapter, income security programs and the income tax system still help to moderate these income inequalities. A final point: the average family market income among the 10 percent of families with the highest incomes rose by 22 percent from 1989 to 2004. Meanwhile, among the 10 percent of families with the lowest incomes, it fell by 11 percent (Heisz, 2007). A recent study showed that during the 1981–2007 period, the

Gini coefficient of after-tax income increased by 12.9 percent, from 0.348 in 1981 to 0.393 in 2007, indicating increasing inequalities among Canadians, even when studies are based on after-tax income (Sharpe & Arsenault, 2009).

Some scholars attribute this growing inequality to the deregulation of financial markets and industry, and the reduction of taxes for the rich (Hacker & Pierson, 2010). The impact of economic inequality on society is profound. Over the past 30 years, social science has provided convincing evidence that a variety of health and social problems are significantly worse in societies that have greater economic inequality: physical health, mental health, drug abuse, education, imprisonment, obesity, social mobility, trust and community life, violence, teenage pregnancies, and child well-being (Wilkinson & Pickett, 2009). In part, these problems occur because unequal societies have less economic redistribution and less commitment to social and health programs for people with lower and middle incomes. Many people, it should be pointed out, are assuming greater personal debt, as noted in Figure 4.4 (Grant, 2010). The same is true of governments and other institutions. Figure 4.5 compares Canada's debt with that of other countries (Coggan, 2010).

It is essential to note some of the changing parameters of poverty in Canada. A 2005 study by the Organisation for Economic Co-operation and Development (OECD) compares Canada's record in combating poverty relative to those of 21 other OECD countries (Forster & d'Ercole, 2005). As Figure 4.6 shows, Canada has maintained a similar poverty rate across all three time periods and has not

FIGURE 4.4   Household Indebtedness

Sources: Adapted from the Statistics Canada CANSIM database http://cansim2.statcan.gc.ca, table number 380-0004 and 378-0085, December 2010, Board of Governors of the Federal Reserve System, Household Debt, Flow of Funds Accounts of the United States, http://www.federalreserve.gov/releases/z1/default.htm, and U.S. Bureau of Economic Analysis, Disposable Income, http://www.bea.gov/national/nipaweb/SelectTable.asp?Selected=Y. Reproduced with permission, 2010.

FIGURE 4.5   Debt by Sector as Percentage of GDP

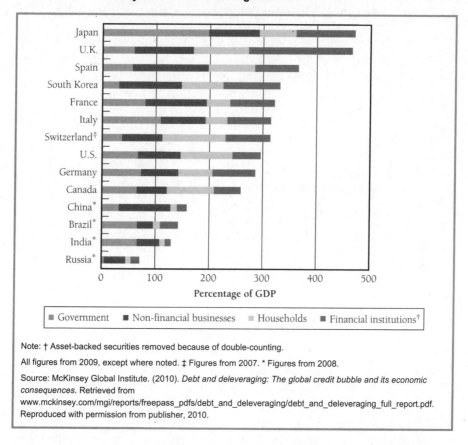

Note: † Asset-backed securities removed because of double-counting.

All figures from 2009, except where noted. ‡ Figures from 2007. * Figures from 2008.

Source: McKinsey Global Institute. (2010). *Debt and deleveraging: The global credit bubble and its economic consequences*. Retrieved from www.mckinsey.com/mgi/reports/freepass_pdfs/debt_and_deleveraging/debt_and_deleveraging_full_report.pdf. Reproduced with permission from publisher, 2010.

effectively lowered poverty levels. This result does not suggest that people are in a constant state of poverty. Some move in and out of poverty. In 2004, 11.2 percent of Canadians were in a low-income category (Statistics Canada, 2007), compared to 15.7 percent in 1996 (Statistics Canada, 2006a). Using LICO as a measure, an OECD study shows that in the mid-2000s, 12 percent of Canadians experienced low-income conditions, a rate slightly higher than that of the average for 30 OECD member countries of 11 percent (OECD, 2008).

Rates of low income for seniors have dropped over the last two decades. During the early 1980s, for example, approximately 17.5 percent of seniors had an after-tax income less than the Statistics Canada LICO measure, compared to 5.4 percent of seniors fitting into this category in 2004 (Hick, 2007). The low-income rate among seniors decreased below that of the overall population in 1990 and continued to fall, reaching 4.8 percent in 2007 (Statistics Canada, 2009). Many assert that the income security programs discussed in Chapter 3, such as Old Age Security and the CPP/QPP, have been especially important in reducing poverty among seniors. But within this cohort, there is a profound gender bias:

FIGURE 4.6   **Poverty in Canada Compared with Other OECD Countries—Poverty as a Percentage of Population, Mid-1980s, Mid-1990s, and Mid-2000s**

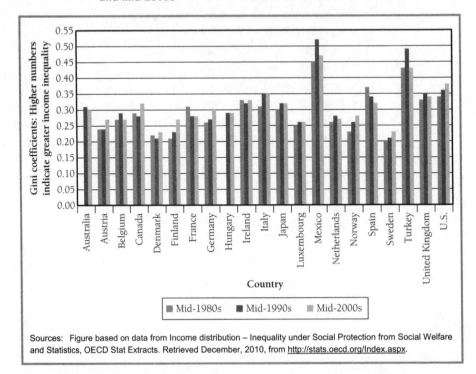

Sources: Figure based on data from Income distribution – Inequality under Social Protection from Social Welfare and Statistics, OECD Stat Extracts. Retrieved December, 2010, from http://stats.oecd.org/Index.aspx.

elderly men—a reflection, in part, of the inequalities in workplace earnings that subsequently were translated into unequal pension rates upon retirement. However, with the possible exception of individuals in the top quintile—where men enjoyed slightly higher income levels than women—trends in income levels did not differ much by gender. Note that among top quintile seniors, CPP/QPP, OAS, and GIS accounted for only 18 percent of income, while private pensions, investments, and capital gains accounted for 60 percent (Statistics Canada, Income Statistics Division, 2008). Finally, it is important to emphasize that many elderly households have only barely been lifted above poverty levels, and, in fact, a significant proportion of the elderly fall into the category of *nearly poor*.

Younger families are more likely to be poor than older families. What is more, poverty has increased dramatically among younger families. In 1981, approximately 20 percent of young families (in which the oldest/only adult is younger than age 25) were poor. By 1991, this figure had increased to 41.5 percent and, by 2001, to approximately 57 percent—a rate that most readers will agree is deeply troubling (Campaign, 2000, 2007). The next age cohort, those parents between 24 and 35 years of age, has also experienced increases in poverty rates (Morissette & Zhang, 2006). Within this family age cohort there was a 31.1 percent increase in the incidence of poverty between 1981 and 2001 (Campaign, 2000, 2007). The risk of poverty has increased in young two-parent families with only one wage earner. In 1980, 17 percent of these families lived in poverty; by 1995, this figure had risen to 27 percent.

Child poverty rates continue to be a great concern. In 2004, 865 000 Canadian children under the age of 18 were living in poverty (National Council of Welfare, 2006a). This number represents 12.8 percent of all Canadian children, a figure that still falls short of many advocates' demands for a total end to childhood poverty. Lone-parent families, particularly female-headed families, continue to be most vulnerable to poverty. In 2004, of the 550 000 lone-parent families headed by women, statistics showed a shocking 36 percent with low income. According to Crossley and Curtis (2006), the poverty rate among children rose slightly between 1986 and 1998 and then settled back to the 1986 level in 2000. The consumption poverty rate among children declined slightly between 1986 and 1998 but then climbed to the 1986 level in 2000, so that both income and consumption poverty rates are almost unchanged between 1986 and 2000. As noted in Figure 4.7, Canada's child poverty rates are higher than those of many other advanced industrialized countries.

The face of poverty has likewise changed in Canada's provinces and regions. The percentage of all poor families in Newfoundland and Labrador dropped from 18.1 percent in 1981 to 12.8 percent in 2003. A similar trend has occurred in all Atlantic provinces and Quebec (National Council of Welfare, 2006a). But during this same period, in Alberta and British Columbia, the share

FIGURE 4.7   Child Poverty in Canada Compared with Other Countries, 2007

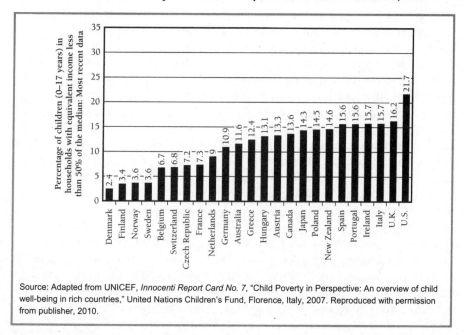

Source: Adapted from UNICEF, *Innocenti Report Card No. 7*, "Child Poverty in Perspective: An overview of child well-being in rich countries," United Nations Children's Fund, Florence, Italy, 2007. Reproduced with permission from publisher, 2010.

of poor families increased from 11.3 percent to 15.7 percent in British Columbia, and from 11.8 percent to 14.6 percent in Alberta. Much of Western Canada's increase in poverty occurred in the 1980s (National Council of Welfare, 2006a). In the 1990s, Ontario's share of poor families rose by more than 7 percent above the late-1980s rates of poverty. But by 2003, it decreased somewhat to 11.3 percent of families, compared to 10.8 percent in 1981. Poverty rates across family and unattached individual categories climbed during the 1990s but lessened during the early years of the twenty-first century. In 2007, 9.2 percent of Canadians living in the 10 provinces were below the after-tax LICO, compared to 10.5 percent in 2006. This poverty rate was the lowest observed in 30 years. For example, in Saskatchewan, the rate decreased to 4.6 percent in 2007 from 7.0 percent in 2006. British Columbia and Ontario experienced a decline of almost two percentage points, to 6.7 percent and 5.9 percent respectively. Among those living alone, only those residing in Alberta experienced a drop in the low-income rate from 23.1 percent to 18.2 percent in 2007 (Statistics Canada, 2007).

Aboriginal peoples, minority peoples, and people with disabilities are particularly vulnerable to poverty, both historically and at present (Ross, Scott, & Smith, 2000; Statistics Canada, 2003). In 2002, based on the LICO measure, 38.0 percent of Aboriginal people and 38.0 percent of visible minorities were poor; and based on the MBM, 35.8 percent of persons with disabilities were poor (Human Resources and Social Development Canada, 2006; Statistics Canada, 2003). These rates are significantly higher than the 2002 national average of 11.6 percent, based on the Statistics Canada after-tax LICO measure (Human Resources and Social Development Canada, 2006); and they are also higher than the 13.7 percent national rate determined by the 2002 MBM (Human Resources and Social Development Canada, 2006).

Durations of poverty differ. For roughly 60 percent of the poor, poverty is a temporary state, unlikely to be repeated within a 10-year period. For 40 percent of the poor, poverty is "a more chronic problem, with longer spells of poverty and a greater likelihood of becoming poor again" (Ross, Scott, & Smith, 2000, 119). According to the National Council of Welfare (2006a), between 1996 and 2001, a total of 7.6 million Canadians experienced poverty for at least one year. There is considerable variability from one person to the next; taking aggregate statistics, the average poor person in Canada spends about five years poor—counting single and multiple experiences of poverty—while 5 percent remain poor for 10 years or more. Between 1996 and 2001, 2 million Canadians lived in poverty for only a single year, while 1.5 million people were in poverty across the entire span of those six years (National Council of Welfare, 2006a).

Using data between 1992 and 2004, Picot, Hou, and Coulombe (2008) showed that recent immigrants to Canada are at risk of experiencing chronic poverty (defined as being in poverty for at least four of their first five years in Canada). After three years, less than one-third of the 1997 cohort was still in the first poverty spell; among the 2001 cohort, this figure rose to 36 percent. About one-quarter of immigrants in poverty remained in the first spell after five years, and after ten years, about 10 percent did so. Thus, chronic poverty appears to be quite persistent, even over a 10-year horizon. Evidently, certain groups of people are more likely to experience longer spells of poverty: lone parents, people with disabilities, members of visible minority communities, recent immigrants, individuals with low levels of education, and single people. The longer that one is poor, the more difficult it is to escape poverty. In examining poverty dynamics (i.e., the poverty flow patterns that underlie the observed poverty rate at a point in time) between the North American countries and their European counterparts, Valletta (2006) found that poverty persistence is high in Canada, where transfer payments lift a smaller share of individuals from working-age families out of poverty than do social transfers in Germany and Great Britain.

Since the economic downturn starting in the fall of 2008, there has been considerably more unemployment, underemployment, and precarious employment (forms of work that involve such things as atypical employment contracts, limited social benefits or statutory entitlements, job insecurity, low job tenure, low wages, or high risks of ill health).

Education remains an important factor in distinguishing the poor from the non-poor, as shown in Figures 4.8 and 4.9. Social policies that encourage people to stay in school and that encourage post-degree continuous learning are potentially useful in reducing lifelong poverty.

FIGURE 4.8   Rates of Unemployment Compared with Highest Education Attained

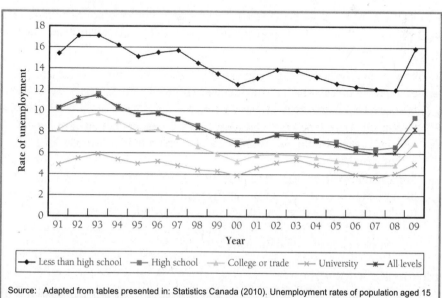

Source: Adapted from tables presented in: Statistics Canada (2010). Unemployment rates of population aged 15 and over, by educational attainment, Canada, 1990 to 2009. Ottawa: Authors. Retrieved from http://www.statcan.gc.ca/pub/81-582-x/2010003/tbl/tble3.1-eng.htm. Reproduced with permission from Statistics Canada, 2010.

FIGURE 4.9   Education Makes a Difference

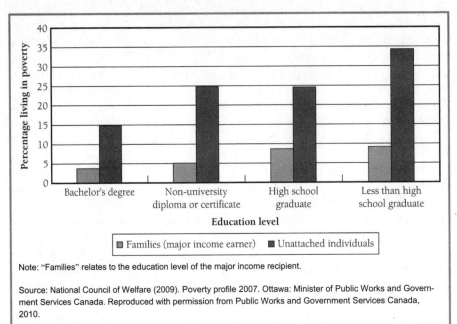

Note: "Families" relates to the education level of the major income recipient.

Source: National Council of Welfare (2009). Poverty profile 2007. Ottawa: Minister of Public Works and Government Services Canada. Reproduced with permission from Public Works and Government Services Canada, 2010.

Social Policy and Economic Policy

Chappell (2006) suggests that Canadian social and economic policies are related in three ways and that these characteristics reflect the Canadian experience of economic insecurity.

1. The state of the economy determines which social programs are needed. For example, in times of high unemployment, the demand for such social services as social assistance, mental and physical health, and child welfare increases.
2. Recent patterns of social spending have been dependent not on need but on the government's economic priority of fiscal restraint in order to reduce deficit spending.
3. Some people believe that social programs discourage economic growth because they decrease the spending power of working individuals and increase the debt/deficit situation. This point, however, is highly debatable. Indeed, several observers argue that social programs promote economic growth by putting more money into more hands (Battle, 1993; Mendelson, 1993).

Income Redistribution

The *Gini coefficient* (see Figure 4.10) is a means of comparing three types of income distribution levels with one another across time. In the Gini coefficient,

FIGURE 4.10   Income Distribution in Canada: The Gini Coefficient

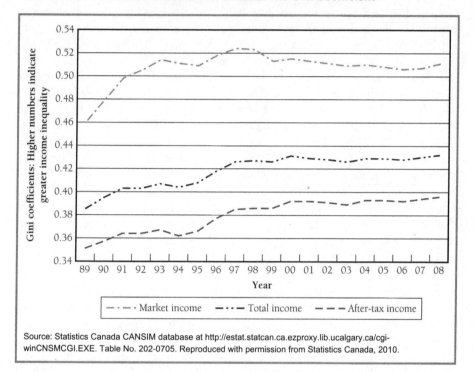

Source: Statistics Canada CANSIM database at http://estat.statcan.ca.ezproxy.lib.ucalgary.ca/cgi-winCNSMCGI.EXE. Table No. 202-0705. Reproduced with permission from Statistics Canada, 2010.

0 indicates perfect equality of income, where every Canadian receives the same amount of money. A score of 1 represents perfect inequality, where one person gets all the income and everyone else receives nothing. Both of these are ideal or theoretical scenarios that would probably never occur. The value of the Gini coefficient is that it provides the extreme parameters (0 and 1) between which we can make comparisons.

Figure 4.10 highlights the influence of income security programs and the tax system as tools of income redistribution. The highest line, which is also the one that shows the least equal income distribution, represents "earned income" prior to taxes. Individuals who do not have income from work are assigned an income of zero. The next highest line shows what happens when "earned income" is combined with income derived from such income security programs as Social Assistance, CPP, and Employment Insurance. This line reveals the equalizing effect of income-security social policies. The third line, which tends to a greater state of income distribution, represents income after taxes, demonstrating the greater equalizing effects of the income tax system.

However, the income tax system does not benefit all Canadians equally. Scholars and policy analysts insist that many tax credits and tax deductions are used by the rich more than the poor, and benefit the rich more than the poor. Two write-offs that favour well-to-do individuals are Registered Retirement Savings Plan (RRSP) contributions and child-care expenses. Far more high-income earners claim RRSP contributions than do low-income earners (Statistics Canada Pensions and Wealth

Surveys Section, 2005). In addition, as one policy document remarks, "High-income Canadians are much more able than low- and middle-income Canadians to put money towards RRSPs, and, because tax assistance is provided in the form of a deduction, RRSP owners in the top bracket enjoy larger tax savings" (Torjman & Battle, 1995a, 5). Moreover and more generally, tax breaks to individuals and corporations drain billions of dollars from government budgets and thereby contribute to the retrenchment of social programs (Torjman & Battle, 1995a, 5; Guest, 1997, 188–189; Muszynski, 1987). For example, tax break measures implemented in the 2007–08 Federal Budget resulted in just over $3 billion of forgone government revenue in that fiscal year alone (Department of Finance Canada, 2007). Overall, the tax break measures taken by the government since 2006, including those in Canada's Economic Action Plan, will reduce taxes on individuals, families, and businesses by an estimated $220 billion over 2008–09 and the following five fiscal years (Department of Finance Canada, 2010). This tax reduction will have serious implications if the government plans to erode funding for social programs, which in turn hurts all Canadians, particularly those who are poorer and hence particularly vulnerable.

Paying Taxes

Death and taxes are claimed to be the two things in life that are unavoidable. Typically, Canadians are most aware of two types of taxes: personal income tax and consumption taxes, especially the goods and services tax (GST) and provincial sales tax (PST). In some provinces, there is a harmonized sales tax (HST), which combines the GST with the PST. Personal income tax is the largest source of government revenue in Canada (Martineau, 2005). In 2009–10, personal income tax revenues stood at 47.6 percent of total revenues collected by the government (Department of Finance Canada, 2010). Although the GST and PST are the most noticeable forms of consumption taxes, "sin taxes" on such consumer items as tobacco and alcohol have received increased public attention. Payroll taxes, business taxes, import taxes, property taxes, and resource taxes are other levies made upon the citizens of Canada. The proportion of Canadian income going toward income taxes has increased over the past several decades, as shown in Figure 4.11. In 2008, the average Canadian family spent 43.9 percent of its income on taxes, a small improvement over 2007 and 2006, when it spent 44.6 percent and 46.1 percent, respectively (Fraser Forum, 2009).

Tax systems generally operate on either regressive or progressive principles (or on a combination of both). *Regressive tax systems* impose the same tax level on all citizens, which, in effect, imposes the greatest burden on those least able to pay (Muszynski, 1987). The PST is a Canadian example of a regressive tax. It is levied on a particular good at the same percentage regardless of a person's income. Because they have less disposable income, persons with low incomes pay a greater portion of their incomes in PST payments than do those in higher income brackets.

A *progressive tax system* bases the level of taxation on a person's ability to pay, such that those with higher incomes pay proportionately higher taxes. Canada's current income tax system contains both progressive and regressive elements. It is progressive insofar as it has multiple tax brackets, with a progressive

FIGURE 4.11   Income Tax Payment in Canada

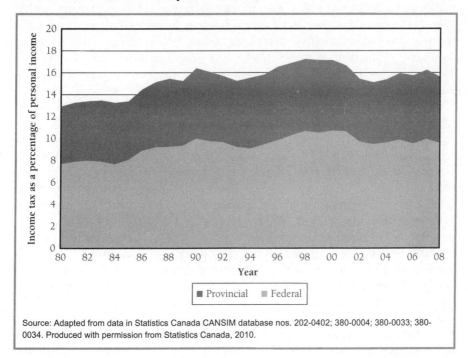

Source: Adapted from data in Statistics Canada CANSIM database nos. 202-0402; 380-0004; 380-0033; 380-0034. Produced with permission from Statistics Canada, 2010.

increase in the percentage of taxable income paid as one's income rises. In this sense, the income tax system differentiates between those with less money (and in lower tax brackets) and those with more (and in higher brackets). But critics point out that it could still be *more* progressive, with richer people and corporations paying more. Because poor people pay a greater proportion of their income to taxes than do rich people, the system has definite regressive elements. If well-to-do individuals and corporations paid more, the system would be more progressive and less regressive.

A recent income tax option that is not based on this progressive principle is the "flat tax." Alberta's provincial income tax is no longer calculated as a percentage of federal tax payable. Rather, as of 2009, it is 10 percent of taxable income (hence a flat tax) above the personal exemption of $16 775 per year; it has a small progressive aspect in that people under the threshold are not responsible for the 10 percent payable (Canada Revenue Agency, 2010). A flat tax brings a simplicity and efficiency to the current complex tax system with less emphasis on tax loopholes than the present system. But it tends to make the income tax system less progressive, and hence a less powerful instrument of income redistribution.

Changing Demographics

An international trend reflects what is described as a "vast gulf in birth and death rates amongst the world's countries" (Kent & Haub, 2005, 5). The wealthier, more urban nations—particularly in Europe—have shrinking and aging populations, while poorer, rural countries—particularly in Asia and Africa—have demographic growth and younger populations (Kent & Haub, 2005). Largely because of Latin immigration, the United States does not face as strong a demographic pressure as Europe. But Canada is close, experiencing the twin themes of birth rate decline and the aging of its population. In partial response to both, immigration has become increasingly important to the growth of the Canadian population over the last 30 years (Figure 4.12). In 2005, immigration accounted for 66 percent of all population growth in Canada (Lapointe, Dunn, Tremblay-Cote, Bergeron, & Ignakzac, 2006). Canada recorded the highest net migration rate (0.61 percent) of all G8 member countries between 1994 and 2004 (Human Resources and Skills Development Canada, 2010a). According to the 2006 Census, the most recent immigrants represented one in five (19.8 percent) of the total population of Canada (Statistics Canada, 2007). As Figure 4.12 illustrates, immigration will become increasingly more important to the sustainability of population growth in Canada in the future. This is not to downplay the problems of population growth, particularly as outlined in the next chapter in its comments about sustainable economic growth.

Age and retirement have become a topic of focus in national and international contexts over the last decade. Some critics describe the situation as a "demographic crisis" in which people throughout the developed world are not bearing enough children to sustain themselves economically (Cohen, 2006). Today, nearly half of the world's population lives in countries with fertility at or below replacement levels. Further, by the mid-twenty-first century, three of four countries now described as *developing* are projected to reach or slip below replacement fertility rates (Morgan & Taylor, 2006).

FIGURE 4.12   Change in Total Population in Canada, 1976 to 2051

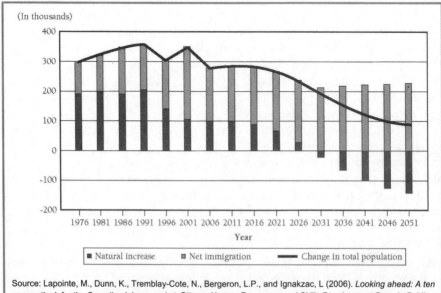

Source: Lapointe, M., Dunn, K., Tremblay-Cote, N., Bergeron, L.P., and Ignakzac, L (2006). *Looking ahead: A ten year outlook for the Canadian labour market.* Ottawa: Human Resources and Skills Development Canada Publications Centre. Reproduced with the permission of Her Majesty the Queen in Right of Canada 2010.

Another major demographic factor is that people in advanced industrialized countries are living longer and retiring earlier (Townson, 2006; United Nations, 2002). During the Paleolithic era, life expectancy at birth was 20 years. Ten thousand years later, for those in the Roman Empire, it had risen to 27 years. People living in fifteenth-century England and Wales had a life expectancy of 33 years; by the mid-nineteenth century, life expectancy had risen to 40 years and, by 1900, to 50 years (Usher, 2003, 5). Major changes in life expectancy occurred during the twentieth century. In 1920, Canada had life expectancies of 59 for men and 61 for women: the average person was not expected to make it to 65, the age of retirement that emerged as an OECD gold standard several decades after Bismarck's Germany introduced an old age social insurance program in 1889 (Germany originally set the age at 70). By 1950, average Canadian life expectancies were 66 for men and 71 for women. In 2004, they were over 82 years for women and 78 for men—and rising yearly (Statistics Canada, Health Statistics Division, 2006). In the early 1970s, working age people (18–64) accounted for 57 percent of the population, climbing to 64 percent in 1995 (Chui, 1996). All growth scenarios considered, and using the population estimates for July 1, 2009, the proportion of the working age population aged 15 to 64 is projected to decline steadily from about 70 percent to about 60 percent in 2036 (Statistics Canada, 2010c). The culmination of these two factors (low fertility and longer life expectancy) has created a situation known as *demographic aging* (Cheal, 2002). In response to this challenge, in 1998, the OECD published a report suggesting that national governments throughout the developed world need to reform legislation to remove incentives for early retirement to reduce the economic implications of an aging population (Townson, 2006). The Canadian government needs to make such adjustments soon to avoid a clash of generations—that is, fewer working age people will have to support the great number of people born between 1945 and the early 1960s, who are sometimes known as the *baby boomers*. The baby boomers have a good portion of society's wealth, but as the baby boomers age, younger workers will have the burden of contributing to their retirement funds, health costs, and other age-related expenditures, which are destined to grow over time (Willetts, 2010).

Many Canadians, particularly when the issue came to the media's attention in the 1990s, wondered how social programs and retirement funds (private and public) could be sustained. Available projections show that people aged 65 and above will account for between 23 percent and 25 percent of the total population by 2036, nearly double the 13.9 percent figure from 2009 (Statistics Canada, 2010c). A similar study, using 2006 as the base year, shows that the ratio of the population aged 65 and over to the population of traditional working age (18–64) will rise from 20 percent to 46 percent in 2050 (Guillemette & Robson, 2006, 1). A further possibility looms on the horizon. Future projections in labour market characteristics suggest that between 2006 and 2015, 70 percent of all newly available jobs will result from people retiring (Lapointe et al., 2006; Human Resources and Skills Development Canada, 2007). A combination of factors—the shrinking proportion of available workers to retired people and the increase in available jobs as a result of retirement—could essentially lead to higher numbers of jobs than there will be available or than there will be qualified workers to fill them (Lapointe et al., 2006). What is the future of the notion of "unemployment," as well as such social programs as health care and retirement, both of which are heavily used by retired people but are funded particularly by those who work (through the income tax system and payroll deductions)?

Some Consequences of Social Policy

Paradoxes of intervening in the economic life of some Canadians have long been recognized. For example, financial assistance programs may sometimes decrease the incentive to paid work for some recipients; that is, some programs contain inherent labour force participation disincentives. The authors of this textbook, like other progressive observers, insist on the need for plentiful jobs offering meaningful employment and decent wages. More than any other factor, decent jobs would alleviate much of the problem of such labour force participation disincentives (Clarke, 1997). In addition, some observers blame social policies themselves for the absence of a full-employment economy. The following components of social welfare programs tend to act as disincentives to paid work:

> the decreased purchasing power of current "minimum wages";

> health-care benefits that exceed those of many jobs;

> insufficient coverage for back-to-work expenses;

> high tax-back rates for earning exemptions; and

> lack of affordable, accessible childcare (National Council of Welfare, 1993).

Canada's transition from an institutional approach to a market-state approach has reduced the scope and impact of such programs as Employment Insurance. As a result, "social assistance has moved from its original intent. It has grown into a major front-line program—larger than Employment Insurance in some provinces. An unpopular and stigmatizing program, it nonetheless has proved stubbornly resistant to reform" (Torjman, 2007, 1). Some proposed changes would particularly assist the unemployed who can seek work, as well as the precariously employed. These changes include making social assistance a genuine program of last resort; providing earnings supplementation measurements separate from social assistance; making work more remunerative than welfare; improving minimum wage levels; introducing working income tax benefits for the working poor; and improving childcare benefits for the working poor (National Council of Welfare, 2007; Torjman, 2007).

Other critics stress that the demoralization of Canadians receiving welfare should be addressed by mandatory workfare programs as a condition for receiving social assistance and EI services (Handler & Hasenfeld, 1991). Proponents of workfare suggest that it promotes the "moral merit of work" in a "failed system of subsidized poverty" (Sirico, 1997). Self-respect, taking responsibility, the development of a "worker" identity, and the acquisition of work skills and work experience are among the moral benefits suggested by advocates of workfare programs. Such programs are based on separating out the able-bodied recipients from those who are unable to work. To some, this division seems a throwback to the nineteenth-century Poor Laws and their delineation of the deserving and undeserving poor. These laws were heavily influenced by the moral overtones of the view that poverty was a state resulting from idleness and immoral behaviour.

One of the key points to analyzing social policy is determining the extent to which individual versus societal factors can be conceived as a source and solution to social problems. Sociologist C. Wright Mills (1959) frames it well, suggesting an inextricable link between the private troubles of an individual and the public issues of which they form a part. He believed that private troubles "have to do with an individual's character and with those limited areas of social life of which s/he is directly and personally aware." Public issues "have to do with matters that transcend these local environments of the individual and the limited range of his/her life. They have to do with the organization of institutions of society" (Mills, 1959, 395–396). One can infer from Mills and like-minded thinkers that both society and the individual are implicated in the construction, definition, and solution of social problems. Thus, difficulties that some social work clients experience getting off income security programs represent both individual trouble *and* a public issue. Some authors—particularly those from the political right—emphasize the individual component. Political scientist Tom Flanagan, as an example, was campaign manager and has been mentor to University of Calgary alumnus Prime Minister Stephen Harper. To Flanagan, the locus is the individual and family:

There is no mystery about the road to success; it can be summarised in six rules: Go to school and graduate. Get a job and stick with it till you find a better one. Get married and stay married. Have children and invest in their future. Don't acquire a criminal record. Don't drink too much, use illegal drugs, or gamble excessively. Anyone who follows these Six Rules of Success cannot help but thrive in Canada. The rules are not absolutely inflexible. Some successful people are divorced, or never married, or childless, or alcoholics, or high-school dropouts. But all of the Six Rules are correlated with success, and anyone who violates several of them is headed for trouble. (Flanagan, 2007, 177)

Similar discourse is common in published reports commissioned by such organizations as the Atlantic Institute for Market Studies, the Canadian Council of Chief Executives, the Fraser Institute, or various banks. Other institutes to the left, such as the Caledon Institute for Social Policy, the Canadian Centre for Policy Alternatives, and the Canadian Council on Social Development, tend to emphasize societal issues as more prevalent causes of social problems.

Conclusion

As this chapter has discussed, a variety of ideological, economic, and social factors influence the nature of social policies, the contexts in which they were conceived and carried out, and the reasons why they change over time. The next chapter sheds light on important additional phenomena—globalization, the environmental movement, and social inclusion—which are now rightly seen as crucial considerations for social policies.

Chapter (5)

Social Policy and Emerging Realities

The issues discussed in this book affect everyone: What level of entitlement is considered fair when determining benefit rates for income security programs such as social assistance? What should be the minimum number of weeks of paid employment to enable a claimant to obtain Employment Insurance benefits? How much money per capita should the state allocate to daycare programs? Should health insurance programs be universal, selective, or a combination of both? These questions and others like them reflect societal values and determine the basic structures of social policies.

The answers vary from place to place and over time. The welfare state of early twenty-first-century Canada is manifestly different from that of the early twentieth century.

As difficult as predictions into the future are to make, this chapter considers the following five essential issues that we expect to shape Canadian social policies in the new millennium:

1. the environmental imperative;
2. globalization;
3. social welfare retrenchment;
4. changing conceptions of social welfare in relation to citizenship and social inclusion; and
5. the growing impact of social movements.

The Environmental Imperative

Rachel Carson's *The Silent Spring*, first published in 1962, was one of the earliest modern-day environmental treatises. Since then, an emergent environmental movement has sought to change social consciousness and legislation in developed countries, such as Canada, and in the developing nations of Asia, Central and South America, and elsewhere. Critical evidence of the ecological crisis throughout the globe is found in the staggering yearly figures of species extinctions (both animal and plant). A recent publication reports that the rate of species extinction is approximately 3000 per annum, a figure that is continually increasing (Meyer, 2006). Oceans cover almost three-quarters of Earth's surface and contain 97 percent of the world's water. Sediments, oils, wastes, and a damaged ozone layer, among other phenomena, increasingly assault them. The annual tonnage of fish caught in the world's oceans increased 1600 percent over the twentieth century (Sachs, Loske, & Linz, 1998, 74). This increase reflects the advent of industrial fishing in the 1950s; as a result of which, by 2003, big-fish stocks had been reduced globally by 90 percent over those five decades (Myers & Worm, 2003). Evidence from global bird and mammal species supports the hypothesis that large-bodied species are indeed more susceptible to extinction (Olden, Hogan, & Zen, 2007). The tragic decline and fall of a once-prolific cod fishery is well-known to the Atlantic provinces in Canada.

In more global terms, at the end of the twentieth century, one-third of the world's tropical forests, one-quarter of its available fresh water, and one-quarter of its fish resources were gone (World Wildlife Fund, 2006). To some extent, as Meyer (2006), Lovelock (2006), Sale (2006), and others argue, overpopulation is the problem. The current global population is more than 6 billion people, compared to 1 billion in 1850 and 2 billion in 1930. The United Nations, through its World Population Plan policy response, has initiated intensive family-planning programs to prevent unwanted pregnancy, coinciding with and bolstering similar programs in some developing countries (Van Wormer, 1997, 652).

But, as relevant as overpopulation, and of particular significance to this textbook, is the fact that the current ecological crisis is a problem largely caused by the developed world. The *ecological footprint* represents the impact of each person on the environment, through consumption of fossil fuels, agricultural production of food and other products, misuses of forests and water, human settlement, and so on. Canadians have an average ecological footprint of 7.01 global hectares per person, and Americans have an ecological footprint of 8.00 global hectares per person (Global Footprint Network, 2010). Likewise, throughout Europe, ecological footprints range from approximately 1.4 to 8.4 global hectares per person; while for Asian countries, they range from 0.6 to 10.7 global hectares per person and African countries have ecological footprints of between 0.7 and 4.3 global hectares per person (Global Footprint Network, 2010). For example, the consumption of fossil fuels alone illustrates the severity of the crisis. Carbon dioxide (CO_2) is released into the atmosphere through the burning of fossil fuels in cars and industries, by forest fires, and through other natural and human sources, causing a greenhouse effect in the atmosphere that steadily increases the world's temperature. The results are potentially calamitous: the possibility of the polar ice caps melting, resulting in the massive flooding of a considerable portion of Earth's land mass, not to mention the drought conditions created in many regions throughout the Global South, which result in the loss of economic and social sustainability for some of the world's poorest people (United Nations Development Programme, 2006). Today, 3 billion people live on less than US$2/day, and of these, over 1 billion live on less than $1/day.

How can Canada respond? With today's world population of more than 6 billion and levels of annual emission of CO_2 close to 29 billion tonnes (in 2007) (United Nations Statistics Division, 2010), an "equal rights of emission" world-wide would assume 5 tonnes per person annually. But in Canada, current annual domestic production of CO_2 (557 million tonnes in 2007) is equivalent to between 15 and 20 tonnes per person. Assume, as is the consensus among many demographers, current projections of a world population of 10 billion by 2050. In this scenario, Canada would need to diminish CO_2 emissions by 80 percent over the next 50 years to achieve even the objective of equal utilization rights with other countries (Flannery, 2006; Sachs, Loske, & Linz, 1998, 30).

Such a reduction would require a profoundly different approach to economic arrangements. *Sustainability* is an economic, political, and environmental world view that promotes present and future generations of stewardship of the physical world. Sustainable development, a resulting concept, "creates a process that ensures that natural resources are replenished, and that future generations continue to have the resources they need to meet their own needs" (Van Wormer, 1997, 650). Myriad non-governmental organizations (NGOs)—such as Greenpeace, Friends of the Earth, and the world scientific community—continue to influence public debate. The 1987 Brundtland Report, commissioned by the United Nations (UN), was an important document in the evolution of this latter concept. The Brundtland Report clearly links economic and environmental development issues. Also significant was the 1992 Rio de Janeiro Earth Summit, a UN conference that produced a 500-page document elaborating global partnerships that could achieve sustainability. This summit led to the 1997 Kyoto Protocol on Climate Change, which now has more than 160 signatories, Canada included. Canada's inability to honour its Kyoto commitments has garnered international media attention.

But the temptations to continue apace are strong. Consider that one barrel of oil is the equivalent in kilojoules of energy to 12 people working for you year-round, or 25 000 hours of human labour. Readily available energy has become intrinsic to all aspects of our lives, from travel to home heating, to consumer good transportation and personal transit. If the world were to immediately stop using hydrocarbons and convert, say, to nuclear energy, it would require 10 000 nuclear plants to meet the demand that oil is supplying now; and were this to happen, some predict that within 10 years the world's uranium reserves would be depleted. Other alternatives—biomass, ethanol, biodiesel, wind, solar, and tidal power—are small players in the world's energy markets (Tertzakian, 2006). Current research suggests massive changes in lifestyle and reductions in consumption will be required; yet the political will to realize these changes seems elusive, as does the public opinion required to make the changes happen.

Oil resources are finite. Yet the world uses approximately 1000 barrels of oil per second, or 87 million barrels of oil per day (Tertzakian, 2006). Canadian consumption is approximately 2.3 million barrels per day (Central Intelligence Agency, 2010; U.S. Energy Information Administration, 2010) or 24.86 barrels per capita per annum. In the 1950s, geophysicist M.K. Hubbert predicted that the world's discovery of finite oil resources would peak in the form of a bell curve, after which point oil and gas would become more expensive in direct proportion to their diminishing abundance. Some scholars think we have already hit "Hubbert's Peak" and are going to experience a difficult, impoverishing transition to a post-oil economy (Deffeyes, 2006). Geographer Jared Diamond (2005) argues convincingly that ecological factors have led to the collapse of many human societies in the past. Meanwhile, Wright (2004) worries that our species may be prone to ecologically induced self-destruction. In either case, the significance of physical ecology to social policy development will be significant. The institutional period of social welfare went hand in glove with the coal- and oil-based economies of massive industrial capitalism. The Canadian market state is liberal in ideology, capitalist in economy, and continues to be powered by hydrocarbons. Will the stage of social welfare that proceeds from the market state be both post-oil in energy and sustainable in philosophy? Will there be a choice?

To the extent that sustainability challenges previous notions of economic growth, the attending basis upon which social policies are conceived may also need rethinking. Moreover, the crisis of worsening public and environmental health concerns is, to stress an important point, an international phenomenon, not just a Canadian one (Garret, 2000). This crisis influences international political and economic relationships too. Perhaps a necessary condition of sustainability is a new world view that equates spiritual growth and self-realization with stewardship of Earth (Lonergan & Richards, 1988; Schumacher, 1973, 54–57).

The 1974 "Group of 77" developing countries (now numbering more than 100) proposed to the UN General Assembly a new international economic order (NIEO) that would address North–South inequalities (the developed world and the developing world, respectively). Thinking about sustainability in that context, Sachs and other environmentalists propose significant changes to the way in which ordinary Canadians think about and act on their patterns of consumption:

> ➤ sharing such goods as skis, cars, and other commodities that are not required on a daily basis;
>
> ➤ using and further developing public transportation infrastructures, rather than roads, highways, and other car-oriented patterns of movement;
>
> ➤ planning cities in ways that revive notions of greater densities of population and greater built-in proximity among homes, schools, places of work, entertainment, and leisure (Sachs, Loske, & Linz, 1998, 123, 133); and
>
> ➤ reducing, reusing, and recycling consumer products.

Several other low-cost strategies that could reduce Canadian greenhouse gas emissions by 50 percent over 30 years include use of increased insulation in houses, increased efficiency in the engineering of heating and cars, and increased use of more efficient, smaller power plants in place of larger-scale plants (Torrie, 2000).

Beyond these immediate courses of action, social policies have scarcely begun to integrate issues of social justice for people with the imperative of physical ecology. Indeed, many social welfare organizations have had only very loose connections with environmental NGOs. Greater collaboration might be useful. According to one Canadian research report, Canada ranks among the worst five OECD nations on 25 environmental indicators (with a ranking among OECD nations of twenty-eighth out of twenty-ninth), including greenhouse gas emissions, air pollution, water consumption, energy consumption, energy efficiency, fertilizer consumption, and generation of hazardous and nuclear waste (Boyd, 2001). A 2006 report by Canada's environment and sustainable development commissioner (Commissioner of the Environment and Sustainable Development, 2006) is likewise critical of the federal government's lack of resolve in implementing larger programs to reduce the amount of greenhouse gases emitted by individuals and industry. Among other concerns, the country's environment commissioner points out, are problems of unregulated livestock sewage and nitrogen in farm fertilizers contaminating water tables (Mittlestaedt, 2001) and pharmaceutical and cosmetic residue traces in water sources (Mittlestaedt, 2006). A recent study released by Simon Fraser University and the David Suzuki Foundation shows that if Canada's environmental policies were strengthened so they reflected the guidelines used in such developed countries as Sweden and Norway, Canada's environmental ranking would move from almost dead last to first place (Gunton & Calbick, 2010). Many observers are worried about government cutbacks to departments that monitor and ensure safe drinking water; such cutbacks, it is argued, are part of the wider phenomenon of government retreat from the social milieu.

Globalization

Globalization refers to the current, pervasive trend of internationalized finance, communication, ideology, and political arrangements. As a result of globalization, money is invested quickly and easily across national borders. Corporations follow principles of transnational competition for lucrative markets and actively pursue inexpensive labour. What is more, in the absence of powerfully constraining national legislation or intra-national structures, multinational corporations achieve growing sovereignty to pursue these objectives. Globalization has contributed to the rise of the market-state era of social welfare, as discussed in Chapter 2.

The Economic Context of Globalization

Two aspects of globalization need to be examined: economics and politics. Global economics is vastly different from any of the economic systems that preceded it. In the sixteenth, seventeenth, and eighteenth centuries, the European economic system was a system of mercantilism: colonial powers created foreign empires to cultivate worldwide systems of primary extraction abroad and production at home. Late-eighteenth-century England—and nineteenth-century France, Canada, the United States, and other countries—underwent an industrial revolution, featuring increased urbanization, steam manufacturing, coal extraction, and railway and other industrial infrastructures. As shown in Chapter 2, capitalism was further transformed in the 1930s, with the advent of an interventionist state and the post–World War II comprehensive welfare state of the institutional era. These structures started to unravel in the 1970s. In the 1990s, a very different basis for economic arrangements emerged: the market state. The market state, in turn, has experienced a profound transition after the severe stock market crash and credit crunch beginning in the fall of 2008.

Like all things, political and economic power are capable of change. In 1000, Chinese per capita incomes were slightly higher than Europe's. In the succeeding period, China lost growth, and Europe surged, so that by 1820, Chinese per capita income levels were half of Europe's (King, 2010, 30). Our economy is in perpetual pursuit of novelty and renewal; the basic roots of capitalism are a type of "creative destruction": as some things (e.g., the horse and buggy) become obsolete, new things (e.g., the automobile) rise in their stead.

One school of thought argues that the basic workings of capitalism started to change in the 1970s. At this time, as we shall elaborate in the next several pages, with the encouragement of government, capital started to flow more freely across national boundaries. As a result, production moved to less-expensive labour markets, depressing workers' incomes in the West. Money loans—credit—became progressively easier to obtain, which in part helped workers and the middle class in the West to reduce the impact on a diminishing standard of living (as discussed in Chapter 4). Beginning in the 1990s, the finance sector proliferated worldwide and a variety of increasingly complicated, and unregulated, trading instruments were developed, among them derivatives, futures, hedge funds, options, and swaps (Harvey, 2010). A real estate boom flowered in growing economies, fuelled by greed, low interest rates, and abundant credit. In some countries, such as the United States, income tax policies encouraged the purchase of mortgages, allowing filers to reduce taxes on the basis of their mortgages. Mortgage brokers, operating without sufficient regulation, and solely on the number of mortgages sold, encouraged people to buy housing they could not afford, passing on the bad debt to others in a dizzyingly complex finance sector. In many instances, these same bad loans in the United States and elsewhere were carved up into collateralized debt obligations (CDOs) and sold on international markets under the false impression that they were secure investments. When the credit crunch set in, in 2008, these CDOs became more difficult to sell and lost trading value.

Quite a few governments (Canada is a notable exception) failed to regulate their financial sectors properly; some financial institutions, particularly in the United States and the United Kingdom, were impervious to self-regulation. Greed overtook large portions of the financial sector and many ordinary investors, particularly those who sought mortgages they could not realistically afford. When the financial bubble burst in the fall of 2008, as it was destined to do at some point, many U.S. and U.K. banks discovered they had insufficient reserves to cover costs. Panic swelled quickly across markets, and historic government bailouts of major companies, which were previously deemed too big to fail, became prevalent. A widespread economic depression was avoided.

Another school of thought sees this several-decade change in economic relations as part of a shift of power from the West to other parts of the world (King, 2010). In the 1960s, the Japanese economy grew stronger, followed by the economies of South Korea, Taiwan, Singapore, and Hong Kong in the 1970s, and then by China in the

1980s. The Organization for Petroleum Exporting Countries (OPEC) was established in 1960. In the 1970s, its member states—including Algeria, the Arab states of the Persian Gulf, Nigeria, and Venezuela—expanded their wealth and influence in the wake of the growing scarcity and costs of oil and gas. Between 1990 and 2008, the middle class in some parts of the developing world increased markedly; by one estimate, their numbers grew from one-third to more than one-half of the world's population ("Burgeoning Bourgeoisie," 2009). (Ways of calculating the middle class in the Global South are different from the methods we would deploy in Canada. One estimate, for instance, claims anyone earning more than US$10/day in some Global South contexts may be considered middle class.) Considerable economic growth occurred in Brazil, China, India, and Indonesia and, to a lesser extent, in Bangladesh, Russia, and elsewhere. This increase may be seen as the third most significant surge of the middle class in modern history; the first surge was the rise of the middle class in nineteenth-century Europe, and the second, the baby boom in the West from 1945 to the early 1960s. When the poor start to enter the middle class in the millions, social and economic changes occur; as Marx and Engels (1848, trans. 1998) put it more than 160 years ago, the bourgeoisie "cannot exist without constantly revolutionizing the instruments of production, and thereby the relations of production, and with them the whole relations of society" (3). The middle class is able to allocate some of its discretionary income and to cease living hand-to-mouth, day-to-day, and season-to-season. They develop expectations for the present and the future. Between 1981 and 2007, the World Values Survey and the European Values Study carried out five waves of representative national surveys in many countries, covering almost 90 percent of the world's population (www.worldvaluessurvey.org). These studies show that when the poorest in a society become middle class, their beliefs and motivations change. They are more likely to seek education for their children, to desire prosperity, to insist on greater accountability from those who govern, and to be less deferential to prevailing structures of authority (Inglehart & Welzel, 2009).

The results of a growing middle class are therefore not universally undesirable. Indeed, many contemporary political scientists see economic modernization as the gateway to improvements in social and political arrangements:

Modernization is a syndrome of social changes linked to industrialization. Once set in motion, it tends to penetrate all aspects of life, bringing occupational specialization, urbanization, rising educational levels, rising life expectancy, and rapid economic growth. These create a self-reinforcing process that transforms social life and political institutions, bringing rising mass participation in politics and—in the long run—making the establishment of democratic political institutions increasingly likely. (Inglehart & Welzel, 2009, 33)

But as several scholars emphasize, modernization and its positive consequences are not automatic; they need to be nurtured continuously (Hufbauer & Suominen, 2010; Rodrik, 2011). Volatile world economies make peoples' lives unpredictable, particularly the lives of the people who are most economically and socially vulnerable. Regimes in Bangladesh, Nigeria, the Philippines, Russia, and

Thailand may stall democratic reform; but, in the long run, modernization tends to promote change, making democratization increasingly possible. Change does not occur linearly; it is rooted to a country's history. Nor is *change* synonymous with *Westernization*. Finally, as part of globalization, the experiences of one country influence another's. Worldwide inflationary food prices, to cite one example, are in part a product of a growing international middle class that possesses greater resources to purchase food.

The 1980s and 1990s saw the ushering in of trade blocs, or free-trade agreements. The most comprehensive example of this was the emergence of the European Union (EU), which included a common Parliament, an extensive legal system that often overrides domestic legislation, a court of justice, a common currency, and a central bank. In addition, people within the EU have the right to invest, live, travel, and work in other member states. On this continent, the United States and Canada struck the Free Trade Agreement (FTA) in 1989, after four years of intense negotiations involving the governments of Brian Mulroney in Canada and Ronald Reagan in the United States. As the economy continues to falter after the fall of 2008, and our ties to the U.S. economy are so profound, some wonder whether we might seek greater trade alliances with China, India, Brazil, and Indonesia: those countries that are seen as emerging economies. In any case, it is important to remember that countries have political choices. Indeed, some political leaders, such as Hugo Chávez in Venezuela, assert active resistance to American hegemony and the myriad global social movements that challenge globalization.

The Political Context of Globalization

Politically, globalization has profoundly transformed international relations during the past decade. The Cold War, which began with the cessation of World War II, came to an abrupt end with the series of collapsed Communist governments in the former Soviet Bloc during the late 1980s and early 1990s. In the aftermath, the old antagonism between the United States and its allies (sometimes referred to as *the West*), and the Soviet Union and its allies (sometimes referred to as *the Eastern or Soviet Bloc*), ceased to be *the* defining facet of global affairs. Commentators such as Fukuyama (1992) declared that liberal democracy had triumphed over communism; many others agreed, implying that the West had "won" the Cold War.

Immediately following World War II, there was a relatively widespread consensus in favour of a universal welfare state and an interventionist government. But by the 1990s, social democratic governments in France, Canada, and other countries appeared to have lost touch with their ideological roots, and globalization proponents eagerly sought opportunities to transform Eastern European societies into capitalist enclaves. (So, too, have other marketplaces—in Asia and in Central and South America—become heightened targets for international capitalism.)

After the fall of 2008, however, it became increasingly apparent that the West's victory in the Cold War—if that is what it was—was brief. We are entering a new era of global political arrangements in which China, in particular, but also other emerging powers such as Brazil, India, and Indonesia, are exerting greater prominence economically and politically.

FIGURE 5.1   Canada in the Global Economy

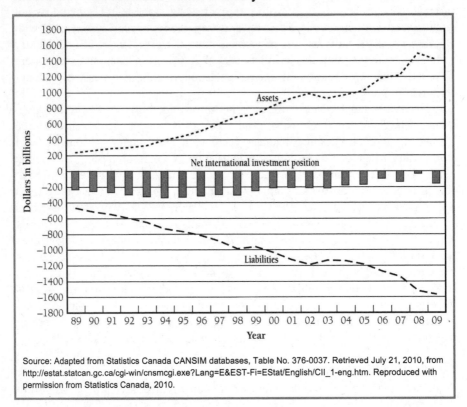

Source: Adapted from Statistics Canada CANSIM databases, Table No. 376-0037. Retrieved July 21, 2010, from http://estat.statcan.gc.ca/cgi-win/cnsmcgi.exe?Lang=E&EST-Fi=EStat/English/CII_1-eng.htm. Reproduced with permission from Statistics Canada, 2010.

One of the main problems with the U.S. economy is consumer debt, the balance of trade deficit and indebtedness through government bonds to other countries, such as China. This deficit is particularly important, given the growing importance of international finance structures on the global economy. The sheer volume of money crossing borders daily has increased exponentially since the 1960s. Figure 5.1 identifies trends for the past two decades, but some of these patterns began as early as the 1970s. It shows the increase in Canadian assets abroad, particularly since the late 1980s, despite evidence indicating that the volume of trading of international currencies increased during that period. Meanwhile, as Figure 5.2 demonstrates, the proportion of households using the Internet for a multitude of tasks—unheard of in mass consumption prior to the 1990s—is now very significant, as is the considerable reduction in costs of long-distance phone calls and the increased use of faxes and other media to reduce global distances. Finally, foreign direct investment—the amount of money invested outside of an individual country—increased fivefold worldwide over the course of the 1980s. By the early 1990s, the world's 300 largest multinational corporations—the major players in foreign direct investment—had gained control of one-quarter of the world's total capital (Marfleet, 1998, 15). More recently, "a third of wealth is now in the hands

FIGURE 5.2   How Canadians Are Wired

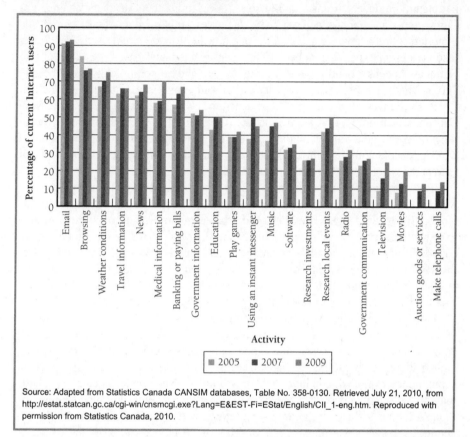

Source: Adapted from Statistics Canada CANSIM databases, Table No. 358-0130. Retrieved July 21, 2010, from http://estat.statcan.gc.ca/cgi-win/cnsmcgi.exe?Lang=E&EST-Fi=EStat/English/CII_1-eng.htm. Reproduced with permission from Statistics Canada, 2010.

of some 200 corporations" (Mackey, 2003, 72). As a result of these trends, the world has entered an era of "turbo-capitalism," in which efficiency, insecurity, and uniformity prevail. Also prevalent—in a temporary way at least—is the generation of new wealth as older forms of practices, companies, and entire industries give way to the new (Luttwak, 1999). These forces create profound workplace changes, as discussed above.

As for the assumptions underpinning this global financial network, the changes in ideology are nothing short of revolutionary. As one scholar points out, globalization "redefine[s] all the fundamental reference points of human society. . . . and requires a modification of all existing paradigms" (Robinson, 1996, as cited in Marfleet, 1998, 2). Gone are the previous principles of a mixed economy during the institutional era of social welfare, where governments of nation-states extensively regulated capitalism. Indeed, in the market-state era, capital often tries to elude any countervailing forces, such as governments, unions, public interest groups, and populations. In Canada, several neo-liberal institutions that actively advocate for corporate interests are entirely aligned with the market-state approach to social welfare described in Chapter 2 and are increasingly influential in policy development.

These institutions consist of business associations (e.g., Canadian Association of Petroleum Producers, Canadian Bankers Association, the Canadian Chamber of Commerce, Canadian Council of Chief Executives, and Canadian Manufacturers and Exporters), think tanks (e.g., Atlantic Institute for Market Studies and the Fraser Institute), groups speaking on behalf of citizens (Canadian Taxpayers Federation and National Citizens Coalition), and various private and corporate lobbyists (Abelson, 2009). These groups have enormous power and scope; the Canadian Council of Chief Executives, for example, represents the top 150 leading corporations in Canada, which hold $4.5 trillion in assets (CCCE, 2010). Some of these organizations object to government funding for civil society groups speaking on behalf of women, people with disabilities, or other communities, calling them *interest groups* (and perhaps not seeing themselves under the same moniker).

Between the 1980s and the fall of 2008, corporations' major remaining check was the marketplace itself. After the autumn of 2008, it became apparent in the United States, the United Kingdom, and other economies that government needed to regulate the private sector, particularly the financial sector, to ensure that major banks did not crash. Canada's situation, thanks largely to Liberal governments of the 1990s and the early part of the 2000s, was far more favourable. In any case, public–private sector relations have most certainly evolved over time. Prior to the first labour legislation, described in Chapter 2, nineteenth-century capitalism during the Industrial Revolution was similarly unhindered by safety and health regulations, urban zoning codes, environmental regulations, and a strong trade union tradition, "and so could send ten-year-olds into coal mines" (Gwyn, 1995, 98). Today, "transnational corporations . . . can make their products in a 'hands-off' plant in some underdeveloped country," where workplace and environmental standards may be profoundly lax (Gwyn, 1995, 98). Moreover, as Gwyn and others argue, the threat of transnational corporations moving production to plants in developing countries "tames governments, and workers of developed nation-states," such as Canada, into reducing environmental, workplace, and social policy standards to compete for jobs (Gwyn, 1995, 98). The very powers of the nation-state—and the extent to which governments can exercise choices—have become highly contested.

Associated with these factors is the growing fetishism about and fascination with the rich. Corporate evidence that Canada long ago left the institutional stage of social welfare for the market state can be found in Peter C. Newman's *The Canadian Establishment* (1975), a biography of major business leaders in Canada at that time. Corporate leaders of the country's institutional welfare-state period frequently complained that politicians were hostile to business and that the public did not understand the needs of business (Newman, 1975). Not so today. Take Alberta, where—as former premier Ralph Klein discovered as he took employment in the oil sector within months of resigning as premier—the transition from government to business is seamless: Alberta's elected governments take many of their marching orders from the oil sector, which is responsible for 40 percent of provincial revenues, as well as for provisioning healthy campaign coffers for the political parties on the right (Nikiforuk, 2007).

Throughout and beyond the OECD, corporate graft (the high salaries of corporate leaders) has been increasing at appalling rates. A recent study of 292 companies in the S&P 500 Index shows that the average annual compensation of CEOs in 2009 stood at $9.25 million (American Federation of Labor—Congress of Industrial Organizations, 2010). Meanwhile, in 2010, there were 24 billionaires in Canada, with David Thomson controlling US$19 billion, thus leading the pack in Canada and taking the title of the twentieth richest person in the world ("The World's Billionaire," 2010). But the question remains: Where precisely does power reside? Political scientist Donald Savoie (2010) argues that because organizations and institutions have become so complicated and because the extent of the problems they deal with are so complex, we seek individuals to create solutions to major social problems, be they "rock star" development economists who hang out with Bono, or CEOs of major companies. The hyper-rich and hyperconnected of today's world—such as Bill Gates and David Thomson—have more power than the capitalists of the Gilded Age (1860s to 1900), during which time industrialization took root and a small cabal controlled critical economic sectors (Cannadine, 2006). Most concerning of all, the new corporate elite has the power to transform and control consciousness. The popular media, which are owned either by corporations or by governments supporting corporations, rarely question the values of the corporate world; governments and civil society increasingly imbibe the corporate world's values, methods, and terminologies (Amernic & Craig, 2006). With the seamless transition of people between corporate and political sectors, boundaries and norms become blurred, and government power is diminished. Moreover, as anarchist scholar Noam Chomsky puts it, "With services privatized, democratic institutions may exist, but they will be mostly formalities because the most important decisions . . . will have been removed from the public arena" (2010, as cited in Pearson, 2010, 25).

Chomsky has long criticized democracy in advanced industrial nations, including the ability of corporate, political, and other leaders to divert attention away from true power within societal structures. As he wrote, "One fundamental goal of any well-crafted indoctrination program is to direct attention elsewhere, away from effective power, its roots, and the disguises it assumes" (1991, 303). On strictly ideological grounds, many advocates of globalization extol its virtues: the promotion of new wealth and competition, and competition equated with human freedom. And yet all of these assumed virtues can be challenged. With the forces of global capitalism weakening governments, trade unions, and social policy legislation, "corporations, above all transnational ones, [remain] free to reshape the world to suit their convenience" (Gwyn, 1995, 262). Unlike governments, corporations are not democratically answerable to a mass electorate; they are accountable only to their shareholders, boards of directors, and to some extent the consumers who buy their products, as well as whatever forms of legislation remain to constrain them. The single operating principle of a corporation is accumulation (Bakan, 2004). Stock market guru and multimillionaire George Soros sounded an important alarm in his 1997 article in *Atlantic Monthly* and his 1998 follow-up book. "Market fundamentalism," he argues, "is a greater threat to an open society than any totalitarian ideology" (3). Like the communism of closed societies, Soros contends, the ardent belief that markets can solve all social, economic, and political questions has become hegemonic—all-powerful. The free flow of ideas, the bedrock of an open society, falls by the wayside.

Social Welfare Retrenchment

Since the advent of the market state, a clear trend across Canada over the past 30 years has been the withdrawal of both federal and provincial governments from commitments to social welfare programs. This withdrawal has not appreciably changed since the fall of 2008 and the resulting credit and economic crisis. Common themes in the past 30 years have included political platforms based on program cuts and public pronouncements that the welfare state has proven too expensive and is a cause of "dependency." Programs affecting even the most vulnerable populations are being cut, privatized, or redesigned to reduce usage and eligibility. Some familiar programs have been renamed to signify this shift. Unemployment Insurance, previously a hallmark of the social safety net, is now known as Employment Insurance. This new name, and indeed the entire program, is intended to emphasize the enhancement of employment opportunities, rather than the subsidization of unemployment. Social assistance programs have been renamed and restructured to focus on paid employment (such as Ontario Works, the new name for what was previously known as General Welfare Assistance) and to "target" those most in need (such as the Assured Income for the Severely Handicapped program in Alberta). Health-care programs and services have suffered harsh cuts, and hospitals are being closed across the country. Although homelessness has become an increasingly visible problem in Canadian cities, until 2009, the federal government had largely withdrawn from social housing commitments; however, the January 2009 Federal Budget has provided more funding in support of social housing than we have seen in a generation. At the same time, homelessness represents a case example of the multiple sectors that are involved in social policy: local, provincial, and federal governments, as well as a battery of NGOs, including locally based initiatives to end homelessness, which are sometimes the genesis of NGOs and sometimes collaborations with government and NGO sectors.

Governments are using several strategies to justify this reduction in public resources for social welfare. One is the device of targeting resources only to those presumed to be most in need, a strategy illustrated by the Canada Child Tax Benefit (CCTB). Through this policy, federal and provincial income security programs are integrated, creating a single benefit paid to all low-income families with dependent children. This program was the latest effort to replace universal family allowances with resources targeted to low-income families.

Another justification of reduced public spending is an increased focus on job training and "social preparation" for employment, expressed in the idea of workfare. Workfare programs take a variety of forms but are generally characterized by requirements that employable recipients of social assistance either provide "approved" labour or participate in activities designed to increase their employment possibilities in return for benefits. Examples of participation requirements are job searches and active preparation for work, such as training and "upgrading" programs (Evans, Jacobs, Noel, & Reynolds, 1995). Penalties for failure to comply can include being cut off from assistance or having benefits reduced. This scheme, which is being operated in some form in virtually all Canadian provinces (Evans, 1995), has deep roots in the tradition of the worthy and unworthy poor, and in the concept of less eligibility (Schragge, 1997). Researchers are critical of workfare programs in relation to their stated objectives. So far, workfare does not appear to improve employment prospects for most participants, to reduce their poverty, or to remove the stigma of being on welfare.

Changing Conceptions of Social Welfare in Relation to Citizenship and Social Inclusion

How are notions of social welfare changing in the face of the realities of globalizing economies and retrenching welfare states? Examination of this question involves exploration of the changing nature of citizenship.

Social Citizenship

Current trends in economic and social welfare policy constitute an important change in the way social citizenship is perceived and experienced. The work of T.H. Marshall is widely acknowledged as the starting point for discussion of social citizenship. His 1949 essay, "Citizenship and Social Class," examines the meaning of citizenship, which he thought had developed in three stages. The first stage, forged in the eighteenth century, established the civil rights of citizenship, leading to property and legal rights, due process, and so on. During the nineteenth century, the second stage developed the political rights of citizenship, including the franchise and the right to hold office. In the twentieth century, citizenship expanded to include social rights, through which the developing welfare state administered basic social and economic security (Morrison, 1997). Many critiques of Marshall's work have pointed out the unevenness of access to these rights for all but reasonably well-off white males. Nevertheless, the creation of the welfare state during the twentieth century has certainly involved the emergence of entitlements through social citizenship, although these entitlements were often more tenuous than is generally realized.

In Canada, the social rights of citizens have been protected to some extent through federal social programs. The Canada Assistance Plan (CAP), for instance, obligated provinces to provide for people in need, included prohibitions against workfare and discrimination, and required the development of appeals systems at the provincial level. But when the Canada Health and Social Transfer (CHST) replaced the CAP in 1996, the federal government ended its commitment to a social "floor" below which federal funding for provincially administered social programs would not be cut (Morrison, 1997). The repatriation of the Constitution and development of the 1982 Charter of Rights and Freedoms might seem to provide new protections, but in fact the Charter contains no explicit protections of social rights. Further, hopes for additional Charter protections via legal challenges now being mounted do not appear to hold much promise for protection of social rights. Some social advocates fear that a two-tiered system of citizenship is being advanced—one tier for those who depend on public resources and another (superior) system for those whose main relationships are with the marketplace.

Considerable concern about this shift in direction has been expressed. Pascal (1993) notes that the logical endpoint of such a shift is that even the most basic needs of able-bodied adults and their dependent children might eventually fail to constitute legitimate claims to entitlement. Schragge and Deniger (1997) conclude their discussion of workfare with a warning that these programs may herald an era of profound social change and inequality, in which large sections of the population will be excluded from stable, meaningful, and reasonably paid employment, as the recession beginning in 2008 has clearly demonstrated. As Swift and Callahan (2009) suggest, the alternative is to insist on formulating and evaluating social programs in line not with efficiency principles but with principles of social justice.

As noted earlier, a primary concern has been whether the nation-state itself—and therefore its ability to develop distinct social welfare policy—is under threat of demise. As trade zones and agreements proliferate and supersede national law and policy, we need to question to what extent national governments can control internal economic forces (Delaney, Brownlee, & Sellick, 2001) and whether states can retain the capacity to provide basic welfare provisions for their citizens. Most social critics now recognize that powerful transnational corporate interests actually do not wish for the demise of the state but rather hope for the reshaping of states to better support their profit-based interests. As Barlow (2001) argues, national governments still provide the security forces required to protect global economic interests. Lamarche (1999) points out that the state is also needed to manage the problems of poverty, which intensify with globalization. This kind of state management, however, transforms the notion of "good governance" from ensuring equality, citizenship, rights, and benefits to the project of producing better consumers. The "citizen" in this scenario becomes less a rights-bearing individual and more a "functional citizen," whose goal is intended to be success in the new and changing global market.

Conversations about citizenship used to assume the existence of the welfare state, along with the justice system, as the grounds within which claims and entitlements were legitimized. Unions were among the beneficiaries, because the resources, stability, and power of the welfare state provided the conditions for unions to build strength and credibility during the mid-1900s (Hargrove, 1999). The benefits of the "rights revolution" of the 1960s (Ignatieff, 2000) appeared to be thoroughly entrenched in the Canadian consciousness and embedded in social institutions.

Current developments have brought this assumption into doubt. Of course, the September 11, 2001, attack on New York's World Trade Center led directly to new federal legislation curtailing a variety of accepted civil and legal liberties in the name of security. But well before that event, research had noted that the reorganization and delegitimization of many traditional welfare-state functions were rapidly eroding citizenship rights, especially for the poor (Little, 1999; Swift, 2001). Marshall and many others believed that the welfare state laid the foundation for full social citizenship. Those who agree with this belief decry the dismantling or diminution of welfare-state structures. Others, however, argue that the welfare state, with its "false universalism" (Hansen, 1999), was never capable of developing either the conditions or the content of authentic citizenship because it does not recognize the unique differences among individuals. The claims of diverse groups for increased entitlements and recognition, discussed at more length in Chapter 6, reflect this problem. Further, social welfare does not encourage the associative ties implied by the idea of full citizenship. Social welfare serves, but it does not identify, nor does it involve. It creates "clients," Hansen argues, not citizens.

In any case, recent examinations of welfare-state activities suggest that they are shifting away from service to a function of assessing "risk" and mediating accountability for risk. The goals of this new welfare ideology are calculating and managing risk for individuals deemed unable to exercise self-management. Certainly, widespread use of risk-assessment tools has become standard practice in health, justice, and child welfare, to name a few domains of the welfare state (Swift & Callahan, 2009). In this conception of welfare, even the service function, already in doubt as useful grounds for promoting citizenship, has diminished.

Recently, discussions have linked citizenship to the idea of "civil society" rather than to the welfare state. But traditional theorists conceptualized the idea of civil society differently. Marx, for instance, saw *civil society* as synonymous with *bourgeois society* (Hansen, 1999). In this view, civil society is the site of market transactions for personal, self-serving activity and therefore a space to be challenged and replaced. Hegel regarded civil society as a social space, developed to address the tensions between individual autonomy and communal interests, a tension that Hansen (1999) suggests is reflected in the welfare state. Feminists raise the question of whether "family" is separate from or included in the civil society (Howell & Mulligan, 2005). Most contemporary activists equate civil society with "the third sector"—neither government nor market.

This non-governmental, non-profit, associational sector is estimated by some to be the fastest-growing sector of society, expanding at four times the rate of the economy, according to one political scientist (Barlow, 2001). This growth has no doubt been facilitated by widespread Internet use, which has allowed activists and groups to make connections far beyond their own communities and countries. Many organizations formerly grounded either in particular countries or in international organizations, are transcending these boundaries to become coalitions of groups claiming the right to have input into wide-ranging decisions in both government and corporate arenas (Florini, 2000). As this trend continues, the natures of civil society and of citizenship are shifting, along with ideas about the nature and auspices of social welfare.

Edwards (2005) defines civil society broadly as "collective" activity that acts as a counterweight to individualism. He suggests incorporating a variety of views into the definition, with the intent of strengthening associational life, and he offers several proposals for the promotion of a healthy civil society. His first proposal is an attack on all forms of discrimination and inequality, which he describes as "poison" for civil society. Second, he recommends supporting innovations to encourage citizen action, including the creation of links between policy groups and across different interests to break down the "silos" that discourage collective action. Finally, he suggests openness to "surprises," meaning the powerful action occasionally seen from unexpected sources. For instance, we do not ordinarily expect mothers to create global interest in an issue, but the Mothers of the Plaza de Mayo, through their persistence and passion, managed to create globally backed resistance to military dictatorship in Argentina several decades ago through demonstrations on behalf of their "disappeared" children.

Rebick (2000) describes in some detail the idea of "active citizenship"—the participation of individuals not only in voting rights, but also in political, social, economic, and cultural decision-making. Thus, while some social critics have predicted the narrowing and even the demise of social citizenship, especially for vulnerable populations, others are now beginning to reconceptualize its possibilities with more breadth and depth. Reduced citizenship will surely mean a concomitantly reduced social welfare arena, one much more likely to be shaped in support of economic interests. An expanded concept of citizenship, however, might result in forms of social welfare that are more responsive to diversity and social justice. In this potential scenario, the relationship of social welfare to civil society would have to be renegotiated to account for the needs of "active citizens."

Social Inclusion

In the last several decades, the issues of "belonging" (implied in Hansen's critique of the welfare state) and of active citizen participation (as examined by Edwards and Rebick) have become issues for Western nations with advanced welfare states, as various groups have identified themselves as "excluded" from society and its opportunities. Social exclusion and social inclusion have consequently become useful concepts in contemporary discussions of the meanings of citizenship.

The concept of social inclusion arises from discussions about its opposite: social exclusion. This term was first used in France in the 1970s to identify people unprotected by social insurance programs. Through the 1980s and 1990s, the term's meaning expanded to include those left behind by the effects of globalizing economies. These discussions about social exclusion were generally undertaken with a goal of enhancing possibilities of social cohesion. In both Europe and North America, the notion of exclusion has begun to replace the discourse of poverty, because it captures not only the conditions of the poor, but also the underlying social and economic processes leading to marginalization of many populations, including areas relating to health, education, debt, access to services, housing, and overall quality of life (Good-Gingrich, 2003).

Barata (2000), on the one hand, has argued that there are several advantages to moving toward the language of social exclusion and social inclusion instead of using the old language of poverty lines, disadvantaged populations, and underclass. The language of exclusion/inclusion (1) includes power relations in the analysis; (2) has the potential to incorporate many levels of experience, for instance, health, quality of life, and rights; (3) involves "the social," implicating society in general as the focus of discussion rather than just "the poor"; and (4) stresses process over established outcomes, such as contentious "poverty lines." Mitchell and Shillington (2005), on the other hand, argue that the focus should remain on poverty and inequality to emphasize the responsibility of society to develop inclusive circumstances.

Concerns with and critiques of the language of exclusion include the obvious problem of deciding what it is that people are excluded from and what they should be included in. If not used with care and precision, exclusion could imply that the goal is conformity with the status quo and a homogeneity of experience. In addition, critics warn that important analysis of poverty levels could be lost altogether in an imprecise discourse of exclusion.

Implementing a process of social exclusion involves processes, policies, and practices that "assign value, determine entitlement and judge legitimacy" (Good-Gingrich, 2003, 12). Good-Gingrich (2003) emphasizes that assimilation, exploitation, domination, abandonment, and indifference are all processes that lead to exclusion. She argues for a framework that is dynamic, multidimensional, and relational as opposed to approaches that focus on the individual as the unit of analysis and concentrate on attachment to the labour force as the primary concern (Good-Gingrich, 2008).

Many theorists are working to sharpen and clarify meanings of exclusion. Klasen (1998), for example, has identified four different sources of exclusion. One source is economic exclusion, relating to the problems of unemployment and poverty captured in previous examinations of disadvantage. A second type is social exclusion, based, for instance, on neighbourhood or family type. Exclusion by birth or background is another source, referring to such issues as disability. Finally, Klasen identifies socio-political exclusion, referring, for instance, to discrimination by race, culture, or gender. Good-Gingrich (2003) has expanded on these categories of exclusion to include political exclusion, which refers to an inability to participate in political processes; geographic exclusion, which consists of labelling places and spaces as, for instance, economically deprived or high-crime areas; and subjective exclusion, which means personal internalization of judgments.

The apparent opposite of social exclusion is *social inclusion*, a term that has come into common usage in North American social policy discourse, and one that Freiler (2000) argues has the capacity to bridge social and economic policy. A major contributor to the international discussion of social inclusion is Amartya Sen (1992). Sen explores the notion of "capability enhancement" as a feature of inclusionary policies. In this case, *capability* means having access to resources necessary for the creation of a life one values. Sen identifies two levels of capability, basic and complex, each important in itself. According to Sen, social welfare goals, now often framed in "risk" terminology, should focus instead on enhancing basic capabilities, such as food security and literacy, as well as complex capabilities, such as civic participation. Capability may be enhanced by social, economic, cultural, and political structures. Analysis of social welfare and social policy then becomes an examination not of risk and accountability, but of the way legislation and policy enhance or inhibit capacity building for individuals and identity groups.

Critics of the widespread use of social inclusion point out that this terminology can be used to support any political position. Silver (1994) has investigated this issue, identifying three ideological uses of this discourse: neo-liberal, social democratic, and social change. Her analysis shows that both British and North American usages of these terms are primarily neo-liberal. In Canada, *The Senate Report on Social Cohesion* (The Standing Senate Committee on Social Affairs, Science and Technology, 1999), for instance, developed strategies for inclusion that relied on neo-liberal terminology such as *investing in human capital* and *removing barriers to social and economic participation*. These objectives signal workfare and other programs designed to enforce participation in a labour force that is increasingly insecure.

Used with specificity and caution, however, the ideas of social exclusion and social inclusion have produced useful tools for reconceptualizing social citizenship, and they are also helpful in considering how social welfare might be redesigned. Jenson's (1998) conceptual framework identifying dimensions of social cohesion provides an example. She shows five continua useful for analyzing inclusion:

Belonging ⟶ ◀— Isolation

Inclusion ⟶ ◀— Exclusion

Participation ⟶ ◀— Non-involvement

Recognition ⟶ ◀— Rejection

Legitimacy ⟶ ◀— Illegitimacy

This framework identifies life possibilities and capabilities that allow individuals to become fully participating members of a society. As Hansen points out, the welfare state falls short on some of these dimensions, such as in its capacity to legitimize its users and to involve its "clients" as active participants. The notion of inclusion may help to provide new language and analytical tools that enhance the possibility for recognizing what is needed for authentic citizenship for a diverse population.

Richmond and Saloojee (2005) explore dimensions of inclusion related to specific groups, including women, children, visible minorities, First Nations, and people with disabilities. One author in this collection (Bach, 2005) argues that a "social solidarity" agenda is needed as a way of enabling currently devalued voices to be heard and to promote change that creates new paths to well-being. Good-Gingrich (2003) suggests that "Change is possible, as the dynamic relations of power that work to inscribe boundaries marking difference and exclusion are interrupted and contested with tenacious acts of collective resistance" (21). Amid the changing dynamics of social citizenship and the increasingly exclusionary processes within the global economic system, it becomes apparent that citizen participation is becoming the catalyst for improved social welfare. After performing a thorough review of relevant literature, Good-Gingrich (2003) suggests that resistance has become a significant concept within the present system and that evidence suggests the need to reject binaries, form alliances with other individuals and groups that are excluded, increase the role of civil society, and undermine the homogenization of the excluded group in order to reject the exclusion of people and groups within the present system.

Social Movements

Chapter 4 outlined current ideologies and their expression through political parties. Today, ideological stances and political party allegiances have been shifting dramatically. Neo-liberal ideology has become the dominant political force in Canada and other Western nations. Even political parties without true neo-liberal platforms are developing policies not dissimilar to those of the conservative parties. During the Liberal government of 1992 to 2005, policy directions developed by the previous Progressive Conservative government had continued. Meanwhile, enthusiasm for the Marxist/socialist vision has dimmed in North America, largely because of world events, such as the breakup of the Soviet Union in the 1990s, followed by revelations of extreme social dislocations in Eastern Bloc countries. Adherents of leftist ideas are also in a state of some disillusionment and difficulty because the public has been encouraged to think of global market forces as overwhelming and unstoppable (McQuaig, 1998).

At the same time, traditional "spaces" for public interchange and participation have diminished. Canadians are being coached to accept the neo-liberal beliefs that our social values and attachment to the social safety net need to be filtered through the realities of globalization and fiscal restraint (Armitage, 2003). Low voter turnout provides an example of withdrawal from civil participation of many people in Western democracies. In 1988, 75 percent of eligible Canadians voted in the federal election. In 2008, 59.1 percent voted, the lowest turnout in Canadian history (CBC News, 2008).

The former strength of unions in challenging employers has eroded over the past decade. Unions are faced with tough choices: to fight hard—by using strike tactics—to retain what they have gained over decades of struggle or to compromise in hopes of retaining at least some benefits and their union status. In a global market, transnational companies can move jobs to more profitable locations, so strikes may prove to be counterproductive. In addition, given its new partnership with business, the state is more likely to pass laws—as Ontario has recently done—to make unionization much more difficult and union decertification much easier. The NDP is the traditional political partner of unions, although some of the large Canadian unions have been critical of the direction and leadership of the party for some time. Some analysts suggest that traditional ideological subtleties and differences will dissolve into two loose coalitions: those defending the accumulation of capital and those opposing it. This division may mean that traditional elements of the right will form alliances to strengthen their political and economic control, and that they will be opposed by a coalition of various political parties and grass-roots groups brought together by a common interest in social justice and a willingness to challenge the idea that there is any genuine benefit in developing a single capital pool (Laxer, 1997). Saul (1995) calls this the politics of "disinterest"—that is, political activity based not on personal gain but on a willingness to struggle for the common good.

What would this "social justice" coalition look like? Esping-Anderson (1990) speaks of a "red–green" alliance, involving traditional leftists and environmentalists, including both rural groups and urban dwellers. Laxer (1997) cites such groups and organizations as trade unions, feminists, childcare advocates, environmentalists, and anti-poverty organizations as having the potential to oppose right-wing policies if they are willing to act in concert. McNally (2006) also suggests alliances on all fronts—unions, anti-poverty groups, feminists, anti-racist organizations, students, and greens—to "articulate a common emancipatory project" (390).

Esping-Anderson's vision involves politics outside Parliament, for he and others (Teeple, 1995) believe that the political parties of the past have either joined in advancing right-wing economics or have lost the ability to oppose the neo-liberal direction effectively within formal government structures. McNally (2006) further suggests that party politics have become ineffective because the economy and market forces operate almost entirely outside the reach of formal government and its laws. In any case, as Esping-Anderson (1990) points out, it is virtually impossible for the left to form a government, since the working class does not constitute a majority. In effect, the rise of the middle class has diluted socialist possibilities. However, a middle class hit with high unemployment and taxes coupled with a reduction in benefits from the welfare state, such as health care and pensions, may itself now be shrinking and becoming more cynical about its future prospects, a development that could help to inspire new coalitions of interests. It is possible that the future will see some elements of the middle class in alliance with various marginalized groups against a small but wealthy and powerful ruling elite.

These visions are largely based on familiar groups and movements using mostly traditional strategies to challenge the status quo. Participants and leaders are likely to be people with long service and ties to political parties, unions, and existing social movements, such as feminism and the established environmental advocates. The collapse of communism in the early 1990s has to some extent shifted the political terrain of these movements, as popular opinion reflects a belief that capitalism has "won" and class analysis therefore no longer has much relevance. Barker (1999) disagrees, suggesting instead that class analysis has become more complicated as a result of "cross-class influences," such as culture, religion, and organizational affiliations. The high end of the class structure has become more unified by the reward system of the new capitalism, Barker contends, while the lower end of the hierarchy has become divided and fragmented by competing loyalties, such as culture, gender, and religion.

McNally (2006) also sees promise in the new left-leaning and socialist governments forming particularly in South America. Elected leaders in Bolivia, Brazil, and Venezuela have openly challenged the neo-liberal politics of the Global North and have loudly proclaimed their intentions to redistribute wealth in their countries. These electoral results have been made possible, McNally contends, through mass popular movements, termed *socialism from below*. Numerous struggles over such basic issues as the privatization of water and the World Bank's "structural adjustment programs," which further impoverish debtor nations, illustrate the ongoing potential for positive social change of social movements. These movements rely on self-mobilization and participatory forms of democracy that develop their own questions and challenges to the existing order. While all of these countries continue to have major problems, including compromises made by their elected leaders, they demonstrate that socialism is still an idea with currency, especially when adapted to the conditions of the twenty-first century.

The context for social movement development and activity is in continual flux, and the tactics and strategies that might be tried are hotly contested. In 2008, the global economy experienced what was often described as the worst meltdown since the Great Depression of the 1930s. Although not as damaged as the U.S. economy, the Canadian economy also suffered. Well before that, the gap between the rich and the poor in Canada had widened, and the gap continues to grow. As reported by Yalnizyan (2010), the richest 1 percent of Canadians now takes one-third of all income growth, leaving the other 99 percent of the population to share two-thirds of the income growth. Unemployment rates remain high at 7.6 percent; although they are slowly falling after a steep spike in 2009 to nearly 9 percent (*The Daily*, January 7, 2011). Also in play are a series of disasters, some natural and some political, around the globe. Naomi Klein (2007) examines the relationship of these disasters to the workings of contemporary capitalism, suggesting that disasters of all kinds provide opportunities for corporate engineering of societies in crisis. These conditions would seem to provide rich terrain for social change; however, there are some problems to overcome.

NGOs, often thought of by social advocates as positive members of civil society and sometimes as drivers of social movements, have been caught up in these relationships. Many NGOs, large and small, step in to develop the capacity to rebuild in disaster zones, without necessarily having any mandate to do so. Recently, NGOs have been criticized from both the right and the left (Hardesty & Furdon, 2004). Neo-liberal critics claim that the boundaries between NGOs and government are too blurred, with NGO leaders becoming consultants and advisers to government and the organizations themselves acting more like special interest groups. The right recommends that NGOs stick to service and stay out of policy and politics if they want government financing. From the left, NGOs are called to account for putting their own fundraising interests ahead of the interests of those they presume to assist. Issues cited include lack of evidence of actual effectiveness and accountability, along with commercializing tendencies and ideologically based performance (Richmond & Carey, 2005). The NGO sector, which plays an important role in civil society, may be somewhat weakened by these critiques.

Developing global social movements fuelled by Internet communication, which appeared so promising at the turn of the century, now have their critics as well as supporters. Critiques suggest that the Internet alone does not provide a sufficient grounding for lasting action. "Members" of various groups can too easily lose focus, referred to as *slacktivism*, because "easy clicks produce big numbers but very little commitment" (Derbyshire, 2011). Also, those in power can cut off access to the Web, isolating activists, as we saw in the Egyptian uprising of 2011. Alternatively, some claim that the Internet can be a breeding ground for activists and that Internet-organized activism can help to shape public opinion and demand a response from politicians (Derbyshire, 2011).

Canel (n.d.) describes two approaches taken by contemporary social movements. The first, new social movements (NSM), arises from a serious challenge to an "oversimplified Marxism" centred mainly in Europe. The second, resource mobilization (RM), challenges the idea that social action develops in a relatively straightforward fashion from perceived conditions of deprivation and the frustrations associated with these perceptions. Both perspectives emphasize the *cultural* nature of the new social change movements and view them as struggles for control over the production of meaning and the constitution of new collective identities. From Canel's perspective, social movements are clearly placed in the terrain of civil society rather than that of the state, and they emphasize the political nature of their activities. In contrast to older movements, the new paradigms, according to Canel, propose that social change is "a contingent and open process" rather than the linear process previously theorized.

Addressing the American and Canadian scene, Tilly (1999) examines the new work of social movement organizers—that of addressing competing loyalties and fragmented organizations. Tilly conceptualizes two major identity formations. One is "embedded identities"—especially religious and cultural identities—that operate in and shape everyday life to a significant extent. The other is "detached identities"—identification with organizations not as part of everyday life but rather as a selective identity, invoked for particular reasons. The work of social movements often involves two processes in relation to the identities of participants: embedding detached identities into everyday life to increase the loyalties of activists and, working the other way, generalizing and detaching embedded identities to blur divisions among participants and facilitate the development of alliances. The actual work of organizers, Tilly notes, involves the piecing together of conditional and impermanent coalitions, involving numerous agendas and ongoing negotiations, while ensuring that these struggles are hidden from public view.

Gramsci's notion of hegemony (1971) helps to explain the current challenges facing social activists. Gramsci theorized that power by ruling elites is secured through two routes: overt force, which we have seen more of since 9/11, and ideology. By *ideology*, Gramsci means not a body of thought, as discussed in Chapter 4, but mechanisms and ways of thinking that influence people to conform to the status quo, even when it operates against their own interests. Ideology in this sense involves mass acceptance and internalization of the values of ruling classes, and regularly acting on those values. This process of accepting the necessity of diminishing civil and political rights in order to "fight terrorism" concerns many of today's social advocates. How are the successes and failures of today's social movements to be studied and judged? Giugni (1999) proposes examining both the "durability and direction" of change, focusing on policy shifts and short-term effects on the one hand, and institutional outcomes and longer-term effects on the other. Social movements, always aiming to change the status quo, face a contradiction. The possibility of success is greater if the goal is short-term policy change, rather than durable, long-term structural change.

Studies on social movement organization (Barker, 1999) suggest that local politics and action by themselves are no match for the power of global forces. Such action must be connected to wider networks of information and to more broadly based organizations, as well as to centres of power within government and anywhere else that has an impact on the local arena.

Conclusion

Historically, social policies have reflected the national will to some extent. Yet globalization influences the range of choices exercised by governments. As companies compete in an increasingly international marketplace, the demands upon governments to restrict the welfare state may grow. Some corporate leaders, for example, seek minimalist tax structures and minimal corporate contributions to income security, health insurance, and other forms of publicly administered programs. Canadians are also subject to American political, cultural, and economic values (Grant, 1965, 1969). Given its growing presence, in part reinforced by the North American Free Trade Agreement, Canadian politicians, particularly those on the right, have looked to the United States for political precedents. Many policy analysts, in fact, are struck by the strongly American influences in contemporary Canadian social welfare retrenchment and workfare (Torjman, 1997, 1998b).

The influence of social movements, citizenship, and social inclusion, likewise, will have a strong bearing on future social welfare development. But given the growing forces of globalization and North American political and economic integration, will the social policy choices Canadians make reflect what they agree as a society *should* be their destiny?

Chapter 6

Diversity and Social Policy

This chapter considers three questions. First, what is meant by *diversity*? Second, what are the relationships between diversity and social policy? And third, what is the "correct" balance between recognition of the interests of specific groups and the needs of Canada's population as a whole?

Three premises, in turn, guide the chapter. One premise is that social workers need to avoid thinking too universally about social policy. "Minority" groups have often been treated differently in social policy terms. Different groups of people, for instance, received the franchise at different times, some very recently. In the early part of the twentieth century, women were not recognized as "persons," and lesbians and gay men have only recently begun to achieve access to benefits long since accorded other Canadians and permanent residents.

A second basic premise is that a major goal of Canadian social policy has always been the goal of equity. However, social policy that purports to be equitable and potentially universal is being challenged for being too crude when universally applied and for failing to reflect the particularities of human experience. This is not a challenge to the idea of equality but a recognition that the provision of the same services for all is not always appropriate or desired.

The third premise is that Canadian social policy has been built on principles drawn from European and especially British traditions. A focus on paid "work" and a concomitant notion of the "dependence" of those who are not breadwinners are basic to our social policy framework. Basic principles also include the somewhat contradictory traditions of individual initiative and "the family" as the building blocks of society. The groups discussed in this chapter have in various ways challenged the relevance of these principles in contemporary times. The goals of these populations often do not fit well with tradition, and challenges to traditions, policies, and practices are the result.

What Is Meant by *Diversity?*

In everyday usage, *diversity* refers to characteristics of individuals such as race, culture, gender, and sexual orientation. These characteristics are those that especially affect access to opportunity and resources. Consequently, the term *minority group* does not necessarily reflect the size of the membership but rather the relative social and economic power of the group. In relation to social policy, the term *diversity* reflects the reality that different people in Canada occupy different statuses and social locations in relation to the state and its policies. In this sense, diverse groups become categories and are often treated this way in social policy. One problem with this approach is that it tends to focus on people as members of categories. A related problem is that it becomes difficult to see that people fit into more than one kind of category.

Kallen (2004) speaks of "diverse" groups as subordinate populations. She views society as socially stratified, with unequal group relations constitutionally predicated on the inegalitarian notion of special group status. She endorses a human rights perspective based on "universal" ideals of equality and social justice, as expressed in such international documents as the United Nations Charter (1945) and the International Bill of Human Rights (1978, 1988). She explores the tensions between individual and community rights and considers how these tensions might be resolved by adopting a human rights approach based on the common humanity of all people, rather than on any single attribute of a person or group. Marumba (1998) elaborates this idea by suggesting that in the globalizing twenty-first century, people should adopt conceptions of human rights that include both the individual and group culture when defining what it means to be human.

Previous chapters have discussed basic provisions of Canadian social policy. However, people's different physical, mental, emotional, and experiential attributes mean they have different needs and variable access to these general social provisions. Further, the recognition of diverse needs in the Canadian population has produced social policies specific to the issues of different groups. Social workers need to be aware not only of basic policy and welfare provisions, but also of the related policies that reflect needs not addressed by these policies and/or that affect access to basic social provisions by specific groups.

Two British traditions have influenced Canadian social policy. One is the tradition of the British Poor Laws, which continue to inform social welfare policy. The Poor Laws, as noted in Chapter 2, established the concepts of deserving and undeserving poor, concepts that apportion blame to individuals for their own problems. Poor Laws also implied different expectations of males and females from the outset. A second tradition infused into social policy is social Darwinism (Christensen, 1995), which justified suppression and resource extraction from non-white populations and supported racial hierarchies. This ideology has shaped both immigration policy and majority–minority relations, and in turn has created the need for anti-discriminatory policies and protections. Along the way, built into social policy of almost every kind has been "familism" (Williams, 1989), a belief that strong families ensure a stable society. The so-called traditional family, embedded in Canadian thought and policy, is that of the heterosexual nuclear family, with a male breadwinner, a female engaged in reproductive work, and children who are "in training" to become productive and reproductive members of society.

Canada does not really have a set of coherent family policies. Rather, implicit assumptions and understandings about "the family" are infused into its laws and policies. Because there is no coherent family policy, there are some contradictions among policies and levels of government. Many policies have sought to define the family for purposes of benefit eligibility. Such definitions are currently subject to challenges from different quarters. For example, in the early 1990s, immigration policy attempted to enforce a very narrow definition of the family for purposes of sponsorship: a person could sponsor only an opposite-sex spouse or a child. This nuclear family model continues to be criticized by many cultural communities for whom the family is an extended kinship network (grandparents, adult siblings, aunts, etc.). The policy was eventually softened (but not rescinded). In another example, some lesbian women and gay men have challenged the definition of family as exclusively heterosexual, a definition that has direct implications for workplace benefits. An additional example includes women who have spent significant parts of their lives caring for others; they are concerned that their own pension benefits will be inadequate to support them in old age because they have not contributed to employee pension programs.

During the 1980s, various groups began to criticize the welfare state and its policies. "Interest groups," formed around cultural, racial, gender, and other "identities," have brought new demands and pressures for change and different directions in policy. In addition, because people are more aware of their identities, many have challenged policies previously assumed to be equitable and accessible to everyone. The 1982 Constitution also had an impact on the way Canadians think about social policy. Court challenges based on the Charter of Rights and Freedoms have brought new attention to the issue of rights. In turn, new rights have influenced policies and the way they are implemented (Canadian Council on Social Development, 1991), bringing attention to the identification and enforcement of anti-discriminatory policies.

Lessard (1997) and Kallen (1995, 2010) argue that despite these advances, entrenchment of rights may also have the effect of entrenching existing relations of subordination. Kallen has shown that the Charter entrenches the rights of three different specific populations in the Constitution, and that different and hierarchical sets of rights have been developed to protect these groups. The group with the most rights protection is termed the *founding peoples*, who are mainly of French and British extraction. Founding peoples are guaranteed positive rights that obligate the state in specified ways. Their rights are spelled out in some detail, involving, as an example, protection of Protestant and Catholic denominational educational rights. The second group is Aboriginal peoples, who are guaranteed collective rights under the Charter, but the rights guaranteed are "negative" ones, often involving non-interference rather than specific obligations of the state. The third group comprises other ethnic minorities, who are not specifically named, or *enumerated*, and who are protected only by negative, unspecified, and undefined rights. Furthermore, because certain minorities are enumerated in the Charter, and others are not, a hierarchy of rights has been established between these two groups.

History and Social Context of Diverse Populations in Canada

Canada's social policy was developed to redress specific inequalities, mainly those of class, income level and source, age, and family type. In general, state interventions were designed to mitigate poverty arising from problems with the market economy system (Williams, 1989). These policies generally related to the ability of an individual or family to access income and resources and were based on two principles: (1) ensuring that vulnerable populations did not fall below an established quality-of-life level and (2) acting to effect some redistribution of wealth from those with sufficient resources to those in need. For several decades, the building blocks of social policy addressing these issues were considered sufficient and at times path-breaking. The health-care system is an example.

In reality, social policy has never been "the same for all" in Canada. Different social policies and limitations in access to resources have always existed for specific populations. This chapter describes several specific groups and the policies that affect them. These are certainly not the only populations representing the diversity of Canadians, but they do represent major groups around which social policy has been developed. It is important to keep in mind that these groups are not mutually exclusive. An individual may belong to one or more of these groups and identify with other diversities as well. Nor are these groups homogeneous; many within-group differences and disagreements are apparent. This reality, not always overtly acknowledged in policy discussions, is one of the significant features of contemporary social policy development. Many social policy texts and discussions have assumed a universal "Canadian" who can access programs given certain eligibility requirements. In the postmodern era, however, this assumption is continually challenged. This chapter describes historical differences among various populations with a view to making visible their particular relationships to and claims upon the state. The discussion is intended to elaborate information presented in previous chapters, as well as to examine some challenges to the traditional foundations of Canadian social policy.

Ethnoracial Minorities

References to diversity often focus on racial and cultural groups. This may be because Canada's cultural and racial groups have been changing rapidly over the past several decades. It may also be because explicit social policies designed to address these shifts have been made. Certainly, Canada's population is changing. Early in the twentieth century, the majority of the Canadian population was white and of European descent. Today, no single ethnic group accounts for a majority of the Canadian population (Statistics Canada, 2006b). Changes in immigration policy account for this shift. Until 1967, immigration to Canada was restricted to "preferred nations." Immigrants seeking and allowed entry varied somewhat, depending on world events and the needs of the country; however, they were overwhelmingly white Europeans, since Europe, and especially Northern and Western Europe, comprised the most preferred countries. British immigrants remained the largest group until World War II. During this period, immigrants were differentiated largely by language, and they tended to settle in regional concentrations of ethnocultural groups (Christensen, 1995).

In 1967, a new liberalized immigration policy came into force, one that focused not on source country—by then considered discriminatory—but on the characteristics of individual immigrants. During the 1970s and 1980s, source countries of immigrants to Canada changed dramatically—from European to Asian, African, South American, and Caribbean. The result has been a change in Canadian demographics, one of considerable interest to social workers. Immigrants now come from several dozen different source countries. According to the 2006 Census, about one in five people in Canada, or 19.8 percent of the total population, are foreign-born. Most of these immigrants are from Asia (58.3 percent), including the Middle East. Europeans are the second-largest group at 16.1 percent. Toronto, Montreal, and Vancouver are the primary settlement areas; 68.9 percent of recent immigrants settled in one of these three cities in 2006. However, increasing numbers of people are now choosing to settle in smaller cities. The majority of immigrants—more than 85 percent—become citizens. In the major urban reception centres, many different languages are spoken, and a broad spectrum of cultural groups require services previously offered only in English and/or French (*The Daily*, December 4, 2007).

As noted in Chapter 2, major policy responses to these population changes were announced in 1971 and again in 1988 legislation (An Act for the Preservation and Enhancement of Multiculturalism in Canada). The 1988 Act recognizes diversity as a basic characteristic of Canada and promotes participation of people of all origins in Canadian society. Despite these apparently worthwhile goals, the policy has come under attack. People question whether the policy will result in a hierarchy of ethnic groups, isolation of communities of immigrants, and perhaps even intergroup dissension (Bissoondath, 1994). In any case, the legislation and policy provide an ideal espoused by many majority and minority Canadians, rather than a guarantee of equality. Legal protection of rights, however, was established in the Charter of Rights and Freedoms (1982), which is intended to guarantee cultural and racial pluralism and provide anti-discrimination mandates for social welfare law, policies, programs, and practices (Herberg & Herberg, 1995). The forerunners of this policy were laws after World War II that mandated "fair" access to housing, education, and employment for minorities. In the 1960s, these laws evolved into more comprehensive federal and provincial human rights codes. Kallen's argument suggesting that even these guaranteed rights are stratified for various groups of Canadian citizens and residents, with immigrants near the bottom, serves as a reminder that equality under the law remains elusive (1995, 2010).

Information from Statistics Canada shows that the numbers of people immigrating to Canada have varied over the second half of the twentieth century (see Figure 6.1). The Statistics Canada definition of an immigrant is anyone who was born in another country and given permanent resident status in Canada. By this broad definition, the percentage of immigrants in the total Canadian population is not particularly high. Figure 6.2 shows that the number of immigrants was quite low at the beginning of the twentieth century and has gradually increased from the 1950s to the present. As of 2006, there were about 6.2 million immigrants in Canada.

FIGURE 6.1   Number of Immigrants to Canada, from 1860 to 2008

Source: Citizenship and Immigration Canada. (2008). Facts and Figures 2008 – Immigration overview: Permanent and temporary residents. http://www.cic.gc.ca/english/resources/statistics/facts2008/permanent/index.asp. Reproduced with permission from Citizenship and Immigration Canada, 2011.

FIGURE 6.2   Number and Share of the Foreign-Born Population in Canada, 1901 to 2006

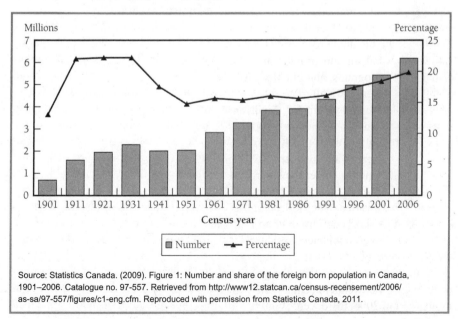

Source: Statistics Canada. (2009). Figure 1: Number and share of the foreign born population in Canada, 1901–2006. Catalogue no. 97-557. Retrieved from http://www12.statcan.ca/census-recensement/2006/as-sa/97-557/figures/c1-eng.cfm. Reproduced with permission from Statistics Canada, 2011.

The major change in recent immigration policy is the source countries. In the 1950s, more than 80 percent of immigrants arriving in Canada were from Europe, with many from Great Britain. In 1994, only 17 percent were European, while 64 percent were from Asian countries. In that year, 6 percent were from Africa and 4 percent each were from South America and the Caribbean. In 2006, Asian countries remained the greatest source of immigration, with South Asians surpassing Chinese for the first time (*The Daily*, April 2, 2008).

Another important change in immigration patterns is the classes of immigrants now arriving. In the 1950s and 1960s, the majority of arrivals were "family-class" immigrants—that is, sponsored by relatives already established in the country. In 1994, 46 percent of new arrivals were "economic" immigrants. By 2009, the most recent year for which accurate figures are available, economic immigrants were just over 60 percent of the 252 179 permanent residents admitted to Canada. These are the applicants demonstrating the requisite skills, education, work history, or money to enable entry into the country. That same year, only about 26 percent of immigrants entered the country as family-class immigrants, about 9 percent entered as refugees, and a small percentage arrived in a catch-all "other" category that includes temporary residents and people admitted on "humanitarian grounds" (Citizenship and Immigration Canada, 2009).

The most recent census shows the majority of recent immigrants to Canada live in Ontario (52.3 percent), followed by 17.5 percent in Quebec, 16 percent in British Columbia, and 9.3 percent in Alberta (*The Daily*, December 4, 2007).

Anderson and Marr (1987) acknowledge the importance of the new wave of immigrants by calling them the "third force" in Canadian politics, not only because of their numbers, but also because many recent immigrants come from different cultural backgrounds and languages than either of the two "founding groups" and therefore bring different social policy issues to the fore. Also, many new immigrants and refugees over the past three decades are people of colour. While immigrants do not constitute a large percentage of the total Canadian population, many settle in urban areas and are substantially changing the racial composition of cities. It is estimated, for example, that by 2031, people of colour could make up 29 to 32 percent of the population (*The Daily*, March 9, 2010). These demographic changes not only put pressure on service organizations to adapt to different kinds of needs, but also call into question the policy frameworks that have traditionally guided service development and delivery. In past decades, social workers often worked as though cultural differences were a small side issue. That is, approaches to professional social work could be considered generalizable to all populations. This belief was given credibility by the fact that the clients social workers faced were often born in Canada or were of European descent. Today's diversity of source countries makes this approach much more difficult to justify. In reality, of course, there have always been diversities that social workers might have noticed.

The federal government sets policy determining classes and levels of immigration and provides several settlement and adjustment programs from federal sources. The Adjustment Assistance Program, for instance, provides financial assistance for basic needs of poor immigrants on arrival. The Immigrant Settlement and Adaptation Program directs the federal government to contract services through voluntary agencies for basic settlement services, such as translation and counselling. Changes in immigration policy have included specification of access to services.

In 2002, Canadian immigration law was revised somewhat through passage of Bill C-11, the Immigration and Refugee Protection Act. This legislation requires that immigration policy fulfill Canada's international obligations (George, 2006). This law permits three basic groups to enter Canada as permanent residents: economic immigrants, family-class immigrants, and refugees. Each of these groups is positioned differently in relation to the state and its resources. Economic immigrants are allowed into the country on the basis of financial assets and/or skills considered important to the country and have generally been granted permanent resident status before arrival. Recent changes in immigration qualifications for skilled workers place more emphasis on employment "flexibility" based on education and language skills, rather than on specific occupations. The introduction of the Provincial Nominee Program, first adopted by Manitoba in 1999 and then by other provinces, and the Canadian Experience Class (created in 2008) mean that an increasing number of these immigrants will arrive and work in Canada for a minimum of two years prior to receiving permanent status (Gates-Gasse, 2010), after which they will have access to the same social programs as Canadian citizens. Family-class immigrants, on the other hand, are permitted entry into the country on the basis of their relationship to a citizen or permanent resident already in the country. Entry of family members is contingent on a promise that the sponsoring relative will provide for the arriving family member(s) for three years (previously ten years) following arrival. Arriving family members are therefore not eligible for many programs and resources available to other residents. In some provinces they are not eligible for welfare, even if the sponsoring relative abdicates responsibility for them. These immigrants can, however, access health care through provincial auspices. These restrictions present some difficult problems for social workers, who may be attempting to assist people ineligible for services available to others. In addition, the new law expands the temporary worker program, which allows temporary residence status for foreign workers, students, and some people on humanitarian grounds.

Canadian immigration law defines two types of refugees. "Convention" refugees are those designated under the terms of the United Nations Convention Relating to the Status of Refugees. They may be selected either in Canada or abroad and are accorded full participation rights. A range of basic programs, including housing and financial assistance, are available to government-sponsored refugees in their first year in Canada. The other refugee group consists of people in need of protection. These claimants enter Canada without documentation with the hope of establishing a "credible claim" to stay in the country. Those who pass successfully through an initial screening become eligible for work permits and some provincial and municipal services, including health care.

Aboriginal Peoples

Aboriginal peoples, including those of mixed origin, constitute about 4.5 percent of Canada's population (Indian and Northern Affairs, 2007). However, they are often overrepresented as clients in the service sector. Of relevance to social work and social policy is the fact that many different First Nations groups exist; for instance, there are 11 Aboriginal language families in Canada (Morrison & Willson, 1986, as cited in Frideres & Gadacz, 2005), several dozen dialects among these language groups, and about 600 recognized First Nations governments or bands. Also, different Aboriginal peoples stand in different relationships to the Canadian state. The term *Aboriginal* came into common usage following passage of the Constitution Act, 1982. It can refer both to status Indians, who are registered by the federal government, and to non-status Indians, who are not registered. Inuit are Aboriginal people who are culturally and legally distinct from Indian peoples and who are not considered to be registered Indians. Métis people are those whose heritage is mixed Aboriginal and non-Aboriginal. Métis do not have rights under the Indian Act.

It is generally acknowledged that most of Canada's Aboriginal peoples live in difficult and often impoverished conditions and that they have for many decades experienced severe structural inequities. This reality is the result of events of the past as well as continued relations between First Nations and the Canadian state. Before contact with Europeans, Aboriginal peoples generally lived in small communities, and although there are significant variations among groups, many operated on principles that all members of the community would share resources and have a valued role in the group (Mawhiney, 1995). Contact with Europeans, who were determined to dominate both Aboriginal peoples and their land, resulted in severe damage to and reorganization of Aboriginal cultural forms (Bourgeault, 1988). Currently, more than one-half of status Indians, now more often called *First Nations*, reside on reserves, most of them quite small. The Aboriginal population is projected to increase substantially more than the general population over the next two decades, and the population of registered Indians is expected to increase by 40 percent by 2029 (Indian and Northern Affairs, n.d.). This growth is due to several factors, including rising birth rates, reinstatement or inheritance of status, and migration.

The Indian Act of 1876—passed shortly after the British North America Act (1867), now known as the Constitution Act, 1982—marked the end of Indian self-government, which was replaced by federal control over the cultural, social, economic, and political activities of those defined in the Act as registered Indians. This definition was limited; those who fell outside this category became ineligible for the benefits of health, education, and social services provided in the Indian Act. Until recently, the definition of status was patrilineal: Indian women who married non-registered men lost their status. In February 1985, legislation was brought to Parliament to establish more gender equality in the Act. The changes allowed bands in Canada to determine their own eligibility criteria for band membership and assured the protection of rights for those who are band members. Aboriginal women who married non-registered men now have their status back and have access to federal programs as well as services off the reserves (Castellano, 2002). Further, in 2008, Bill C-21 repealed Section 67 of the Canadian Human Rights Act, which shielded the federal and First Nations governments from human rights complaints related to actions arising from the Indian Act. Section 67 was seen as especially prejudicial to Aboriginal women deprived of their status through marriage.

Aboriginal peoples who fall under the Indian Act access many programs and funding sources differently than other Canadians do. In fact, the Indian Act of 1876 gave the federal government jurisdiction over Indians and their land (Patterson, 1987), and agents employed by Indian Affairs administered both benefits and sanctions. Also regulated by the Indian Act were legal rights, inheritance, taxation, wills, and many other matters. Until 1960, registered Indians who voted in a Canadian election lost their Aboriginal status and rights under this Act. Unlike for other citizens and residents of Canada, the health and welfare services received by registered Indians flow through the federal rather than the provincial governments, which otherwise claim these areas as their jurisdiction. Over time, exceptions to this rule have been worked out by intergovernmental arrangements (McGilly, 1998, 7).

These measures have had profound effects on Aboriginal peoples in Canada. For example, education, which is provided provincially to other Canadians, used to be administered entirely by the federal government for registered Indians. Residential schools were the required form of education for Aboriginal children between the late nineteenth and mid-twentieth centuries, with the result that many Aboriginal children were removed from their families at an early age and sent to boarding schools outside their own communities. Similarly, child welfare, normally a provincially administered service, was supposed to be delivered by the federal government to registered Indians. But since many children attended residential schools a large part of the year, little service was provided (Johnston, 1983). In 1951, the Indian Act was revised to recognize provincial law as applying to First Nations (Mawhiney, 1995). Aboriginal children were increasingly encouraged to attend provincially funded schools and access provincial services. After 1951, child welfare services were increasingly extended to reserves, with the result that many children over the next several decades came into the care of child protection authorities (Johnston, 1983). Many of these children were adopted by families outside the province or even the country, and records of the whereabouts of many of these children disappeared. Others were raised in non-Indian care and became alienated from their own parents and communities. Today, most child welfare services on reserves are administered by bands through a variety of funding mechanisms (Indian and Northern Affairs, 2007).

Other services to Aboriginal peoples came primarily from the federal government after 1951; however, these services existed at a very low level, as revealed by the 1966 Hawthorn Report. The Hawthorn Report revealed that the ideal of equality among different groups of people in Canada was not being met for Aboriginal peoples. Subsequently, a 1969 White Paper recommended that Indian people receive services through the same channels and government agencies as other Canadians; but this proposal was rejected by Indian leaders and organizations because it implied the phasing out of rights guaranteed by the Indian Act. Currently, with the exception of child welfare, most provincial governments do not extend services to reserves. In the North, where about half the population is Aboriginal but where there are few reserves, services are generally delivered by the territorial governments (Indian and Northern Affairs, 2007). The funding and delivery of health, education, and welfare services to Indians on reserves is a federal responsibility. Section 91(24) of the Constitution gives the federal government the power to provide universal welfare benefits to registered Indians without encroaching on provincial powers. Access to services is at the band level. Bands are empowered under Section 81 of the Indian Act to enact and administer bylaws. In addition, most bands have developed sufficient administrative structure and capacity to deliver federally funded programs and services (Shewell & Spagnut, 1995). There are wide variations in how these tasks are accomplished, but generally speaking, service delivery through the bands has replaced administration by employees of Indian and Northern Affairs (INAC) across Canada. In 2006–07, INAC transferred about $5.5 billion to Aboriginal recipients (Indian and Northern Affairs, 2007).

In addition, under the auspices of the Indian Act, the federal government funds the Social Development Program, which administers several services. These include child and family services; adult care, involving basic homemaker services for the chronically ill and elderly; and social assistance. The latter continues to be governed primarily by INAC, a situation that symbolizes a continuing "dependent" relationship of First Nations peoples on the government of Canada. At the start of the twenty-first century, INAC social services formed the sole source of support for many Aboriginals. A recent study shows the median incomes of Aboriginal people living on reserve are no more than $15 000 (Wilson & Macdonald, 2010). INAC acknowledges that almost half of First Nations people on reserve have incomes of less than $10 000 (Indian and Northern Affairs Canada, n.d.). Since the 1960s, the federal government has made many efforts to implement economic development programs intended to increase First Nations self-sufficiency. These programs, however, have not resulted in improvements to the economic fortunes of many reserves across Canada (Shewell, 2007).

Since the early 1800s, the overall policy of the federal government has been the assimilation of Aboriginal peoples into the general population. Many efforts to achieve this goal have been made, but Aboriginal peoples have been determined to avoid this outcome. Over the past three decades, Aboriginal organizations and leaders have pressed for increasing rights and self-government. Advances in this direction have been made—for instance, in control of education and child welfare in particular locations. The Constitution Act of 1982 recognizes Aboriginal rights, specifically identifying Indian, Inuit, and Métis peoples. The wording of the Act places Aboriginal peoples in a new relationship with both federal and provincial governments, and represents a new phase in the long relationship between Canada and First Nations (Patterson, 1987).

Three main themes have been pursued in the recent political activities of First Nations peoples: (1) ending the paternalistic relationship that is the legacy of the

Indian Act; (2) devolving social programs from federal and provincial auspices to First Nations' control; and (3) working toward self-government (Shewell & Spagnut, 1995). Another significant goal is the "revitalization" of Aboriginal communities (Castellano, 2002). The scope of self-government negotiations concerned with social welfare is inclusive—health, justice, education, housing, social security, child welfare, and social services are all "on the table." Control of child welfare has been of particular importance to First Nations peoples. To stem the outflow of their children from their communities and to control the socialization of their children, First Nations representatives will likely pursue full jurisdiction in this and other social policy areas in future talks.

Women

Social work has traditionally focused on women as clients, and the field is dominated by women as workers. However, until the "second wave" of feminism in the 1970s, many social workers were not aware of the special interests of women as a group. Of course, this lack of awareness is no longer the case. Social workers work with women more often than men because women are more disadvantaged in relation to social welfare and face different kinds of life tasks than men, tasks that often involve dependants as well as themselves. As a result of these differences, policies addressing women's particular needs have been promoted and in some cases adopted. Social workers need to be aware of these policies and the debates surrounding them to work effectively with both male and female populations.

Changing demography is a different issue with respect to gender than with some other minority groups. Females generally compose just over half of the total Canadian population. However, females tend to dominate in older age groups. In 2006, about 56 percent of the population aged 65 and over were female (*The Daily*, July 17, 2007).

In addition, until relatively recently, women have been situated quite differently from men in relation to the law. Eichler (1987) notes that women were not considered to be "persons" under English Common Law. Following this tradition, the Dominion Elections Act (1906) contained a clause stating that "no woman, idiot, lunatic, or criminal shall vote" (CBC, 2000). Not until 1918 were Canadian women accorded the federal vote. In 1929, they were granted legal identity as "persons," and it remained for the 1982 Charter of Rights and Freedoms to guarantee women equality before the law.

Women have also been situated differently from men in relation to the paid labour force and its programs and benefits. The arrangements of industrial capitalism led to separation of the public and the private worlds of labour in the early part of the twentieth century. While men came increasingly to occupy the public and higher-status domain of paid work, women were consigned to the private world of unpaid and often invisible caring and household labour. Historically, there has been meagre support for women who were not attached to a breadwinning male. While a succession of policies has addressed this situation, the separation of the public and private worlds continues to have repercussions for women (and men) today. As Eichler (1987) notes, the husband as breadwinner was the statistical norm until the 1980s. More recently, women have entered the paid labour force in large numbers. Many of these women are employed part time, however, often because of child care or other responsibilities, and most women continue to work in female-dominated occupations, which provide lower status and pay (Statistics Canada, 2006, March 7).

A report developed for the Canadian Research Institute for the Advancement of Women (Morris, 2007) confirms that women make up the majority of the poor in Canada, noting that even the United Nations has commented on the high rate of Canadian women who live in poverty. Today, one in seven Canadian women, or 2.4 million, are poor. The report demonstrates how membership in more than one disadvantaged group increases women's vulnerability. Women with disabilities are especially vulnerable to poverty. Those living in a household rather than an institution earn an average of $13 000 per year. Recent figures show that the average annual income for Aboriginal women is $13 300 compared to $18 200 for Aboriginal men. Visible minority women fare slightly better than Aboriginal women, with an annual average income of $16 621. Employment does not necessarily improve these results.

There were substantial changes in the relationship of women to the paid labour force during the twentieth century. At the beginning of the century, women made up 13.3 percent of the total labour force. In 2006, women constituted 47 percent of the labour force (Almey, n.d.). Along with this change have come other changes in women's life paths. Women marry later and on average have their first baby at a later age. Availability of consumer goods has increased the possibility of spending less time doing domestic labour, thus freeing women to enter the paid labour force. At the same time, the rising cost of basic needs has come to require increased paid labour to cover expenses. Women have often taken paid jobs to close the gap between expenses and income, but their earnings continue to lag behind those of men. In 1994, women still earned only 62.3 percent of men's earnings. However, the wage gap between women and men in full-time work has been narrowing. In 1967, women earned 58 percent of men's wages; in 2004, the ratio was 71 percent (Pay Equity Task Force, 2004, 13), causing some women to declare September 17 of each year "Now You're Working for Free" day (Cornish & Faraday, 2008). According to Jackson and Robinson (2000), this narrowing gap was due only in part to rising earnings of women; other causes are increased time worked by women and the falling wages of men. Although women made strides in public sector labour force participation during the 1980s and early 1990s, they are still placed differently in the labour market than men. Women continue to be highly overrepresented in the 10 lowest-paid occupations and underrepresented in the 10 highest-paid occupations (Pay Equity Task Force, 2004, Tables 1.4 and 1.5). Also, women represent 70 percent of all part-time employees, about the same proportion as in the 1970s (*The Daily*, March 7, 2006).

As feminist scholars have been reporting for the past two decades, women do not access or benefit from social welfare policies in the same way that men do. Pateman (1992) analyzed the income security system as two-tiered. The top tier provides benefits to people based on participation in the paid labour force.

Canadian examples are the CPP/QPP, EI, and provincial workers' compensation programs. The second tier is available to the dependants of people in the first category. Canadian examples include provincially/municipally administered welfare assistance programs and selective daycare programs. Women are much more likely to make claims on the state through family or dependency status than as "workers" or as public persons (Pateman, 1992, as cited in Evans, 1997, 95). These second-tier policies deliver low benefit levels and have stringent eligibility requirements and means tests, and typically involve considerable scrutiny. Men are much more likely to access first-tier programs that generally carry less stigma, provide higher benefits, and are accessed through administrative means (Evans, 1997). When women do access these programs, as they increasingly do because of greater labour force participation, they still benefit less as a group because of lower pay and higher proportions of part-time work. Women aged 65 and older are almost twice as likely to be poor than men of the same age. Also, more older women than men living alone are poor—43 percent compared with 31 percent of men living alone (Pay Equity Task Force, 2004).

Historically, there have been social policies specific to women, especially in their roles as mothers of dependent children. The provincially mounted "mothers' pension" program, initiated in Manitoba in 1916, is an example. This selective policy provided benefits to mothers only if they were raising children alone and were deemed "worthy." The universal Family Allowance (1940–92), a federally financed and administered direct transfer to mothers for each child in their care on a monthly basis, was another example. Contemporary assistance policies are couched in gender-neutral terms; however, women continue to be the primary recipients of assistance claimed on the basis of providing care for young children. In fact, it was not until 1984 that single fathers were able to access assistance benefits on the same terms as single mothers.

Over the past several decades, a range of policy initiatives dealing with the special concerns of women have been developed. Provincial policies funding women's shelters and other supports for victims of domestic violence are specific to women. Policies dealing with childcare, pornography, sexual assault, sexual harassment, and sexual abuse are not necessarily confined to women but arose from women's concerns and experiences and are generally considered to apply to females much more often than to males. Equal pay legislation and policies are specifically aimed at reducing salary inequalities for women. These policies provide the legal framework to enforce equal pay for women who do the same work as men or who do work of "equal value." In addition, there are calls to redress policy directions that leave women in old age at a disadvantage in terms of pensions and benefits (Sayeed, 2002). Wages for housework and some form of pension credit for women whose labour has primarily been in the home are examples of suggested policy directions. The Pay Equity Task Force noted that women of colour, Aboriginal women, and women with disabilities suffer "double discrimination" in their wages and recommended that the framework for examining pay equity be broadened to focus on these groups. Recommendations have also been made for more proactive pay equity legislation (National Association of Women and the Law, 2007), but the federal government has so far refused to act on this recommendation.

Over the past three decades, the federal government has created an elaborate structure for incorporating women's issues into public policy. During the 1970s and 1980s, this structure came to include a minister responsible for the status of women, an Advisory Council on the Status of Women (SWC) at "arm's-length" from the government, and a Women's Program at the Secretary of State, which funded many women's organizations (Eichler, 1987). In 2006, the federal government announced a 40 percent ($5 million) funding cut to SWC. In 2007, the funding was restored, although only a small amount is allocated to existing programs (Status of Women Canada, 2007). In addition, provinces have their own organizational structures specific to women's issues and concerns. In the era of downsizing and downloading, women's groups are concerned that these structures and the funding for women's groups they have supported are diminishing. In 2010, the federal government has defunded or reduced funding for a number of women's groups, including the Canadian Research Institute for the Advancement of Women (CRIAW) and the Sisters in Spirit initiative, which has brought to public attention the number of Aboriginal women who are murdered or missing (Airdrie, 2010).

Women's participation in the paid labour force increased dramatically during the twentieth century and especially in the past three or four decades. In spite of this, most recent studies suggest that women continue to perform most of the labour in the household, including child care. In addition, women are increasingly required to compensate for the recent downsizing of many former programs and services by caring for vulnerable and dependent family members. For many years, women's organizations have lobbied for a national childcare policy that would support supervised, safe care for children while their mothers are in the paid labour force. Although repeatedly promised, as of now there is no such policy, a situation that continues to disadvantage women in the labour force. Instead, the federal government created the "child care allowance" in 2006, which provides $1200 per year for each child under the age of six to support costs of care, a mere fraction of the real cost. This program has been criticized by many as insufficient for this purpose. Only Quebec has an accessible childcare program, one offering subsidized childcare spaces at a rate of $7.00 per day.

The economic downturn of 2008 affected employment prospects for both men and women. The unemployment rate was below 6 percent before the downturn but reached a high of nearly 9 percent in 2009 and declined to around 8 percent in 2010 (Statistics Canada, 2010c). Gains in employment are greater in part-time work, where many women are employed. These changes in market conditions are far-reaching, and social workers will need to inform themselves regularly about the gender implications of current labour-market trends.

Sexual Orientation

Not all groups in Canada have historically viewed same-sex relationships in negative terms. Some Aboriginal people, for instance, recognize the existence of people who combine aspects of both female and male. These "two-spirited" people are regarded as especially fortunate and associated with power and generosity. In contrast, European settlers, both English and French, adopted punitive positions toward same-sex relations. At times, Canadians of European background have shown tolerance toward same-sex relationships—for instance, in all-male situations of long duration, such as lumbering or mining camps (O'Brien & Weir, 1995). The general Canadian climate regarding homosexuality, however, has been one of hostility, with discrimination of many kinds evident in both public and private life. In recent years, the identification of sexually diverse populations has expanded to include not only lesbians and gays, but also bisexual, transgendered and transsexual people, two-spirit, intersex, queer, and/or questioning individuals (LGBTTTIQQ, or LGBTQ for short), thus disrupting the binaries of sexual orientation (female/male, gay/straight) and somewhat complicating our understanding of what social policies may need to account for.

Canada has long had a single national law governing same-sex sexual activity: the Criminal Code. As recently as 1967, men engaging in sexual activity with other men were considered "dangerous sexual offenders" under the Code and were subject to imprisonment. In 1969, provisions of the Code dealing with this issue were amended to decriminalize sexual behaviour between consenting adults.

Since the end of World War II, challenges to discrimination against gay, lesbian, and bisexual individuals have been increasingly raised at every level of government around the world, including the United Nations (Wintemute, 1995). Representatives of these populations have been trying to establish a general principle that discrimination based on sexual orientation is inherently wrong. The adoption of such a principle would place the onus of responsibility on those who practise discrimination to demonstrate why such discrimination should be permitted. In Canada, two strategies can be used to establish this principle. One is the political strategy designed to create, change, or repeal laws in order to develop a non-discriminatory legislative framework. The second strategy is a legal one, carried out through courts and human rights tribunals designed to demonstrate that a particular instance of discrimination violates existing human rights legislation.

Through the 1970s and into the 1980s, several legal battles, some at the level of the Supreme Court of Canada, were fought concerning issues of discrimination against, or unequal treatment of, gay and lesbian individuals and groups. The advent of the Charter of Rights gave the Court the power to strike down laws depriving individuals of their rights. Section 15 of the Charter guarantees equal treatment under the law without discrimination. Although sexual orientation is not specifically enumerated in this section, court challenges have produced precedents confirming sexual orientation as grounds for protection under Section 15 (Young, 1994). The Charter of Rights and Freedoms has also helped to produce new debates, litigation, and directions concerning issues of sexual orientation (Woodford, Newman, Brotman, & Ryan, 2010).

Over the past several decades, there has been increased acceptance of gay and lesbian people, decreasing discrimination, and progress on social policy issues (O'Neill, 2006). For instance, Canada's Immigration Act at one time did not permit entry of gay people into Canada. This provision was dropped in 1977, but gay people were still prevented from sponsoring same-sex partners. In 2002, Bill C-11, the Immigration and Refugee Protection Act, replaced the old law. The new law allows sponsorship of a same-sex partner and additionally allows the admission of refugees on grounds of discrimination based on sexual orientation. A 1998 Supreme Court decision concerning employment discrimination because of sexual orientation ordered Alberta to include the words *sexual orientation* in its discrimination statute (*Vriend v. Alta*, 1998). As L'Heureux-Dubé (2000) notes, this decision shows the importance of looking beyond the Charter in the search for protection of equality rights. There have also been many political campaigns and court challenges over several decades based on the goal of including sexual orientation in human rights codes. All provinces and territories now include sexual orientation in their codes, and the Canadian Human Rights Act was amended in 1996 to include protection for gay and lesbian people (O'Neill, 2006).

Undoubtedly, the most significant policy shift in the last few years has been the legalization of gay marriage. In the past, both social policy and discourse tended to pose "the family" as separate and different from homosexuality, with the family symbolizing stability, responsibility, and happiness, and homosexuality representing a threat to this valued institution (O'Brien & Weir, 1995). Legal and social precedents defined *marriage* as inherently involving opposite-sex couples, with at least the theoretical possibility of procreation. In the 1990s, advocates mounted challenges to these traditional ideas about the family. From a social policy perspective, a central issue was whether "the family" can or ought to include lesbian and gay couples. From a human rights standpoint, the issue was whether it was discriminatory to deny same-sex couples benefits and entitlements enjoyed by heterosexual couples.

The Charter of Rights, Section 15, has been successfully used to challenge traditional laws related to marriage. In 2002, the House of Commons Justice Committee debated the question of gay marriage, finding a majority of witnesses in favour. By 2003, most provincial jurisdictions had passed laws allowing same-sex marriage, based on Section 15 of the Charter guaranteeing equal treatment under the law. The following year, the Supreme Court of Canada decided that the federal government had the power to legislate on the issue. The Civil Marriage Act, Bill C-38, permitting legal marriage between same-sex partners, was passed in 2005 by a narrow but convincing majority vote in Parliament. The Conservative government revisited the issue the following year, initiating a free vote on whether to reopen discussion on the legality of same-sex marriages, essentially with the intention of revoking the law. The initiative failed by a decisive margin, the subject was declared to be settled, and gay marriage remains the law of the land. The law means that same-sex partners have equal rights, obligations, and benefits of the marital relationship. Some issues continue to be challenged. The Supreme Court decision on the Hislop case in 2007 reiterates that surviving same-sex partners are eligible for equal CPP benefits, but it did not sanction retroactive payments past the preceding year (Egale, 2006).

While this policy shift has received much national and international attention and has been advocated by many gay and lesbian people and groups, it is not viewed by some members of this community as the most important or even an appropriate social goal. Inclusion in law on the same basis as heterosexual couples is referred to by Cossman (1996) and many others (e.g., Mulé, 2010) as an assimilationist position. There are substantial differences among advocates, however, concerning whether assimilation is the most advantageous policy direction. Mulé (2005) describes the assimilationist position as a pursuit for equality leading to tolerance and legitimization of a sexually diverse population by the mainstream society. It is based on liberal notions of equal rights and tends to equate legal change with social change. In contrast, he describes a "liberationist" position held by many gay and lesbian people and groups as a challenge to existing social codes, freedom from traditional constraints, and self-fulfillment based on creation of new forms of social organization, including the notion of registered domestic partnerships (RDPs), a proposal involving the replacement of government-sanctioned marriage with registration schemes allowing "private ordering of both conjugal and non-conjugal relationships" (Mulé, 2010, 76). Mulé cautions against too rigid a division between the assimilationist and liberationist positions, noting that each position exists on a continuum and each applies the strategies of the other at times. However, it is certainly the assimilationist or "equality" approach that is dominating issues of social policy at present.

Gay and lesbian people currently have other policy issues on their agenda. One relates to consultations and proposed legislation dealing with "sex laws" (Mulé, 2005). Proposed changes would include revision of laws dealing with definitions of "indecent acts," the age of consent for sexual activity, and the definition of a "common bawdy house." Parliamentary discussion of such issues as solicitation began a few years ago. Bill C-2, first introduced in 2005, was intended to alter sections of the Code related to exploitation of children and age of consent for sexual activity. Advocacy groups were divided somewhat along assimilationist and liberationist lines on provisions in this Bill, especially with respect to the age of consent for sexual activity. The Bill was passed in 2008, as Part 2 of the Tackling Violent Crime Act, in which the age of consent was changed from 14 to 16. Health policy, especially at the organizational level, is also an issue documented in literature (Ryan, Brotman, & Rowe, 2000; Mulé et al, 2009). Public policy awareness of gay and lesbian health issues has typically not gone beyond acknowledgment of HIV/AIDS. Issues relevant to gay and lesbian people include recognition of the impact on health of their status as a group subject to homophobia, as well as problems specific to this population, such as family planning, certain cancers, and barriers to accessing health care.

These challenges raise questions about social policy. One is why minorities such as those included in the LGBTQ communities have not been more readily recognized by social policy experts. Fiona Williams (1989) argues that social policies have always been intertwined with subordinations based on gender and race, but that these diversities have been hidden by the more universal categories of the social policy field, such as class and poverty. Certainly, those discriminated against on the basis of sexual orientation remain a marginal voice in social policy discourse, and the policy-based literature focused on them remains very small.

Another question is what constitutes social policy itself. Writing from a feminist perspective, Linda Gordon (1990) criticizes traditional approaches to social policy for being preoccupied with legislation and formal programs. Many writers in the field, she contends, do not understand that policy is constructed of practices as well as written legislation. This reality, as O'Brien (1998) notes, challenges traditional assumptions that the state is the primary site of power. Other critics suggest instead that state power is more fragmented and less coherent than the traditional field of social policy has assumed. However, it is important to note that much of the policy discourse related to sexual orientation, as well as policies themselves, are shaped through such state-sponsored processes as court challenges, rather than through traditional processes of policy analysis and development. In fact, in the case of sexual orientation, court challenges currently appear to be the primary instrument for change.

Sexual orientation is now included in the Social Work Code of Ethics (CASW, 2005). This addition means that the profession now formally recognizes the existence of these groups and bears some responsibility for taking action to reduce discrimination against them. However, Mulé (2008) argues that the profession needs to push harder for social policy that recognizes and addresses the specific needs and issues of members of these communities, rather than continuing to rely on human rights legislation.

Disablement

People with disabilities have at different times in history been seen as symbols of divine punishment, as sacred beings, and as members of the deserving poor (Roeher Institute, 1996). In ancient Greek philosophy, disability was viewed as a deficit to humanness. In Western liberal thinking, disability has constituted a reason for exclusion from society and civil life. Canada's first residential institution for people with intellectual disabilities opened in 1859 in Ontario. Over the following century, institutional care dominated as the preferred form of service (Roeher Institute, 1996). The eugenics movement in the early part of the twentieth century, spawned partly by new technology, led to very punitive measures for people with both physical and intellectual disabilities, including institutionalization, sterilization, segregation, and medication (Stainton, 1994). Only within the past two decades have community-based services become the preferred service policy.

Vocabulary in the area of disablement has been confusing and has led to the misunderstanding of policy issues. The term *disability* itself covers a wide range of descriptors. Disabilities may be physical, intellectual, or emotional, and may be congenital or the result of life circumstances. Some disabilities are visible, and some, such as deafness, are invisible. An individual's disability status may change over time. Wide-ranging specifics of disability may be partly responsible for the fragmentation of social policy in this area. The 1980 publication of the International Classification of Impairments, Disabilities and Handicaps (ICIDH) by the World Health Organization was significant in clarifying terminology. This report identifies three dimensions of disablement. *Impairment* is defined in the report as an abnormality of physiological or anatomical structure or function. A *disability* is any limitation in ability to perform functions considered "normal" for a human being or required for a social role or occupation. A *handicap* is the resulting disadvantage. The term *disablement* refers to all three dimensions (Bickenbach, 1993). A Canadian perspective on terminology is presented in the glossary of a report called *Disability-Related Policy in Canada* (The Disability-Related Policy Website, n.d.).

Canada is signatory to a number of international laws guaranteeing protection for human rights generally and for rights for people with disabilities particularly. The Universal Declaration of Human Rights (UDHR, 1948) is based on three principles: freedom, equality, and dignity. A subsequent U.N. document, the International Bill of Human Rights (IBHR, 1978), articulates rights of access to the economic resources required for participation in social and economic life, participation in decisions affecting one's own life, and affirmation of the worth of each person. Two further relevant U.N. documents are the Declaration on the Rights of Mentally Retarded Persons (1971) and the Declaration on the Rights of Disabled Persons (1975). Although not legally binding, these documents provide a moral basis for the formation of national legislation and policy commitments to people with disabilities. They express the principles of care, economic security, guardianship when necessary, freedom from exploitation, and rights of consent to the full extent possible given individual circumstances. A variety of more recent U.N. documents, most of which are not binding, indicate a trend in the direction of an international human rights framework for addressing issues related to disability (Rioux & Samson, 2006).

Critics of these international instruments note that the framers represent Western philosophy and attention to the individual, largely ignoring collective interests and rights (Rioux & Samson, 2006). Nevertheless, it is clear that both national and international human rights movements have strongly influenced relations between people with disabilities and the state (Stainton, 1994). Significant support and publicity for disability issues resulted from the U.N. designation of 1981 as the International Year of Disabled Persons. Later, the United Nations announced the International Decade of Disabled Persons, leading to a sustained focus on issues of disability rights for a longer period of time. Part of the Canadian response to this attention was a report tabled in 1981 called *Obstacles*, written by the Special Committee on the Disabled and the Handicapped. In it, three aspirations by and for people with disabilities were articulated: (1) respect and dignity, (2) empowerment to participate in decisions regarding their own lives and futures, and (3) accommodations providing the *means* to participate.

Also in the early 1980s, the Canadian Charter of Rights and Freedoms was adopted. Section 15 of the Charter, which enumerates specific groups protected under the Charter, includes those with a "mental or physical disability." Although Kallen (1989) notes that no right is beyond encroachment by state action, she also describes inclusion of disability in the Charter as a "monumental constitutional breakthrough." Inclusion provides rights protection as well as the potential for specific legal challenges based on this section.

In addition, persons with disabilities are one of four designated groups specifically mentioned in Canada's Employment Equity Act of 1986. This legislation requires federally regulated employers to implement equity programs and report annually on their results. In 1987, the Standing Committee on Human Rights and the Status of Disabled Persons was established by the House of Commons; and in 1991, the federal government launched the five-year National Strategy for the Integration of Persons with Disabilities. Both initiatives have been instrumental in advocacy efforts. Disability is also included in the human rights legislation of provinces, territories, and the federal government.

In the 1990s, several reports issued at the federal level provided more focus and commitment to policy relevant to disablement. In the mid-1990s, the Federal–Provincial–Territorial Council on Social Policy Renewal considered this area a major focus. In 1996, the Scott Task Force, representing several federal departments, was charged with the task of defining the role of the federal government as it relates to the disability community. *In Unison: A Canadian Approach to Disability Issues*, a vision paper following up recommendations of the Scott Report, was issued in 1998. This document includes principles for ensuring full citizenship, including removal of barriers to full civic participation, for the estimated 14.3 percent of Canadians who identified themselves in 2006 as having a disability (Human Resources and Skills Development Canada, 2009; Gilmour, 2010). In 2005, the federal government announced improvements to tax measures related to disability, including the Disability Tax Credit. While important, critics also say that fairness and inclusion for people with disabilities must also involve investment in technical and personal supports for this population (Torjman, 2005).

Rioux and Samson (2006) suggest that two basic approaches to disabilities have shaped social policy over the past few decades. The most prominent is the biomedical model, which assumes an individual "abnormality" that can be prevented or ameliorated through intervention by qualified professionals. In one version of this approach, people with disabilities are positioned as "other" (113) and may then be considered as having little to contribute to society. Another version of this approach focuses less on the impairment itself and more on the limitations imposed on an individual's functional capacity. This idea leads to a goal of living as "normally" as possible. Second, a more recent approach to understanding disabilities is a focus on the social and economic conditions that impede full participation in social, political, and economic life. One aspect of this approach is to focus on sites for state intervention, resulting in the adaptation of the social and physical environments that act as barriers to participation. A "human rights" model, which is the most recent version of this approach, looks beyond specific contexts to examine broad underlying factors that prevent "some groups from participating in society as equals" (Rioux & Samson, 2006, 115). Impairment is then one of many determinants of exclusion. This idea leads to a much broader policy approach, one requiring a paradigm shift and substantive policy changes at many levels.

Bickenbach (2006) argues that anti-discrimination laws should be based on particular definitions of disability. He suggests that the International Classification of Functioning, Disability, and Health (ICF), a document of the World Health

Organization, provides a solid framework of "body, personal capacity and social functioning" (79). In this view, disability is universal because functional capacity is universal: "disability is normality" (82), something everyone shares at some point. Social inequality as it relates to disability then becomes an issue of distributive justice—or injustice.

Canadian social policy concerning disablement is quite diverse, involving all three levels of government and reflecting both the medical and social models described above (Rioux & Samson, 2006). Bickenbach (1993, 5) lists 14 distinct policy areas through which services related to disablement are considered and delivered:

1. biomedical services;
2. employment programs;
3. autonomy protection;
4. rehabilitation and institutional care;
5. independent living;
6. housing;
7. income security;
8. physical access;
9. compensation;
10. communications and access to information/education;
11. health and safety legislation;
12. research;
13. human rights; and
14. anti-discrimination.

A 1990 report issued by the House of Commons Standing Committee on Human Rights and the Status of Disabled Persons noted the fragmentation of policy concerning disability. The report, *A Consensus of Action: The Economic Integration of Disabled Persons*, demonstrated that policy in this arena is inconsistent, ambiguous, contradictory, and often merely an "add-on" to other social policy.

Prior to the 1970s, disability of any kind was generally viewed as illness or abnormality in Canadian policy. Since that time, perceptions of disability have changed as a result of the advocacy efforts of Canadians with disabilities. Advocacy has been pursued in the form of three challenges to Canadian society and government (Valentine, 2001). One asserts the right of people with disabilities to organize autonomously, outside of the health care and policy sectors. The second asserts the right of disabled people to equal treatment as individuals with full citizenship. The third develops the argument that disability is a social construction, often more reflective of the fears and feelings of others than of the experiences of people with disabilities.

In Canada, as in the United States, a policy of deinstitutionalization has been in effect for more than two decades. Stroman (1989) identifies three dimensions to deinstitutionalization: (1) the release of people from institutions, (2) specific practices designed to prevent people from entering institutions, (3) and modification of institutional practices to make them less institutional in character. Five forces converged to cause the movement away from institutional care:

> the growth of an advocacy movement, involving parents and organized associations;

> indictment and exposure of large institutions as dehumanizing and harmful;

> acceptance of the "normalization" principle—that people with disabilities can and should have access to normal living conditions;

> development of community-based services; and

> escalating costs of care in institutional settings.

Community services to supplement and replace institutional care have been initiated largely by local organizations, often with funding from federal or provincial governments. In this era of cutbacks, developing a sufficient funding base and service infrastructure (as well as the social commitment required) for the wide range of community-based services required for people with disabilities to participate to the fullest extent possible in public life has become a serious policy issue. There is now a disability tax credit designed to provide tax relief to individuals with impairments who need assistance with basic daily living activities. The credit amount is fully indexed to inflation. The CPP also has a component intended to protect "working Canadians" (Lawand & Kloosterman, 2006, 268) against loss of income from any kind of disability, provided the disability is "severe" and "prolonged." Requirements to qualify for benefits are quite stringent, and although there has been a recent trend to encourage beneficiaries to return to work, most receive benefits for long periods of time, often until they are 65 years of age, when they become eligible for other benefits. Quebec operates a similar program under the QPP (Lawand & Kloosterman, 2006). There are also programs designed to enhance the employability of Canadians with disabilities (Jongbloed, 2006). In spite of these programs, employment rates of Canadians with disabilities remain far below those without (53.5 percent versus 75.1 percent, respectively) and incomes of Canadians with disabilities are only about two-thirds of those without (Human Resources and Skills Development Canada, 2009).

Increased attention to children with disabilities is currently being encouraged by community advocates. Available research shows that about 3.7 percent of Canadian children aged 0 to 19 have disabilities (Human Resources and Skills Development Canada, 2009), and this percentage is expected to increase as medical technology helps to save the lives of more infants compromised at birth and in early childhood. Valentine (2001) shows that many of these children have multiple disadvantages. For instance, he found that children with disabilities are more likely than other children to live in poor families and in "problem" housing. However, there is as yet no integrated and clear policy focus on this population. Valentine (2001) recommends three "enabling conditions" for improving services: adequate income, sufficient services for effective parenting to occur, and a supportive community environment.

Advocacy groups generally articulate the most important social policy goals as self-determination and equality. Self-determination for people with disabilities should mean the same thing it does for the non-disabled: the opportunity to participate in making decisions about matters that affect their lives and support in developing capacities enabling them to reach their goals. Equality means having the support needed (including special accommodations where necessary) to provide all people with an equal claim on society's offerings (Roeher Institute, 1996). Stainton (2005) distinguishes the current approach from the past. The concern now is capacity rather than outcome—with how choices are made rather than what choices are made. Also, the ability to act on that choice is key. Finally, Stainton calls attention to the "difference dilemma," referring to the issue of what people require to achieve full citizenship. Different people, he notes, require different treatment to achieve the same capacity for citizenship. Some critics warn that these goals may be difficult to achieve in a neo-liberal era that places more responsibility on individuals to guide their own fates. In this context, "ableness" may increasingly be seen as a necessary condition of inclusion and participation (Chouinard & Crooks, 2005).

Geography

A final area of diversity, of particular significance to Canada given the country's vast size, is geography. Historian Maurice Careless (1954) aptly describes the Canadian experience as a tension between metropolis and hinterland. Externally, much of our history has been that of a colony, subject to the norms and will of a faraway political/economic system, be it Great Britain, or, more recently, the United States. Internally, powerful centres—economically, socially, and politically— have dominated those areas that are farther removed from such power (Careless, 1954). Toronto, and Southern Ontario in general, has been the metropolis to a hinterland, resource-based Northern Ontario (Nelles, 1974). Central Canada may be seen to have been a metropolis to Western provinces and to Atlantic Canada (Morton, 1969). But these hinterland areas, too, have their own complex networks of metropolis–hinterland relationships within them. St. John's, as an example, has been a metropolis to the rest of Newfoundland and Labrador; Calgary and Edmonton are metropolises to Northern Alberta.

In social work, much literature has been imported from other countries, the United States in particular. In social policy, as we have seen, many factors existing outside the country have influenced Canadian developments. Social policies and the way in which social policies are conceived have had other biases beyond these. They have been overwhelmingly urban in orientation and have overlooked important differences relevant to rural, northern, and remote Canada (Delaney & Brownlee, 1995; Delaney, Brownlee, & Zapf, 1996; Delaney, Brownlee, & Graham, 1997). As Zapf (1999) points out, in one social policy textbook published many years ago, "rural areas were dismissed as exhibiting 'all the same problems as their larger metropolitan counterpart'" (345), and more generally still, "few pages" within any social policy text delved into "Native issues" (346), among other areas of concern to the country's traditional hinterlands.

Canada's population dispersion patterns are striking. A century ago, about half the population lived in rural areas. In 2006, only 20 percent were classified as rural (Statistics Canada, 2009). Only 1 percent of the population occupies the northern 80 percent of the country's land mass. And 80 percent of the population lives within 400 kilometres of the American border, with a significant proportion in a narrow, and largely urban, corridor between Quebec City and Windsor. In Canada's North, small, disparate communities numbering under 250 are scattered across a territory as large as Europe, with only a handful of these small settlements approaching 10 000 inhabitants (Zapf, 1999, 348–349). In northern regions too, like their remote and rural counterparts, differential policy needs have been overlooked, and metropolis assumptions and metaphors have been systematically—and inappropriately—applied. As Zapf (1999) remarks, "Social policy and program planners have tended to view their own separate northern regions as variations of the south posing some service delivery problems" (349). Hinterland regions continue to be economically exploited, and when their natural resources are depleted or no longer valued, problems of unemployment, poverty, and limited labour mobility are intensified. Social policies have tended to reinforce metropolis–hinterland power imbalances and inequalities, so much so that some authors refer to areas of northern and rural Canada as a domestic Third World (Zapf, 1999, 349).

Soon after Confederation, the federal government began to implement economic policies and programs that affected regions of the country in different ways (Chappell, 2006). However, it was not until the 1940s and 1950s that serious examination of the way policies affected different parts of the country were undertaken. The Rowell–Sirois Commission of 1940 marked the beginning of the idea of equalization payments from richer to poorer provinces, based on recognition that uniform national tax rates did not provide equal services to all Canadians. The later Gordon Commission (1957) examined regional disparities further, especially those that persisted over time. A long-standing problem has been whether to define the issues in relation to provinces, regions, or subregions. Generally, provinces have been the identified unit of policy, since data are organized by province.

Since the 1960s, the federal government has run regional development programs in some parts of the country. These were initially aimed at depressed rural regions, but the mandate was later broadened. A Department of Regional Economic Expansion (DREE), established in 1969, was integrated in 1982 into the Department of Regional Industrial Expansion (DRIE). DRIE was dismantled in 1988. Critics of these federal efforts have generally felt that these policies placed inappropriate emphasis on the manufacturing sector and on job creation to spur economic growth in rural areas, rather than creating plans for sustainable economic development. DRIE was replaced by four regionally based agencies: Western Economic Diversification (WD); Atlantic Canada Opportunities Agency (ACOA); Canada Economic Development for Quebec Regions; and Federal Economic Development Initiative in Northern Ontario (FedNor). These agencies have attempted to promote local industries through financial supports to local firms and entrepreneurs and through previously established government programs. As one economist points out, regional development programs "encompass a broad range of policies, including grants, special depreciation allowances and loans to encourage the location of firms in designated areas. Federal departments and agencies have also entered into general development agreements with the provinces, which can include infrastructure programs, mineral exploration, industrial restructuring incentives, rural development schemes, etc." (Polese, 1998).

Collier (2006) examines the nature of social policy relevant to Canada's rural areas in relation to the differences among foraging, agricultural, and industrial economies. Foraging, or hunting and gathering, societies involved all members in subsistence provision. Kinship systems were of primary importance for survival, and decision-making was carried out by the whole group, rather than by representatives of the group, creating a relatively egalitarian society. Agricultural economies involve more permanent residence than foraging. Also, some people will be employed by others, and some will become much richer than others. Institutions like the church, schools, and charities emerge as supports and keepers of social order. As industrial economies developed and expanded, urbanization increased, and the modern state was born. Today, Canada's rural areas, Collier maintains, cannot escape the incursions of industrialism, and they are likely subject to various kinds of exploitation by industrial centres. They become, in his words, "peripheral" economies that are often subject to the needs of monopolies and multinational businesses rather than local needs. Of course, welfare services and supports are present, although not necessarily as accessible as in cities. Collier recommends a "generalist" approach for social workers in remote regions where aspects of a foraging economy still exist and in rural agricultural societies. Knowledge of social forms and histories that still shape life in these regions is required, and a wide variety of skills is necessary, ranging from counselling to political and organizing expertise. As Zapf (1999) notes, a sense of community and local identity helps to create and sustain a worker mindset that will lead to advocating more geographically sensitive social policy practices.

How Diversity Challenges Social Policy

Traditionally, treating everyone alike or with like intentions has been a valued social goal in the service sector. Diversity raises the question of whether these are appropriate objectives. The extension of equal child welfare services onto reserves, for example, has produced unequal results in terms of children taken into care (Swift, 1995). And, as many feminists point out, assumptions of gender neutrality are embedded in policies. In reality, the consequences of social policies have proven to be different for women than for men and different in many cases for minorities as well. Issues concerning definitions of the "family" are especially at issue. Lesbians and gay men have challenged the meaning of the family as being necessarily heterosexual, and members of various cultures, especially of non-European cultures, do not necessarily see the family as nuclear.

A related challenge involves the relationship of labour to social policy. This issue is especially relevant to work traditionally done by women in the private household. The caring labour performed mostly by women is a crucial and assumed piece of Canada's social structure. Current examples include the return to "family care," which translates into invisible free care often given by women. In fact, without this unpaid and usually invisible labour, most of our social policies would not be at all workable. If this form of labour were compensated, even at minimum-wage rates, the costs of social programs would substantially escalate. And as Eichler (1987) points out, until caring responsibility is equally shared—in actual practice—by men and women, social policy will necessarily be accessed by and will affect men and women quite differently, with potentially different policy outcomes.

At a fundamental level, diversity challenges the concepts, assumptions, and structure of the Canadian social policy framework, including conventional ideas of need. In the developing neo-conservative/neo-liberal context, the idea of need is increasingly personalized and attached to individual problems and failings, in the tradition of the Poor Laws. An alternative and useful way to think about social policy and diversity is in relation to the concept of "thick" and "thin" needs, introduced by Fraser (1989) and elaborated by Kerans (1994). We will examine thin needs first.

A thin need is characterized as "objective, universal, and abstract" (Kerans, 1994, 45). A thin need is rooted either in human physiology or in obligations imposed on the individual by society. This concept of need has been crucial in the development of social welfare policy because, as Kerans points out, the idea of universal need carries the moral weight required to justify redistribution of resources. Most social policy shaping the welfare state has been based on a notion of thin needs. Programs flowing from this idea were socially supported because of the presumed universality of the needs they were intended to meet.

Of course, universality of need does not translate directly into universality of claims on the public purse. Western societies, as Kerans notes, assume the market as the "normal" route for need fulfillment (1994, 48). Claims on the state are legitimized through evidence showing that the special circumstances of individuals and families mean that their needs cannot be met through this usual route. These circumstances typically include age, disability, caring responsibilities, job loss, and so forth. Nonetheless, a thin concept of need is an important assumption underlying social policy because it allows the possibility of claims by those in need. Thin needs as the basis for provision also enhance the possibility for justice and equity. An important characteristic of Canadian social policy is impersonal provision for socially legitimated needs. That is, it is not supposed to be patronage, or payoff, or promises of votes that justify provision; rather, it is the universality of need that justifies resource distribution. The goal is to ensure "standard treatment of all individuals, regardless of their ethnic identity, class position, or gender, as the basis for intervention with disadvantaged persons and populations" (Mawhiney, 1995, 223).

A problem with using thin or universal need as a basis for social provision, as Kerans notes, is that it is necessarily abstract. Thin need is an idea assumed to apply to all. Since it is not grounded in variations of real life, it cannot account for or express the multiplicity of experience and collective and individual differences that shape and give meaning to *need* in the everyday world. This reality has accounted for substantial dissatisfaction with social policies intended to address need as a universal experience. Bureaucratic procedures that objectify need for purposes of resource distribution (one-size-fits-all) have become sources of frustration for both receivers and providers of social programs. In other words, the attempt to create policy that addresses universally experienced needs runs the risk of "universalizing" human experience in unacceptable ways. Also, social policy is not created by all people. Policy formulation in fact is dominated by white males. Policy has a tendency to represent the viewpoints of its authors, which may erroneously appear as "universal" ideas.

Thick needs, in contrast, represent needs within a particular cultural context. Diversity is central to this concept of need. Thick need is not objectified and measurable but rather is viewed as subjective. Its meaning is constructed by individuals or groups through their particular experiences. As Kerans notes, neither category of need is as clear as definitions presume, and neither can stand on its own as the basis for social policy. However, application of thick and thin ideas of need can help us explore the relationship between diversity and social policy. Challenges to the welfare state by diverse groups can be understood as insistence upon recognition of "thick" conceptions of need. That is, diverse groups are insisting upon their particular history and experience as factors in defining need and in satisfying it through social policy initiatives.

Conclusion

Fraser and Honneth (2003) pose two important understandings of injustice. One is socio-economic, which is rooted in the "political-economic structure" of society. This is the primary kind of injustice addressed by redistributive social safety net policies discussed in other chapters of this book. The other kind of injustice, referred to as insufficient "recognition," is cultural and symbolic rather than material. Members of subordinate populations (Kallen, 2004) are subject to both kinds of injustice, which frequently interact to reinforce each other.

Fraser (1995) argues that in the current era, class has become decentred; group identity and calls for recognition have to some extent supplanted class interests as the "chief medium of political mobilization." The goals of recognition politics stand in some contradiction to the goals of the first form of injustice. Whereas redistributive forms of redress call for dissolving differences in the quest for equality, groups seeking recognition of identity seek acknowledgment of their differences from others. Fraser's challenge is to acknowledge both forms of injustice and to better understand the kinds of redress needed for each of them. She concludes that a transformative social and political agenda is the only way to address the goals of both kinds of injustice.

Chapter 7

Social Policy and Social Work Practice

Social work is about helping people. But the assistance a social worker provides—be it to an individual, a family, a group, or a community—occurs in a social policy context. This chapter elaborates why and how social workers need to understand social policy and policy processes. Without this understanding, social workers can never be fully effective, and the help that they provide their clients will never be fully satisfactory. This chapter also explains how the relationship between social policy and social work processes has evolved in the literature. Understanding this relationship is crucial to a final objective of the chapter: appreciating the relationships between the practice skills of direct intervention and the skills of social policy comprehension and analysis.

Why Study Social Policy?

Social policy students and practitioners in Canada may be more aware of relationships between policy and practice now than in past decades. An overall shift in general policy from support for the welfare state to the dismantling of programs and the restricting of access to social services has made social workers aware of the ways policy affects direct practice. Since the 1990s, social workers have seen the effects of job loss and long-term unemployment. Many found themselves in the position of refusing clients services previously offered; many have observed substantial withdrawal of funding and cutbacks to the programs they run. Yet social work training programs and literature often maintain a sharp division between the ideas and skills of direct practice and those of social policy development and analysis. This chapter focuses on exploring those relationships, as well as examining policy-based knowledge and skills useful in practising social work.

In spite of the recognized importance of social policy to direct practice, few students enter social work hoping to focus on social policy itself. Many social work students in Canada express the goal of "helping others." Familiarity with social policy may appear a remote and dubious route to this goal. The social policy

152

field has been dominated by white males, who have tended to write and talk about this field in a somewhat abstract and impersonal manner. Perhaps one reason social work students so often avoid social policy is that it has indeed been too far removed from the messy "real life" experience of practice and does not seem to assist them in obtaining the resources their clients need. Universalizing tendencies aggravate this problem, for students cannot easily recognize, in abstract descriptions, the individuals and problems they work with in direct practice settings. Finally, as Wharf and McKenzie (2004) point out, practitioners and their clients are generally not included in the policy-making process.

One of the unique features of social work is its focus on the individual in a wider context (within a family system, an organizational system, a community, or a society), as well as the complex relationships between the individual and these broader structures. This emphasis on appreciating the individual in broad contexts is sometimes called understanding "the person in environment"—a key skill that social workers must cultivate.

In the early years of social work, this "environment" clearly included social policies and the requirement to use, develop, and change them for the benefit of clients. Pioneers of social work, such as Mary Richmond, Bertha Reynolds, and Jane Addams, focused on both the personal and the social context when framing ideas about the new profession. As Wharf (1990) notes, agencies such as settlement houses, located in inner cities, provided appropriate settings for social workers to observe the effects of social policies on individuals and to apply their efforts to individuals and to social causes simultaneously. In fact, these early social workers became leaders because of their commitment to social causes. "They cared desperately about people, they had a vision of the good life, and they were morally indignant about social evil" (Burns, as cited in Wharf, 1990, 16). These leaders considered social action, along with the promotion of legislation that would alter the conditions of life for individuals they cared about, to be a natural part of their work. But in 1915, Abraham Flexner, addressing a social work conference, issued a stinging indictment of this approach to social work. He urged social workers to enhance their own status as a profession by emulating the medical profession. Flexner said that if social work wanted to become a "real" profession, its members would have to develop a recognizable technology as doctors had done and would have to demonstrate this technology in their everyday practice with individuals where it could easily be seen.

As Popple and Leighninger (2001) argue, after Flexner, the social work profession focused on individuals and families as the route to professional success and largely abandoned social action. Flexner's work was important for highlighting the individualism that pervaded social work through the rest of the century. Certainly, by the 1920s, casework had established itself as the "nuclear skill" of social work (Lubove, 1965). Supported by the curriculum of most schools of social work, the majority of social workers have since been directed toward and trained in interventions with individuals and families. This trend reached a peak in the psychoanalytic training of the 1950s. During the 1960s and early 1970s, intense focus on social issues shifted emphasis back toward social action for many members of the profession.

However, social workers have continued to find pressing reasons to maintain their focus on individuals. One reason is that individuals and families present themselves directly to us; they are immediately available as the focus of possible changes, whereas policy changes are slow. In the political climate of the new millennium, many social workers may even believe that larger social change is beyond possibility. In *The Cult of Impotence*, McQuaig (1998) explores the widespread belief that social forces affecting individuals are now too powerful and overwhelming to be changed. Such disempowering myths reinforce for social workers the idea that the only useful point of intervention is the individual. McQuaig argues that the Canadian public has been fooled into believing that access to social programs and good jobs is now out of reach because of globalization and that social change is impossible. Finkel (2006) provides an example showing that rapid, significant, and positive social change is still possible. In the 1980s, the Cree people of Northern Quebec were considered among the most impoverished in the developed world. A decade later, following active protests and social development efforts, the same community was named by the United Nations as one of 50 "exemplary communities in the world" (325).

Changes in the Canadian political and economic context may make social workers aware of the importance of understanding and changing social policies. Downsizing, for instance, has eroded job security for social workers themselves. Cutbacks mean that some of the traditional casework jobs on which social work relied are disappearing. Cutbacks in related sectors, such as nursing, mean other professions may claim traditional areas of social work as their own. The substantial reduction in the size and number of institutions, such as hospitals, has meant that clients previously counselled in institutional settings are now living "in the community" and requiring assistance to find resources. Social workers must be intimately familiar with the relevant social policies and their related service provisions to be useful. Neo-liberal social agendas mean that a profession geared toward seeking social justice must become knowledgeable about and insistent upon policy development and change to work toward justice goals.

Theory: Understanding the Person in Their Social Context

Over the century of its existence, social work has struggled to theorize connections between individuals and their environment. Mary Richmond is generally recognized as the first to theorize and extensively explore this relationship. In *The Long View* (1930), she expanded on the idea of casework:

One perfectly good definition of social casework is the development of the character and welfare of the individual through adjustments effected between him (or her) and his social surroundings. Sometimes the surroundings need to be radically changed, sometimes the person needs to be, but more often a change, to be permanent, must be effected in both. (577)

She recommended that caseworkers "consciously and deliberately" examine their work at the points of intersection with social movements, and strive to improve their work at these points. The casework movement, she thought, would inform the caseworker and in turn direct the workers toward the movement.

Sociologist C. Wright Mills' notions of private troubles and public issues have also been crucial to the exploration of the personal and the social. He said a "trouble," on the one hand, is a problem that has to do with the self and the limited areas of social life with which a person is involved. "Issues," on the other hand, have to do with matters that transcend local involvement. An issue is a public matter, incapable of private resolution. In the conclusion to his important work *The Sociological Imagination* (1959), Mills offered this advice: "Do not study merely one small milieu after another; study the social structure in which milieux are organized. . . . Know that many personal troubles cannot be solved merely as troubles, but must be understood in terms of public issues . . . and know the human meaning of public issues must be revealed by relating them to private troubles" (224–226).

Feminists later explored this general terrain, elaborating on it and changing the emphasis to create the slogan "the personal is political." This notion, expanded in models of feminist practice (Dominelli & McLeod, 1989), suggests that private troubles are intricately connected to the public and political worlds. Through feminist analysis, problems previously viewed as private and personal came to be seen as common and widespread (Callahan, 2004). For example, a man's violent behaviour toward his female partner is now widely understood as part of a larger social problem of violence against women, not just as an interpersonal problem between one man and one woman. The arrangements of society, including social policy, are implicated in creating and maintaining problems experienced by individuals. These insights reveal the reluctance of the Canadian state to establish policies that address private troubles as public issues. Recently, the concept of "provisioning" has been employed by economists and social theorists to reveal this reluctance (Neysmith, Reitsma-Street, Baker-Collins, Porter, & Tam, 2010). *Provisioning*, defined as labour tied to relationships, does not fit neatly into the public/private dichotomy. Instead, provisioning labour shifts through time and with changing tasks and relationships. In the neo-liberal context, this labour often includes responsibility for labour market activity, however poorly paid, as well as a wealth of invisible, unpaid tasks attached to and created by networks of women's kin, social, and community relationships (Neysmith et al., 2010). Many feminists (e.g., Little, 2005) have examined the ways social programs reinforce the unpaid, undervalued labour expected of women in both the public and private realms. These approaches show the importance of changing the fundamental principles upon which social policy is based as a strategy for changing the daily realities of individual women.

Some social work theorists and writers have employed ideas from Marx and the Critical School to explore the relationship between the person and the social environment. Marx and Engels (1846, trans. 1947) observed that the state is itself based on the contradiction between public and private, and between general and particular interests. Social work's original purpose was to mediate this contradiction, helping to soften the worst effects of public life on individuals and proposing remedial public policies. A Marxist perspective also theorizes that society and individuals have mutually constructing relations; in other words, people both create and are created by their social world. Writing about this idea from a social work perspective, Leonard (1975, 1984) examined how individuals internalize ideological constructs that help to shape their personality. In the aggregate, the characteristics of these individuals then appear to justify public policy. Internalized constructs tend to be those that support and recreate the status quo. Girls, for instance, have traditionally been socialized to be caring and passive, qualities that, if internalized, ensure the continuation of unpaid provisioning labour upon which the economy depends. Social work has at least two possible responses to this public/private dilemma. According to Pearson (1975), it might come to rest on a "false split" between society and individuals; or it can enhance the potential of people in both the private and social realms (Leonard, 1975).

A related view of the policy–practice relationship is the idea that social policy creates the world in which it practises. Rein (1983) points out that "the things we think about and the ways we think about them, as well as the ways we act, are shaped by the institutional arrangements of the society we live in" (223). Of course, practice also contributes to policy. The activities of front-line workers are not merely neutral instruments of broad objectives. The activities themselves act to alter intentions (Rein, 1983, 40). "The lowest field officer," as Handler (1979) notes, interprets rules and guidelines for specific cases. This idea was taken up in considerable detail in Lipsky's book *Street Level Bureaucracy* (1980). According to Lipsky, each encounter with a client represents an instance of "policy delivery." These encounters help to entrench policy on the personal level. For instance, they help to socialize citizens about social expectations and rules. Through the creation of precedents, these encounters determine eligibility for the services created through policy. Lipsky focuses on the collective behaviour of staff in public service organizations, arguing that their practical behaviour actually *becomes* the policy they carry out. "Street-level" workers actually make policy in two ways. First, they exercise discretion on an individual basis, which is an expression of policy. Second, in its aggregate form, this discretion then becomes agency policy.

Swift (1995) used the terrain of child welfare to explore the way social workers help to create social policy development through their casework practices, including agency records. She examined how the individual decisions of "anonymous" social workers become the raw material through which the concepts of child abuse and neglect are developed and legitimized. Simultaneously, their records have been used as evidence of the individual failings of the clientele. This idea had previously been explored by Rein (1983), who observed that service intervention can actually magnify problems, especially for vulnerable populations. He noted that the rich, on the one hand, are able to sort out their problems, using their own private resources to do so. The poor, on the other hand, become subject to a "problem formulation process," which then legitimizes the organization of services and creates identifiable "targets" for social policy.

Lipsky also identified the mediating influence of the organization in the dialectic (or interaction) between individual workers and the policy level. Perhaps one reason social workers often fail to recognize the relationship between social policy and their own everyday work is that policy is filtered through organizational processes and practices. Agencies themselves also set policy, which is much more visible to front-line workers than macro-level policy is likely to be; but, social workers may view this not as policy but merely as agency "rules." Lipsky shows the importance of the "mezzo" or organizational level in the processes of both enacting and making policy.

What most of these theoretical perspectives have in common is the idea that policy is not simply a top-down process carried out by the social worker in everyday practice. Rather, there is a dialectic relationship between policy and practice through which policy is not only carried out but also created, maintained, and changed by social workers in their everyday practice.

Practice Models

An impressive literature has developed exploring the ways social work can integrate direct practice skills and policy skills to forge a more effective practice. These models are discussed separately below. Most share certain core values and ideas, such as the dialectic between practice and policy, the "social justice imperative" (Figuera-McDonough, 1993), and the belief that the intersection of direct practice and social policy is the natural terrain and most powerful field of endeavour for social work.

Systems and Ecological Approaches

Beginning in the 1960s, social workers began to use and promote systems theory and its heir, ecological theory. These theories focus on the relationship between individuals and their social contexts (the "person in environment" as social work frames the idea) as a method of integrating direct practice with social issues. Building on the sociological writings of Talcott Parsons and other sociologists, systems theory explored the interactions between people and the systems they are enmeshed in. Applied to social work (Schwartz, 1974), systems theory regarded the social worker as a bridge between the individual and the environment. A systems approach called for a "generalist" social worker, comfortable working and intervening in the social environment as well as directly with the individual. Johnson (1986), for instance, describes the generalist approach as requiring social workers to determine which "system" is the appropriate unit of attention for the change effort. She lists 26 social work approaches that might be employed, from those focused on the individual to models of social action and social planning. Since the 1980s, ecological theory, as espoused in the writings of Germain and Gitterman (1980, 1996), has found favour among social work students and educators. Ecological theory seems to capture the relationships between people and their immediate surroundings in a concrete way that social workers can visualize and work with. Both systems and ecological theories focus on helping people cope with and develop within a social context. Although both approaches are intended to create a balance in social work activity between the two spheres, in practice, they usually emphasize direct work with individuals and families and recommend knowledge and skill development in that area.

Certainly, both models have been criticized. A serious criticism has been the assumption that once a need for social change is identified, it is easy to achieve it. Canadian society has continued to reproduce and legitimize major social inequities —including child poverty, racism, and violence against women—in spite of many advocacy efforts to create change. A related criticism is that these approaches fail to conceptualize power and power relations adequately. The knowledge and skill base evolving from systems and ecological theories does not include analysis of power elites, power bases, or power processes common in Canadian society. This critique suggests that social workers hoping to challenge and change oppressive social policies by using systems or ecological approaches are left without appropriate tools to carry out this work.

The Critical Paradigm

Karen Healy (2005) outlines a group of practice types she labels as "critical." These practice types are based on Marx and Marxist thinking and are generally focused on macro social structures and their relationship to the oppression of individuals and groups. Among the most significant of these approaches is the "radical" model popularized by Galper (1975) and Bailey and Brake (1975). Their approach to social work focuses on the position and problems of oppressed people within the social and economic structures of their lives. Leonard's (1975) contribution describes the aims of radical practice:

1. improving education, referring primarily to consciousness raising;
2. linking people with systems to serve their interests; and
3. building counter-systems.

Referring to Marxist thought and analysis, Leonard proposed exploring the "contradiction" as a primary method of radical practice. Through this exploration, social workers can identify and supply both misinformation and missing information to help explain relations between public and private experience. For instance, social workers could look for relevant information about clients' living conditions that is not asked for in agency forms. A problem labelled as child neglect might then be viewed as a problem of poverty. Recognition of contradictions experienced in everyday practice can reveal to social workers the discrepancies between expressed aims of social policy and the actual experiences of their clients (Fook & Gardner, 2007).

According to Thompson (1993), only toward the end of the 1980s did social work education begin to take seriously the impact of racial oppression and discrimination on clients and communities. Earlier "radical" texts focused primarily on class analysis and referred infrequently to issues of race (and even to gender, notwithstanding the substantial contribution of feminists). Most of the major published theorists of radical practice were themselves white males. Furthermore, much of this work was premised on classical Marxist analysis, which did not include race, gender, or other forms of "difference" in its scope.

Dominelli's work *Anti-Racist Practice* (1988) and Thompson's work *Anti-Discriminatory Practice* (1993), both published in Great Britain, and Mullaly's publications on challenging oppression (2002, 2007) offer well-developed analyses of the relationships between oppression and social work practice. They also explore practice methods and propose the kinds of policy challenges social workers must deal with at the policy–practice intersection. They propose using anti-discriminatory practice to move away from the individualistic approach to an approach that emphasizes "difference." Social workers need to focus on the impacts of policies that assume, entrench, or subtly allow racism and other forms of discrimination, and on the impacts and experiences of discrimination on the individual and the group. Thompson (1993) argues that any model of social work practice that does not take account of oppression cannot be seen as good practice, regardless of whether standards are high in other respects. Social workers play the role of mediators between clients and the state and its apparatus. If policy is misused or used for inappropriate control purposes, lives of clients can be made worse, as when social workers moved many Aboriginal children from their homes to residential schools and foster homes during the "sixties scoop" (Johnston, 1983). The practitioner, Thompson notes, may be encouraged through policy to provide either care or control, and to enhance either the empowerment or the oppression of individual clients. Similarly, Leonard (1975) notes that social systems and policies can be both oppressive and supportive: it is a crucial function of social work to enhance the possibilities of the latter and reduce the potential for the former.

Thompson (1993) identified the three essential building blocks of radical practice:

1. the understanding of the social and political contexts within which their clients' experiences occur;
2. the acknowledgment of the danger that their own practice could contribute to and reinforce oppression; and
3. the recognition and use of opportunities for the emancipation of clients from oppressive circumstances.

These three precepts also inform related models of practice that attempt to explore the relationships between policy and practice, including feminist practice, the structural approach, and anti-discriminatory and anti-oppressive practice.

Closely related to both radical and anti-discriminatory models is the structural model, developed by Moreau (1989) and elaborated by Mullaly (1993, 2007). The structural approach pays systematic attention to race, class, and gender in the assessment of individual problems presented to social workers. The practitioner's tasks include helping clients to recognize the structural antecedents of their problems and the social changes that need to occur in these social structures. The client–practitioner relationship is less focused on therapeutic processes than on consciousness raising and mutual social critique. Roles of the practitioner emphasize advocacy, mediation, and brokerage.

Community Development Models

For several decades beginning in the 1960s, schools of social work recognized community organization and development as comparable in importance to casework and group work. Community work could involve helping communities become more self-sufficient, participating in social planning tasks, and, most prominently, taking social action. For some years, however, the community development approach has been in decline, perhaps largely because policy-makers who grant funds do not value social action and the possibility of public policy challenges, as many in the social work profession do. The principles of community development can help to build bridges between the macro and micro areas of practice. They also help raise clients' consciousness concerning social change by involving them explicitly in efforts to change social structures. Furthermore, community organization is helpful in strengthening communities that are under stress as the result of neo-liberal political agendas.

Wharf and McKenzie (2004) distinguish between the organization of geographic communities and the organization of interest or policy communities. Geographic communities share common interest and common space. Policy communities are "loosely knit groups of individuals interested in and knowledgeable about a particular aspect of public policy" (99). An example of a policy community is Campaign 2000, an effort to pressure the federal government to make good on its United Nations commitment to end child poverty by 2000 (www.campaign2000.ca). Through this campaign, organized largely by social work practitioners and academics, a national coalition of individuals, schools of social work, and community groups has obtained funding, carried out research, and participated in widespread lobbying efforts. The campaign has given the issue of child poverty a high profile and has produced media and public support for the goal of changing social policy to provide more generously for poor children and their parents. The goal of ending child poverty is far from realized, but this campaign has successfully pressured the federal government to re-examine policy options and to create a different approach, including the Canada Child Tax Benefit (CCTB), which demonstrates that social workers committed to improving the lives of vulnerable children can collectively reshape the policy agenda.

Closely related to community organization approaches to social work are "alliance" models that connect practice and policy. This approach is described in Bishop's (2002) work *Becoming an Ally*. Alliance models encourage social workers to ally themselves with social movements, such as labour unions, the women's movement, poor people's organizations, First Nations groups, and various coalitions, and to provide supporting activity and expertise in targeting social change goals. Texts advocating this approach often speak not to professionals at all but to large groups of like-minded people, such as "activists" (Bishop, 2002) or "women" (Ricciutelli, Larkin, & O'Neill, 1998). Alliance-building approaches ask social workers to move beyond the "elitist" professional sphere to work with a wide variety of people toward common goals. This approach is often, but not only, pursued after-hours by committed social workers who have strong community ties and interests in addition to their day jobs. It asks social workers to contribute to a cause that uses both their professional knowledge regarding the effects of policy on individuals, and their professional practice skills in organizing and in policy development. This approach specifically works toward coalition building, combining skills and experiences to develop a stronger challenge for change.

Postmodern Approaches

Healy (2005) and others (Payne, 2005) describe the most recent change in social work as postmodernism, which is often associated with Foucault. This approach attends to ideas of discourse, subjectivity, and power. It claims that local and specific differences among people have been ignored by the more sweeping ideas of previous critical models. Instead, a postmodern approach examines the discourses that construct meanings, analyze whose voices count and whose do not, and create spaces for subjugated voices to be heard. The subjectivity of individuals—that is, the sense we have of ourselves—is explored, and the idea of any fixed identity is challenged. Power, in accordance with Foucault, is perceived as something that is exercised rather than possessed, and that is not necessarily oppressive but rather productive. Social workers using this model attempt to reconstruct the stories of clients—for instance, replacing "victim" identities with those of survival and courage.

Postmodern approaches are generally credited with attending to issues of "difference," allowing individuals and groups to formulate specific goals for change rather than having their aspirations defined by such overarching categories as class or gender. Dualisms, such as male/female and middle class/working class, are decentred and deconstructed, allowing the fluid subjectivities of people a space for expression and a format for policy development.

Postmodern approaches are criticized for ignoring the material realities that clients face (Healy, 2005). Some theorists see them as conservatizing, encouraging individualism rather than group cohesiveness and action. Some theorists, notably Leonard (1997), suggest that the value of a postmodern approach is the newfound visibility of difference and its presence as a policy and practice challenge, as opposed to the one-size-fits-all approach of the welfare state. Leonard proposes that we need both the postmodern and the critical models for contemporary social work and social policy development.

Everyday Relationships between Policy and Practice

In the everyday world of work, social workers specializing in direct practice may find themselves feeling cut off from social policy and analysis, whereas those in social policy development and analysis may feel cut off from issues of direct practice. Even—or perhaps especially—in social work education, these two fields of endeavour have been conceptualized and organized separately, and they often appear as distinct silos or even bunkers to both students and practitioners. Typically, social work courses are cast as either direct practice or social policy. In the world of work, the skills and tasks of policy and direct practice also tend to be organized in different spheres, so that practitioners do not see themselves as involved in policy development, and policy analysts do not come into frequent contact with the people who are most affected by their policy efforts. In addition, the policy-making process rarely includes those most affected by policy—that is, practitioners and service users (Wharf & McKenzie, 2004). Schorr (1985) pointed out some time ago that social workers in fact "practise policy" when they choose instruments to employ in their interventions, make decisions influencing organizations, and attempt to change policy. However, many social workers and students remain unclear about how policy is practised and how practice reflects policy.

In the dogma of the field, social policy analysts have generally been characterized as "progressive," while direct practitioners frequently labour under the stigma of being the conservatizing agents of the profession. However, as Lecomte (1990) observes, "All methods of social work have the potential to be conservative or progressive" (45). Adams (2002) stresses the relationships between social work and social policy, noting they are both "inseparable from politics" (29): they draw on common theory and concepts, use similar language, and are linked through legislation. Much theory, as we have seen, directs us to see and act on the ongoing connections between these two apparently separate endeavours. This section of the chapter identifies the tasks and skills needed for work in each arena and emphasizes the potential complementarity between them.

Policy Practice

Popple and Leighninger (2001) refer to social work as a "policy-based profession." They suggest that social work and some other professions, such as the law, base their authority on mastery of complex cultural traditions, rather than on precise and specific techniques. This characteristic of social work legitimizes and, in fact, requires social policy as a central feature of the profession. Following theoretical formulations outlined earlier in the chapter, Popple and Leighninger list several ways that social policy, including policy at the organizational level, shapes the tasks and attention of direct service to individuals and families. First, policy determines the major goals of service. For example, public policy is shifting away from universal and accessible social welfare services to a "leaner, meaner" model of reduced budgets and privatization of service delivery. Second, policy determines the characteristics of the clientele. For example, policies may grant services on the basis of marital status, physical or mental abilities, age, immigration status, and so on. At the agency level, eligibility may be further limited geographically, or in terms of religion or other characteristics. Third, policy may specify and restrict service options. For instance, abortion counselling services may be restricted on the basis of the age of the mother. Finally, policy can determine the theoretical or ideological focus of services. In Canada, for instance, multicultural policy underlies ideas of "inclusive" service provision, while human rights policies direct attention to such issues as who is hired to deliver services.

Policy is generally considered to operate at three levels: *macro, mezzo,* and *micro*. Macro-level policy includes legislation and regulations formulated at the federal, provincial/territorial, and municipal levels. These policies, many of which are outlined and described in previous chapters of this book, set the basic framework for the provision of services and benefits. Mezzo policy involves organizational guidelines, rules, protocols, and precedents that "direct and regularize" operations of the agencies where social workers are employed (Popple & Leighninger, 2001). In turn, these operations mediate between macro policy and service delivery, translating policies into response systems. It is often at the mezzo level that social workers attempt to translate and reshape policy. McKenzie (1997) has developed a Canadian model examining the importance of the mezzo level. He points out that it is at the agency level that the connections between policy and practice take on real meaning. Micro policy describes the transactions that occur as social workers deliver services to particular individuals and groups. This is the level of potential discretion described by Lipsky (1980).

Taking a somewhat different tack, Jansson (1990, 2011) examines the practice component of social welfare policy. He suggests that contemporary realities and the reform tradition of social work require social work practitioners to become conscious and active participants in the shaping of social policy. In the current neo-liberal era, wealth is accumulating at the top (Wilkinson & Pickett, 2010), and public resources are shrinking. Jansson (1990) suggests that serving the needs of clients in this climate of increasing inequality requires social workers to become more proactive in policy development. His "policy practice" approach is defined as "the use of conceptual work, interventions, and value clarification to develop, enact, implement, and assess policies" (25). Skills required for "policy practice" (Jansson, 2011, 86) include the following:

> analytical skills to gather data, identify policy options, compare merits of various options, and draft proposals;

> political skills to gain and use power, explore feasibility, locate power resources, and develop political strategies;

> interactional skills to create contacts, build networks, develop and use group processes, and form individual relationships; and

> value clarification skills to identify and rank moral and ethical considerations in proposals and strategies.

Of course, these same skills may be and frequently are used in direct practice. For example, in working with a client who has been cut off from assistance, a social worker will analyze the relevant policy to determine if the client meets eligibility requirements, employ political skills to locate allies with the power to support access, use interactional skills to tap into potential helping networks, and evaluate and act on the moral considerations of potential courses of action. Jansson argues that conscious application of these skills extends a social worker's options because it uses knowledge of policy to help solve client problems.

Practice to Policy

A different yet ultimately similar approach has been taken by McInnis-Dittrich (1994). This approach begins with the traditional problem-solving skills of direct practice and shows how they can be used in policy development. Steps in this model include the following:

> assessment of the problem, including information gathering, problem identifi-
  cation, identification of resources and obstacles, needs assessment and goal
  setting. In this phase, specific facts and figures are accumulated to answer
  specific questions;

> exploration of alternatives, considering a wide range of possibilities and their
  potential consequences;

> development of an action plan and selection of alternatives;

> implementation—translating plans into specific tasks and allocating them to
  particular people; and

> evaluation of results.

The recommendations of Jansson and McInnis-Dittrich regarding both direct
practice and policy work overlap considerably. Both require conceptual and planning tasks, political and relational skills, and ethical considerations, although the
language used is somewhat different.

Use of Power

Central—although often implicit—to all discussions concerning the interaction
between policy and practice is the issue of power. Traditionally, social workers
have been taught less about power than about authority. Lukes (2005) defines
authority as a form of power exerted and complied with because both parties agree
on its legitimacy. Certainly, social workers accept the authority of supervisors
(most of the time), of executive directors, and so on. However, this traditional
definition suggests that the existing relations that vest authority in some people are
reasonable and normal and should not be challenged.

The social work functions of authority and helping are not necessarily mutually exclusive (Kadushin & Martin, 1988). However, social workers often have
considerable difficulty negotiating these apparently opposing functions in their
everyday work (Swift, 1995). Furthermore, the business of challenging existing
policies and practices very likely involves questions about appropriate authority,
including the authority vested in organizational bureaucracies through which most
agency policy is made. Authority and the way social work literature has addressed
it have not offered sufficient or clear guidance to social workers about how to
relieve oppressive conditions. A direct focus on power may be more helpful.
Recent attention to the work of Foucault (1972) has made many social workers
and students aware of the complexity of the concept of power. However, social
workers have often been reluctant to acknowledge its importance in their work.

The concept of power, as Lukes (2005) points out, has deep historical roots
and has been written about by many of the most authoritative scholars of the last
two centuries. Lukes has developed a conceptual map of power that considers
power in four dimensions. First is the scope or range of issues over which power
is being exerted. Second is the contextual range or circumstances in which power
is operative. The third dimension is the relationship between power and intention.

The fourth dimension distinguishes between active and inactive power, demonstrating that power can be effective even if not actively pursued.

Power—perhaps several kinds of power—is present in all relationships, and power held by each person continually shifts in the course of action. Jansson (1990, 2011) describes power as transactional rather than unilateral. He identifies several kinds of power that may appear in "policy practice."

One kind of power is *person-to-person power*. Expertise, coercion, reward, charisma, and authority characterize this kind of power. It is perhaps most familiar to direct practitioners, since they engage in much person-to-person interaction and are made aware in education and training of the potential for misuse and abuse of personal power. In a client–worker relationship, the worker may be presumed to be more powerful most of the time, because he or she brings the mandates, policies, and resources of the organization and of macro-level policy to the encounter. However, clients find ways to exert power as well. Resistance, withholding, avoidance, withdrawal, aggression, deception, and dishonesty are all strategies employed by clients to assert themselves in relations they consider to be to their disadvantage. Clients, individually and in groups, may also try to influence a social worker to become interested in an issue or to take up a cause. Both kinds of power can provide social workers with information about social policies that have an impact on the people with whom they work.

Substantive power refers to the content of policy proposals. Those who attempt to shape policy spend considerable time compiling arguments and evidence supporting one position or another and discrediting alternatives. Constantly at play in this work is the question of how particular content will be received by different parties and with what consequences. Attempts to make policy changes appear non-threatening, and the inclusion of such provisos as time limitations demonstrates how this type of power is deployed.

Another kind of power is *procedural power*, which is often overlooked in discussions of power exerted by social workers. The skills of controlling the agenda, chairing, and participating in meetings are used by all social workers at some time or other. Procedural skills can help to ensure that a topic reaches the floor for discussion, that challengers are satisfied or avoided, that barriers are bypassed, and that rules of order are used to advantage.

A related type of power is *process power*, through which the tenor or scope of an issue is set. Social workers generally become familiar with and use complex and sophisticated means to develop and encourage processes favourable to their cause. Team-building skills, tact, emphasis on opportunities for key players, timing, and broadening or restricting participation are all strategies used to influence processes, and therefore the outcome of a cause.

Jansson also identifies the *power of autonomy*, the ability to develop policies of one's own, at times in defiance of existing policies. Social workers have considerable latitude in some circumstances to use this kind of power. In some situations, a group of social workers might discover and share a common issue and prepare a proposal for dealing with the problem. A proposal might request a grant to fund a programmatic response, suggest a change in organizational policy, or move to challenge macro policy. Social workers are also at times inventive in resisting unwanted policies—for instance, by circumventing rules they consider damaging to clients and by ignoring meaningless recording requirements. As Spicker (2006, 25) notes, practitioners may also engage in other kinds of tactics. For example, they might plan to divide and conquer their opposition, play "shell games" with statistics, bring in outside experts and call for studies, and bypass normal channels to influence the way policy is shaped or changed.

Finally, Jansson (2011) discusses the power of *coercion and reward*. The threat of penalties may be hinted at or openly disclosed, while the promise of various kinds of supports or a quid pro quo may be suggested or actually offered. Coercive power tends to be overused in mandated forms of social work and underused when challenging oppressive policies. Social workers need to be aware of their own power and to put it to use in service of the client. Because many social workers are women, and because women are not generally socialized or encouraged to take and use power, this remains an arena for further exploration and skill development. Of course, there are also more overt forms of power. Physical threat or actual violence is one. Usually this kind of power is more common in the police and military, but it may be an important factor in the lives of some clients. Economic power is also relevant for social work practitioners. Capital, as Finkel (2006) points out, is sometimes invisible but is always an important player in social policy. The power to grant or withhold money or resources can be exercised not only by the state, but also by corporations, employers, agencies, and intimate partners.

In direct social work practice, uneven power relations between worker and client are somewhat hidden by the concept of the "helping relationship." As radical social workers have warned, unacknowledged power can increase oppression for the client. Social workers who want to decrease oppressive experiences need to be aware of how power operates in various facets of social work. They also need to be aware of the risks to themselves in challenging established authority.

Moreau (1989) and Jansson (2011) have identified several specific kinds of power that can be learned, practised, and brought to bear on behalf of clients. One kind is *expert power*, including access to information, resources, and networks of help. Another type is *referent power*, meaning the ability to attract others to a cause. The third is the *power of numbers*: direct social work provides many opportunities to gather data about individuals and their experiences. In the aggregate, these data can provide powerful support for a cause. Fourth is *legitimate power*, the power that parole officers, welfare workers, and child protection workers have.

Empowerment has become almost a cliché in social work, to the point that some people no longer use this word. However, there can be no doubt that significant contributions to professional work have been developed under the label of *empowerment*. Quoting Rappaport, Wharf (1990) defines empowerment as "the process by which people, organizations, and communities gain mastery over their lives" (158). For Chamberlin (1997), a psychiatric survivor, empowerment is a process rather than an event. Popple and Leighninger (2001) also define empowerment as a process, one that increases personal, interpersonal, or political power in an "active, self-creating process" (123).

Conclusion

Social workers are developing new visions for resolving contradictions between the policy and practice worlds. These proposals grow out of concerns about the market-state characteristics of the welfare state, described in Chapter 2. A generally shared proposition is that social work has the potential to redirect social welfare from control to caring. Writing from a sociological perspective, Dominelli (1997) suggests that social work can be profoundly revolutionary, challenging governments' current focus on economic priorities, and arguing that human needs must be the organizing force in the development of new forms of welfare. Leonard (1997) and Swift and Callahan (2009) also speak of human need as a crucial focus for social work in the future, describing social welfare as an emancipatory project, requiring not only cool analysis but also courage and the strength of moral outrage. Wharf and McKenzie (1998) say the task of building a more humane social environment requires social workers to give up the need to control. They recommend focusing instead on an "inclusionary practice" as the most important reform in human services.

How would social workers begin to address such a goal? Wharf and McKenzie (2004) recommend developing genuine alliances between practitioners and service users. In the long term, such alliances can be practical and effective for influencing the policy development process. Without the serious input of those who need and use services, social policies are doomed to be incomplete and inappropriate, at best. Wharf and McKenzie also propose the development of "vertical-slice policy groups" as a mechanism for creating a more inclusive practice. These are groups that involve people at all levels of a policy process, including social workers and service users.

To increase the potential for creating and changing social policy, Dominelli (1997) suggests that local issues be brought to national and international attention. An example is the appearance of Canadian social workers at the United Nations, protesting that the country's rating as the "best place to live" ignores our escalating rates of child poverty. Dominelli further suggests that social workers focus on making connections among different forms of oppression and help to develop new paradigms that account for these connections. Leonard's (1997) proposal is "welfare building"—the construction of new policies and practices promoting human welfare. This project, of course, would require the power and resources of the state. His suggested strategy is the development of a "confederation of diversities"—a movement or even a political party with sufficient power to wrest needed resources from the state. Such a movement, he suggests, might involve feminists, trade unions, anti-racist groups, and the ecology movement, as these are some of the more active and solidified social movements in contemporary times.

These and other emerging proposals require work, knowledge, and skills at the micro, mezzo, and macro levels. Among the threads that tie these visions together is the insistence that social work move beyond the "silo" approach so that the potential power of the practice–policy relationship can be fully realized. The HST case study in Chapter 8 provides an up-to-date and relevant example of an important policy issue for social work. The study demonstrates how macro tax policy directly affects those with whom we work; the usefulness of critically analyzing policy; and how coalitions of activists, including social work, can affect and change public policy.

The Policy-Making Process

This chapter discusses how social policy moves from ideas into action. The first part explains how world views shape unique perceptions about society, people, and people in society and how these perceptions simplify reality to conform to each world view. Not only does each world view correspond to a social policy, but each also prescribes how to convert that social policy into public policies, programs, and services. For example, a neo-liberal world view would accept inequality as a mechanism for promoting competition and stimulating individual initiative and would be relatively unconcerned about equality issues in policies and programs. In contrast, a social democrat world view would highly value equality and insist that public policies and programs promote greater equality. Moreover, each of these world views would also prescribe who is to be involved in the policy-making process and how power and decision-making authority would be distributed.

This chapter examines different approaches to the policy-making process, including comprehensive, incremental, and other approaches. As noted in Chapter 1, each model for policy-making has advocates who believe that their model best serves the people of Canada. Much like world views, models for policy-making are based on notions that assign value to citizen participation, political and economic power, evaluation and feedback, and other related areas, which are discussed in Chapter 9.

The following four short stories convey the notion of world views or social constructions of reality and show how these affect how we see the world.

Story 1: You and a friend are walking down a country road on a beautiful autumn day. As you turn a corner, you spot a cluster of maple, oak, and elm trees sporting a magnificent array of fall colours. For a moment, you are enthralled by the beauty of these colours reflecting against the brilliant blue of the sky. You experience a sense of wonder at nature's glory and feel content. Then your friend says, "Look at those poor leaves. All spring and summer they work to provide nourishment for the tree. Then in the fall, the trees remove the chlorophyll, the leaves return to their natural colour, and they are condemned to die. What a shame! Can you imagine anyone admiring a dying leaf?" You feel deflated and say nothing.

Story 2: It is June, and you are driving along the Trans-Canada Highway in Northwestern Ontario. You see a beautiful lake surrounded by trees and wild grass, so you stop to take a photograph at the roadside. As you exit your car, you are immediately attacked by hordes of blackflies. Fighting off the flies, you quickly take a picture and get back into your car. At home, you proudly display an enlargement of the photograph, which always attracts comments about how beautiful and peaceful the location looks and how people wish they were there right now. You remember the blackflies.

Story 3: It is 1944, and the International Red Cross is sending a delegation to visit Theresienstadt, a ghetto the Germans claim to be a paradise for Jews. Prior to the visit, the ghetto sees a flurry of activity, as fresh paint is applied, rooms are refurbished, activity centres are created, and the Jewish people are clothed and cleaned. When the delegation arrives, children are playing, music from live bands fills the air, food is available, arts and crafts are on display, and the Jewish people themselves are friendly and open. The delegation members, even with some reservations, speak highly of this ghetto and the Germans' treatment of these Jewish people. When the delegation leaves, all food, furnishings, and clothes are removed, and the Jewish people begin an exodus from this camp by cattle trains to the death camps and eventual "final solution."

Story 4: It is 1998, and Canada is experiencing positive economic growth. New jobs are being created, and the federal government and many of the provinces are moving toward balanced and surplus budgets. Employment Insurance (EI) is experiencing a billion-dollar surplus, and workfare is being introduced in some provinces to give the poor an opportunity to get back into the workforce. Companies and governments are becoming more efficient, and private interests are being encouraged to become involved in public-sector activities. Canada is a viable member of the North American Free Trade Agreement (NAFTA) and has been invited to join an international consortium through the Multilateral Agreement on Investment (MAI). The economic health of Canada is vastly improving as governments free the private sector to conduct business.

World Views and the Policy-Making Process

What do these stories have in common? Each illustrates how a world view or social construction can frame our notions of "reality" and why it is sometimes easier to believe stories than to try to confront "reality" as critical thinkers. The first story, about the dying leaves, shows how difficult it can be when our assumptions about reality are challenged. One such reality today is the issue of poverty. Neo-liberal domination of Canada's media has resulted in a constant negative image of the poor: women having children so they do not have to work; people cheating on welfare; unemployed people taking advantage of EI premiums; young people going on welfare so they do not have to live with their parents; lack of common sense among the poor; and so forth (Saul, 1995). This representation creates the impression that everyone is relatively well-off in our society, and if they are not, then it is probably due to a character flaw or bad life choices. Yet as the Senate Committee on Poverty (1971) stated a generation ago, "The time has come for a little common honesty. The poor, after all, are not, as some still pretend, poor of their own accord. . . . They are casualties of the way we manage our economy and our society" (xxvii).

The second story, about the photograph and the blackflies, relates to what it is like to view society from a distance. When one is removed from the helplessness and hopelessness, the poor-quality housing and food, the violence, the tensions, the frustrations, and the pain and the emotional injury, it seems as if people choose to remain poor and refuse to be responsible citizens. When one is far away enough not to see poverty, soup kitchens, hostels, street kids, low-paying, no-benefit part-time and casual jobs, pay inequity, and minority discrimination, Canada seems to be doing very well in the global economy.

The story about the Jewish ghetto alludes to the social cosmetics and "spin" that can be placed on reality. In Ontario, the recent decision to introduce private sector "boot camps" for young offenders was carefully orchestrated—only the best candidates were chosen, the process was carefully followed, and the results were well publicized and even mentioned in the Throne Speech. Young offenders are presented as really bad people needing to be shamed and disciplined with a firm hand—often the very reality that has shaped these young people in the first place. Positive publicity for boot camps is given prominence by newspapers essentially owned by those supporting conservative government reforms.

The final story, about Canada's current economic growth, shows why social policy analysts must constantly listen past the stories created by those in positions of public and economic power. Through the clever use of rhetoric and propaganda, power groups perpetuate social myths to minimize criticism and maximize conformity (Saul, 1995). For example, instead of acknowledging that companies are firing large numbers of employees, a power group might say these companies are "down-sizing." Furthermore, these companies are not downsizing to increase profits but to demonstrate "fiscal responsibility." Today, governments are not in the business of promoting equality and protecting the welfare of their citizens, but in the business of making profits (called *surpluses*). Just as the Gulf War created new media euphemisms, such as "sanitizing" to mean "killing people," corporations are inventing euphemisms that make government programs and public workers seem uncaring and uneconomical and other euphemisms to suggest that corporate models and corporate leaders are necessary for proper management of human resources, especially where there is "a rush to use machinery—inanimate or human—while these are still at full value, before they suffer a depreciation" (Saul, 1995, 162). Moreover, Clarke (1997) asserts that the Business Council on National Issues and its allied corporations have heavily funded the Fraser Institute, the C.D. Howe Institute, and the Reform Party in order to manufacture opposition to government interventionism. Not only have these think tanks been successful in creating a negative image of government, but they have also been able to hide the fact that they play a powerful, behind-the-scenes role in determining public policy-making in Canada.

The policy-making process is manifold. On the one hand, the prevailing world view implicitly creates the social policy-making process of the time by ascribing privilege and power to those it favours and ascribing a reduced or nominal role for those it does not favour. It answers such questions as the following: To whom do politicians listen? How are people appointed on commissions and other bodies studying public and social policy? Is there a process for making social policies? Do some people have a greater say on which social policies will drive society? The answers determine how social policy will be made.

Many people are involved directly and indirectly in the policy-making process. Some of these people, such as members of the governing party, have the power to legislate policies into law. Others, such as business leaders, wealthy individuals and families, labour leaders, and entertainment notables, may become involved as advocates for policies that best reflect their own interests or values. Still others, such as consumers, average citizens, or interested people, may become involved in the policy process as advocates for policy options that are relevant to the communities in which they live.

As noted at the beginning of the chapter, everyone who becomes involved in the policy-making process brings their own world views and life experiences into the policy debate. From a social work perspective, Wharf and McKenzie (2010) suggest that policy-makers have a professional responsibility to ensure that issues of social development and social justice are included in the policy-making process. Citing Flynn (1992), they recommend that policy-makers keep the acronym SCRAPs (sexism, classism, racism, ageism, and poverty) in mind as a reminder that many of society's victims of discrimination receive only "scraps" from most policy initiatives. To evaluate the impact of policies on people, Reamer (1993) recommends exploring how the concept of equality is being applied. Reamer suggests that equality has a range of definitions:

➤ *Absolute equality* exists where resources, such as wealth, property, and access to services, are divided equally among all people (also known as *equality of result*).

➤ *Equality of opportunity* is concerned with the opportunity individuals have to gain access to desired resources. This type of equality might also include remedial services to enhance opportunities to compete for scarce or limited resources.

Reamer recommends that to enhance equality and minimize inequality, policy-makers should use the following mechanisms:

> *Maximum policy*, which seeks to maximize the minimum—that is, to raise minimum standards for such items as income, housing, health care, and education;

> The *ratio of inequality* approach, which seeks to increase the resources of those worse off in relation to those who are better off;

> The *least difference policy*, which seeks to reduce the range of inequality;

> The *mini-max principle*, which seeks to reduce the advantage of those who are most privileged—that is, to minimize the maximum (27).

Review the exercise "Are You a Number One?" at the end of Chapter 1. Advocates of social justice seek a social order where the societal distribution of resources and rewards is as just as possible and where exploitive inequalities are removed. Again, examine your own reality within the existing social order. What policy solutions would benefit you in relation to the distribution of resources and rewards and exploitive inequalities? You might wish to identify existing policies that continue to promote inequalities in your own life. You might wish to break into groups and share your discoveries. Are there common themes? Are there common solutions? Do you or members of your group feel disempowered to remedy inequality in your lives?

Gil (1998) suggests that social work's Code of Ethics requires all social workers to integrate a social justice approach to their practice setting, regardless of the resistance they receive. Similarly, Titmuss (1974) warns that because social policies are simply choices that direct government action toward given social ends, they may very well promote or create social injustice, discrimination, and oppression. For example, apartheid in South Africa was a social policy, as was racial segregation in several American states. It is important to question all policy initiatives. Are current neo-liberal and liberal initiatives toward the poor, women, children, and the unemployed further promoting social injustices, discrimination, poverty, and oppression? Keep in mind that these same initiatives have resulted in workfare, limited insurance for unemployment, reduced benefits for welfare recipients, reduced support for women's and minorities' programs, reduced support for all levels of education, and reduced health-care benefits.

Powerful groups justify the policies they create by appealing to the public about needs and responsibilities. For example, recent leaders have justified cutbacks to social programming because of the "need" to reduce government debts and deficits. But evidence suggests that a large portion of Canada's national debt is due more to tax breaks and loopholes for wealthy individuals and corporations and to high interest rates than to government spending on social programs (Turk & Wilson, 1996; McQuaig, 1993; Minoto & Cross, 1991). Yet government spending is where the majority of cuts have been directed.

The world views of the rich and powerful shape Canada's social policies and help to determine who influences policy decisions and the policy-making process. Of major concern to social workers is the constant decrease in government funding to support organizations that promote the interests of those who are not rich and powerful. This, of course, means that not everyone is in the same position to influence the policy-making process, and indeed, some people may be deliberately ignored. Being ignored as partners in the constitutional debates leading to the Charlottetown Accord was one of the complaints of Aboriginal groups. Many people on social assistance have been upset by the failure of some provincial governments to invite or to include their opinions, experience, and knowledge in the policy-making process. This disregard is especially true of neo-liberal governments, whose view of the poor is often hostile and dehumanizing. In 1996 in Ontario, advocates of the poor attempted to use both public protest and the court system to stop the severe cuts to social assistance implemented by Mike Harris's Conservative government, on the basis that these cuts infringed on their human rights. These efforts failed, and the cuts remained and even deepened. Yet when the medical profession and the legal profession were angered over anticipated cuts to their domain, the same government backed down and granted concessions.

Given that many people representing many interests and world views are involved in the policy-making process at many different levels of power and influence, understanding the process is not easy. It can best be understood within a framework that incorporates models of policy-making, the role of political ideology and power, institutional structures supporting the policy-making process, and participation in the policy-making process. The policy-making process is constantly influenced by such factors as globalization; dominant political ideologies; institutional structures; public values; social and economic power holders; economic prosperity; degrees of social and economic equality and equity; quality of social, political, and civil rights; and the degree of public participation. These important variables must be considered when examining the various approaches to the social policy-making process.

Models of Social Policy-Making

The Comprehensive Approach

When comparing the social policies of different countries, researchers often use social indicators representing quality-of-life measures. These social indicators reflect how public policies, social institutions, social programs, and social services work in each country and how they influence the various elements that make up a society of people. For example, countries may be compared to each other based on child poverty, the social equality of women, the quality and availability of educational institutions and health (physical and mental) resources, social welfare spending as a percentage of gross national product, criminality and correctional resources, child welfare services, and income security levels, among others. As such, social indicators provide a comprehensive overview of each nation's social policies in practice and, in turn, allow nations to be ranked based on the various social indicators.

This approach is called the *comprehensive approach* to policy-making because it begins with global objectives based on social values and then translates these policies into public policies, social institutions, social programs, and social services. The advantage of this highly centralized approach is that policy is equally applied to all parts of a country.

The following summaries of representative models of social policy will be helpful to review and revisit as you proceed through the chapter.

The Rational Model (Simon, 1957) The rational decision-making model uses the following sequence of tasks:

a. identify and clarify a social problem;

b. identify and rank goals with respect to that problem;

c. develop strategies that can remedy the problems (or achieve the goals);

d. carefully examine all possible consequences; and

e. decide on which policy best achieves government/organizational goals.

The Incremental Model (Braybrooke & Lindblom, 1963) The incremental model suggests that the rational model fails because it cannot account for everything and therefore must be incomplete at design level. This model instead views policy-making as "muddling through" by making incremental adjustments to existing policies.

The Mixed-Scanning Model (Etzioni, 1968) The mixed-scanning model suggests that substantive (political or social) issues need to be addressed by rational decision-making; then adjustments need to be made to the policy to reflect unforeseen social realities and unintended consequences.

The Rights Model (Marshall, 1965) The rights model argues that the best way to ensure the welfare of citizens is to institute universal entitlement to the following three rights: (1) civil rights that guarantee individual liberty and equality before the law; (2) political rights that ensure the right to vote and seek political office; and (3) social rights that ensure equal access and opportunities to all social institutions. Social policy advocates rely on the legal system to monitor and correct any abuses of these rights.

Titmuss's Three Historical Models (1974)

1. *The Residual Welfare Model of Social Policy* The residual welfare model argues that the private market and the family are responsible for meeting an individual's needs. Only when these break down should social welfare institutions come into play. This model is favoured by the neo-liberals and economists such as Friedman and Hayek.

2. *The Industrial Achievement-Performance Model of Social Policy* The industrial achievement-performance model argues that social needs should be met on the basis of merit, work performance, and productivity. Known as the *handmaiden model*, it is favoured by positivists and other economic and psychological theorists who advocate incentives, effort, and reward.

3. *The Institutional Redistributive Model of Social Policy* The institutional redistributive model argues that social welfare is a major integrated institution in society, providing universal services outside the market based on the principle of need. It is based on a model incorporating systems of redistribution in command over resources through time. In other words, society must ensure that major income redistribution systems, such as income tax and regional distribution transfers, are moving constantly toward achieving equality.

Titmuss also coined the phrase "The Iceberg Phenomenon of Welfare" to compare perceived and real welfare spending. *Occupational welfare* (benefits, such as pensions and health insurance, which are derived by workers through employment) and *fiscal welfare* (tax benefits to individuals and corporations, including all deductions) formed the majority of the iceberg that is hidden under the water, whereas social assistance welfare is a smaller portion visible above the water. In other words, many people other than the poor benefit from welfare, but this other welfare is concealed. Titmuss found that the majority of welfare spending actually is distributed upward to the rich through "hidden welfare benefits" (pensions, work-related benefits, tax deductions).

Values Competition Model (Rein, 1974) The values competition model suggests that social policy is, above all, concerned with choice among competing values. Society consists of people holding diverse values (world views) who are in competition with one another and, consequently, with one another's values, in an effort to achieve maximum power. Values are so ingrained in every aspect of social, economic, and public policies that a major role of policy-makers is to learn how to control their own values and prejudices.

Social Justice and the Comprehensive Model of Social Policy (Gil, 1970, 1992) The comprehensive model suggests that social policies are guidelines for behaviour that have evolved through societal processes. They specify, maintain, or transform the structures, relations, values, and dynamics of a society's particular way of life. As such, comprehensive and rational social policies govern societal life and are therefore of great concern to social workers and other human-service personnel. Good social policies should be concerned not only with life-sustaining activities that ensure minimum basic needs, but also with life-enhancing activities that stimulate human potential.

The Value Criteria Model (Haskins & Gallagher, 1981; Wharf & Mackenzie, 2004) The value criteria model suggests that after determining what the problem is and what policy alternatives are available to address the problem, policy-makers must use value criteria, informed by universal and selective values, and cost–benefit analysis to evaluate each policy alternative. In short, the best policy is the one that maximally reflects these value criteria.

The Garbage Can Model (Kingdom, 1995) The garbage can model suggests that the three types of policy processes—problems, solutions, and politics—operate individually and independently until a crisis occurs that requires all three to come together. Resolving the crisis is dependent on (1) how the public perceive the problem, (2) what the current political agenda is, and (3) who the participants are. Getting an issue on the policy agenda becomes a function of whether or not there is a crisis or situation that creates a need for the three processes to come together.

Drawbacks of Comprehensive Approaches

Some advocates believe that social policy should work along the lines of the garbage can model. Politicians and policy analysts should determine what each country's social policies should be and then put these policies into practice. Social policy is thus the aggregate of all social indicators and a statement about society's values. But applying programs universally does not guarantee equality. For example, when the Canada Assistance Plan was enacted in the late 1960s, the federal government was able to ensure that all Canadians received equal treatment under the act, regardless of what province they lived in. The same is true for the health-care system, which also ensures that all Canadians have equal access to health care. In contrast, the recent creation of EI signalled a limiting of benefits to the unemployed. The disadvantage of the comprehensive approach for EI is its universality and equality: it ends up being less sensitive to Canada's social and regional diversities, especially regarding seasonal employment.

Comprehensive policy approaches can also backfire if they are not solid. Consider the Canada Assistance Plan (1966), which the federal Liberal government replaced in 1995. To balance the budget and reduce the public debt, the government determined that it was more advantageous to negotiate lump-sum transfers of money to provinces than to make transfers based on actual cost. The Canada Assistance Plan originally paid dollar for dollar what the provinces paid for programs that qualified under the Act, including social assistance. It also allowed for assistance to be granted to people in need or likely to become in need, thus allowing for prevention services. In 1996, the Canada Assistance Plan was replaced by Canada Health and Social Transfer Regulations, with enabling legislation in the Federal–Provincial Fiscal Arrangements Act (1985, 1995). The federal government no longer cost-shares the actual program costs of each province, nor does it enforce uniform standards. Canada's poor are no longer protected; soup kitchens and flophouses have reappeared; and Canada has lost an Act that provided public-policy protection.

At the same time, even though health costs have been greatly increasing, the government did not substantively change the Health Act (1984) to compensate for these increases. The Health Act simply restricted the provinces from instituting direct patient charges. Moreover, even though the core principles of universality, comprehensiveness, accessibility, portability, and public administration remained, the means to provide for them did not.

Yet the political right remains committed to dismantling comprehensive programs and reinstating needs- and means-based programs that require meeting eligibility criteria. The argument is that this approach ensures that those most in need receive the benefits, while those who are better off do not. Given this logic, what is next for the health-care system, one of the last remaining universal programs in Canada? The provinces of Alberta, Quebec, and Ontario have begun to challenge the Health Act and have committed to privatizing some parts of health care. Moreover, most provinces have reduced medical and prescription services covered by the health-care system. What do you believe it will take to turn around this process? How empowered do you feel in being a part of the effort to redirect these policies? Comprehensive policies often have a "power-over" feel to them, and solutions are often limited to "power-over" strategies. You may wish to examine these issues by exploring the concerns raised by Jackson and Sanger (1998); Blake, Bryden, and Strain (1997); Finlayson (1996); McQuaig (1995); Wein (1991); and Carniol (1987).

The comprehensive view of social policy maintains that a scientific, rational approach to social policy-making is feasible and desirable. But social policy is about accomplishing what is termed *net value achievement*, rather than about pleasing everyone on every issue. Net value achievement means that the rewards gained from society's common values, as chosen by the policy-makers, more than compensate for any values that may have been sacrificed. For example, a country may value stable economic growth to the point where it chooses to control inflation by increasing interest rates. These increased interest rates will result in higher borrowing costs, making it more expensive for companies to borrow money and to have large inventories. This process usually concludes with companies laying off staff and creating more unemployment. Although the country may value employment and regret the layoffs, it may value stable economic growth more and be prepared to sacrifice employment for stability. The choice about which values to sacrifice is often a function of the value preferences of those who have the power to determine social and public policies. Analyzing social and public policy-making from a net value achievement perspective often focuses on issues of economic, social, and political power and how this power influences value-based policy choices that serve the interests of the powerful. In the above example, had the workers themselves been consulted, they might very well have preferred to sacrifice some economic stability in favour of maintaining or increasing employment levels.

Rein's Model

Social and public policies are often about struggles between value preferences and how some values become dominant and why. Rein (1974) suggests that social policy is about choice between competing values. From his perspective (see Figure 8.1), the social policy process stresses the interaction between values (input), operating principles (conversion process), and outcomes (output). Because Rein's model provides a comprehensive view of the policy-making process, it will be examined in some detail.

FIGURE 8.1   Rein's Overview of the Policy-Making Process

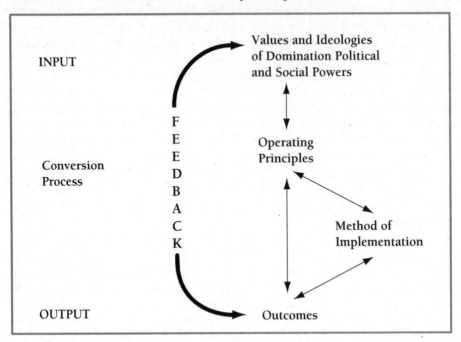

People who hold positions of political and/or social power disproportionately influence which values (input) win. When the debate about values is limited to ideology and world views, rather than the real world and the needs of real people, then social policy process suffers from what Rein calls *detached ideology*—that is, choices are made strictly in accordance with values, regardless of the outcome and consequences to others. Statements such as "It is important to reduce employment in order to control inflation"; "Adjustments to the safety net are required if Canada is to overcome its national debt"; or "Social services must be limited to what a country can afford" are simply instances of the values of the people in power (in this case, economic well-being) being used to justify reduced opportunities and services (i.e., reductions in another value) for the average Canadian (social well-being).

Input for social policy design and analysis consists of the values and ideologies of dominant political and social powers. In Canada and all democratic societies, governments are elected by the people to lead the nation. Part of that leadership is the implementation of the "political platform," which states the vision the party has for the country or the province. This vision reflects the world views and ideologies that constitute the value base for that political party. In other words, different political parties—such as the Liberal Party, the Bloc Québécois, the New Democratic Party, and the Conservative Party—inform the public of what they will do if elected.

Consider the following holes that detached ideology creates in social policy. The political right believes in deregulation, decentralization, and free enterprise. A pro-globalization orientation gives corporations freedom from government intervention and advocates for minimal government programs and a balanced or surplus (profit) government budget. What options are available to advocates of this ideology when confronted with rising costs, such as those associated with health care? The Canadian Institute for Health Information reports that the cost of drugs is the fast-est-growing segment of health care and is now second only to hospital costs. Obvi-ously, controlling drug costs would seem to be a logical policy direction; but how likely is it that people holding the current ideology will introduce new health-care coverage? Would a corporate world view not prefer to reduce health costs associ-ated with hospital and doctor care, while allowing drug costs to spiral upward?

Discuss the following questions in small groups: How important is balancing the federal, provincial/territorial, and municipal budgets, and what priority should this goal have relative to other problems? What factors have contributed to Canada's determination to balance budgets and to allow globalization to direct Canadian social and economic policies? Who do these policies benefit the most? Are poor and marginal income groups being asked to carry the major burden in reducing the public debt? Is it possible for any government to escape its own detached ideology? How much of the discussion that you are having is being influ-enced by each participant's detached ideology?

Once in power, a majority government can pass legislation that creates new social policies and alters existing policies. These policies, called *public policies*, are a purposive course of government action designed to deal with issues of public concern (Anderson, 1990). Berkowitz (1980) notes that social choices made in the policy process only rarely benefit the interests of all without being adversely con-sequential to some. Thus, the political influence held by various alliances and interest groups in Canada can limit universality. These influential groups can include the economic/business sector; special interest groups, such as the elderly, women, or people with disabilities; and international monetary institutions.

As noted in Chapter 1, when social policy becomes public policy, it also becomes legitimate and universal and controls the forces of coercion. For example, in the early 1990s, Canada underwent a debate about gun registration, with many people disagreeing with or wanting amendments to the proposed registration policy. In 1995, Bill C-68 was introduced; it contained stricter gun control legislation and a requirement for all guns to be registered. However, once the policy became law in late 1998, gun registration became mandatory regardless of different opinions (legitimacy); it applied to everyone in Canada (universal); and the police were sanctioned to enforce the law (monopoly of coercion). In another example, physician-assisted suicide has not become legal in Canada, and it is therefore illegal (illegitimate) for anyone to assist in suicide, regardless of personal beliefs, with prison or a criminal record awaiting any who choose to do so (use of coercion). In Holland, physician-assisted suicide is legal, provided all criteria are met, and there are no social sanctions. Further discussion of the law-making process can be found in Chapter 9.

If a political party comes to power with a pro-business and anti-welfare agenda, social workers can anticipate negative public policies regarding the poor and the disadvantaged. Wharf and Cossom (1987) warn of potential efforts to restrict the role of citizens in policy-making and policy decisions through *consociational democracy*—that is, "government of elite control designed to turn a democracy with a fragmented political culture into a stable democracy" (267). Marchak (1988) goes so far as to speculate that should the demands for the redistribution of power and wealth become public policy, the elites of Canada would break away from democracy and take power by force.

While these may seem like dire warnings, Saul (1995) identifies the modern corporate advocate as promoting economic objectives that are similar to those that were advocated by fascists in the early 1930s:

1. to shift power directly to economic and social interest groups;
2. to push entrepreneurial initiatives in areas normally reserved for public bodies; and
3. to obliterate the boundaries between public and private interest—that is, to challenge the idea of the public interest (91).

A recent example of the use of power by Canada's economic elite is the 1989 Canada–United States Free Trade Agreement (FTA), which eventually became the 1994 North American Free Trade Agreement (NAFTA). As Trudeau (1990) noted,

The commendable goal of promoting freer trade has led to a monstrous swindle under which the Canadian government has ceded to the United States of America a large slice of the country's sovereignty over its economy and natural resources in exchange for advantages we already had, or were going to obtain in a few years anyway through the normal operation of the GATT. (385)

GATT is the General Agreement on Tariffs and Trade, which was adopted in January 1948. Not only did Canada give up a large measure of sovereignty, but thousands of Canadians lost their jobs as well.

Another major problem for social workers working with communities and the poor is "social dumping," which occurs when corporations invest in countries with fewer labour rights and lower wages, thus driving down the wages and job security in Canada. The push to join the MAI would have enhanced the rights of investing corporations and further weakened Canada's sovereignty (Clarke, 1997).

Social policies are based on operating principles, which combine with implementation methods and create a *throughput* or *conversion process*. *Operating principles* are "attempt[s] to integrate various social ideals with a practicable rule of application" (Rein, 1974, 297–298). These ideals include universality, citizen participation, housing and in-kind benefit subsidies, earned access, equity, and other such principles that are held to be of value by society. Not all of these principles support a social work value system, and it is incumbent on social workers to carefully analyze and articulate the operating principles associated with social policy decisions and positions.

The *methods of implementation* consist of organizations, including social agencies, specifically designed or altered to provide the services prescribed by implemented social policies. For example, social policies and public policies regarding children have resulted in the establishment of myriad social agencies, such as schools, children's aid societies, children's mental health clinics, and young offender facilities. However, many of these agencies and the professionals within them can prefer a particular value (e.g., children/youth should or should not be involved in agency policy-making; family is or is not the primary institution in a child's life; or children have or do not have the same human rights as adults) or a particular practice methodology (e.g., psychotherapy, brief therapy, task-centred therapy, or community-based practice). This prescribed value or practice methodology can in fact compromise the policy and operating principles to the extent that they become congruent with the prevailing value or practice methodologies. In effect, the agency or staff members could be doing the same thing but under a different name and could be acting in a manner that is counterproductive to the values and objectives of the new policy. This debate about the principles of implementation is known as *doctrinaire insulation* (Rein, 1974, 298). In Canada, other examples of doctrinaire insulation include situations where southern-based practice methodologies and specializations are applied directly to northern environments without adaptation or citizen consensus, and situations where public policies do not account for the values and views of groups other than the policymakers, such as women's groups, ethnic groups, religious groups, and gay groups (Delaney & Brownlee, 1995).

The output of social policy is its outcome. The importance of outcome centres on whether the outcome and the purpose of the social policy are congruent and *in whose estimation*. Often social policy success is measured by social impact studies or by feedback from those whom the social policy was intended to benefit. However, the degree to which citizens are allowed to give feedback and influence social policy is in itself a fundamental issue for social policy analysis.

Rein views values, operating principles, and outcomes as inseparable and in fact completely interrelated. Rein (1974) explains this interrelationship in the following manner:

Policies are in fact interdependent systems of: (1) the abstract values we cherish; (2) the operating principles which give these values form in specific programs and institutional arrangements judged acceptable for public support; (3) the outcomes of these

programs which enable us to contrast ideals and reality; and (4) the often weak link-
ages among aims, means, and outcomes, and the feasible strategies of change this
pattern suggests. (298)

Gil's Model

Another social policy theorist who supports Rein's notions of value-driven social policy is David Gil (1998, 1992). Gil maintains that human beings and human development should form the basis of social policy. Gil believes that throughout history, systemic inequalities have resulted in social arrangements that benefit selected members of society and disadvantage the remaining members of society. He calls this process *patterned inequalities* and suggests that, over time, people do not even recognize the injustice or the inequalities. The result is the creation of social institutions that serve to benefit the interests of the few, while dehumanizing, marginalizing, discriminating against, and/or oppressing the many. Gil believes that most societal violence stems from the damage these social institutions do to people.

Gil argues that social policy must promote and enhance human development and potential and in doing so, serve as "guidelines for behaviour, evolved through societal processes, which specify and maintain or transform the structures, relations, values, and dynamics of a society's particular way of life" (Gil, 1992, 21–22). Gil defines social policy as a set of guiding principles that govern societal life and that therefore must be of great concern to social workers and other human service personnel. In effect, social policies should control all other public policies, excluding religion and foreign trade, but including economic policies.

From this perspective, social policy should reflect long-range visions of what a just and non-oppressive society would look like (Gil, 1998). Gil's vision also stresses values and ideologies affirming equality, individuality, liberty, coopera-tion, community, and global solidarity, rather than the currently prevailing values and ideologies that support inequality, individualism, selfishness, domination, competition, and disregard for community. For example, if Canada and other nations used the Universal Declaration of Human Rights, as adopted by the United Nations in 1948, as the centrepiece for all social policy, then all social policies would have to conform to this declaration to be established as public policies. By signing the U.N. document, Canada committed itself to eradicating poverty and ensuring basic human rights—and then did not do it.

Gil's comprehensive view of the social policy-making process suggests that social policies should govern natural and human-created resources; all aspects of employment, including human issues; the production of life-sustaining and life-enhancing resources; social, political, and civil rights; mechanisms for the distri-bution of rights and privileges; and mechanisms for the assignment of social status (Gil, 1992, 24–25). Therefore, all social problems are the result of a flawed social policy; thus, the policy, not the problem, needs to be redressed. As such, social policies are "potentially powerful instruments for planned, comprehensive, and systematic social change rather than reactive measures designed to ameliorate (in a fragmented fashion) undesirable circumstances" (Gil, 1970, 413). The primary domain of social policy is "all possible sets of human relationships and the quality of life or level of well-being in a given society" (415).

An important feature of Gil's approach to social policy is his insistence that social policies must address not only life-sustaining activities that ensure minimum basic needs, but also life-enhancing activities that promote and support human growth and potential. Social change theorist Paulo Freire (1968) argued that every person has an "ontological vocation"—that is, all people are born with the desire to search for meaning in their lives. Oppressive societies thwart this drive to maximize one's humanity. In this sense, Gil agrees with Freire that the ontological vocation for humans is to become more fully human and that social policy should be a mechanism to ensure that all humans have equal opportunity and equal access to society's resources to this end.

Swift (1995) suggests that existing social policies do in fact discriminate against the poor and, in particular, poor women. To gain resources, mothers "must appear incompetent in order to qualify for the resources" (125) and, in effect, present themselves as failed mothers. And yet the alternative is to live in poverty with inadequate resources, with the result of many mothers being labelled "bad mothers," rather than people who have been failed by society. Similar criticisms of social policies, as they relate to other areas of social diversity, are outlined in Chapter 4.

For social workers, Gil's notion of social policy conforms to the profession's value and ethical base. Having social policy address the challenges and realities of the human condition is certainly an ideal worth seeking. Making the interests of all people, their families, and their communities the first principle for societal governance emphasizes the *common good* rather than the *public* or *private interest*. As social welfare philosopher Frederic Reamer (1993) puts it, there is a substantive difference between the common good and the public interest, with commensurate implications to social policies. The common good refers to "that which constitutes the well-being of the community—its safety, the integrity of its basic institutions and practices, the preservation of its core values," and human end-states such as human flourishing and moral development (35). While originally referring to national security and prosperity goals, because of the neo-liberal world view, the *public interest* has now come to mean "a rational alliance of primarily self-interested individuals whose collective good is constituted by the collection or aggregation of private interests" (Reamer, 1993, 35). Thus, powerful groups can argue that they are promoting public interest by enhancing the individual pursuit of self-interest. Thus, social workers, who have a particular commitment to social justice for society's most marginalized, must hold notions of the common good as sacrosanct, despite changing notions about the public interest.

Implementing Gil's approach would require society to agree on what set of values should govern social policies. But in societies where political, ideological, and economic power is in the hands of fewer and fewer people (Bishop, 2002), this degree of social transformation is unlikely to occur. In the neo-liberal world view, life enhancement is something to earn, and society is responsible only to provide the minimal life-sustaining needs.

An Incremental Approach

Other social policy theorists do not take as comprehensive a view of social policy as Rein and Gil do. Wharf (1992) distinguishes between the *ordinary* and *grand* issues of social policy. *Grand* issues are "those pertaining to the fundamental structure of political–economic life" (14), including distribution of income and wealth, political power, and corporate prerogatives. *Ordinary* issues of social policy include "the governance of child welfare services, deinstitutionalization and the development of community support programs, the struggle to raise social welfare rates in Ontario, and the debate about abortion politics in Nanaimo" (15). Wharf argues that *ordinary* issues should be of concern to social workers because these issues directly affect the lives of people, can be managed and redressed by community-based organizations, and are sometimes the unintended consequence of earlier reforms.

When dealing directly with the *ordinary* issues of social policy, social workers often employ the rational decision-making model used by incrementalists. The incremental model views the social policy-maker as having to do the following:

> define and rank governing values;

> specify objectives compatible with these values;

> identify all relevant options or means of achieving these objectives;

> calculate all the consequences of these options and compare them; and

> choose the option or combination of options that would maximize the values earlier defined as being important (Hogwood & Gunn, 1984, 46–47).

Wharf (1992) makes note of the "goal-directed-muddling-through" approach to the policy process (where goals emerge in a way that might not be clear at the outset of the intervention) that community workers use. This inductive approach allows the community worker to ensure that the people's interest is known and that the policy process is "anchored in a philosophical position and a vision for change" (233). Because it permits a high degree of flexibility, practice wisdom, and discretion in pursuing objectives, Wharf believes it is an adaptive approach to policy-making. For most social workers, who will only rarely be exposed to global social policy issues, the values and ethics of social work are often the only firm base they have in policy.

A criticism of the incremental approach is that social workers and other human service workers become too preoccupied with resolving local or immediate issues stemming from social policy and do not pay sufficient attention to the social issues that may be creating the problem in the first place. For example, when the new EI program limited the time people were able to collect benefits, many regions with high seasonal unemployment organized against this policy. But the Liberal government did not alter it, which suggests that it was committed to globalization and a right-wing policy agenda (Clarke, 1997). How then should regional groups have attacked the Liberal government's policy position? Would they have obtained better results from local (incremental) efforts that challenged this policy within the region, or from national (comprehensive) initiatives that challenged the national policy direction?

The Mixed-Scanning Model

Etzioni (1968) argues that there may be a method of reconciling the differences between a comprehensive policy-making process and an incremental policy-making process. The mixed-scanning model can bridge the gap between these two approaches. After making a rational, comprehensive policy decision, policy-makers adjust the policy incrementally, based on information gained from its implementation. Thus, policy-makers can focus on the greater issues without becoming bogged down in details (Hess, 1993).

Table 8.1 compares the sequences of tasks for each approach. The *policy agenda* refers to the need to identify problems in a priority manner and to make policy-makers aware of this priority. *Policy formulation* refers to the development of clear and acceptable ways of solving problems or at least addressing them in a policy. *Policy adaptation* refers to the development of support and acceptance for the policy by such means as advocacy and accommodation. *Policy implementation* refers to the actual application of policy to the problem. *Policy evaluation* seeks to answer whether or not the policy worked.

Table 8.1 shows that each theory has its strengths and weaknesses. Anderson's sequence is rational and easy to understand, but it fails to address who is benefiting from these policies and why policies are directed to their benefit (Mason, Talbott, & Leavitt, 1993). While Wharf's sequencing appears similar to Anderson's, his approach is much more analytical and substantive, with a very clear community-organization perspective. Wharf's sequence addresses concern about which people are involved in the policy-initiation process; whether the problem the policy is addressing is correctly defined or whether it can be redefined; and whether sufficient resources, including people and funding, are available. Like Wharf, Rein recognizes that the policy-making process is not linear and that each stage is subject to problems and to political manipulation.

TABLE 8.1   Sequencing the Policy-Making Process

Anderson (1990)	Wharf (1992)	Wharf & McKenzie (2010)	Rein (1974)
Policy agenda	Initiation	Problem identification	Values
Policy formulation	Formation	Identification of value criteria	Operating principles
Policy adaptation	Execution	Assessing alternatives	Method of implementation
Policy implementation	Implementation	Feasibility assessment	
Policy evaluation	Evaluation	Recommendations	Outcomes

In the mixed-scanning model, policy-makers choose different paths through the sequence. They can start with Wharf and McKenzie's value criteria model (2010), which requires them to evaluate costs, benefits, and alternatives after defining the problem and the policy alternatives. Or they can use the garbage can model's three types of policy processes (problems, solutions, and politics), allowing them to operate independently until a situation or crisis arises. If a particular issue does not get on the policy agenda, then it may have to wait until a new opportunity arises or may have to be removed if it appears to be resolved. In other words, whenever there is a public concern, such as those being expressed over water quality in Ontario or farm subsidies in the Western provinces, then all components come together. When the crisis is over, they separate again, only to be re-engaged when another crisis strikes. While these processes are separated, there is little opportunity for social change.

The mixed-scanning approach is important because it allows social workers to understand both the anticipated and unanticipated impacts of social policy, as well as potential or actual shifts in social policy in Canada. Pierce (1984) notes, "Social workers also need to be able to identify policies that actually constitute a part of their practice world. If policy is to be used in generalist practice, its definition must come from the practice parameters and perspectives of line social workers" (4). However, the policy analyst should be aware of Wharf's (1990) cautions regarding four limitations associated with generalist practice models based on the ecological systems perspective:

> The mixed-scanning approach assumes that problems, once identified, will generate a demand for change—that is, change will occur and the problem will be solved.

> This approach ignores power and its distribution in Canada—that is, goodness-of-fit for the rich is good to excellent, while the goodness-of-fit for the poor is bad to terrible. Who has the power and the will to change this—the rich who are benefiting?

> This approach does not assign social workers responsibility to bring about change.

> This approach does not address the issue of auspices—that is, the fact that social workers work in agencies that are given their mandates by those holding political power. The social worker's efforts to change the system are limited by each agency's political and social agenda.

Controlling the Policy-Making Process

If anything is apparent from the preceding discussion on policy-making approaches, it's the number of factors that can derail the policy-making process. In Canada, there are four major types of pressure groups involving social policy:

> business groups, including the Canadian Manufacturers' Association and the Business Council on National Issues;

> labour groups, including the Canadian Labour Congress;

> professional groups, including the Canadian Association of Social Workers and the Canadian Association for Schools of Social Work Education; and

> advocacy groups, including the Canadian Council of Social Development, the National Anti-Poverty Organization, and the National Council of Welfare.

The most successful groups over the past few decades have been the business pressure groups. Corporate models essentially reflect a "power-over" (Bishop, 1994) approach, promoting the value of competition, hierarchy, and separation. *Separation* here refers to groups of citizens uniting to promote their best interests against the best interests of others. Bishop suggests that the end product of this type of "power-over" approach is a society infused with "sexism, racism, ageism, adultism, heterosexism, and ableism" (21). The question is simply this: What is needed to motivate people who are benefiting from the existing system (and who have the political, economic, and ideological power to maintain their advantage) to share their benefits with those less fortunate?

Consider the following example. Cancer patients in Southern Ontario who have to travel to Northern Ontario for radiation treatment have their travel, hotel, and food expenses covered; Northern Ontario residents who travel to Southern Ontario are not reimbursed equally. In one example reported in *The Globe and Mail* (Nikiforuk, 2007), a cancer patient from Iroquois Falls travelling to Sudbury (about 360 kilometres) a half-dozen times received $109.89 in support payments. Cancer patients travelling from Southern Ontario cities to Northern Ontario hospitals received approximately $5000. The reason: Northern Ontario patients are covered by Northern Health Travel Grants, whereas Southern Ontario residents are covered by the more generous Cancer Care Ontario. The same problem in opposite directions makes a difference of $4890.

By limiting the resources provided to those less well-off (such as the geographically isolated, the unemployed, the poor, the marginal income earners, and many postsecondary students) or those in need of protection (such as abused children, battered women, and dependent elderly), power groups create an environment of competition for funds. For example, the simple tightening of EI criteria has prevented thousands of seasonal workers from receiving benefits. Reducing social assistance and introducing tighter eligibility criteria has forced thousands of people off welfare. Reducing public housing projects ensures that thousands of people live in inadequate housing, which many cannot even afford. Reducing subsidies for women's shelters ensures that many women are left with horrific options should they need to flee a dangerous home situation. These are all current examples of human deprivation and suffering in one of the world's richest countries. How can a nation such as Canada justify there being more food banks than McDonald's restaurants?

Social policy advocates, such as Bishop (2005), Banks and Mangan (1999), and Wharf (1992), have increasingly focused on the need to engage the community in the policy-making process. By engaging the community, policy advocates can also link with existing community resources, such as local social and economic planning councils and citizen advocacy groups. These linkages ensure not only that the policy issues being discussed are relevant to the community, but also that obstacles to policy development are identified. Policy advocates can also translate new policy initiatives and existing public policies into terms that communities can understand.

Controlling the policy-making process is one of the major challenges facing policy advocates. Not only do political interest groups control the government public policy-making mechanisms; they also play a large role in the economic life of Canada and its communities. Advocates for progressive social policies must put away their individual differences (avoiding separation) and unite as allies seeking the same end despite different self-interests. As Bishop (1994) notes, "Commitment to social justice means beginning a completely unknown journey—a journey that can unfold only one step at a time, with confusion and danger along the way" (124).

Figure 8.2 presents an overview of the policy-making process as discussed in this chapter.

Figure 8.2 shows that the tensions created by the conflicts in globalization and social transformation challenge the ideologies that influence Canada's economic and social policies. Currently, the forces supporting globalization have been moving policies away from social transformation and citizenship and more toward a social responsibility and accountability model. At the policy analysis level, the dominant neo-liberal world views shape the policy debate by infusing its ideological interpretations of social and economic benefits and corresponding social and economic costs into public policy. At the next level, the theoretical and critical analysis of academic policy analysis comes into conflict with the applied policy

FIGURE 8.2   An Overview of the Policy-Making Process

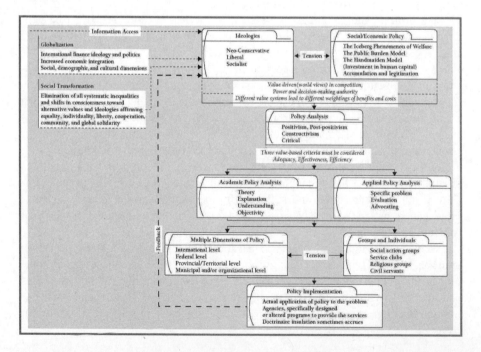

analysis process—the process of actually transforming policy into structure. The next level represents tensions between the political dimensions of a policy and the positions of interest and advocacy groups. Policy committee representatives (selected individuals who represent affected constituencies) tend simply to represent their constituencies, rather than providing direct feedback. Neysmith, Bezanson, and O'Connell (2005) advocate using a direct feedback mechanism, one that lets people understand "how policies play out in the lives of citizens from the perspective of those who experience them—those for whom . . . they are designed" (14). At the bottom level, policy becomes implemented in practice. A final feedback loop assesses whether the policy in structure is congruent with the original objectives. But whose voice actually is heard in the feedback process? And if concerns are raised, is anybody listening?

The following overview and discussion of the recent implementation of harmonized sales tax in Ontario and British Columbia is meant to provide a case example of the policy-making process as shown in Figure 8.2. An overview of the policy will be provided, followed by an analysis of the policy by using Figure 8.2.

A Policy-Making Process Case Study: An Overview of the HST

The global economic crisis and recession beginning in 2008 impacted the Ontario economy particularly hard. Ontario's reliance on the U.S.-dependent manufacturing, forestry, and automobile industries meant that over half of all jobs lost in Canada during the recession were lost in Ontario (Pasma, 2010). The B.C. economy was also hit hard because of weak forest product exports and declining levels of home construction. The provincial governments of both provinces experienced dramatic decreases in tax revenues combined with huge bills for "stimulus" infrastructure spending. This spending meant ballooning deficits and harsh criticism for the Liberal governments of Ontario and British Columbia in a political climate demanding "fiscal restraint" and "balanced budgets." Ontario and British Columbia were in trouble, with essential programs, such as health care, education, and social services, facing significant cuts because of plummeting provincial revenues.

Enter the federal Conservative government. Since the early 1990s, successive federal governments have made harmonizing provincial and federal retail sales taxes a priority, and four provinces had already implemented such a tax. At the time of the recession, Ontario and British Columbia both had a dual sales tax system in which some purchases were subject to only federal sales tax (GST) while others were also subject to provincial sales tax (PST). A harmonized sales tax (HST) would combine the GST and PST into one tax, administered by the federal government, and be applied according to the broader tax base of the GST. The federal Conservatives entered into talks with the Ontario Liberals, and on March 26, 2009, Ontario Finance Minister Dwight Duncan announced that Ontario would harmonize its PST with the GST in exchange for $4.3 billion in transfer payments from the federal government to assist with the province's transition to the new system. The B.C. Liberals soon followed suit, announcing their plans to implement a harmonized sales tax, which would come into effect the same day as the Ontario tax, July 1, 2010. British Columbia's new tax was made possible by $1.6 billion in federal incentive money.

The move to a harmonized sales tax was designed to make Ontario and British Columbia (and thus Canada) more appealing to business investment and create jobs in the struggling economies. How would this new tax initiative be effective in attracting business investment? The HST is meant to "simplify" retail taxes for business owners. Under the PST/GST system, business owners had to comply with two different sales tax systems at two different levels of government. In addition, business owners were required to pay GST and PST on purchases needed to run their businesses (called *input taxes*) but were able to claim and receive rebates only for the GST paid. In the new harmonized system, business owners are able to submit claims for the entire HST amount, effectively paying no input sales taxes and drastically lowering operating costs. Proponents of HST claim that businesses will eventually pass on their tax savings to customers in the form of lower prices.

The lost revenues from retail sales taxes previously generated from businesses are made up for by consumers who must now pay the combined HST amount on items previously only subject to GST. This change means consumers spend an additional 8 percent in Ontario and 7 percent in British Columbia on a variety of purchases, including home utilities, gasoline, professional services, new home purchases, membership fees, and even funerals. To offset the increased burden on families and individuals, the governments of British Columbia and Ontario also introduced other tax policy reforms, including decreases in personal and corporate income tax rates, temporary transition payments, and permanent sales tax credits to low-income families.

HST is important from a social policy-making perspective because its implementation, along with the simultaneous reductions in personal and corporate income taxes, represents an overall shift in Canadian tax policy toward regressive taxation. As discussed in Chapter 4, regressive taxes, such as retail sales tax, impose the same tax level on all citizens, disproportionately burdening those least able to pay, while more progressive taxes, such as income taxes, base the level of taxation on a person's ability to pay. Analysis of HST policy also highlights the current forces influencing the policy-making process, as shown in Figure 8.2.

Analyzing the HST Policy-Making Process by Using Figure 8.2 We will begin by looking at the tension created by the conflicts in *globalization* and *social transformation*. HST policy is an example of how the forces of globalization have prevailed in pressuring the governments of British Columbia, Ontario, and Canada to enact social and economic policies favouring business in an effort to become more "competitive" in global markets. With HST and regressive taxation, social policy moves away from the ideals of equality and social transformation and toward a policy that benefits an elite minority.

The current dominant neo-liberal *ideology*, with its emphasis on the state of the economy as the key indicator of the well-being of a nation, views the market as the primary solution to all social issues, and job creation is seen as effective and beneficial to *all* in society. With a neo-liberal ideology informing policy planning and implementation, the economy has become the priority for all levels of government. Priority for new policy initiatives is given to those policies that seem to promote economic growth and support the goals of the private sector, as is the case with HST. In this view, taxes, especially taxes on business, are viewed as inhibitors to economic growth and, thus, are undesirable.

The garbage can model of policy-making suggests that getting an issue on the *social/economic policy* agenda becomes a function of whether or not a crisis creates a need for the policy processes to come together. In the case of tax harmonization, the global economic crisis and domestic recession created a policy window in which the governments were able to introduce a policy based on a regressive model of taxation because it was portrayed as necessary for economic growth and job production.

We now come to *value driven world views* and *power and decision-making authority*. In Canadian politics, the *world views* and *values* of those in power are those reflected in social policy. Those in power tend to value economic production, GDP, strength in global markets, and tax cuts for the rich. As a result, less weight is given to policies that promote social welfare and equality. Concern over the effects of regressive forms of taxation, as well as the effects of reduced government revenue because of corporate tax cuts are heavily outweighed by concern over productivity and growth. The values reflected by a progressive tax system are absent or ignored.

Thus, the *policy analysis* of the move to HST and regressive taxation is limited by the neo-liberal ideology of those in power and the dominant values and world views that are taken into account. Policy analysis and discourse is confined to the potential effects of the new policy on the economy only. Little attention is paid to the effects of the policy on the population. Citizens are described only as consumers in the HST tax policy debate. The dominant values define *taxes* as undesirable constraints on business investment and economic growth, rather than as valuable and important means of generating revenues for social welfare programs and services. Discussion of the new HST policy is limited only to its desired effects on the economy and job production, with no discussion regarding what the move to a more regressive tax system means to the people of those provinces affected or a discussion about what this move says about the Canadian social welfare system.

The *critical* policy analysis voice that should attack this move to regressive taxation—based on the belief that it is fundamentally wrong for the government to raise revenues through regressive taxation of basic necessities rather than a suitably progressive income-based taxation system—is silenced. A critical analysis would view the move to HST as representing further government intrusion into the ability of individuals and families to survive. Families are sacrificed to put more money into the bank accounts of large international corporations that answer to no one and contribute less and less to the welfare of Canadians.

Those in power use three *value-based criteria* to justify the move to a regressive tax. First, in terms of *efficiency*, HST is described as easier for business owners to understand and comply with and as simpler and less costly to administrate. The previous PST/GST system is described as outdated, and rhetoric supports the necessity of moving to a more "modern" tax system. Second, the government introduces tax credits and tax cuts that are just *adequate* enough to appease the opposition and squelch any strong public outcry by seeming to protect those least well-off. The low-income credits and personal income tax cuts offer an incentive for "buy-in" from leftist organizations and potential opposition. Finally, the *effectiveness* of the policy is judged only in terms of its ability to achieve the desired goals of job creation and economic productivity.

The *academic* and *theoretical analysis* regarding the costs and benefits of regressive versus progressive forms of taxation are overshadowed by the *applied analysis* regarding benefits to business and the economy. HST policy discussion becomes a "public interest" argument about the "necessity" of competing in global markets and a cautionary tale about how easily businesses and business owners can move their factories and companies (cross-border or cross-province). The academic analysis of what a move to regressive taxation means to the provinces and the country is virtually non-existent. The "common good" argument is ignored in favour of business interests.

HST policy certainly encompasses *multiple dimensions of policy* and has received support and opposition at both the federal and provincial levels from different political parties, business groups, think tanks, and interest groups. Most notable in terms of opposition has been the Fight HST campaign in British Columbia led by former premier William Vander Zalm. This group has been the first to successfully file a petition under B.C.'s unique Recall and Initiative Act (1991). This Act makes it possible for voters to propose new laws or changes to existing laws that fall within the jurisdiction of the provincial government. Vander Zalm and his group collected more than 500 000 signatures opposing the new HST policy and demanded that the legislation enacting it be repealed. A referendum scheduled to take place in September 2011 will allow B.C. voters to decide the issue.

Policy implementation has taken place in both provinces, and the population now pays HST on purchases of goods and services. The new tax rules and regulations are being enforced by the Canada Revenue Agency. It is yet to be determined how future policy analysis in regard to HST will view the effects of this change and whose voices will form the *feedback* that informs future policy decisions.

Conclusion

This chapter explored how different world views shape unique perceptions about society, people, and people in society. It also examined the power of world views to convert social policy into public policies, programs, and services; to prescribe who is to be involved in the policy-making process; and to distribute power and decision-making authority. Finally, it discussed different approaches to the policy-making process.

Every model of social policy-making has its supporters and detractors. Academic debate still flourishes around which model is most effective. However, the tightening of control over Canadian policy-making process by those with the most economic and political power signals a challenge to advocates for social justice to unite in a common cause—to let Canadians know "the other side of the story." Chapter 9 discusses issues associated with implementing social policies and strategies to bring social justice to the forefront of Canadian public policy.

Chapter 9

Implementing Social Policies

The goal for all advocates of a specific social policy is to shape the public land-scape in a manner that reflects the values and objective of their policy position. This chapter discusses how these goals are accomplished. Having political power, especially in the form of a majority government, allows a group to introduce its social and economic policies into public policy with little opposition. This process is evident in such provinces as British Columbia and Ontario, where reform governments over the past 10 to 20 years have created tremendous public policy changes. Dare (1997) details major public policy changes made by Ontario's Harris government in its first five months in office:

> dismantling the Workplace Health and Safety Agency (incorporated by Workers' Compensation) and eliminating worker input; and limiting the Wage Protection Fund, which had included wages, benefits, severance, and termination pay, to only wages and benefits;

> reinstating the "spouse-in-the-house" rule, where single women who are alleged to be living with a man are cut off from welfare;

> imposing a three-month wait for welfare if applicants quit their jobs;

> cancelling 390 co-op and non-profit housing projects and Jobs Ontario, and closing 25 halfway houses for offenders;

> cutting welfare rates by 21.6 percent, the Ministry of Health budget by $1.5 billion, school board budgets by $1 billion, and grants to municipalities by 48 percent over two years.

Even when the Harper government ruled with a minority government, it sought to create changes in areas that tend to support multinational businesses and negate unions and the environment. For example, the decision to support the SPP (Security and Prosperity Partnership of North America) provided an opportunity for business leaders to participate in semi-secret policy debates. Unions and advocates for the environment and for various groups (such as women and immigrants) were not invited to these meetings. It will be important for advocates for social justice to monitor how the majority federal Conservative party deals with social welfare and justice issues.

This chapter will explore how laws are made in Canada (both federally and provincially/territorially); what laws look like and why they are important; the role of courts in the policy-making process; how power and influence play a major role in policy selection; and the role of citizen participation in this process.

The Canadian Political System

Like the United States, Switzerland, and Australia, Canada is a federal state. A federal state has two levels of government: national and state/provincial. The role of the national government is to promote the best interests of the whole country, to offset the diversity and chaos that could be created if each province or state sought its own best interests. Canada has two major forms of government—federal and provincial—built on a parliamentary model with a constitutional monarchy. The British North America Act, 1867 (now known as the Constitution Act, 1867), and the Constitution Act, 1982, established the governance domains for both the federal and provincial governments. While the territories—Nunavut, Northwest Territories, and Yukon—are based on similar parliamentary models as the provinces, they are headed by a commissioner, rather than a lieutenant-governor.

The federal parliament governs issues associated with Canada as a nation and makes laws to support the peace, order, and good government of Canada, such as international agreements and the right to levy taxes across the country. The provincial parliaments govern issues associated with the province, including hospitals (except marine hospitals), natural resources, municipal and provincial institutions, property rights, marriages, and social services; they have the right to levy taxes for provincial purposes.

> To learn more about the history of the Canadian parliamentary system of government, visit www.parl.gc.ca/parlinfo/, or check out Landes, R. (1998), *The Canadian Polity: A Comparative Introduction* (5th ed.). Scarborough: Pearson.

At the federal level, Canada has a governor general (representing the Queen of England), a Senate, and a House of Commons. The governor general appoints members of the Senate on the recommendation of the prime minister. The 105 members of the Canadian Senate, called senators, are appointed on the basis of 24 seats for the Western provinces, 24 seats for Ontario, 24 seats for Quebec, and 24 seats for the Maritime provinces. The remaining 9 seats represent Newfoundland and Labrador, the Northwest Territories, Yukon, and Nunavut. Senators maintain their seats until 75 years of age.

The 308 members of the House of Commons, known as *members of Parliament (MPs)*, are elected from across Canada and its territories. The executive authority for Canada is vested in the Queen, who is represented by the governor general (the lieutenant governor in provinces). By tradition, the governor general conforms to the will of the Cabinet, which is headed by the prime minister, who is the leader of the political party with a majority of seats (or the largest minority party, if no majority is elected, as determined by the governor general). The Cabinet, which is the executive branch of government, consists of a small group of MPs, known as *ministers*, who have been selected by the prime minister and assigned specific ministries. These ministers are responsible for all policy development within their ministerial portfolio and the promotion of these policies in Cabinet. Obviously, a strong minister will achieve greater success in moving policy to law or programs.

The legislative branch of government essentially consists of the House of Commons, including all parliamentary committees. Should the governor general become incapacitated, the chief justice of the Canadian Supreme Court becomes administrator of Canada and serves on behalf of the governor general.

At the provincial level, a lieutenant governor represents the Queen of England for a provincial parliament. Provincial parliaments follow the same process as the federal government, except that the head of the provincial Cabinet is called a *premier*, and there is no provincial senate. The Quebec provincial parliament is called the *National Assembly*, and members are called *Members of the National Assembly (MNA)*. The Newfoundland and Labrador provincial parliament is called the *House of Assembly*, and members are called *Members of the House of Assembly (MHA)*. The Ontario provincial parliament is called the *Provincial Parliament* and members are called *Members of Provincial Parliament (MPP)*. All other provinces and territories call their provincial parliament the *Legislative Assembly*, and members are called *Members of the Legislative Assembly (MLA)*.

Making Laws

The initiative to create a new law or reform an existing one can come from various sources. For example, strong public opinion, such as the current fear of terrorism, can influence ministers, as can people lobbying for industry or other interest groups. As noted in the beginning of this chapter, the political platform of newly elected governments can also shape political opinion. In addition, the bureaucracy for each ministry can promote public policy initiatives based on their own operations, including program evaluations and need surveys.

Essential policy debate on a proposed legislation (called a *bill*) occurs in Cabinet, often in secret, before it ever reaches Parliament. Committees of Cabinet, including the Treasury Board, examine the bill. Other constituents, such as the party's caucus (elected members of the ruling party), may be involved in discussions, particularly for controversial or marginally supported bills.

Laws can originate in many ways, but some routes are more effective than others. Explore this further by reading newspapers, magazines, and public opinion surveys and searching for the answers to the following questions: Who is sponsoring the proposed new or reformed legislation? Who is likely to benefit from this legislative initiative? Who is likely to be negatively affected?

When a draft of the bill is ready, the minister introduces it to the House of Commons or Legislative Assembly. It must then pass three separate readings and votes. By use of a "party whip," the governing party ensures that party members who are not in Cabinet (known as *backbenchers*) vote in support of the proposed legislation. Sometimes, when a piece of legislation has deep moral or social meaning, party members are allowed to vote according to their own conscience and not necessarily with the party's position. If the bill is passed, Parliament sends it to committees composed of representatives from all parties for fine-tuning and minor amendments.

There are two common types of bills. *Public bills* are proposals that will impact the public as a whole, and they are usually introduced by the appropriate minister. *Private bills* usually concern individuals or local matters. However, there are also private members' public bills, private senators' public bills (federal only), private senators' private bills (federal only), and senate government bills.

Once a federal bill passes three readings in the House of Commons, it then goes to the Senate, where the process is repeated. If it passes all three readings in the Senate, the bill goes to the governor general for royal assent. Once the governor general signs it, the bill becomes law. Provincially, the bill becomes law once it passes its three readings in the provincial Legislative Assembly and receives royal assent by the lieutenant governor.

Each department or ministry in the federal and provincial government has statutes (acts) that empower these ministries and departments to do their business. For example, the minister assigned to the Department of Family and Community Services in New Brunswick works under the following statutes: Charitable Donation of Food, Family Income Security, Health Services, Intercountry Adoption, Nursing Homes, Family Services (except Part 7), and Vocational Rehabilitation of Disabled Persons. As well, it operates under some sections of Change of Name, Education, Employment Standards, Hospital, and Reciprocal Enforcement of Maintenance Orders statutes. It is important for social policy advocates to know which acts govern which ministries or departments and to become familiar with those acts that affect their work.

Municipal governments, which govern cities, towns, villages, counties, districts, and metropolitan regions, are established by the provincial legislatures. Provincial and territorial legislatures grant municipalities all their powers. Officials such as mayors, reeves, and councillors are elected on a basis determined by the provincial legislature.

The Internet provides ready access to provincial and federal ministries and departments. Most sites allow downloading or printing of acts and regulations associated with the different ministries. Try looking up ministries or departments that interest you, and examine the statutes that govern their activities. Provincial/territorial government sites can be found at www.gov.nf.ca (Newfoundland and Labrador); www.gov.pe.ca (Prince Edward Island); www.gov.ns.ca (Nova Scotia); www.gnb.ca (New Brunswick); www.gouv.qc.ca (Quebec); www.ontario.ca (Ontario); www.gov.mb.ca (Manitoba); www.gov.sk.ca (Saskatchewan); http://alberta.ca (Alberta); www.gov.bc.ca (British Columbia); www.gov.nt.ca (Northwest Territories); www.gov.yk.ca (Yukon); and www.gov.nu.ca (Nunavut).

Municipal governments provide an array of local services, including water supply, sewage and garbage disposal, roads, sidewalks, street lighting, building codes, parks, playgrounds, and libraries. Some provinces, such as Ontario, have granted municipalities a greater role in social welfare programs. For example, Ontario Works (1997) downloaded workfare and social assistance to municipalities. Schools are generally looked after by school boards or commissions elected under provincial education acts but are often funded at the municipal level.

As noted in Chapter 1, laws are powerful instruments that impact all Canadians. Despite controversy and opposition, once a bill becomes law, all citizens must obey it or suffer sanctions, such as fines or even imprisonment. Certainly, such issues as capital punishment, abortion, and marriage definitions are still being debated in the general public, but existing laws frame what options are legal. Nevertheless, people who believe their rights are being infringed have options.

The Court Option

People who believe they have a legitimate case against an existing law can take their case to court. Canada has two levels of courts: federal and provincial. While the Constitution provides that most courts are created by provincial legislatures, judges from county courts up are appointed by the federal government (with the exception of probate courts in Nova Scotia and New Brunswick). Under the Judges Act (1952), the federal government in Canada appoints and pays all federally appointed judges. However, removing judges is a different issue. Judges of the provincial supreme courts (called the *Superior Court* in Quebec), the Federal Court, and the Supreme Court of Canada may be removed only by the governor general. This rule provides these courts with a great deal of independence from governing parties. Nevertheless, judges are appointed by a governing party, and there is a tendency for parties to select judges who reflect their political ideology or orientation. A judge with a neo-conservative orientation may adjudicate differently on the same issue than a judge with a social democratic orientation.

People who believe their rights are being violated or who wish to contend with how a particular act is being interpreted may address their grievances through the court system. What is important is that the ruling of the Supreme Court of Canada is final. This process is very expensive and time-consuming, but is still an option for advocates of human and social rights to redress social injustices. For example, the Supreme Court has been asked to rule on such issues as the right of gay partners to receive the same employee benefits as the partners of heterosexual employees; the right of an individual to choose physician-assisted suicide; and the right of citizens to practise active euthanasia.

Power and Ideology

Power has been defined by Etzioni (1975) as the ability to enforce compliance to authority, and by Brager, Specht, and Torczyner (1987) as the potential for and the exercise of influence. Other theorists (Gil, 1992) have viewed power in terms of its ability both to create compliance and to resist being made compliant. This ability to resist being made compliant is a critical issue for social work and all the helping professions. In terms of social policy, Wharf (1992) suggests that power is, in effect, the capacity to alter policies and decisions.

This capacity may be exercised through persuasion, rewards, or other means of securing compliance; but where these strategies fail, policy-makers can bring about change on a unilateral basis. *Influence* refers to any attempt to convince policy-makers of the need for change. Policy-makers have power, even though their ability to secure compliance may at times be slight because of the pitfalls of implementation. On the contrary, social reform organizations possess influence but not power (Wharf, 1992, 25–26).

In terms of political advocacy, Gil (1990) reminds social workers that they cannot be politically neutral if they value the social well-being of those they serve, because their practice "either confronts or challenges established societal institutions or it conforms to them openly or tacitly" (20).

According to Woodsworth (1986), while power operates on many levels, it takes many forms:

➤ big business and big government;

➤ management and bureaucracy;

➤ professional and interpersonal relationships;

➤ religious organizations; and

➤ professional, scientific, and technical leaders.

While acknowledging *pluralism* as a central concept in Canadian political life, Woodsworth (1986) notes that there is also an elite group in Canada that wields considerable power. *Pluralism* means that "there are many competing influences on the way people behave toward each other" (71). *Elitism* refers to the chosen or most carefully selected part of a group or society. Elitism in social policy terms implies that social and public policy do not reflect the demands of the people so much as they do the interests and values of the powerful few. Elitism views the masses as largely passive, apathetic, and poorly informed—a situation that allows the elite to manipulate mass sentiments by the use of power gained from monopolistic control of the boards of major corporations and financial institutions and by their overwhelming presence in government. This presence leads to a situation where the elite "develop policies to favour big business, and when in business they find ways of influencing public policy" (71). Woodsworth (1986) goes on to say, "Perhaps the central question for social workers is the extent to which the methods and goals of government and business (aimed at standardization and control) are accepted and continued by professionals in their ways of working with clients" (70).

Galbraith (1983) suggests that power is derived from three sources: (1) personality (with leadership a major asset); (2) wealth or property (including disposable income); and (3) organization (viewed as most important). Wharf (1986) views politicians, bureaucrats, and pressure groups as having the most influence on policies, with provincial and federal cabinets being the most important units in the Canadian political system. In terms of pressure groups, Wharf notes that having well-organized groups with influential people who are known to those in power is essential for successful influencing. Canadian Manufacturers and Exporters, the International Bank for Reconstruction and Development, the Chamber of Commerce, the Canadian Medical Association, and the Canadian Bar Association are examples of business and professional groups. The National Council of Welfare, the National Anti-Poverty Organization, the Canadian National Institute for the Blind, and the Canadian Council on Social Development are all examples of pressure groups from the social welfare arena.

The influence of an ideology supported by powerful political and economic forces is enormous. *Ideology* is essentially a confirmed belief that a political and social order is correct. In effect, an ideology with political, economic, and sometimes religious clout becomes so dominant that other perspectives are viewed as dangerous or irrelevant. In effect, oppression and "power-over" thinking comes to pervade the policy-making process. For example, Schragge (1997) suggests that the new political agenda of the 1990s promoted an ideology that not only "bashed the poor," but also created a whole new ideology about the "underclasses." Not only have social programs been cut after being blamed for creating the public debt, but a meaner and dehumanized ideology has also ascended into policy prominence, legitimating workfare as progressive policy development despite research that suggests it is repressive and counterproductive. The following quote from a conservative writer exemplifies how neo-conservative ideology blames the poor for their social conditions:

Social Work's reluctance to see that personal failings play a role in poverty is worse than unrealistic: it positively hurts the poor. Modern social workers have taken the position that environmental factors—the economy, racism, sexism, and so on—account for neediness, and sadly, many have preached this doctrine to their clients. By telling them that someone else is to blame for their fate, they encourage scapegoating and whining, and undermine the motivation to succeed. (Payne, 1998, 109–110)

An oppressor's goal is to maintain absolute control by planting fear and doubt in the minds of the oppressed, who are only rewarded for public docility and compliance. As Fromm (1967) notes, human freedom has historically been restricted by "the use of force on the part of the rulers . . . and, more importantly, the threat of starvation against all who are unwilling to accept the conditions of work and social existence that were imposed on them" (183).

Institutional Structures Supporting the Policy-Making Process

The primary policy-making bodies in Canada are the federal, provincial, and territorial parliaments. All public policies stem from these bodies, and the power granted to municipalities stems from the provincial and territorial governments. As discussed in Chapters 2 and 3, under the Canadian Constitution, provincial governments historically have jurisdiction over health, welfare, and education. Any federal government intrusion into these jurisdictions—such as occurred with Unemployment Insurance (1940, Section 91, 2A), Old Age Pensions (1951, Section 94A) and pensions extended to cover survivors, disability, and supplementary benefits (1964)—requires constitutional amendments. The provinces did contest Family Allowances (1944) (*Angers v. Minister of National Revenue*), but it was eventually allowed under the constitutional provision of "peace, order, and good government" (Report for the Interprovincial Conference of Ministers Responsible for Social Services, 1980).

The two most important components of the policy-making process are the prime minister/premiers and the Cabinet (Yelaja, 1987). The prime minister and premiers have the power to appoint Cabinet members and to remove them as well. Each Cabinet minister is given a specific area of government responsibility called a *portfolio*. This portfolio may be just one ministry or department or it may include more than one. For example, Alberta has the Ministry of Family and Social Services; Ontario has the Ministry of Community and Social Services; New Brunswick has the Department of Health and a Department of Family and Community Services; Prince Edward Island has a Department of Community and Cultural Affairs and a Department of Social Services and Seniors; the Northwest Territories have a Department of Health and Social Services; British Columbia has a Ministry of Children and Family Development and a Ministry of Community Services; and Manitoba has both a Department of Family Services and Housing and a Department of Health. The titles of these ministerial portfolios change often with the election of new governments.

The Charter of Rights and Freedoms (1982) is a major piece of social policy legislation that has the potential to ensure that citizens have the opportunity to challenge any legislation or amendments that might restrict, interfere, or impinge on those rights and freedoms claimed in the Charter. However, as Hess notes,

When interpreting complex and sometimes ambiguous sections of the Charter, the courts will inevitably play an increasing role in social policy, despite the fact that many

people in Canada's judicial system have limited experience and understanding of social policy issues and the implication of their decisions on policies and programs. (1993, 45)

Citizen Participation

Citizens can participate in the social policy-making process in many ways. Before exploring the options, we need to explore the issue of citizen participation. The role of citizens in the policy-making process is a major concern for social workers, in terms of both social work's value base and its code of ethics. People in a democratic country have a right to participate in issues affecting the public interest and the common good. However, there are problems in motivating people to participate.

Wharf and Cossom (1987) suggest that the *principle of affected interest* is a major issue in promoting citizen participation. This principle states that everyone "who is affected by the decisions of a government should have a right to participate in that government" (271), especially in terms of the following three criteria:

> *Personal choice* reflects the degree to which a person wants to be involved, especially in terms of how much people believe the policy will affect them. For example, university students may become involved in decisions to raise tuition but not feel affected or interested in decisions to raise the price of admission to local swimming pools.

> *Competence* suggests that some decisions are accepted because experts made them. As well, for issues of complexity, such as pollution and nuclear waste, citizens need a degree of knowledge to participate. Complexities, such as the overuse of rules of order or presentations by technocrats, can intimidate people into not participating.

> *Economy* suggests issues of efficiency, rationality, and preservation of scarce resources. It also refers to the time, energy, and money people have to participate. For example, single mothers may not be able to attend meetings because they do not have money for bus fare or babysitters.

Another problem stems from Canada's political process. Canada's political system is based on the principle of representative democracy. Each political party in Canada is permitted to choose a candidate to represent that party in each federal/provincial electoral riding. In each riding, members of the party select from among a number of eligible candidates the person they wish to represent the party at the next election. Once an election is called, this member then runs against candidates selected by other parties in the same way. The winner is supposed to represent all those in the riding, including all members of other parties. Yet the member becomes a member of the party caucus and is expected (and even coerced) to vote along party lines. It is easy to see why people can feel alienated and powerless in getting their voices heard when the very system that is there to represent them is so removed from them as individuals. Moreover, it is difficult for an elected member not to feel a sense of obligation to those who helped them to win the election and to feel fewer obligations to those who were trying to defeat them.

Governments can involve citizens in the policy-making process in several ways. At the input or formative stage, governments can establish commissions with the mandate to explore a public issue in depth and to bring back a community-informed recommendation on actions the government should take. The Senate Committee on Poverty in the late 1960s is an example of such a commission. This committee visited several cities in Canada and listened to thousands of delegations representing multiple interests. It prepared a final report including these recommendations, which was made public.

Also at the input level, the government may appoint policy committees. The recent popularity of policy committees reflects the disparity of influence between "the haves" and "the have-nots." The core of policy committees consists of representatives from government, agencies, and institutionalized interest groups, who have the real power in the policy-making process (Hess, 1993). Other groups that lack status or resources, such as academics and advocacy groups, are given the status of "attentive public," and their contribution is limited to what they contribute to the public debate and the policy discussion.

This unequal power and influence means that the power of specific pressure groups can increase the probability of a policy outcome (Hage & Hollingsworth, 1977). Mishra (1995) notes that pressure or lobby groups "are associations of people with common interests which seek to influence public policy" (67–68). Pressure groups can either be interest groups that seek to enhance members' interests (such as chambers of commerce, rifle associations, trade and business associations) or promotional groups that "espouse a cause . . . or advocate on behalf of a particular group (such as the poor, the homeless, the disabled)" (68). Wharf (1986) recommends that any group wishing to influence public policy must be well organized and made up of influential people who are known by senior civil servants and politicians.

In other words, influencing public policy at the input stage is both strategic and expensive. Large corporations hire lobbyists who are often ex-politicians or ex-senior civil servants to advance their causes and to ensure that public policies reflect their best interests. The poor, the injured, the unemployed, the sick, people with disabilities, and dependent groups cannot compete and are often dependent on the policy advocacy of others, such as the National Council on Welfare, National Anti-Poverty Organization, the Canadian Council on Social Development, Canadian Association of Social Workers, and other promotional groups.

At the policy evaluation stage, governments once again seek citizen input. However, many of the problems that reduce citizen involvement at the input level also affect it at the evaluation level. Some people assume that policy-makers reflect on their policy decisions because of the feedback. However, Grob (1992) and Galster (1996) suggest that this is not the case. Essentially, policy-makers are receptive to research findings that support their ideology, especially when the research is easy to understand and to use. Timing is another important factor, because research becomes attractive when there is a current, controversial public issue, and less attractive when there is no public controversy.

Unfortunately, very few built-in structures in Canada ensure that citizens—both those directly affected by policy or those with an interest in policy—have the opportunity to be heard. Certainly, not voting for a party in the next election is one means of protest; but if one is a member of a minority group, it is of little consequence unless the majority understands the issues as seen by the minority.

Getting information to the public is another means of consciousness-raising that can influence policy. However, in a country where the vast majority of media—such as television, newspapers, radio, and magazines—are owned by the privileged few, it is unlikely that the minority and politically left views will be deemed newsworthy. Meanwhile, the media are more likely to accept reports from a neo-conservative ally source, such as the Fraser Institute, without question or analysis. Those in power are able to maintain a "power-over" posture that maintains hierarchy (who rules, who follows), separation (we are not responsible for one another), and competition (the proving ground for competence and character), because decision-makers favour their own group and give themselves increasing power.

These powers serve to sever those with limited power or no power from any substantive role in the policy-making process. It is essential that social workers and other human service professionals strive to open the channels for citizen involvement.

The Role of the Social Worker in the Policy-Making Process

The call to use community as a basis for policy-making development is not new (Wharf, 1992); nor is the *strengths perspective*, which views the strengths and resources of people and their environment as the central focus of social work (Chapin, 1995). Together, they provide an excellent framework for conceptualizing societal needs in new ways to allow a more inclusive approach to policy formulation and a wider opportunity to develop more meaningful and realistic policy options. Communities have personal, first-hand knowledge of *respect, collaboration, caring, trust, sacredness, vision,* and *neighbourliness,* and they are familiar with ways these ideas translate into community needs.

Obviously, the trust and value the community places in the social worker plays an important part in how well these resources work together. Earning this trust without violating or compromising one's social work values and ethical base requires great skill and time. The knowledge social workers gain through their position of trust gives them a unique ability to relate the policy-making process to social impacts by doing the following:

➢ objectively analyzing the anticipated and unanticipated impacts of social and public policies on the communities they serve;

➢ examining the congruence between social policies and agency policies (their own and other agencies) and advocating for adjustments to align these policies;

> increasing community consciousness regarding existing social and economic policies and any potential consequences for these communities;

> organizing community responses to social policies with negative consequences;

> developing coalitions between communities to enhance the response to negative social policies;

> ensuring that those social policies that benefit communities are acknowledged;

> developing a research capacity of sufficient sophistication to allow information pertaining to the community to be collected; and

> developing mechanisms to ensure this research information is made available and acknowledged by policy-makers, even if lobby or pressure groups must be employed.

For many social workers, social policies often seem abstract concepts with little or no connection to social work practice. However, policy advocacy and policy practice are both instrumental components of social work practice.

Conclusion

At a time when social programs and agencies are being downsized and even eliminated, social workers need to become involved in the policy-making process. As political and economic interest groups dominate Canada's policy-making process, the helping professions, especially those in the public sector, are being called on to engage in collaborative partnerships with their client groups and their communities (Barter, 1996; Delaney & Brownlee, 1995; Graham & Barter, 1999) to fight for their inclusion as citizens who can take part in policy-making, and not just as citizens who are passively affected by social and public policies.

While there are and probably will continue to be many different approaches to the policy-making process, social workers should advocate for citizen participation in all policy-making activities. Within the framework of social justice and equality, social workers can go a long way toward ensuring that all voices are heard by policy-makers and that no voice is given preference over others. The objective is not to make social policy a matter of easy choices but of informed choices that benefit all the people of Canada.

Social work is being called on to resist neo-conservative interpretations of social realities and to maintain its own vision and critical analysis to promote social and human justice. Social workers and human service professionals must maintain their ideals in a storm of cynicism about people and human value. As Homan (1994) states, "Idealism is not to be confused with naiveté. Idealism is a purposeful, powerful belief. . . . An idealist simply refuses to capitulate to a prodding dullness of spirit. . . . Someone may say to you, 'You are an idealist.' Take it as a compliment." (32).

Appendix

Canadian Chronology of Social Welfare

Prior to European colonization, Aboriginal peoples are in North America and have long-established traditions of social care.

1520s–1763: European settlement along the St. Lawrence River; establishment and growth of French colony in North America—Nouvelle France. Formal European contact had preceded this date along the eastern coast of North America. European colonization in North America transformed Aboriginal communities across the continent. Colonization brought with it European social welfare institutions, such as education, hospitals, and charity.

1759: The fall of Nouvelle France led to the 1763 Treaty of Paris and the creation of a British colony. British social welfare institutions, like their French counterparts, assume limited, local government (parish) responsibility for the poor and indigent. A residual approach to social welfare.

1867: The British North America Act established constitutional jurisdiction over provinces for health, social services, and education. Residual approach persisted. There was an increase in the scope and number of voluntary charitable services during the latter half of the nineteenth century.

1872: The Nine-Hour Movement, in defiance of the existing law stipulating that labour unions were illegal, resulted in labour rights rallies throughout Ontario and Quebec. Later that year the Trade Unions Act was passed, making trade unions legal. But it would require several decades of strikes, and the subsequent deaths of several strikers, to gain union recognition in many employment sectors.

1873–1878: The Canadian Labour Union (the first national organization for unions in Canada) was created and abolished. Local unions, though, would continue to flourish—by 1890 there were approximately 240 local unions across the country.

1876:   The Indian Act established the Crown as a separate authority for services to Aboriginal peoples based on treaty obligations. The Act placed Aboriginal peoples in a distinct legal category, as wards of the federal government, without the privileges of full citizenship. To gain citizenship rights, Aboriginal people would have to apply for enfranchisement (a culturally insensitive and completely discriminatory process of total assimilation within Canadian society), a condition of which included relinquishing their status rights and cultural identity.

1883:   The Labour Congress of Canada was created out of meetings with the Toronto Trades and Labour Council and the Knights of Labour, and was later renamed the Trade and Labour Congress of Canada (1886–1956).

1886:   Early forms of Workers' Compensation legislation were introduced. Voluntary welfare organizations emerged over the early to mid-nineteenth century, with greater intensity at century's end. Highlights included the Toronto Children's Aid Society (1891), Red Cross (1896), and Victorian Order of Nurses (1897).

1900:   Dominion Elections Act was passed, permitting only those people considered eligible to vote in provincial elections the right to vote in federal elections. As a result, Aboriginal people, visible minorities, and women did not gain voting rights.

1914:   The country's oldest social work school was established at the University of Toronto. Others followed at McGill University (1918) and the University of British Columbia (1928).

1914:   Workers' Compensation was established in Ontario; other provinces followed.

1914–1918:   World War I. Returning veterans provided retirement annuity insurance assistance (1920), settlement assistance (1927), and allowances (1930) to veterans, widows, or orphans with insufficient means.

1914:   Voluntary welfare organizations proliferated after World War I. They included the Toronto Family Service Agency (1914), Canadian Mental Health Association (1918), Canadian National Institute for the Blind (1918), Canadian Council on Social Development (1920), and Canadian Association of Social Workers (1926).

1916:   Mothers' Allowances, a selective program, was established in Manitoba; other provinces followed.

1916–1920:   During this period approximately 1600 worker strikes were undertaken. Workers were requesting standards to be implemented that legally only allow for an eight-hour work day, that unions become recognized, and that wages be improved.

1919:   The Winnipeg General Strike, consisting of 25 000 to 30 000 strikers, began on May 15 and ended on June 26. During these few weeks, two Canadian workers were killed and a few dozen others were injured.

1920: Amendments were made to the Dominion Elections Act. Voting rights were extended to all except Aboriginal people and visible minorities. The vote was accorded to women federally; between 1916 and 1920, seven provinces also accorded women the vote. Prince Edward Island gave women the vote in 1922, followed by Quebec in 1939.

1927: Old Age Pension Act was introduced. It was federal, selective, and cost-shared with provinces.

1928: The Sexual Sterilization Act was passed in Alberta, forcing the sterilization of all those in mental institutions. The Act was not repealed until 1972.

1929: Five Canadian women successfully sought legal recognition as persons under the British North America Act.

1930s: The Great Depression. In 1933, the national unemployment rate was 25 percent. Municipal governments faced difficulties paying for Unemployment Relief; many went bankrupt. An uploading of responsibilities to higher levels of government occurred.

1937: The Rowell–Sirois Commission on dominion–provincial relations was established, releasing its report in 1940. The report examined the economic and financial basis of Confederation. It advocated greater taxing provisions for the federal government; a national system of Unemployment Insurance and pensions; and revenue transfers to provinces.

1939–1945: World War II. Domestic conditions set the stage for the onset of a universal welfare state.

1940: Unemployment Insurance (1940–1996), a federal program resulting from constitutional amendment, was introduced.

1943: The Marsh Report, a wartime blueprint for a federal welfare state, was released.

1944: The Privy Council Order 1003, an emergency order by the federal government, in response to the growing number of strikers across the country, was passed in Parliament. The order further solidified in law the right for workers to organize, and it ordered that businesses recognize the unions chosen by the majority of workers.

1944: Family Allowances (1944–1992), a universal program, was introduced.

1945: The United Nations was created.

1946: Supreme Court Justice Ivan Rand ruled that workers were obligated to pay union dues (known as *the Rand Formula*) regardless of status within the union. This, coupled with legislation similar to the Privy Council Order 1003 being passed in all provinces during 1946 and 1948, solidified the role of unions in negotiating labour standards and worker rights.

1948:   Discriminatory sections that provided voting rights based on race were repealed from the Dominion Elections Act.

1948:   The United Nations General Assembly passed the Universal Declaration of Human Rights.

1951:   The Old Age Security program became universal.

1954:   Ontario became the first government in Canada to establish that it was illegal to deny to any person service or accommodation by passing the Fair Accommodations Act. The other provinces followed suit shortly thereafter.

1956:   The Hospital Insurance and Diagnostic Services Act saw the federal government agree to set up a plan in cooperation with the provinces to provide hospital care for everyone.

1956:   The federal government passed the Female Employee Equal Pay Act, entitling women to pay equal to men's for the same work.

1956:   The Canadian Labour Congress (1956–present) was formed by merging the Trade and Labour Congress of Canada and the Canadian Congress of Labour (1940–1956).

1960:   Aboriginal people were granted the right to vote in federal elections without giving up their treaty rights and entitlements first.

1960:   The federal government passed the Canadian Bill of Rights, which guaranteed such rights as freedom of the press, freedom of association and assembly, freedoms of speech and religion, equality rights before the law, and the right of the individual to life, liberty, security of the person, and enjoyment of property.

1962:   The Saskatchewan government of T.C. Douglas proposed the first medicare plan in North America (it had been announced in 1959 and was preceded by other initiatives from his government in 1947 covering hospital insurance). Medicare allowed doctors to collect their fees only from the government.

1962:   The federal system of immigration selection began to become more objective, yet individuals from European countries continued to be favoured in selection processes.

1966:   The Medical Care Act of the federal government extended health insurance to cover doctors' services. It was finally implemented in 1968, and it would take six years for all of the provinces to join. The Medical Care Insurance Act implemented cost-shared programs between the federal and provincial governments to finance provincially run health-care programs.

1966:   The Canada Assistance Plan (CAP, 1966–1996), a cost-sharing agreement between the federal government and the provinces to split fifty–fifty the costs of provincially delivered education and social services, was introduced.

1966:	The Canada Pension Plan (CPP) and Quebec Pension Plan (QPP) were established. Intended to cover all working Canadians, the plans transferred income from workers to retired persons.
1966:	The Guaranteed Income Supplement (GIS), a supplement to Old Age Security for low-income earners, was introduced.
1967:	A points system was introduced to Canadian immigration in an effort to reduce the selection process's racial biases. Subsequent legislation further revised the immigration selection process.
1968:	The Employment Standards Act was introduced by the federal government. This Act established a national labour code that set minimum wage standards ($1.25 per hour at this time), the eight-hour workday and the 40-hour workweek, and the entitlement to vacation time by employees.
1969:	The federal government's White Paper on Indian Affairs proposed the repeal of the Indian Act, the end of separate legal status for Aboriginal peoples, and conversion of reserve lands to private tenure. It was widely rejected by Aboriginal leaders, who began a sustained campaign for separate constitutional and policy recognition.
1969:	Following the Royal Commission on Bilingualism and Biculturalism, the Official Languages Act was passed. This federal legislation recognized English and French as official languages in the operations of all federal departments and agencies.
1971:	The federal government announced an official policy of multiculturalism. These principles were further elaborated in the 1988 Multiculturalism Act, among other policy documents.
1971:	The Unemployment Insurance program was considerably expanded in scope.
1971:	The Senate Committee on Poverty coincided with the creation of the National Council of Welfare and with more comprehensive publication of poverty data by Statistics Canada.
1973:	The Canadian Council on the Status of Women was established following the recommendations of a royal commission on the status of women.
1976:	The Coalition of Provincial Organizations of the Handicapped (COPOH) was formed (currently known as the *Council of Canadians with Disabilities*), acting as a national lobbying group to further the rights of people with disabilities in Canada.
1977:	The Established Programs Financing (EPF) Act, signalling changes to funding arrangements of the CAP and the Medical Care Act, was passed.
1977:	The Canada Human Rights Act was passed. An important inclusion of this legislation, which was missing from other human rights

documents, was the disallowance of discrimination on the basis of a person's ability. Sexual orientation was not amended into the Act, as a ground to disallow discrimination, until 1996.

1981: The Special Committee on the Disabled and the Handicapped published a report consisting of narratives about the barriers and obstacles that people with disabilities were facing in Canadian society. Policy outcomes developed from the recommendations in this report around improving the ways in which people with disabilities were integrated into Canadian society.

1982: The Charter of Rights and Freedoms, expanding previous legislation, provided individual rights and group rights to various communities in Canadian society. Marital status and sexual orientation have been recognized as categories for protection from discrimination by the Supreme Court of Canada (*Miron v. Trudel* and *Egan v. Canada*, both in 1995), but currently have not been added to the Charter.

1982: Mandatory retirement was abolished in Quebec, followed by Manitoba in 1983. This practice was not recognized elsewhere in the country until the twenty-first century: Ontario, 2006; Saskatchewan, 2007.

1984: The federal government's Canada Health Act, outlining the conditions of universality—portability, public administration, comprehensiveness, and accessibility—was passed.

1985: The Indian Act was amended to eliminate discriminatory practices that were present in prior amended versions. For example, women no longer gained or lost their entitlement to register as a result of becoming married, and marriage of parents no longer determined the entitlement of a child. The concept of enfranchisement was removed from the Indian Act, and all entitlements that had been a result of this policy were reinstated after application.

1989: Changes to the income tax system made Old Age Security effectively a selective program. Over the 1980s and 1990s, other programs were systematically eroded.

1992: Family Allowances were abolished and replaced with selective child tax benefits.

1996: Unemployment Insurance was replaced with Employment Insurance. Retrenchment of the terms/conditions of this program and others continued.

1996: CAP and the funding arrangements for health care under EPF were replaced with the Canada Health and Social Transfer.

1998: The National Child Benefit Supplement (NCB), which provided supplemental income to low-income families over and above the amount received through the Canada Child Tax Benefit, was introduced.

1999: The federal and provincial governments joined in a Social Union initiative to co-ordinate delivery of social and related programs.

2000: In response to a 1999 Supreme Court of Canada decision regarding same-sex couples, legislation defining spouses to be opposite or same-sex for Canada Pension Plan, Old Age Security, and other income security programs was introduced.

2002: The Superior Court of Ontario determined that disallowing same-sex marriages was discriminatory and unconstitutional in the *Halpern v. Canada* case (similar rulings were passed down from the courts in Quebec and British Columbia) but allotted two years for the federal government to amend applicable legislation. The federal government later in the year appealed this decision in the Ontario Court of Appeal.

2003: The Ontario Court of Appeal passed a ruling upholding the decision of the Superior Court of Ontario in *Halpern v. Canada*. Within this new decision, the Ontario Court of Appeal removed the interim period and stated that the ruling will be effective immediately. An opposition motion to uphold the historic definition of marriage was defeated in the House of Commons.

2004: The Canada Health and Social Transfer was divided into two separate transfer arrangements: the Canada Health Transfer (for health-related programs) and the Canada Social Transfer (for programs related to education, social services and support, and child development).

2005: The equal marriage law (Bill C-38) was passed in the House of Commons, extending equal marriage rights for same-sex couples across all of Canada.

2006: A motion was introduced and defeated in the House of Commons that would allow the government to vote again on Bill C-38, with the government's intention to repeal the law.

2006: The Universal Child Care Benefit (UCCB) was introduced. It provided a monthly payment to the primary caregiver of a child under the age of six at a rate of $100 per month. The program was universal and was provided to all families with children meeting the age requirements regardless of financial need.

2007: The Supreme Court of Canada issued a ruling on the case *Health Services and Support—Facilities Subsector Bargaining Assn. v. British Columbia, 2007 SCC 27*, stipulating that collective bargaining was protected by the Canadian Charter of Rights and Freedoms.

2008: In the fall of 2008, major banks, such as Bear Stearns, Merrill Lynch, Lehman Brothers (United States), and the Royal Bank of Scotland either went bankrupt or were bought at fire-sale prices. The financial crisis of post-2008, described by many as the worst economic crisis since the 1930s Great Depression, precipitated trillions of dollars in government bailouts of companies previously deemed "too big to fail." A credit crunch hit many advanced industrialized countries after the fall of 2008.

2009: The Group of 6 (established 1975) expanded to the Group of 7 (1976, to include Canada) and the Group of 8 (1996, to include Russia). By 2009, in the aftermath of the great recession, it became increasingly apparent that the Group of 8 might be superseded by the Group of 20. The G8 members were Canada, France, Germany, Great Britain, Italy, Japan, Russia, and the United States. The G20 originated out of the financial crises of the late 1990s and added such member states as Argentina, Australia, Brazil, China, India, Indonesia, Mexico, Saudi Arabia, South Africa, South Korea, and Turkey. The G20, like its predecessors, provided those countries with the world's leading economies an opportunity to meet on issues of consultation and cooperation in economic issues.

2010: HST was introduced in Ontario and British Columbia.

Glossary

Aboriginal peoples: Native persons indigenous to Canada. Aboriginal communities consist of First Nations peoples (those Aboriginal peoples with treaty status), Métis (Aboriginal people who, following eighteenth- and nineteenth-century intermarriage of First Nations peoples with traders/settlers, founded distinct societies in Western Canada), and Inuit (Aboriginal peoples who live north of the tree line).

Alms: A historical term describing charity in cash or kind provided to the needy.

Block grant: A cash transfer provided by one level of government to another, the amount of the transfer being fixed independently of the purpose to which the funds are put. Also known as a general-purpose grant. Its opposite is a *specific-purpose grant.*

Breadwinner male: A term coined by scholars to describe the social construction of men as the principal income earners. Notions of the breadwinner male have had mutually reinforcing relationships with some social programs but have been challenged by feminist thinking and some contemporary social programs. See also *women's domesticity.*

Canada Assistance Plan (CAP): Introduced in 1966, this program allowed provinces and the federal government to cost-share on a fifty–fifty basis education, health care, and social welfare services. Provinces administered these services and received federal money, subject to federal standards. The CAP gradually eroded during the latter part of the 1970s, 1980s, and 1990s, and was ultimately replaced in 1996 by the Canada Health and Social Transfer (CHST), with looser federal standards.

Canada Health Act: Federal legislation enacted in 1984 that reaffirms five principles of our universal health care system: its universality, comprehensiveness, accessibility, portability, and public administration.

Canada Pension Plan/Quebec Pension Plan (CPP/QPP): Both pension plans were introduced in 1966. The CPP applies to all working Canadians except for those in Quebec, which has its own contributory pension plan, the QPP. Both are publicly administered and are based on employees' workplace contributions.

Canadian Charter of Rights and Freedoms: The only Charter of Rights entrenched in the Canadian Constitution. It came into force in 1982.

Canadian Constitution: A body of fundamental principles and established precedents on which the Canadian state operates and which determine legislative and administrative responsibilities among the three levels of government: federal, provincial, and municipal. Named the British North America Act in 1867, it was renamed the Constitution Act in 1982. Every law that is inconsistent with the Constitution is, to the extent of the inconsistency, of no force and effect.

Capitalism: An economic system in which the production and distribution of goods and services are controlled through private ownership and open competition.

Collectivism: A world view wherein the rights and welfare of the group or society are placed above those of the individual.

Comparative needs: Needs that are determined by comparing one individual or group to another.

Conditional grant: A transfer of money from one level of government to another, and tied directly to an expected type of service delivery. The Canada Assistance Plan (1966–96) is an example of a conditional grant. CAP provided federal transfers to provincial governments to cover the latter's delivery of health, education, and social services.

Consumer Price Index (CPI): An economic measurement consisting of a typical and predetermined "basket" of consumer items from which analysts may measure and compare changes in inflation over time.

Debt: A cumulative, multiyear calculation based on the total amount of money that is owed.

Deficit: A yearly calculation based on annual operating costs. It occurs when spending exceeds revenue.

Detached ideology: Those political values that create policy choices that are made strictly in accordance with one's values, regardless of the outcome and consequences to others.

Dictatorship of the proletariat: According to Marxist theory, the control of communist parties that begins immediately following a revolution. Marxist theory projects the dictatorship as ending with the development of a classless society.

Diversity: A concept that conveys differences between people on the basis of age, culture, ethnicity, gender, nationality, race, range of ability, religion, and sexual orientation, among other social factors.

Egalitarianism: A world view that values human equality politically, socially, and economically.

Elitism: A world view that sees society organized around groups that are unequal in power and resources.

Employment Insurance (EI): Formerly Unemployment Insurance (introduced 1940), this publicly administered, universal, employment-based contributory insurance program was initially intended to provide for the hazards of temporary unemployment but has been expanded to include other reasons for temporary cessation of work, including maternity and parental benefits. Renamed *Employment Insurance* in 1996.

Equalization payment: Also known as an unconditional grant, an equalization payment is a transfer of money from one level of government to another; no particular commitment by the recipient government to tie the grant to an expected type of expenditure is required. Its opposite is a *conditional grant*.

Expressed needs: Needs that are communicated to others.

Family Allowance (FA): A universal program, introduced in 1944 and withdrawn in 1992, that provided mothers a monthly payment for each child under their care. In 1992, the universal FA program was replaced by a refundable, income-tested (i.e., selective) tax credit.

Federal system of government: In this type of system, political power is divided between the national and provincial governments. Canada is a federal system. Most countries are unitary, meaning that political power is centralized in one national level of government.

Felt needs: Needs that are defined on a personal or subjective level.

Fiscal capacity: A particular level of government's ability to change the total or composition of its revenues (e.g., taxes) or expenditures (e.g., a social program).

Globalization: A current, pervasive trend of international finance, ideology, and political arrangements. As a result of globalization, money is invested quickly and easily across national borders. Principles of transnational competition for lucrative markets and inexpensive labour are actively pursued. In the absence of powerfully constraining national legislation or intra-national structures, multinational corporations have growing sovereignty to pursue their objectives.

Grand issues of social policy: Those issues relating to the fundamental structures of political–economic life. Examples include distribution of income and wealth, political power, and corporate prerogatives. Grand issues are contrasted with *ordinary issues of social policy*.

Gross domestic product (GDP): A measurement of a country's economic productivity over time.

Horizontal imbalance: An unequal relationship in fiscal capacity between richer and poorer provinces.

Human rights: Those legal, social, and political entitlements that are justly claimed to belong to any individual in society. These include, but are not restricted to, the right to justice, equality of opportunity, and religious freedom.

Ideology: A pattern of ideas based on experiences, values, and beliefs, and profoundly influencing one's political views. Ideologies shape, organize, and justify a course of action, and are used to legitimize the power held by the active political party.

Individualism: A world view wherein freedom, worth, and self-determination are foremost attributed to the individual rather than a group.

Intergovernmental finance: The web of financial movement that links governments in a federal system.

Low-income cut-off (LICO): A relative measure of *poverty* and the standard *poverty line* used by the federal government since 1959. It is calculated based on information from a survey of family spending patterns conducted by Statistics Canada.

Means of production: According to Marxist theory, the land, labour, and capital that are used by a society to produce material goods.

Normative needs: Needs that are determined by someone other than the individual by applying some benchmark or standard to the individual case.

Old Age Security (OAS): Introduced as a selective, means-tested program in 1927, Old Age Security was transformed into a universal program in 1952, providing all Canadian senior citizens a monthly income. The introduction in the late 1980s of income tax "claw-backs" for individuals and couples having or surpassing a particular net income has called into question whether OAS may truly be considered a universal program today.

Operating principles: The policy results that occur when various social ideals are integrated with a practicable rule of application.

Ordinary issues of social policy: Those policy issues that directly affect the lives of people in a community and the technical operating principles of direct social work intervention. These are often managed and redressed by community-based organizations, and are sometimes the unintended consequence of earlier reforms. Examples include how child welfare service organizations are structurally administered, or the deinstitutionalization and development of community support programs. Ordinary issues of social policy are contrasted with *grand issues of social policy*.

Poverty: A state of deficiency in money or in the means of subsistence.

Poverty gap: How far below a particular *poverty line* (such as the *low-income cut-off*, or *LICO*) one's income falls. If the poverty line is $15 020/year, and one's income is $13 020, then the poverty gap would be $2000.

Poverty line: A measure representing a minimal level of human need. An absolute poverty line presumes that there is some fairly objective means for determining the absolute minimum an individual or household requires for food, shelter, clothing, and any other physical necessities. A relative poverty line assumes that poverty is to be defined relative to prevailing community standards, as opposed to absolute criteria.

Power: In social policy, power refers to the capacity to alter policies and decisions.

Principle of affected interest: A principle of social policy relating to community or citizen participation, and affirming that anyone who is affected by the decisions of a government should have a right to participate in that government.

Proletariat: According to Marxist theory, the proletariat consists of individuals and families who are members of the working class, particularly manual and industrial labourers.

Public policies: Legislated acts, regulations, and bylaws (including all associated policies in the ministerial, agency, and public arenas) at the federal, provincial/territorial, and municipal levels of government.

Selective programs: Social welfare programs implemented on the basis of assessed need. Eligibility for benefits is determined through means testing. Selective programs are distinct from *universal programs*.

Social assistance: An income security program that uses a "means" or "needs" test to determine eligibility.

Social insurance: An income security program in which eligibility for benefits is determined on the basis of a record of contribution and the occurrence of a foreseen contingency, such as injury, retirement, unemployment, or the death of an income-earning spouse.

Social policy: The statements of the selected social goals and objectives to which a group—be it professional, governmental, or private—is committed.

Social welfare: A complex network of personal relationships, institutions, policies, and services that a society creates to contribute to the well-being, or welfare, of its members.

Specific-purpose grant: A cash transfer provided by one level of government to another. The amount of the transfer is tied to its intended purpose; an example would be a matched or shared-cost program. Its opposite is a *block grant*.

Standard of living: A term denoting the necessities and luxuries required for living in a particular circumstance.

Sustainability: An economic, political, and environmental world view that promotes present and future generations of stewardship of the physical world.

Universal programs: Social welfare programs based on national and categorical membership. These programs are available to all persons regardless of need. They are distinct from *selective programs*.

Vertical imbalance: An unequal relationship in fiscal capacity between the federal and a provincial government.

Welfare state: A term coined by the Archbishop of Canterbury during World War II to describe those governments, such as Canada's, that were committing themselves to the use of resources and to the development of social policies for the collective well-being of all.

Women's caring: A term coined by scholars to describe the social construction of women as principal caregivers in family and social relationships.

Women's domesticity: A term coined by scholars to describe the social construction of women in the domestic or home realm—daughters, mothers, wives, or widows. This term contrasts with the gendered social construction that encouraged men to take on economic, political, and social activities outside of the home. See also *breadwinner male*.

World view: An outlook drawn from religious, political, social, and physical information about humans and the societies they create.

References

Abelson, D. E. (2009). *Do think tanks matter?* (2nd ed.). Montreal: McGill-Queen's University Press.

Adams, R. (2002). *Social policy for social work.* Basingstoke, UK: Palgrave Macmillan.

Airdrie, K. (2010). *Canadian Aboriginal women's "Sisters in Spirit" funding cut.* Retrieved from http://www.suite101.com/content/canadian-aboriginal-womens-sisters-in-spirit-funding-cut-a306076

Alberta Health Services. (2010). *Becoming the best: Alberta's 5-Year Health Action Plan 2010–2015.* Edmonton: Alberta Health Wellness Communications.

Allen, R. (1971). *The social passion: Religion and social reform in Canada, 1914–1928.* Toronto: University of Toronto Press.

Almey, M. (n.d.). *Women in Canada: Work chapter updates.* Retrieved from http://www.statcan.gc.ca/pub/89f0133x2006000-eng.htm

American Federation of Labor—Congress of Industrial Organizations. (2010). *Executive paywatch.* Retrieved from http://www.aflcio.org/corporatewatch/paywatch/

Amernic, J., & Craig, R. (2006). *CEO speak: The language of corporate leadership.* Montreal: McGill-Queen's University Press.

Anderson, G., & Marr, W. (1987). Immigration and social policy. In S. Yelaga (Ed.), *Canadian social policy* (Rev. ed., 88–114). Waterloo, ON: Wilfrid Laurier University Press.

Anderson, J. E. (1990). *Public policymaking.* Boston: Houghton Mifflin.

Armitage, A. (1996). *Social welfare in Canada revisited: Facing up to the future* (3rd ed.). Don Mills, ON: Oxford University Press.

Armitage, A. (2003). *Social welfare in Canada* (4th ed.). Oxford: Oxford University Press.

Artibese, A. F. J., & Stelter, G. A. (1985). Urbanization. In *The Canadian encyclopedia* (Vol. 3, 1887). Edmonton: Hurtig.

Babbie, E. (1986). *Observing ourselves: Essays in social research.* Belmont, CA: Wadsworth.

Bach, M. (2005). Social inclusion as solidarity: Rethinking the child rights agenda. In T. Richmond & A. Saloojee (Eds.), *Social inclusion: Canadian perspectives* (126–154). Halifax: Fernwood.

Bailey, R., & Brake, M. (Eds.). (1975). *Radical social work.* London: Edward Arnold.

Bakan, J. (1997). *Just words: Constitutional rights and social wrongs.* Toronto: University of Toronto Press.

Bakan, J. (2004). *The corporation: The pathological pursuit of profit and power.* New York: Simon and Schuster.

Ball, O., & Gready, P. (2006). *The no-nonsense guide to human rights.* Toronto: New Internationalist Publications.

Banks, K., & Mangan, M. (1999). *The company of neighbours: Revitalizing community through action-research.* Toronto: University of Toronto Press.

Bannock, G., Baxter, R. E., & Davis, E. (Eds.). (1998a). Gross domestic product. In *The penguin dictionary of economics.* Retrieved from http://www.xreferplus.com.ezproxy.lib.ucalgary.ca/entry/445411

Bannock, G., Baxter, R. E., & Davis, E. (1998b). Gross national product In *The Penguin dictionary of economics.* Retrieved from http://www.xreferplus.com.ezproxy.lib.ucalgary.ca/entry/445417

Banting, K. G. (1985). Institutional conservatism: Federalism and pension reform. In J. S. Ismael (Ed.), *Canadian social welfare policy: Federal and provincial dimensions* (48–74). Kingston/Montreal: McGill-Queen's University Press.

Barata, P. (2000). *Social exclusion in Europe: Survey of literature.* Unpublished paper. Toronto: Laidlaw Foundation.

Barker, J. (1999.) *Street-level democracy: Political settings at the margins of global power.* Toronto: Between the Lines.

Barker, R. L. (1991). *The social work dictionary.* Washington, DC: National Association of Social Workers.

Barlow (2001). *Global Showdown: How the New Activists Are Fighting Global Corporate Rule* (with Tony Clarke) – Stoddart, Toronto (2001).

Barter, K. (1996). Collaboration: A framework for northern practice. In R. Delaney, K. Brownlee, & K. M. Zapf (Eds.), *Issues in northern social work practice* (pp. 66–78). Thunder Bay, ON: Centre for Northern Studies.

Battle, K. (1993). *Federal social programs: Setting the record straight.* Ottawa: Caledon Institute of Social Policy.

Battle, K. (2001). *Relentless incrementalism: Deconstructing and reconstructing Canadian income security policy.* Ottawa: Caledon Institute of Social Policy.

Battle, K. (2002). *Social policy that works: An agenda.* Ottawa: Caledon Institute of Social Policy.

Battle, K., & Mendelson, M. (1997). *Child benefit reform in Canada: An evaluative framework and future directions.* Ottawa: Caledon Institute of Social Policy.

Battle, K., & Torjman, S. (1993). *Federal social programs: Setting the record straight.* Ottawa: Caledon Institute of Social Policy.

Beach, C. M., Green, A. G., & Reitz, J. G. (Eds.). (2004). *Canadian immigration policy for the 21st century.* Montreal: McGill-Queen's University Press.

Berkowitz, I. (1980). Social choice and policy formulation: Problems and considerations in the construction of the public interest. *Journal of Sociology and Social Welfare, 16*(2), 533–545.

Berman, M. (2000). *Wandering God: A study in nomadic spirituality.* Albany: State University of New York Press.

Bickenbach, J. E. (1993). *Physical disability and social policy.* Toronto: University of Toronto Press.

Bickenbach, J. E. (2006). *Canadian Charter v. American ADA: Individual rights or collective responsibilities.* In M. McColl & L. Jongbloed (Eds.), *Disability and social policy in Canada* (2nd ed., 77–86). Concord, ON: Captus Press.

Bishop, A. (1994). *Becoming an ally: Breaking the cycle of oppression.* Halifax: Fernwood.

Bishop, A. (2002). *Becoming an ally: Breaking the cycle of oppression* (2nd ed.). Halifax: Fernwood.

Bishop, A. (2005). *Beyond token change: Breaking the cycle of oppressive institutions.* Halifax: Fernwood.

Bissoondath, N. (1994). *Selling illusions: The cult of multiculturalism in Canada.* Toronto: Penguin.

Blackburn, R. (2002). *Banking on death, or investing in life: The history and future of pensions.* London: Verso.

Blake, R. B. (2009). *From rights to needs: A history of Family Allowances in Canada, 1929–92.* Vancouver: University of British Columbia Press.

Blake, R., Bryden, P., & Strain, F. (Eds.). (1997). *The welfare state in Canada: Past, present, and future.* Concord, ON: Irwin.

Bobbitt, P. (2002). *The shield of Achilles: War, peace, the course of history.* New York: Anchor Books.

Bopp, J., Bopp, M., Brown, L., & Lane, P. (1985). *The sacred tree.* Lethbridge, AB: Four Worlds Development Press.

Bornstein, D., & Davis, S. (2010). *Social entrepreneurship: What everyone needs to know.* New York: Oxford University Press.

Bourgeault, R. (1988). Race and class under mercantilism: Indigenous people in nineteenth-century Canada. In B. Bolaria &

P. Li (Eds.), *Racial oppression in Canada*. (2nd ed., 41–70). Toronto: Garamond Press.

Boychuk, G. W. (1998). *Patchworks of purpose: The development of provincial social assistance regimes in Canada*. Kingston/Montreal: McGill-Queen's University Press.

Boyd, D. (2001, April 27). They're blowing smoke. *The Globe and Mail*, p. A19.

Brager, G., Specht, H., & Torczyner, J. (1987). *Community organizing*. New York: Columbia University Press.

Braybrooke, D., & Lindblom, C. E. (1963). *The strategy of decision*. New York: Free Press.

Broad, D., & Antony, W. (1999). *Citizens or consumers? Social policy in a market society*. Halifax: Fernwood.

Bruce, M. (1961). *The coming of the welfare state*. London: B.T. Batsford.

Burgeoning bourgeoisie. (2009, February 12). [Special supplement]. *Economist Magazine*, *390*(8618), p. 1.

Burns, T. J., Batavia, A. I., & DeJong, G. (1994). The health insurance work disincentive for persons with disabilities. *Research in the Sociology of Health Care*, *11*, 57–68.

Callahan, M. (2004). Chalk and cheese: Feminist thinking and policy-making. In B. Wharf & B. McKenzie (Eds.), *Connecting policy to practice in the human services* (2nd ed., 128–140). Don Mills, ON: Oxford University Press.

Campaign 2000. (2007). *Raising the falling fortunes of young families of Canada*. Toronto: Family Service Association of Toronto.

Canada. (1966). *Canada Assistance Plan*. Ottawa: Queen's Printer (Repealed in 1995).

Canada. (1984). *The Health Act*. Ottawa: Queen's Printer.

Canada. (1985, 1995). *Federal-Provincial Fiscal Arrangements Act*. Ottawa: Queen's Printer.

Canada. (1997). *Canada Health and Social Transfer Regulations*. Ottawa: Queen's Printer.

Canada Revenue Agency. (2010, December 13). Canada Child Tax Benefit. Retrieved from http://www.cra-arc.gc.ca/bnfts/cctb/menu-eng.html

Canadian Association of Gift Planners. (2010). Who gives: Statistics on giving Canada. Retrieved from Leave a Legacy website: http://www.leavealegacy.ca/program/who/

Canadian Association of Social Workers (CASW). (2005). Code of Ethics.

Canadian Council of Chief Executives. (2010). About CCCE. Retrieved from http://www.ceocouncil.ca/en/about/about.php

Canadian Council on Social Development. (1991). *Social policy in the 1990s: The challenge*. Ottawa/Montreal: CCSD.

Canadian Press, The. (2010, December 18). 2010 a tough year for charity scams, experts say. Retrieved from CTV.ca Ottawa website: http://ottawa.ctv.ca/servlet/an/local/CTVNews/20101218/social-scams-101218/20101218/?hub=OttawaHome

Canel, E. (n.d.). *New social movement theory and resource mobilization theory: The need for integration*. International Development Research Centre. Retrieved from http://www.idrc.ca/en/ev-54446-201-1-DO_TOPIC.html

Cannadine, D. (2006). *Mellon: An American life*. New York: Allen Lane.

Careless, J. M. S. (1954). Frontierism, metropolitanism, and Canadian history. *Canadian Historical Review*, *35*, 1–21.

Carniol, B. (1987). *Case critical: Challenging social work in Canada* (2nd ed.). Toronto: Between the Lines.

Carniol, B. (1995). *Case critical: Challenging social work in Canada* (3rd ed.). Toronto: Between the Lines.

Carson, R. L. (1962). *Silent Spring*. Boston: Houghton Mifflin/Mariner Books.

Carty, R. K., Cross, W., & Young, L. (2000). *Rebuilding Canadian party politics*. Vancouver: University of British Columbia Press.

Cassidy, F. (Ed.). (1991). *Aboriginal self-determination*. BC and Montreal: The Institute for Research on Public Policy and Oolichan Books.

CASSW. (1996). *The manual of standards and procedures for the accreditation of Canadian programs of social work education*. Ottawa: Author.

Castellano, M. (2002). *Aboriginal family trends: Extended families, nuclear families, families of the heart*. Ottawa: The Vanier Institute of the Family.

CBC. (2000). "Nellie McClung: The Sculpting of Angels." *Life and Times*. Retrieved from http://www.cbc.ca/lifeandtimes/ mcclung.html

CBC News. (2008). *Canada votes*. Toronto: CBC. Retrieved from http://www.cbc.ca/ news/canadavotes/story/2008/10/15/ voter-turnout.html

Central Intelligence Agency. (2010). *The world fact book, 2010*. Washington: Author. Retrieved from https://www.cia. gov/library/publications the-world-factbook/

Chamberlin, J. (1997). A working definition of empowerment. *Psychiatric Rehabilitation Journal, 20*(4), 43–46.

Chapin, R. K. (1995). Social policy development: The strengths perspective. *Social Work, 40*(4), 506–514.

Chappell, R. (1997). *Social welfare in Canadian society*. Scarborough, ON: ITP International Thomson Publishing.

Chappell, R. (2006). *Social welfare in Canadian society*. Toronto: Nelson Thompson Learning.

Cheal, D. (Ed.). (2002). *Aging demographic change in Canadian context*. Toronto: University of Toronto Press.

Chomsky, N. (1991). *Deterring democracy*. London: Verso.

Chomsky, N. (2010). *Hopes and prospects*. New York: Haymarket Books.

Chouinard, V., & Crooks, V. (2005). "Because *they* have all the power and I have none": State restructuring of income and employment supports and disabled women's lives in Ontario, Canada. *Disability and Society, 20*(1), 19–32.

Christensen, C. (1995). Immigrant minorities in Canada. In J. Turner & F. Turner (Eds.), *Social welfare in Canada* (3rd ed., 179–212). Scarborough, ON: Allyn and Bacon Canada.

Christian, W., & Campbell, C. (1990). *Political parties and ideologies in Canada* (3rd ed.). Toronto: McGraw-Hill Ryerson Ltd.

Chui, T. (1996). Canada's population: Charting into the 21st century. Catalogue No. 11-008-XPE. Ottawa: Statistics Canada.

Citizenship and Immigration Canada. (2009). *Facts and figures 2009: Summary tables— Permanent and temporary residents*. Ottawa: Author. Retrieved from http://www.cic.gc.ca/english/resources/ statistics/facts2009-summary/permanent/ 01.asp.

Clarke, T. (1997). *Silent coup: Confronting the big business takeover of Canada*. Ottawa/Toronto: Canadian Centre for Policy Initiatives/James Lorimer & Co.

Coggan, P. (2010, June 26). Repent at leisure [A special report on debt]. *Economist Magazine*. Retrieved from http://www.economist.com/node/ 16397110?story_id=16397110&source=hpt extfeature

Cohen, E. (2006). Why have children? *Commentary Magazine*, June, 44–49.

Collier, K. (2006). *Social work with rural peoples*. Vancouver: New Star Books.

Commissioner of the Environment and Sustainable Development. (2006). *2006 Report of the Commissioner of the Environment Sustainable Development*. Ottawa: Office of the Auditor General of Canada. Retrieved from http://www.oag-bvg.gc.ca/domino/ reports.nsf/html/c2006menu_e.html

Cooke, M. (2003). The Canada Pension Plan goes to market. *Canadian Review of Social Policy, 51*, 126–131.

Copp, T. (1974). *The anatomy of poverty: The conditions of the working class in*

Montreal, 1897–1929. Toronto: McClelland and Stewart.

Cornish, M., & Faraday, F. (2008). *Ontario's gender pay gap cheats women workers.* Retrieved from http://www.thestar.com/comment/article/500415

Cossman, B. (1996). Same-sex couples and the politics of family status. In J. Brodie (Ed.), *Women and Canadian Public Policy* (pp. 223–253). Toronto: Harcourt Brace and Company.

Crossley, T., & Curtis, L. (2006). Child Poverty in Canada. *Review of Income & Wealth, 52*(2), 237–260.

CUPE. (2007, November 16). Transfers to municipalities fell billions short in 2006. *CUPE economic brief.* Retrieved from http://cupe.ca/updir/Municipal_Transfer_Shortfall.pdf

Daily, The. (2006, March 7). *Women in Canada.* Ottawa: Statistics Canada.

Daily, The. (2007, July 17). *2006 census: Age and sex.* Ottawa: Statistics Canada.

Daily, The. (2007, December). *2006 census: Immigration, citizenship, language, mobility and migration.* Ottawa: Statistics Canada.

Daily, The. (2008, April 2). *2006 census: Ethnic origin, visible minorities, place of work and mode of transportation.* Ottawa: Statistics Canada.

Daily, The. (2010, March 9). *Study: Projections of the diversity of the Canadian population.* Ottawa: Statistics Canada.

Daily, The. (2011, January 7). *Latest release from the Labour Force Survey.* Ottawa: Statistics Canada. Retrieved from http://www.statcan.gc.ca/subjects-sujets/labour-travail/lfs-epa/lfs-epa-eng.htm

Dare, B. (1997). Harris' first year: Attacks and resistance. In D. Ralph, A. Regimbald, & N. St-Am (Eds.), *Open for business, closed to people* (20–26). Halifax: Fernwood.

Davies, J., Sandstrom, S., Shorrocks, A., & Wolff, E. (2009). The global pattern of household wealth. *Journal of International Development, 21*(8), 1111–1124.

Deffeyes, K. S. (2006). *Beyond oil: The view from Hubbert's Peak.* New York: Hill Wang.

Delaney, R. (1995). The philosophical base. In J. Turner & F. Turner (Eds.), *Canadian social welfare* (3rd ed., 12–27). Scarborough, ON: Allyn and Bacon Canada.

Delaney, R., & Brownlee, K. (Eds.). (1995). *Northern social work practice.* Thunder Bay, ON: Centre for Northern Studies.

Delaney, R., Brownlee, K., & Graham, J. R. (Eds.). (1997). *Strategies in northern social work practice.* Thunder Bay, ON: Centre for Northern Studies.

Delaney, R., Brownlee, K., & Sellick, M. (Eds.). (1999). *Social work with rural and northern communities.* Thunder Bay, ON: Centre for Northern Studies.

Delaney, R., Brownlee, K., & Sellick, M. (2001). Surviving globalization: Empowering rural remote communities in Canada's provincial norths. *Australian Rural Social Work, 6*(3), 4–11.

Delaney, R., Brownlee, K., & Zapf, K. M. (Eds.). (1996). *Issues in northern social work practice.* Thunder Bay, ON: Centre for Northern Studies.

Department of Finance Canada. (2006). The economic fiscal update 2006. Ottawa: Public Works and Government Services Canada. Retrieved from http://www.fin.gc.ca/budtoce/2006/ec06_e.html

Department of Finance Canada. (2007). *Restoring fiscal balance for a stronger federation.* Ottawa: Author. Retrieved from http://www.budget.gc.ca/2007/bp/bpc4e.html#equalization

Department of Finance Canada. (2010). *Canada's finance minister highlights tax breaks for Canadians.* Ottawa: Author. Retrieved from http://www.fin.gc.ca/n10/10-099-eng.asp

Department of Finance Canada. (2011). *Federal support for provinces and territories.* Ottawa: Author. Retrieved from http://www.fin.gc.ca/fedprov/mtp-eng.asp

de Schweinitz, K. (1943). *England's road to social security*. Philadelphia: University of Pennsylvania Press.

Derbyshire, J. (2011, January 8). Internet activism: For and against. *New Statesman*. Retrieved from http://www.newstatesman.com/blogs/the-staggers/2011/01/morozov-internet-netroots

Desert, G. (1976). Une source historique trop oublié: Les archives hospitaliers. *Gazette des Archives*, *94*, 145–164.

Desroches, C. (2009). For them but never really theirs: Finding a place for the "aged" within state-funded institutions in nineteenth century Nova Scotia. *Journal of the Canadian Historical Association*, *20*(1), 57–84.

Diamond, J. (2005). *Collapse: How societies choose to fail or succeed*. New York: Viking Books.

Disability-Related Policy Website. (n.d.). *Disability 101*. Retrieved from http://www.disabilitypolicy.ca/policy/index.php

Doern, B., & Aucoin, P. (Eds.). (1971). *The structures of policy-making in Canada*. Toronto: Macmillan.

Dolgoff, R., & Feldstein, D. (1984). *Understanding social welfare* (2nd ed.). London: Longman.

Dominelli, L. (1988). *Anti-racist social work*. London: Macmillan.

Dominelli, L. (1997). *Sociology for social work*. London: Macmillan.

Dominelli, L., & McLeod, E. (1989). *Feminist social work*. London: Macmillan.

Drover, G. (1988). Social work. In *The Canadian encyclopedia* (2034–2035). Edmonton: Hurtig.

Drover, G. (2000). Redefining social citizenship in a global era [Special issue on social work and globalization]. *Canadian Social Work Review*, *17*, 29–49.

Drover, G., & Kerans, P. (1993). New approaches to welfare theory: Foundations. In G. Drover & P. Kerans (Eds.), *New approaches to welfare theory* (pp. 3–32). Brookfield, VT: Edward Elgar.

Easterbrook, W. T., & Aitken, H. G. J. (1956). *Canadian economic history*. Toronto: Macmillan.

Edwards, M. (2005). Civil society. In *The encyclopedia of informal education*. Retrieved from http://www.infed.org/association/civil_society.htm

Egale. (2006). *Equal marriage backgrounder*. Retrieved from http://www.egale.ca

Eichler, M. (1987). Social policy concerning women. In S. Yelaga (Ed.), *Canadian social policy* (Rev. ed., 139–156). Waterloo, ON: Wilfrid Laurier University Press.

Ellwood, W. (2006). *The no-nonsense guide to globalization*. Toronto: New Internationalist Publications.

Emery, J. C. H., & Emery, G. (1999). *A young man's benefit: The Independent Order of Odd Fellows and sickness insurance in the United States and Canada, 1860–1929*. Montreal: McGill-Queen's University Press.

Esping-Anderson, G. (1990). *The three worlds of welfare capitalism*. Cambridge, UK: Polity Press.

Etzioni, A. (1968). *The active society*. New York: The Free Press.

Etzioni, A. (1975). *A comparative analysis of complex organizations* (2nd ed.). New York: Free Press.

Evans, P. (1995). Women and social welfare: Exploring the connections. In J. C. Turner & F. Turner (Eds.), *Canadian social welfare* (3rd ed., 150–164). Scarborough, ON: Allyn and Bacon Canada.

Evans, P. (1997). Divided citizenship? Gender, income security, and the welfare state. In P. Evans & G. Wekerle (Eds.), *Women and the Canadian welfare state: Challenges and change* (91–116). Toronto: University of Toronto Press.

Evans, P., Jacobs, L., Noel, A., & Reynolds, E. (1995). *Workfare: Does it work? Is it fair?* Montreal: Institute for Research on Public Policy.

Fair taxes, not more taxes. (1995, February 13). *The Globe and Mail*, p. A12.

Federal/Provincial/Territorial Ministerial Council on Social Policy Renewal. (2003). *Three year review: Social union framework agreement.* Ottawa: Social Development Canada. Retrieved from http://socialunion.gc.ca/menu_e.html

Federico, R. (1983). *The social welfare institution* (4th ed.). Toronto: D.C. Heath.

Feehan, K., & Hannis, D. (Eds.). (1993). *From strength to strength. Social work education and Aboriginal people.* Edmonton: Grant MacEwan Community College.

Ferley, P., & Janzen, N. (2009). *Ontario budget 2009: Impact of the recession is evident but is it being sufficiently countered?* Royal Bank of Canada Economics Research.

Figuera-McDonough, J. (1993). Policy practice: The neglected side of social work interventions. *Social Work, 38,* 179–188.

Fingard, J. (1989). *The dark side of life in Victorian Halifax.* Porters Lake, NS: Pottersfield Press.

Finkel, A. (2006). *Social policy and practice in Canada: A history.* Waterloo, ON: Wilfrid Laurier University Press.

Finlayson, A. (1996). *Naming Rumpelstiltskin: Who will profit and who will lose in the workplace of the 21st century.* Toronto: Key Porter Books.

Flanagan, T. (2007). The six rules of success. In R. Griffiths (Ed.), *Great questions of Canada* (177–180). Toronto: Porter Publishing.

Flannery, T. (2006). *The weather makers: The history and future impact of climate change.* Berkeley, CA: Atlantic Monthly Press.

Florini, A. M. (2000). *Third force: The rise of transnational civil society.* Washington D.C.: Carnegie Endowment for International Peace.

Flynn, J. P. (1992). *Social agency policy* (2nd ed.). Chicago: Nelson-Hall.

Fook, J., & Gardner, F. (2007). *Practising critical reflection: A resource handbook.* Maidenhead, UK: Open University Press.

Forster, M., & d'Ercole, M. M. (2005). *Income distribution and poverty in OECD countries in the second half of the 1990s.* Paris: OECD Publications.

Foucault, M. (1972). *Power/knowledge: Selected interviews and other writings.* New York: Pantheon Books.

Frankl, V. (1969). *The will to meaning.* Scarborough: Plume.

Fraser Forum. (2009). *May 2009: The tax burden.* Retrieved from http://www.fraserinstitute.org/research-news/research/display.aspx?id=13199

Fraser, N. (1989). *Unruly practices: Power, discourse and gender in contemporary social theory.* Minneapolis: University of Minneapolis Press.

Fraser, N. (1995). From redistribution to recognition? Dilemmas of justice in a "post-socialist" age. *New Left Review, 212,* 68–93.

Fraser, N., & Honneth, A. (2003). *From redistribution to recognition? A political-philosophical exchange.* London: Verso.

Freeman, H., & Sherwood, C. (1970). *Social research and social policy.* Englewood Cliffs, NJ: Prentice-Hall.

Freiler, C. (2000). *What needs to change? Social inclusion as a focus of well-being for children, families, and communities.* Unpublished paper. Toronto: Laidlaw Foundation.

Freiler, C., & Cerny, J. (1998). *Benefiting Canada's children: Perspectives on gender and social responsibility.* Ottawa: Status of Women Canada.

Freire, P. (1968). *Pedagogy of the oppressed.* New York: Seabury Press.

Freire, P. (1985). *The politics of education: Culture, power and liberation.* South Hadley, MA: Bergin and Garvey.

Freire, P. (1994). *Pedagogy of hope.* New York: Continuum.

Frideres, J., & Gadacz, R. (2005). *Aboriginal peoples in Canada: Contemporary conflicts* (7th ed.). Toronto: Pearson Prentice Hall.

Fromm, E. (1955). *The sane society*. Greenwich, CT: Fawcett.

Fromm, E. (1967). The psychological aspects of the guaranteed income. In R. Theobald (Ed.), *The guaranteed income* (183–193). Garden City: Anchor.

Fukuyama, F. (1992). *The end of history and the last man*. New York: Avon Books.

Galabuzi, G. E. (2006). *Canada's economic apartheid: The social exclusion of racialized groups in the new century*. Toronto: Canadian Scholars Press.

Galbraith, J. K. (1983). *The anatomy of power*. Boston: Houghton Mifflin.

Galper, J. (1975). *The politics of social services*. Englewood Cliffs, NJ: Prentice-Hall.

Galster, G. (1996). *Reality and research: Social science and U.S. urban policy since 1960*. Washington: Urban Institute Press.

Garrett, L. (2000). *Betrayal of trust: The collapse of global public health*. New York: Hyperion.

Gates-Gasse, E. (2010). *"Two Step" immigration: Canada's new immigration system raises troubling issues*. Retrieved from http://www.policyalternatives.ca/publications/monitor/two-step-immigration

George, U. (2006). Immigration and refugee policy in Canada: Past, present, and future. In A. Westhughes (Ed.), *Canadian social policy: Issues and perspectives* (4th ed., 349–374). Waterloo, ON: Wilfrid Laurier University Press.

Germain, C., & Gitterman, A. (1980). *Social work practice, people, and environments: An ecological perspective*. New York: Columbia University Press.

Germain, C., & Gitterman, A. (1996). *The life model of social work practice: Advances in theory practice*. New York: Columbia University Press.

Giddens, A. (1998). *The third way: The renewal of social democracy*. Cambridge: Polity Press.

Gil, D. (1970). A systematic approach to social policy analysis. *Social Service Review*, *44*(4), 411–426.

Gil, D. (1990). Implications of conservative tendencies for practice education in social welfare. *Journal of Sociology Social Welfare*, *XVII*(2) 5–27.

Gil, D. (1992). *Unravelling social policy* (5th ed.). Rochester, NY: Schenkman Books.

Gil, D. (1998). *Confronting injustice and oppression: Concepts and strategies for social workers*. New York: Columbia University Press.

Gilbert, N., & Specht, H. (1974). *Dimensions of social welfare policy*. Englewood Cliffs, NJ: Prentice-Hall.

Gilmour, J. (2010). Retrenchment not Reform: Using Law and Policy to Restrict the Entitlement of Women with Disabilities to Social. In S. Gavigan & D. Chunn (Eds.), *The legal tender of gender* (pp. 189–216). Onati International Series in Law and Society. Oxford: Hart Publishing.

Giugni, M. (1999). Introduction: How social movements matter. Past research, present problems, and future developments. In M. Giugni, D. McAdan, & C. Tilly (Eds.), *How social movements matter* (iii–xxxiii). Minneapolis: University of Minnesota Press.

Global Footprint Network. (2010). *Humanity's ecological footprint biocapacity through time*. Retrieved from http://www.footprintnetwork.org/en/index.php/GFN/page/ecological_footprint_atlas_2008/

Gonthier, N. (1978). Dans le Lyon médiéval: Vie et mort d'un pauvre. *Cahiers d'Histoire*, *23*(3), 335–347.

Good-Gingrich, L. (2003). Theorizing social exclusion: Determinants, mechanisms, dimensions, forms, and acts of resistance. In W. Shera (Ed.), *Emerging perspectives on anti-oppressive practice* (pp. 3–23). Toronto: Canadian Scholars' Press Inc.

Good-Gingrich, L. (2008). Social exclusion and double jeopardy: The management of lone mothers in the market-state social field. *Social Policy and Administration*, *42*(4), 379–395.

Gordon, L. (1990). The new feminist scholarship on the welfare state. In L. Gordon (Ed.), *Women, the state, and welfare* (pp. 78–89). Madison: University of Wisconsin Press.

Gormley, W. T. (2007). Public policy analysis: Ideas and impacts. *Annual Review of Political Science, 10*, 297–313.

Government of Alberta. (2002). *A framework for reform: Report of the Premier's Advisory Council on Health.* Edmonton: Author.

Government of Canada. (2007). *Citizenship and Immigration Canada website*. Retrieved from http://www.cic.gc.ca/english/refugees/asylum-1.html#convention

Government of Canada. (2008, October 8). *Newfoundland and Labrador offshore arrangements*. Retrieved from Department of Finance Canada website: http://www.fin.gc.ca/fedprov/na-eng.asp

Government of Ontario. (2010, November 17). *Ontario guaranteed annual income system*. Retrieved from Ministry of Revenue website: http://www.rev.gov.on.ca/en/credit/gains/

Government of Saskatchewan. (2010). *The seniors income plan*. Retrieved from http://www.socialservices.gov.sk.ca/SIP-factsheet.pdf

Graham, J. R. (1992). The Haven, 1878–1930. A Toronto charity's transition from a religious to a professional ethos. *Histoire Sociale/Social History, 25*(50), 283–306.

Graham, J. R. (1995). Lessons for today: Canadian municipalities and unemployment relief during the 1930s Great Depression. *Canadian Review of Social Policy, 35*, 1–18.

Graham, J. R. (1996a). *A history of the University of Toronto School of Social Work, 1914–1970* (Doctoral dissertation, University of Toronto).

Graham, J. R. (1996b). A practical idealism: A theoretical values conception for northern social work practice. In R. Delaney, K. Brownlee, & J. R. Graham (Eds.), *Strategies in northern social work practice* (95–103). Thunder Bay, ON: Centre for Northern Studies.

Graham, J. R. (1996c). An analysis of Canadian social welfare historical writing. *Social Service Review, 70*(1), 140–158.

Graham, J. R. (2008). Canadian approaches to income security. In J. C. Turner & F. J. Turner (Eds.), *Canadian social welfare* (6th ed., 276–293). Toronto: Prentice Hall.

Graham, J. R., & Barter, K. (1999). Collaboration: A social work practice method. *Families in Society: The Journal of Contemporary Human Services, 80*(1), 6–13.

Graham, J. R., Trew, J. L., Schmidt, J. A, & Kline, T. B. (2007). Influences on the subjective well-being (SWB) of practicing social workers. *Canadian Social Work, 9*(1), 92–105.

Gramsci, A. (1971). *Prison notebooks*. New York: International Publishers.

Grant, G. (1965). *Lament for a nation: The defeat of Canadian nationalism*. Toronto: Anansi.

Grant, G. (1969). *Technology and empire: Perspectives on North America.* Toronto: Anansi.

Grant, T. (2010, October 21). "Excessive" personal debt a concern. *The Globe and Mail*, p. B4.

Greenaway, N. (2004, August 20). Fewer Canadians on welfare: Study. *The Globe and Mail,* p. A9.

Grob, G. (1992). How policy is made and how evaluators can affect it. *Evaluation Practice, 13*(3), 175–183.

Guest, D. (1997). *The emergence of social security in Canada* (3rd ed.). Vancouver: University of British Columbia Press.

Guillemette, Y., & Robson, W. B. P. (2006). No elixir of youth: Immigration cannot keep Canada young. *CD Howe Institute Backgrounder, 96*. Toronto: CD Howe Institute.

Gunton, T., & Calbick, K. S. (2010). *The Maple Leaf in the OECD: Canada's environmental performance*. Report for the David Suzuki Foundation Simon Fraser University.

Gwyn, R. (1995). *Nationalism without walls: The unbearable lightness of being Canadian*. Toronto: McClelland and Stewart.

Haber, A., & Runyon, R. (1986). *Fundamentals of psychology* (4th ed.). New York: McGraw-Hill Company.

Hacker, J. S., & Pierson, P. (2010). *Winner-take-all politics: How Washington made the rich richer—and turned its back on the middle class*. New York: Simon & Schuster.

Hage, J., & Hollingsworth, J. R. (1977). The first steps toward the integration of social theory social policy. *Annals of the American Academy of Political and Social Science, 434*, 1–23.

Hall, M. H., de Wit, M. L., Lasby, D., McIver, D., Evers, T., Johnston, C., et al. (2004). *Cornerstones of community: Highlights of the national survey of non-profit and voluntary organizations*. Ottawa: Minister of Industry.

Handler, J. F. (1979). *Protecting the social service client: Legal and structural controls on official discretion*. New York: Academic Press.

Handler, J. F., & Hasenfeld, Y. (1991). *The moral construction of poverty: Welfare reform in America*. Newbury Park, CA: Sage.

Hansen, P. (1999). The welfare state as political community. In D. Broad & W. Antony (Eds.), *Citizens or consumers? Social policy in a market society* (314–321). Halifax: Fernwood.

Hardesty, J., & Furdon, E. (2004). Policing civil society: NGO watch. *The Public Eye, 18*, 1.

Hargrove, B. (1999). Unions and social policy: Confronting a challenging future. In D. Broad & W. Antony (Eds.), *Citizens or consumers? Social policy in a market society* (73–82). Halifax: Fernwood.

Harischandra, K., & Palacios, M. (2007, March 15). Equalization reforms: Consensus disagreements. Retrieved from http://www.fraserinstitute.org

Harvey, D. (2010). *The enigma of capital and the crises of capitalism*. New York: Oxford University Press.

Haskins, R., & Gallagher, J. J. (1981). *Models for analysis of social policy*. Norwood, NJ: Ablex Publishing Corporation.

Healy, K. (2005). *Social work theories in context: creating frameworks for practice*. New York: Palgrave Macmillan.

Heisz, A. (2007). *Income inequality and redistribution in Canada: 1976 to 2004*. Catalogue No. 11F0019MIE – No. 298. Ottawa: Ministry of Industry, Government of Canada.

Herberg, D., & Herberg, E. (1995). Canada's ethno-racial diversity: Policies and programs for Canadian social welfare. In J. Turner & F. Turner (Eds.), *Social welfare in Canada* (3rd ed., 179–212). Scarborough, ON: Allyn and Bacon Canada.

Hess, M. (1993). *An overview of Canadian social policy*. Ottawa: Canadian Council on Social Development.

Hick, S. (2007). *Social welfare in Canada: Understanding income security* (2nd ed.). Toronto: Thompson Educational Publishing.

Hobsbawm, E. (1995). *Age of extremes: The short twentieth century 1914–1991*. London: Abacus.

Hodgson, G., & Browarski, S. (2008). *Harmonize consumption taxes to improve economic efficiency*. Ottawa: The Conference Board of Canada.

Hogwood, B., & Gunn, L. (1984). *Policy analysis for the real world*. Toronto: Oxford University Press.

Homan, M. (1994). *Promoting community change: Making it happen in the real world*. Pacific Grove, CA: Brooks/Cole Publishing Company.

Hoover, K. R. (1992). Conservatism. In M. Hawkesworth & M. Kogan (Eds.),

Encyclopedia of government and politics (Vol. I, 139–154). New York: Routledge.

Horowitz, G. (1970). Red Tory. In W. Kilbourn (Ed.), *Canada: A guide to the peaceable kingdom* (254–260). Toronto: Macmillan of Canada.

Howell, J. & D. Mulligan, (Eds.). (2005). *Gender and civil society: Transcending boundaries*. London: Routledge.

Hufbauer, G. C., & Suominen, C. (2010). *Globalization at risk: Challenges to finance and trade*. New Haven, CT: Yale University Press.

Human Resources and Skills Development Canada. (2004). *Employment insurance and regular benefits*. Retrieved from http://www.hrsdc.ca

Human Resources and Skills Development Canada. (2007, January 29). *Looking ahead: 10-year outlook for the Canadian labour market (2006–2015)*. Retrieved from http://www.hrsdc.gc.ca/eng/publications_resources/research/categories/labour_market_e/sp_615_10_06/future.shtml

Human Resources and Skills Development Canada. (2009). *Advancing the inclusion of people with disabilities*. Retrieved from http://www.hrsdc.gc.ca/publications

Human Resources and Skills Development Canada. (2010, January 15). *Union membership in Canada 2009*. Retrieved from http://www.hrsdc.gc.ca/eng/labour/labour_relations/info_analysis/union_membership/index2009.shtml

Human Resources and Social Development Canada. (2005). *Social security statistics Canada and provinces 1978–79 to 2002–03 Tables*. Retrieved from http://www.hrsdc.gc.ca/en/cs/sp/sdc/socpol/tables/page02.shtml

Human Resources and Social Development Canada. (2006). *Low income in Canada: 2000–2002: Using the market basket measure*. Ottawa: Author. Retrieved from http://www.hrsdc.gc.ca/en/cs/sp/sdc/pkrf/publications/research/2002-000662/SP-628-05-06e.pdf

Human Resources and Social Development Canada. (2007). *Employment insurance program characteristics*. Ottawa: Author. Retrieved from http://srv200.services.gc.ca/iiws/eiregions/geocont.aspx

Ignatieff, M. (2000). *The rights revolution*. Toronto: Anansi.

Indian and Northern Affairs. (2007). *Annual reports, minister's message*. Retrieved from http://www.tbs-sct.gc.ca

Indian and Northern Affairs Canada. (n.d.). *Social development programs*. Retrieved from http://www.ainc-inac.gc.ca/ai/mr/is/sdpr-eng.asp

Indian and Northern Affairs Canada. (n.d.). *Registered Indian demography—Population, household and family projections, 2004–2029*. INAC Strategic Research and Analysis Directorate, CMHC Policy and Research Division.

Inglehart, R., & Welzel, C. (2009). How development leads to democracy: What we know about modernization. *Foreign Affairs, 88*(3), 33–48.

Inwood, G. J. (2000). Federalism, globalization, and the (anti-)social union. In M. Burke, C. Mooers, & J. Shields (Eds.), *Restructuring and resistance: Canadian public policy in an age of global capitalism* (124–144). Halifax: Fernwood.

Irving, A. (1987). Federal-provincial issues in social policy. In S. A. Yelaja (Ed.), *Canadian social policy* (326–349). Waterloo, ON: Wilfrid Laurier University Press.

Irving, A., Parsons, H., & Bellamy, D. (1995). *Neighbours: Three social settlements in downtown Toronto*. Toronto: Canadian Scholars Press.

Jackson, A., & Robinson. D. (2000). *Falling behind: The state of working Canada, 2000*. Ottawa: Canadian Centre for Policy Alternatives.

Jackson, A., & Sanger, M. (1998). *Dismantling democracy: The multilateral agreement on investment (MAI) and its impact*. Ottawa: Canadian Centre for Policy Alternatives and James Lorimer & Co.

Jackson, A., & Sanger, M. (2003). *When worlds collide: Implications of international trade investment agreements for non-profit social services.* Ottawa: Canadian Centre for Policy Alternatives.

Jansson, B. (1990). *Social welfare policy: From theory to practice.* Belmont, CA: Wadsworth Publishing Company.

Jansson, B. (2011). *Becoming an effective policy advocate.* Belmont, CA: Brooks/Cole.

Jenson, J. (1998). *Mapping social cohesion: The state of Canadian research.* Canadian Policy Research Network Study No. F103. Ottawa: Renouf Publishing.

Johnson, L. (1986). *Social policy: A generalist approach* (2nd ed.). Boston: Allyn and Bacon.

Johnston, P. (1983). *Native children and the child welfare system.* Toronto: James Lorimer and Company.

Jones, A., & Rutman, L. (1981). *In the children's aid: J. J. Kelso and child welfare in Ontario.* Toronto: University of Toronto Press.

Jongbloed, L. (2006). Disability income and employment policies in Canada: Historical development. In M. McColl & L. Jongbloed (Eds.), *Disability and social policy in Canada* (2nd ed., 243–253). Concord, ON: Captus Press.

Kadushin, A., & Martin, J. (1988). *Child welfare services* (4th ed.). New York: Macmillan.

Kahn, A. J., & Kamerman, S. B. (1998). *Big cities in the welfare transition.* New York: Columbia University School of Social Work.

Kallen, E. (1989). *Label me human: Minority rights of stigmatized Canadians.* Toronto: University of Toronto Press.

Kallen, E. (1995). *Ethnicity and human rights in Canada* (2nd ed.). Toronto: Oxford University Press.

Kallen, E. (2004). *Social inequality and social injustice: A human rights perspective.* New York: Palgrave Macmillan.

Kallen, E. (2010). *Ethnicity and human rights in Canada* (3rd ed.). Don Mills, ON: Oxford University Press.

Kealey, G. S. (1980). *The working class response to industrial capitalism in Toronto, 1867–1892.* Toronto: University of Toronto Press.

Kealey, L. (Ed.). (1979). *A not unreasonable claim: Women and reform in Canada, 1880s–1920s.* Toronto: The Women's Press.

Kent, M. M., & Haub, C. (2005). Global demographic divide. *Population Bulletin, 60*(4), 1–25. Retrieved from http://www.prb.org

Kerans, P. (1994). Need and welfare: "Thin" and "thick" approaches. In A. Johnson, S. McBride, & P. Smith (Eds.), *Continuities and discontinuities: The political economy of social welfare and labour market policy in Canada* (44–59). Toronto: University of Toronto Press.

King, S. D. (2010). *Losing control: The emerging threats to Western prosperity.* New Haven, CT: Yale University Press.

Kingdom, J. (1995). *Agendas, alternatives, and public policies* (2nd ed.). New York: Harper/Collins.

Kingdon, G. G., & Knight, J. (2007). Subjective well being poverty vs. income poverty and capabilities poverty. In D. Hulme & J. Toye (Eds.), *Understanding poverty well-being: Bridging the disciplines* (115–140). London: Routledge.

Klasen, S. (1998). *Social exclusion and children in OECD countries.* Paris: OECD Publications.

Klein, N. (2007). *The shock doctrine: The rise of disaster capitalism.* Toronto: A. A. Knopf Canada.

Kleiss, K. (2010, December 9). Leaked document suggests health-care privatization for Alberta. *Edmonton Journal.* Retrieved from the Calgary Herald website: http://www.calgaryherald.com/business/ Leaked+document+suggests+health+care+ privatization+Alberta/3907320/story.html

Krieger, J. (Ed.). (1993). *The Oxford companion to politics of the world.* New York: Oxford University Press.

Lafitte, F. (1962). *Social policy in a free society.* Birmingham, AL: Birmingham University Press.

Lamarche, L. 1999. New governing arrangements, women and social policy. In D. Broad & W. Antony (Eds.), *Citizens or consumers? Social policy in a market society* (5–72). Halifax: Fernwood.

Lapointe, M., Dunn, K., Tremblay-Cote, N., Bergeron, L. P., & Ignakzac, L. (2006). *Looking ahead: A ten year outlook for the Canadian labour market.* Ottawa: Human Resources Social Development Canada Publications Centre.

Lawand, N., & Kloosterman, R. (2006). The Canada Pension Plan Disability Program: Building a solid foundation. In M. McColl & L. Jongbloed (Eds.), *Disability and social policy in Canada* (2nd ed., 267–283). Concord, ON: Captus Press.

Laxer, J. (1997). *In search of a new left: Canadian politics after the neo-conservative assault.* Toronto: Penguin.

Lecomte, R. (1990). Connecting private troubles and public issues in social work education. In B. Wharf (Ed.), *Social work and social change in Canada* (31–51). Toronto: McClelland and Stewart Inc.

Le Grand, J. (2007). *The other invisible hand: Delivering public services through choice and competition.* Princeton University Press.

Leiby, J. (1978). *A history of social welfare and social work in the United States.* New York: Columbia University Press.

Leonard, P. (1975). Towards a paradigm for radical practice. In R. Bailey & M. Brake (Eds.), *Radical social work* (46–61). London: Edward Arnold, Ltd.

Leonard, P. (1984). *Personality and ideology: Towards a materialist understanding of the individual.* Atlantic Highlands, NJ: Humanities Press.

Leonard, P. (1997). *Postmodern welfare: Reconstructing an emancipatory project.* London: Sage Publications.

Lerner, M. (1997). *The politics of meaning: Restoring hope and possibility in an age of cynicism.* Don Mills, ON: Addison-Wesley.

Lessard, H. (1997). Creative stories: Social rights and Canada's Constitution. In P. Evans & C. Wekerle (Eds.), *Women and the Canadian welfare state: Challenges and change* (pp. 71–90). Toronto: University of Toronto Press.

Lewin, A. C., & Hasenfeld, Y. (1995). AFDC marital dissolution: Does welfare policy reduce the gains from marriage? *American Sociological Association Papers.*

Lewis, D., & Kanji, N. (2009). *Non-governmental organizations development.* London: Routledge.

L'Heureux-Dubé, C. (2000). A conversation about equality. *Denver Journal of International Law and Policy, 29*(1), 65.

Lightman, E. (2003). *Social policy in Canada.* Don Mills, ON: Oxford University Press.

Lipsky, M. (1980). *Street-level bureaucracy: Dilemmas of the individual in public services.* New York: Russell Sage Foundation.

Little, B. (2001, May 21). Remarkable progress cutting federal debt. *The Globe and Mail,* p. B7.

Little, M. M. (1999). The limits of Canadian democracy: The citizenship rights of poor women. *Canadian Review of Social Policy, 43,* 59–76.

Little, M. (2005). *If I had a hammer: Retraining that really works.* Vancouver: UBC Press.

Lonergan, A., & Richards, C. (Eds.). (1988). *Thomas Berry and the new cosmology.* Mystic, CT: Twenty-Third Publications.

Lovelock, J. (2006). *The revenge of Gaia: Earth's climate crisis and the fate of humanity.* New York: Basic Books.

Lower, A. (1958). *Canadians in the making: A social history of Canada.* Toronto: Longmans, Green, and Company.

Lubove, R. (1965). *The professional altruist: The emergence of social work as a career, 1880–1930.* Cambridge: Harvard University Press.

Lukes, S. (2005). *Power: A radical view* (2nd ed.). New York: Palgrave-Macmillan.

Luttwak, E. (1999). *Turbo-capitalism: Winners and losers in the global economy.* New York: Harper Collins.

Macarov, D. (1995a). *The design of social welfare.* New York: Holt, Rinehart and Winston.

Macarov, D. (1995b). *Social welfare: Structure and practice.* Thousand Oaks, CA: Sage.

Mackey, W. F. (2003). Forecasting the fate of languages. In J. Maurais & M. A. Morris (Eds.), *Languages in a globalising world* (72). Cambridge, UK: Cambridge University Press.

Makarenko, J. (2007, April 1). 2002 Mazankowski Report on Health Care in Alberta. Retrieved from Maple Leaf Web website: http://www.mapleleafweb.com/features/2002-mazankowski-report-health-care-alberta

Makarenko, J. (2008, April 24). *Equalization Program in Canada: Overview and Contemporary Issues.* Retrieved from Maple Leaf Web website: http://www.mapleleafweb.com/features/equalization-program-canada-overview--contemporary-issues

Mannheim, K. (1936). *Ideology and utopia.* New York: Harcourt, Brace & World.

Marchak, M. P. (1988). *Ideological perspectives on Canada* (3rd ed.). Toronto: McGraw-Hill Ryerson Ltd.

Marfleet, P. (1998). *Against the globalist paradigm.* International conference on globalization: Political, social, and economic perspectives, held at Eastern Mediterranean University (TRNC), November 19–21, 1998.

Marshall, T. H. (1949). Citizenship and social class. Reprinted in D. Held et al., *States societies.* 1983. London: Open University.

Marshall, T. H. (1965). *Social policy.* London: Hutchinson.

Martineau, P. (2005). *Federal personal income tax: Slicing the pie.* Catalogue No. 11-621-MIE. Ottawa: Minister of Industry.

Marumba, S. K. I. (1998). Cross-cultural dimensions of human rights in the twenty-first century. In A. Anghie & G. Sturgess (Eds.), *Legal visions of the 21st century: Essays in honour of Judge Christopher Weeramantry* (201–240). The Hague: Kluwer Law International.

Maslow, A. H. (1954). *Motivation and personality.* New York: Harper.

Mason, D., Talbott, S., & Leavitt, J. (1993). *Policy politics for nurses* (2nd ed.). Toronto: W. B. Saunders Co.

Marx, K., & Engels, F. (1947). The German ideology, parts 1 and 3, (C. J. Arthur, Trans). New York: International Publishers. (Original work published 1846)

Marx, K., & Engels, F. (1998). *The communist manifesto.* New York: Verso. (Original work published 1848)

Maurutto, P. (2009). Charity public welfare in history: A look at Ontario, 1830–1950. *The Philanthropist, 19*(3), 159—167.

Mawhiney, A. (1995). The First Nations in Canada. In J. Turner & F. Turner (Eds.), *Canadian social welfare* (3rd ed., 213–230). Scarborough, ON: Allyn and Bacon Canada.

McGilly, F. (1998). *An introduction to Canada's public social services.* Don Mills, ON: Oxford University Press.

McInnis-Dittrich, K. (1994). *Integrating social welfare policy and social work practice.* Pacific Grove, CA: Brooks/Cole Publishing Company.

McKenzie, B. (1997). Connecting policy and practice in First Nations child and family services: A Manitoba case study. In J. Pulkingham & G. Ternowetsky (Eds.), *Child and family policies: Struggles, strategies and options* (pp. 100–114). Halifax: Fernwood.

McMenemy, J. (1995). *The language of Canadian politics: A guide to important terms and concepts*. Waterloo, ON: Wilfrid Laurier University Press.

McNally, D. (2006). *Another world is possible: Globalization and anti-capitalism* (Rev. ed.). Winnipeg: Arbeiter Ring Publishing.

McPherson, D., & Rabb, D. (1994). *Indian from the inside: A study in ethno-metaphysics*. Thunder Bay, ON: Centre for Northern Studies.

McQuaig, L. (1993). *The wealthy banker's wife*. Toronto: Penguin Books.

McQuaig, L. (1995). *Shooting the hippo: Death by deficit and other Canadian myths*. Toronto: Viking.

McQuaig, L. (1998). *The cult of impotence: Selling the myth of powerlessness in the global economy*. Toronto: Viking.

Mendelson, M. (1993). *Social policy in real time*. Ottawa: Caledon Institute of Social Policy.

Meyer, S. M. (2006). *The end of the wild*. Cambridge, MA: MIT Press.

Mills, C. W. (1959). *The sociological imagination*. Oxford: Oxford University Press.

Minoto, H., & Cross, P. (1991). The growth of the federal debt. *Canadian Economic Observer*, June, 3.1–3.17.

Mishra, R. (1981). *Society and social policy: Theories and practice of welfare* (2nd ed.). London: Macmillan.

Mishra, R. (1995). The political bases of Canadian social welfare. In J. Turner & F. Turner (Eds.), *Canadian social welfare* (3rd ed., 59–74). Scarborough, ON: Allyn and Bacon Canada.

Mitchell, A., & Shillington, R. (2005). Poverty, inequality and social inclusion. In T. Richmond & A. Saloojee (Eds.), *Social inclusion: Canadian perspectives* (33–57). Halifax: Fernwood.

Mittlestaedt, M. (2001, October 3). Commission throws water on Ottawa's lakes cleanup. *The Globe and Mail*, p. A13.

Mittlestaedt, M. (2006, March 6). Drug residue tainting water, report warns. *The Globe and Mail*, p. A5.

Moreau, M. (1989). *Empowerment through a structural approach to social work*. Ottawa: Carleton University School of Social Work.

Morgan, S. P., & Taylor, M. G. (2006). Low fertility at the turn of the twenty-first century. *Annual Review of Sociology, 32*, 375–390.

Morissette, R., Schellenberg, G., & Johnson, A. (2005). Diverging trends in unionization. *Statistics Canada's Perspectives on Labour and Income, 17*(2), n.p. Retrieved from Statistics Canada website: http://www.statcan.ca/bsolc/english/bsolc?catno=75-001-X20050027827

Morissette, R., & Zhang, X. (2006). Revisiting wealth inequality. *Perspectives on Labour and Income, 7*, 12, December. Statistics Canada—Catalogue No. 75-001-XIE.

Morris, M. (2007). *Fact Sheet No 9: Women's experiences of social programs for people of low income*. Canadian Research Institute for the Advancement of Women.

Morrison, I. (1997). Rights and the right: Ending social citizenship in Tory Ontario. In D. Ralph, A. Regimbald, & N. St-Amand (Eds.), *Open for business, closed to people* (pp. 68–79). Halifax: Fernwood.

Morton, W. L. (1969). *The kingdom of Canada*. Toronto: McClelland and Stewart.

Mulé, N. (2005). Equality's limitations, liberation's challenges: Considerations for queer movement strategizing. *Canadian Online Journal of Queer Studies in Education, 2*(1). Retrieved from http://jqstudies.library.utoronto.ca/index.php/jqstudies/article/view/3290/1419

Mulé, N. (2008). Demarcating gender and sexual diversity on the structural landscape of social work. *Critical Social Work, 9*(1). Retrieved from http://www.criticalsocialwork

Mulé, N. (2010). Same-sex marriage and Canadian relationship recognition—One step forward, two steps back: A critical liberationist perspective. *Journal of Gay & Lesbian Social Services, 22,* 74–90.

Mulé, N., Ross, L., Deeprose, B., Jackson, B., Daley, A., Travers, A., & Moore, D. (2009). Promoting LGBT health and wellbeing through inclusive policy development. *International Journal for Equity in Health, 8,*(18). Retrieved from http://www.equityhealthj.com/content/8/1/18

Mullaly, R. (1993). *Structural social work.* Toronto: McClelland and Stewart.

Mullaly, R. (2002). *Challenging oppression: A critical social work approach.* Don Mills, ON: Oxford University Press.

Mullaly, R. (2007). *The new structural social work.* Don Mills, ON: Oxford University Press.

Mulvale, J. P. (2001). *Reimagining social welfare: Beyond the Keynesian welfare state.* Toronto: Garamond.

Muszynski, L. (1987). *Is it fair? What tax reform will do to you.* Ottawa: Canadian Centre for Policy Alternatives.

Myers, R., & Worm, B. (2003). Rapid worldwide depletion of predatory fish communities. *Nature, 423,* May 15, 280–283.

National Association of Women and the Law. (2007). *Pay equity at the heart of equality.* Retrieved from http://www.nawl.ca/ns/en/is-wmnwrk-pe.html

National Council of Welfare. (1993). *Incentives and disincentives to work.* Ottawa: Ministry of Supply and Services Canada.

National Council of Welfare. (1995). *The 1995 budget and block funding.* Ottawa: National Council of Welfare.

National Council of Welfare. (2001). *Child poverty profile 1998.* Ottawa: National Council of Welfare.

National Council of Welfare. (2006a). *Poverty Profile, 2002 and 2003.* Catalogue No. SDZ5-1/2003E. Ottawa: Minister of Public Works and Government Services Canada.

National Council of Welfare. (2006b). *Welfare Incomes 2005.* Ottawa: Minister of Public Works Government Services Canada.

Retrieved from http://www.ncwcnbes.net/en/research/welfare-bienetre.html

National Council of Welfare. (2007). *Solving poverty: Four cornerstones of a workable national strategy for Canada.* Ottawa: National Council of Welfare.

Naylor, C. D. (1986). *Private practice, public payment.* Montreal/Kingston: McGill-Queen's University Press.

Naylor, D., & Martin, R. (2005, February 10). A better way to share. *The Globe and Mail,* p. A23.

Nelles, H. V. (1974). *The politics of development: Forests, mines, and hydro-electric power in Ontario, 1849–1941.* Toronto: Macmillan.

Newman, P. (1975). *The Canadian establishment.* Toronto: McClelland & Stewart.

Neysmith, S., Bezanson, K., & O'Connell, A. (2005). *Telling tales: Living the effects of public policy.* Halifax: Fernwood.

Neysmith, S., Reitsma-Street, M., Baker-Collins, S., Porter, E., & Tam, S. (2010). Provisioning responsibilities: How relationships shape the work that women do. *Canadian Review of Sociology, 47*(2), 149–170.

Nikiforuk, A. (2007, June 11). Is Canada the latest emerging petro-tyranny? *The Globe and Mail,* p. A13.

O'Brien, C. (1998). *Sexual regulation and Ontario social policies in the 1990s* (Doctoral dissertation. Faculty of Social Work, University of Toronto.)

O'Brien, C., & Weir, L. (1995). Lesbians and gay men inside and outside families. In N. Mell & A. Duffy (Eds.), *Canadian families: Diversity, conflict and change* (111–139). Toronto: Harcourt Brace and Company.

O'Neill, B. (2006). Toward inclusion of gay and lesbian people: Social policy changes in relation to sexual orientation. In A. Westhughes (Ed.), *Canadian social policy: Issues perspectives* (4th ed. pp. 331–348). Waterloo, ON: Wilfrid Laurier University Press.

Obituaries, Bessie Touzel. (1997, April 26). *The Globe and Mail.*

Offe, C. (1984). *Contradictions of the welfare state.* Cambridge, MA: MIT Press.

Olden, J., Hogan, Z., & Zen, M. (2007). Small fish, big fish, red fish, blue fish: Size-biased extinction risk of the world's freshwater and marine fishes. *Global Ecology & Biogeography, 16*(6), 694–701.

Palmer, B. D. (1979). *A culture in conflict: Skilled workers and industrial capitalism in Hamilton, Ontario, 1860–1914.* Montreal/ Kingston: McGill-Queen's University Press.

Pascal, G. (1993). Citizenship—A feminist analysis. In G. Drover & P. Kerans (Eds.), *Welfare theory* (pp. 113–126). Aldershot, UK: Edward Elgar Publishing.

Pasma, C. (2010). *Ontario: Bearing the brunt.* Retrieved from Citizens for Public Justice website: http://www.cpj.ca/en/blog/ chandra/ontario-bearing-brunt

Pateman, C. (1992). Equality, difference, subordination: The politics of motherhood and women's citizenship. In S. James & G. Bock (Eds.), *Beyond equality and difference: Citizenship, feminist politics, and female subjectivity* (pp. 17–31). New York: Routledge.

Patterson, E. (1987). Native peoples and social policy. In S. Yelaja (Ed.), *Canadian social policy* (Rev. ed., 175–194). Waterloo, ON: Wilfrid Laurier University Press.

Pay Equity Task Force. (2004). *Pay equity: A new approach to a fundamental right.* Ottawa: Minister of Justice and Attorney General of Canada, and the Minister of Labour.

Payne, J. (1998). *Overcoming welfare: Expecting more from the poor and from ourselves.* New York: Basic Books.

Payne, M. (2005). *Modern social work theory* (3rd ed.). Chicago: Lyceum Books.

Payne, R. K. (2010). *How much is enough? Buddhism, consumerism, and the human environment.* New York: Wisdom Publications.

Payne, S. (1992). Fascism. In M. Hawkesworth & M. Kogan (Eds.), *Encyclopedia of government politics* (Vol. I, 167–178). New York: Routledge.

Pearson, G. (1975). Making social workers: Bad promises and good omens. In R. Bailey & M. Brake (Eds.), *Radical social work* (13–45). London: Edward Arnold, Ltd.

Pearson, J. (2010, November 26). Empire lines. *Times literary supplement.* 5620, 25.

Penner, N. (1992). *From protest to power: Social democracy in Canada 1900–present.* Toronto: Lorimer.

Picot, G., Hou, F., & Coulombe, S. (2007). *Chronic low income and low-income dynamics among recent immigrants.* Catalogue no. 11F0019MIE — No. 294. Ottawa: Statistics Canada.

Picot, G., Hou, F., & Coulombe, S. (2008). Poverty dynamics among recent immigrants to Canada. *International Migration Review, 42*(2), 393–424.

Pierce, D. (1984). *Policy for the social work practitioner.* New York: Longman.

Pierson, C. (1991). *Beyond the welfare state: The new political economy of social welfare.* University Park: Pennsylvania State University Press.

Polese, M. (1998). Regional economics. *The 1998 Canadian and world encyclopedia* [CD ROM]. Toronto: McClelland and Stewart.

Popple, P., & Leighninger, L. (2001). *The policy-based profession: An introduction to social welfare policy for social workers* (2nd ed.). Boston: Allyn and Bacon.

Prentice, A., Bourne, P., Cuthbert-Brandt, G., Light, B., Mitchinson, W., & Black, N. (1988). *Canadian women: A history.* Toronto: Harcourt, Brace, Jovanovich.

Putnam, R. D. (2000). *Bowling alone: The collapse revival of American community.* New York: Simon Schuster.

Raphael, D. (Ed.). (2004). *Social determinants of health: Canadian perspectives.* Toronto: Canadian Scholars' Press.

Reamer, F. (1993). *The philosophical founda-tions of social work*. New York: Columbia University Press.

Rebick, J. (2000). *Imagine democracy*. Toronto: Stoddart.

Rein, M. (1974). Social policy analysis and the interpretation of beliefs. *The American Institute for Planners Journal*, September, 31(3): 297–310.

Rein, M. (1983). *From policy to practice*. Armonk, NY: M. E. Sharpe Inc.

Report for the Interprovincial Conference of Ministers Responsible for Social Services. (1980). *The income security system in Canada*. Ottawa: Canadian Intergovern-mental Conference Secretariat.

Ricciutelli, L., Larkin, J., & O'Neill, E. (1998). *Confronting the cuts: A sourcebook for women in Ontario*. Toronto: Inanna Publications and Education Inc.

Rice, J. J., & Prince, M. J. (2000). *Changing politics of Canadian social policy*. Toronto: University of Toronto Press.

Richmond, M. (1930). *The long view*. New York: Russell Sage Foundation.

Richmond, O., & Carey, H. (Eds.). (2005). *Subcontracting peace: The challenges of the NGO peacebulding*. Aldershot, UK: Ashgate Publishing.

Richmond, T., & Saloojee, A. (Eds.). (2005). *Social inclusion: Canadian perspectives*. Halifax: Fernwood.

Rioux, M., & Samson, R. (2006). Trends impacting disability: National and interna-tional perspectives. In M. McColl & L. Jongbloed (Eds.), *Disability and social policy in Canada* (2nd ed., 112–142). Concord, ON: Captus Press.

Rodrik, D. (2011). *The globalization paradox: Democracy and the future of the world economy*. New York: Norton.

Roeher Institute. (1996). *Disability, community and society*. Toronto: Author.

Rooke, P. T., & Schnell, R. L. (1987). *No bleeding heart: Charlotte Whitton—A fem-inist on the right*. Vancouver: UBC Press.

Ross, D. P., Scott, K. J., & Smith, P. J. (2000). The Canadian fact book on poverty. The Canadian Council on Social Development.

Royal Canadian Legion Ontario Provincial Command. (2009). *WVA rates*. Retrieved from http://www.on.legion.ca/veterans/wvarates.asp

Ryan, B., Brotman, S., & Rowe, B. (2000). *Access to care: Exploring the health and well-being of gay, lesbian, bisexual and two-spirit people in Canada*. Montreal: McGill Centre for Applied Family Studies.

Sachs, W., Loske, R., & Linz, M. (1998). *Greening the North: A post-industrial blueprint for ecology and equity*. New York: Zed.

Sadava, M. (2010). More choice, less educa-tion. *Alberta Views*, *13*(6), 28–30.

Sale, K. (2006). *After Eden: The evolution of human domination*. Durham, NC: Duke University Press.

Saul, J. R. (1995). *The unconscious civilization*. Concord, ON: House of Anansi Press.

Savoie, D. (2010). *Power: Where is it?* Montreal: McGill-Queen's University Press.

Sayeed, A. (2002). *The 1997 Canada Pension Plan changes: Implications for women and men*. Ottawa: Status of Women Canada.

Schansberg, D. E. (1996). *Poor policy: How government harms the poor*. Boulder, CO: Westview Press.

Schorr, A. (1985). Professional practice as policy. *Social Service Review*, *59*(June), 185–86.

Schragge, E. (Ed.). (1997). *Workfare: Ideology for a new under-class*. Toronto: Garamond Press.

Schragge, E., & Deniger, M. (1997). Workfare in Quebec. In E. Schragge (Ed.), *Workfare: Ideology for a new under-class* (59–84). Toronto: Garamond Press.

Schumacher, E. F. (1973). *Small is beautiful: Economics as if people mattered*. New York: Harper and Row.

Schwartz, W. (1974). Private troubles and public issues: One social work job or two?

In P. E. Weinberger (Ed.), *Perspectives on social welfare* (2nd ed., pp. 22–43). New York: Macmillan.

Scott, K. (1998). *Women and the CHST: A profile of women receiving social assistance in 1994*. Ottawa: Status of Women Canada.

Sen, A. (1992). *Inequality reexamined*. New York: Harvard University Press.

Senate Committee on Poverty. (1971). *Poverty in Canada*. Ottawa: Canadian Government Publishing Centre.

Service Canada. (2007). *Employment insurance regular benefits*. Ottawa: Author. Retrieved from http://www1.servicecanada.gc.ca/en/ei/types/regular.shtml#Qualifying

Shah, P. J., & Smith, P. K. (1995). Do welfare benefits cause the welfare caseload? *Public Choice, 85*(1–2), 91–105.

Sharpe, A., & Arsenault, J. (2009). *Living Standards Domain Report. Canadian Index of Wellbeing*. CSLS Research Report (Vol. 4).

Shewell, H. (2007). *Gathering strength or just more welfare? The socio-economic situation of First Nations before and since the Royal Commission on Aboriginal Peoples*. Unpublished paper.

Shewell, H., & Spagnut, A. (1995). The First Nations of Canada: Social welfare and the quest for self-government. In J. Dixon & R. Scheurell (Eds.), *Social welfare with indigenous peoples* (1–15). London: Routledge.

Shirky, C. (2008). *Here comes everybody: The power of organizing without organizations*. London: Penguin Press.

Silver, H. (1994). Social exclusion and social solidarity: Three paradigms. *International Labour Review, 1333*(5–6), 531–578.

Simon, H. (1957). *Administrative behavior: A study of decision-making processes in administrative organization* (3rd ed.). New York: Free Press.

Sirico, R. A. (1997, July 27). Work is moral and so is workfare. *New York Times*, p. E15.

Smiley, D. (1976). *Canada in question: Federalism in the seventies* (2nd ed.). Toronto: McGraw-Hill Ryerson.

Smith, P. K. (1993). Welfare as a cause of poverty: A time series analysis. *Public Choice, 75*(2), 157–170.

Soros, G. (1997). *The crisis of global capitalism: Open society endangered*. New York: Public Affairs.

Speech from the Throne. (2010, February 4). *Third Session of the Twenty-seventh Legislature*. Edmonton: Government of Alberta.

Spicker, P. (2006). *Policy analysis for practice: Applying social policy*. Bristol, UK: The Policy Press.

Splane, R. B. (1965). *Social welfare in Ontario 1791–1893: A study of public welfare administration*. Toronto: University of Toronto Press.

Stainton, T. (1994). *Autonomy and social policy*. Aldershot, UK: Avebury.

Stainton, T. (2005). Empowerment and the architecture of rights based social policy. *Journal of Intellectual Disabilities, 9*, 289–298.

Standing Senate Committee on Social Affairs, Science and Technology, (1999). *Final report on social cohesion*. Retrieved from http://www.parl.gc.ca/36/1/parlbus/commbus/senate/com-e/soci-e/rep-e/repfinaljun99part1-e.htm

Statistics Canada. (2003, December 16). *Total Income Groups in Constant. (2000) Dollars*. File no. 97F0020XCB2001073. Ottawa: Author. Retrieved from http://www12.statcan.ca/english/census01/proucts/standard/themes/RetrieveProductTable.cfm?Temporal=2001&PID=60960&APATH=3&GID=355313&METH=1&PTYPE=55496&THEME=54&FOCUS=0&AID=0&PLACENAME=0&PROVINCE=0&SEARCH=0&GC=99&GK=NA&VID=0&VNAMEE=&VNAMEF=&FL=0&RL=0&FREE=0

Statistics Canada. (2006, March 7). Women in Canada. *The Daily*. Retrieved from http://www.statcan.ca/Daily/English/060307/d060307a.htm

Statistics Canada. (2006a). *Low wage low income.* Catalogue no. 75F0002MIE. Ottawa: Author.

Statistics Canada. (2006b). *Population by selected ethnic origins, by province and territory.* Ottawa: Author. Retrieved from http://www40.statcan.ca/l01/cst01/demo26a-eng.htm.

Statistics Canada. (2007). *Income in Canada.* Catalogue no. 75-202-X. Retrieved from http://dsp-psd.tpsgc.gc.ca/Collection/Statcan/75-202-XIE/75-202-XIE2004000.pdf

Statistics Canada. (2009). *Population urban and rural, by province and territory.* Retrieved from http://www40.statcan.ca/l01/cst01/demo62a-eng.htm

Statistics Canada. (2010a). *Charitable Donors.* Retrieved from http://www40.statcan.gc.ca/l01/cst01/famil90-eng.htm

Statistics Canada. (2010b). *Government finance: Revenue, expenditure and surplus.* Retrieved from *The Daily*: http://www.statcan.gc.ca/daily-quotidien/090616/dq090616a-eng.htm

Statistics Canada. (2010c). *Latest release from the Labour Force Survey.* Retrieved from *The Daily*: http://www.statcan.gc.ca/subjects-sujets/labour-travail/lfs-epa/lfs-epa-eng.htm

Statistics Canada. (2010d). *Satellite account of non-profit institutions volunteering.* Retrieved from *The Daily*: http://www.statcan.gc.ca/daily-quotidien/101217/dq101217b-eng.htm

Statistics Canada, Health Statistics Division. (2006). *Deaths, 2004.* Ottawa: Minister of Industry. Retrieved from http://www.statcan.ca/english/freepub/84F0211XIE/84F0211XIE2004000.htm

Statistics Canada, Income Statistics Division. (2006). *Low income cut-offs for 2005 and low income measures for 2004.* Catalogue no. 75F0003MIE. Ottawa: Statistics Canada.

Statistics Canada, Income Statistics Division. (2007). *Low-income cutoffs for 2006 and low income measures for 2005.* Income Research Paper Series, Catalogue no. 75F0002MIE. Ottawa: Minister of Industry.

Statistics Canada, Income Statistics Division. (2008). *Income security stability during retirement in Canada.* Income Research Paper Series, Catalogue no. 306 - 11F0019M. Retrieved from http://www.statcan.gc.ca/pub/11f0019m/11f0019m2008306-eng.pdf

Statistics Canada, Income Statistics Division. (2010). *2008 Survey of Household Spending.* Retrieved from *The Daily*: http://www.statcan.gc.ca/daily-quotidien/091218/dq091218b-eng.htm

Statistics Canada and the Council of Ministers of Education Canada. (2006). *Education indicators in Canada: Report of the pan-Canadian education indicators program 2005.* Ottawa: Author.

Statistics Canada Pensions and Wealth Surveys Section. (2005). *The wealth of Canadians: An overview of the results of the survey of financial wealth.* Catalogue No. 13—F0026MIE. Ottawa: Author.

Status of Women Canada. (2007). *Status report.* Retrieved from http://www.swc-cfc.gc.ca/index_e.html

Stedman Jones, G. (2004). *An end to poverty? A historical debate.* New York: Columbia University Press.

Stelter, G. A., & Artibese, A. F. J. (Eds.). (1977). The *Canadian city: Essays in urban history.* Toronto: McClelland and Stewart.

Stittle, M. (2010, March 4). *Budget fights deficit with freeze on future spending.* Retrieved from CTV News website: http://toronto.ctv.ca

Stroman, D. (1989). *Mental retardation in social context.* Lanham, MD: University Press of America, Inc.

Strong-Boag, V. (1976). *The parliament of women: The National Council of Women of*

Canada, 1893–1929. Ottawa: National Museum of Man.

Struthers, J. (1983). *No fault of their own: Unemployment and the Canadian welfare state, 1914–1941*. Toronto: University of Toronto Press.

Struthers, J. (1994). *Limits to affluence: Welfare in Ontario, 1920–1970*. Toronto: University of Toronto Press.

Swift, K. (1995). *Manufacturing bad mothers: A critical perspective on child neglect*. Toronto: University of Toronto Press.

Swift, K. (2001). The case for opposition: Challenging contemporary child welfare policy directions. *Canadian Review of Social Policy*, 47, 59–76.

Swift, K., & Callahan, M. (2009). *At risk: Social justice in child welfare and other human services*. Toronto: University of Toronto Press.

Teeple, G. (1995). *Globalization and the decline of social reform*. Toronto: Garamond Press.

Teilhard de Chardin, P. (1955). *The phenomenon of man*. New York: Harper & Brothers.

Tertzakian, P. (2006). *A thousand barrels a second: The coming oil break point and the challenges facing an energy dependent world*. Toronto: McGraw-Hill.

Thomlison, R., & Bradshaw, C. (1999). Canadian political processes and social work practice. In F. Turner (Ed.), *Social work practice: A Canadian perspective* (pp. 264–275). Scarborough, ON: Prentice Hall Canada.

Thompson, N. (1993). *Anti-discriminatory practice*. London: Macmillan.

Thyer, B. (2010). Social justice: A conservative perspective. *Journal of Comparative Social Welfare*, 26(2/3), 261–274.

Tilly, C. (1999). From interactions to outcomes in social movements. In M. Giugni, D. McAdan, & C. Tilly (Eds.), *How social movements matter* (253–270). Minneapolis: University of Minnesota Press.

Titmuss, R. M. (1958). *Essays on the welfare state*. London: George Allen & Unwin.

Titmuss, R. (1970). *The gift relationship: From human blood to social policy*. London: George Allen & Unwin.

Titmuss, R. (1974). *Social policy: An introduction*. London: George Allen & Unwin Ltd.

Torjman, S. (1996a). *Workfare: A poor law*. Ottawa: Caledon Institute of Social Policy.

Torjman, S. (1996b). *History/hysteria*. Ottawa: Caledon Institute of Social Policy.

Torjman, S. (1997). *Welfare warfare*. Ottawa: Caledon Institute of Social Policy.

Torjman, S. (1998a). *Community-based poverty reduction*. Ottawa: Caledon Institute of Social Policy.

Torjman, S. (1998b). *Welfare reform through tailor-made training*. Ottawa: Caledon Institute of Social Policy.

Torjman, S. (1999). *Dumb and dumber governments*. Ottawa: Caledon Institute of Social Policy.

Torjman, S. (2005). *Disability tax: The budget's quiet little secret*. Ottawa: Caledon Institute of Social Policy.

Torjman, S. (2007*). Repairing Canada's social safety net*. Ottawa: Caledon Institute of Social Policy.

Torjman, S., & Battle, K. (1995a). *Can we have national standards?* Ottawa: Caledon Institute of Social Policy.

Torjman, S., & Battle, K. (1995b). *The dangers of block funding*. Ottawa: Caledon Institute of Social Policy.

Torrie, R. (2000, May 19). A clear and present danger: We can cut greenhouse gasses by half and it won't hurt a bit. *The Globe and Mail*, p. A13.

Townson, M. (2006). *Growing older, working longer: The new face of retirement*. Ottawa: Canadian Centre for Policy Alternatives.

Trofimenkoff, S. M. (1983). *The dream of nation*. Toronto: McClelland and Stewart.

Trudeau, P. E. (1990). The values of a just society. In T. Axworthy & P. E. Trudeau (Eds.), *Towards a just society*, (357–385). Markham, ON: Viking.

Turk, J., & Wilson, G. (1996). *Unfair shares: Corporations and taxation in Canada.* Don Mills, ON: Ontario Coalition for Social Justice and Ontario Federation of Labour.

Turner, F. (1995). Social welfare in Canada. In J. Turner & F. Turner (Eds.), *Canadian social welfare* (3rd ed., 1–11). Scarborough, ON: Allyn and Bacon Canada.

United Nations, Department of Economic Social Affairs, Population Division. (2002). *World population ageing: 1950–2050.* New York: United Nations Publications.

United Nations Development Programme. (2006). *Human development report 2006. Beyond scarcity: Power, poverty, and the global water crisis.* New York: Author.

United Nations Development Programme. (2010). *Human Development Index and its components.* Retrieved from http://hdr.undp.org/en/media/HDR_2010_EN_Table1_reprint.pdf

United Nations Statistics Division. (2010). *Millennium development goals indicators: CO_2 emissions, 2007.* Retrieved from http://unstats.un.org/unsd/mdg/SeriesDetail.aspx?srid=749

Ursel, J. (1992). *Private lives and public policy: One hundred years of state intervention in the family.* Toronto: Women's Press.

U.S. Energy Information Administration. (2010). *Canada energy data.* Retrieved from http://www.eia.doe.gov/

Usher, D. (2003). *Political economy.* Oxford: Blackwell.

Valentine, F. (2001). *Enabling citizenship: Full inclusion of children with disabilities and their parents.* Discussion paper No. F/13. Ottawa: Canadian Policy Research Network.

Valletta, R. (2006). The ins and outs of poverty in advanced economies: Government policy poverty dynamics in Canada, Germany, Great Britain, and the United States. *Review of Income & Wealth, 52*(2), 261–284.

Van Wormer, K. (1997). *Social welfare: A world view.* New York: Nelson Hall.

Veterans Affairs Canada. (2009, February 18). *Veterans affairs disability pension program.* Retrieved from http://www.veterans.gc.ca/general/sub.cfm?source=Services

Vosko, L. F. (2006). Precarious employment: Towards an improved understanding of labour market insecurity. In L. F. Vosko (Ed.), *Precarious employment: Understanding labour market insecurity in Canada* (3–39). Montreal/Kingston: McGill-Queen's University Press.

Waldi, P. (2006, November 16). Canadian firms and charity: Are they scrooges? *The Globe and Mail*, p. B2.

Webb, D. (1981). Radical and traditional social work. *British Journal of Social Work, 11,* 143–158.

Weber, M. (1958). *The Protestant ethic and the spirit of capitalism,* (T. Parsons, Trans.). New York: Charles Scribner's Sons. (Original work published 1930)

Wein, F. (1991). *The role of social policy in economic restructuring.* Halifax: The Institute for Research on Public Policy.

Westhues, A. (Ed.). (2003). *Canadian social policy: Issues and perspectives.* Waterloo, ON: Wilfrid Laurier University Press.

Westhues, A. (Ed) (2006). *Canadian social policy* (4th ed.). Waterloo, ON: Wilfrid Laurier University Press.

Wharf, B. (1986). Social welfare and the political system. In J. Turner & F. Turner (Eds.), *Canadian social welfare* (2nd ed., 103–120). Don Mills, ON: Collier Macmillan.

Wharf, B. (Ed.). (1990). *Social work and social change in Canada.* Toronto: McClelland and Stewart.

Wharf, B. (1992). *Community and social policy in Canada.* Toronto: McClelland and Stewart.

Wharf, B., & Cossom, J. (1987). Citizen participation and social welfare policy. In S. Yelaja (Ed.), *Canadian social policy.* (Rev. ed., 266–287). Waterloo, ON: Wilfrid Laurier University Press.

Wharf, B., & McKenzie, B. (1998). *Connecting policy to practice in the human services*. Toronto: Oxford University Press.

Wharf, B., & McKenzie B. (2004). *Connecting policy to practice in the human services* (2nd ed.). Don Mills, ON: Oxford University Press.

Wharf, B. & McKenzie B. (2010). *Connecting policy to practice in the human services*. (3rd ed.). Toronto: Oxford University Press.

Wilensky, H. L., & Lebeaux, C. N. (1958). *Industrial society and social welfare*. New York: Russell Sage Foundation.

Wilkinson, R., & Pickett, K. (2009). *The spirit level: Why more equal societies almost always do better*. London, UK: Allen Lane.

Wilkinson, R., & Pickett, K. (2010). *The spirit level: Why equality is better for everyone*. London, UK: Penguin Books.

Willetts, D. (2010). *The pinch: How the baby boomers took their children's future—and why they should give it back*. London: Atlantic Books.

Williams, F. (1989). *Social policy: A critical introduction*. Cambridge: Polity Press.

Wilson, D., & Macdonald, D. (2010). *The income gap between Aboriginal peoples and the rest of Canada*. Ottawa: Canadian Centre for Policy Alternatives.

Wintemute, R. (1995). *Sexual orientation and human rights*. Oxford: Clarendon Press.

Woodford, M., Newman, P., Brotman, S., & Ryan, B. (2010). Northern enlightenment: Legal recognition of same-sex marriage in Canada: Strengthening social work's advocacy efforts. *Journal of Gay & Lesbian Social Services, 22*, 191–209.

Woodsworth, D. (1986). Canadian realities. (44–66). In J. Turner & F. Turner (Eds.), *Canadian social welfare* (2nd ed.). Don Mills, ON: Collier Macmillan.

Workers' Compensation Board-Alberta, The. (2010). *What Workers' Compensation provides*. Retrieved from http://www.wcb.ab.ca

World Wildlife Fund. (2006). *Living planet report: 2006*. Gland, Switzerland: Author.

The world's billionaire. (2010). *Forbes Magazine*. Retrieved from http://www.forbes.com/2010/03/10/worlds-richest-people-slim-gates-buffett-billionaires-2010_l.html

Wright, R. (2004). *A short history of progress*. Toronto: Anansi.

Yalnizyan, A. (2010). The rise of Canada's richest 1%. *Canadian Centre for Policy Alternatives*. Retrieved from http://www.collectionscanada.gc.ca/caninfo/ep036.htm

Yelaja, S. (Ed.). (1987). *Canadian social policy* (Rev. ed.). Waterloo, ON: Wilfrid Laurier University Press.

Young, C. (1994). Taxing times for lesbians and gay men: Equality at what cost? *Dalhousie Law Journal, 17*(2), 534–559.

Zapf, M. K. (1999). Geographic factors. In F. Turner (Ed.), *Social work practice: A Canadian perspective* (344–358). Scarborough, ON: Allyn and Bacon Canada.

Index